Hidden Gems of the Washington Cascades:

Brief Essays on Climbs, Scrambles and Traverses in Our Most Overlooked Alpine Area and National Park

BY BARRY M. MALETZKY, M.D.

MOUNTAIN AND ROUTE ILLUSTRATIONS BY KARYN SERVIN

FLOWER ILLUSTRATIONS BY SUSI DAVIS

MAP ILLUSTRATIONS BY RACHEL DAVIS

Copyright © 2024 Barry Maletzky

All rights reserved. No part of this publication may be reproduced, distributed or transmitted in any form or by any means, including photocopying, recording, or other electronic or mechanical methods, without the prior written permission of the publisher, except in the case of brief quotations embodied in critical reviews and certain other noncommercial uses permitted by copyright law.

ISBN: 979-8-218-41904-2

Library of Congress Control Number: 2024907965

Front cover: *A scrappy climber stares at the camera on Sahale arm, with some of the Ptarmigan Traverse peaks in the background.* Photo taken by author.

Back cover: taken from the USGS Toplogical Survey website.

Illustrations done by Karyn Servin, Rachel Davis, and Susi Davis

Book Design by Jill Flores

Printed using IngramSpark

First printing edition 2025

Table of Contents

Acknowledgment. I

Dedication. III

Introduction. IV

Chapter One: A Southern Rampart
Mt. Curtis Gilbert (8,184')... 1

Chapter Two: Often Better Than Rainier
The Tatoosh Traverse (5,958'–6,917') 11

Chapter Three: Lakes and Views East of the Crest
Alta (6,250') and Hibox Mountains (~6,547'). 23

Chapter Four: A Five-fingered Riddle
Lemah Mountain (7,480'). 33

Chapter Five: You can do it: Mt. Stuart
The West Ridge (9,415')... 41

Chapter Six: Shaking the Dragon's Tail
Colchuck (8,705') and Dragontail Peaks (8,840').............. 51

Chapter Seven: Slicing the Washington Sky
Prusik Peak (~8,000')... 59

Chapter Eight: Only Lesser in Altitude than in Alpine Experience
The Lesser Enchantments.. 67

Chapter Nine: A Prize South of Route 2
Malachite Peak (6,261')... 75

Chapter Ten: Mines, Mountains and Alpenglow
The Monte Cristo Range (~5,480'–7,172'). 83

Chapter Eleven: The Matterhorn of the Cascades
Sloan Peak (7,835'). 93

Chapter Twelve: A Gem Neglected
Mount Chaval (7,127')... 101

Chapter Thirteen: It's All in the Approach
Mount Buckindy (7,320')... 111

Chapter Fourteen: For the Matchless Views
Buck Mountain (8,573') 121

Chapter Fifteen: Poor Spelling but Great Mountaineering
Dumbell Mountain (8,421') 129

Chapter Sixteen: Two for the Effort of One
Cloudy Peak (7,915') and North Star Mountain (8,096') 139

Chapter Seventeen: From Heaven's Own Campsite
Mts. Maude (9,082') and Seven-Fingered Jack (9,100') 151

Chapter Eighteen: An Enigma Resolved
Bonanza Peak (9,511') 159

Chapter Nineteen: Infrequently Explored, Some Peaks with No Recorded Ascents
Peaks of the South Cascade Glacier (7,188'–8,261') 171

Chapter Twenty: Imposing but not Unclimbable
Mt. Formidable (8,325') 185

Chapter Twenty-one: The Panorama Prevails
Mount Buckner (9,192').. 197

Chapter Twenty-two: A Dance with the Devil
Teebone Ridge (6,985'–7065') 205

Chapter Twenty-three: Spine of the North Cascades
Backbone Ridge (7,040'–8,040').. 219

Chapter Twenty-four: Guaranteed Sunshine East of the Crest
The McAlester Area Ridges: Reynolds Peak (8,512'), Rennie Peak (7,742'), McAlester Mountain (7,928') and Mt. Gibbs (8,142')... 233

Chapter Twenty-five: The Razor Blade Traverse
Scalpel Ridge (7,065'–7,805')... 243

Chapter Twenty-six: It's Worth the Brush
Mt. Blum (7,680') 253

Chapter Twenty-seven: Better Views of the Giants than Climbing Them
Fisher Peak (8,040') 263

Chapter Twenty-eight: The ABC's of the North Cascades
*Arriva (8,215'), Black (8,970') and
Corteo Mountains (8,080')* 273

Chapter Twenty-nine: Running Ragged Ridge
Centerpiece of the National Park (7,310'–8,795') 285

Chapter Thirty: Heeding the Climber's Creed
Mt. Logan's North Face (9,087') 299

Chapter Thirty-one: No Easy Way Up
Jack Mountain (9,066') 309

Chapter Thirty-two: At Last - An Easy One!
Crater Mountain (8,218') 323

Chapter Thirty-three: Jewels of the East
Gilbert Mountain (8,023') and Abernathy Peak (8,321') 331

Chapter Thirty-four: Icon of the North Cascades
The Picket Range (6,819'–8,207') 339

Chapter Thirty-five: Massive but Unjustly Ignored
Mt. Spikard (8,979') 361

Chapter Thirty-six: A Northern Outpost of Mt. Baker
Hadley Peak (7,515') 369

Chapter Thirty-seven: Even Better Views than from Ruth
Icy Peak (7,073') 377

Chapter Thirty-eight: Tip-toe Across the Ridges North of the
Western Giants
*The High Divide/Keep Kool Lakes Traverse
(4,350'–6,415')* 387

Chapter Thirty-nine: Few Goats, but Spectacular Gardens and
Views
Goat Mountain (6,840') 399

Chapter Forty: Close Encounters of the Fourth Kind
Bear Mountain (7,942') 407

Chapter Forty-one: An International Feast for the Eyes and Soul
*The Border Peaks: American (7,994')
and Canadian Peaks (7,516')* 417

Chapter Forty-two: Best Views for the Effort in the Entire Range
Mt. Larrabee (7,861'). 429

A List of Several World-class Campsites in Washington's Cascades. 437

Epilogue, With an Apology to Fred Beckey 459

Bibliography 467

Acknowledgment

No such text could have seen the light of publication day without the benign guidance of Village Books' staff, including Chloe Hovind and Jessica Moreland, who parsed my overly complex sentences and took an ice ax to my purple prose. Their staff accomplished miracles in editing and offering suggestions on the order and progress of each essay, no matter how confused my original manuscript may first have appeared. Moreover, without the assistance of Village Books' marketing team and their personal contacts with well-established distributors, along with their savvy in electronic means of distribution, this book would, in all likelihood, never have been published.

My deepest appreciation goes to Karyn Servin, illustrator extraordinaire, without whose drawings of peaks and routes would have rendered this text useless. I also owe an abundance of appreciation to Rachel Davis, whose elegant renderings of the alpine flowers so pleasantly displays the magnificent botanical abundance of the Cascades in exquisite fashion. Her daughter, Susi Davis, was responsible for the beautiful rendering of the topographical maps, placing sites of crucial importance such as correct summits and campsites superimposed in plain sight. I am in debt as well to Cindy Hervey for her transcription of this manuscript from a page-less mess into a text with a professional appearance.

My gratitude also extends to the many climbing friends who have suffered my whining and ill-timed attempts at humor with uncommon patience. Thanks too, for the many climb leaders who encouraged me through the brush and led me to heights I never imagined I could attain. They shined a spotlight to illuminate strengths I never would have realized without their guidance, counsel, hand-holding (literally), escort and leadership. The two David's, Mike, Bob, Eddie, you all know who you are. To list these all would comprise a book in itself.

It should go without saying that my greatest debt is owed to The Man, Fred Beckey, who, when a steep couloir opened up in heaven, rappelled down a shaft of light to illuminate the darkest of alpine reaches in this, our least-appreciated and most untraveled of American alpine areas: Washington's Cascades. Although I take issue with his text with some of the descriptions, there can be no denying that 99% of the time, he is spot-on.

Perhaps my deepest gratitude and admiration, however, should go to my closest partner, my ex-wife, Marjorie. I recall her earliest outdoor adventure 50 years ago, taking the trail up Table Mountain in the Columbia River Gorge. Crying and angry at me in the upper meadows after just 2,000' of altitude gain, she went on to accomplish multiple ascents of Mts. Rainier, Glacier Peak, Baker, Dome and Shuksan, not to mention a number of summits far abroad in the Alps, Himalaya, Patagonia, and New Zealand. She's climbed Mt. Hood at least seven times, often by different routes. When fear knocked on her door in the form of acrophobia, she answered, and there was no one there.

Thanks to all for allowing an aging climber to revisit his mountain past, and once again savor the pleasure of these heights.

Dedication

Dedicated first to the best partner I've ever had - in the city as well as in the mountains: Marjorie, who transformed fear into courage and insecurity into strength.

Dedicated also to the climbing organizations, The Mountaineers and the Mazamas; it is an irony that the best friends we make on level ground are those we first met on the ups and downs of the mountains.

Introduction

Scope

Millions of nature travelers, the majority vehicle-bound, will visit the Grand Canyon (5,520,726 people in 2024), Zion National Park (4,500,000), Yosemite (4,150,217), and Yellowstone (4,097,710). I've hiked and climbed in them as well. How many folks have taken a journey to the North Cascades? In 2024, the National Park Service counted over 3,700,000 park visits. Although millions of these may have driven Highway 20 or taken a sightseeing boat up Lake Chelan, the Park Service estimates only about 800,000 people have actually *used* the North Cascades National Park in that year; however, that includes folks who might have stopped by the Ranger Station in Marblemount and asked a question or those who may have spent a night in a camper at Colonial Creek Campground.

But the majority of these visitors have, in all likelihood, never ventured into the depths of its mountains, never hiked its trails nor scrambled its easier peaks, much less backpacked or climbed in its jagged ranges. The best estimates for those who have hiked, camped and/or climbed in just the National Park for 2024 are barely 10,000 souls.

As a result, the entire range of peaks beginning just south of Mt. Rainier and continuing north into southern British Columbia is often, I believe, unjustly neglected. It is as if a black hole exists in this far western corridor of Washington State, from which no information has leaked out to the millions of wilderness-loving Americans living outside of its immediate proximity.

All of us who enjoy this montage of mountain miracles, our shared alpine culture, may be partly at fault, as we often display more prejudice than pride as we rarely tout its unique character. This alpine region, unified by the majesty and continuity of its summits, is the mountain province which this text covers. Fortunately, Congress has deemed much of this area worthy of the strongest protection, creating such sanctuaries as the Henry Jackson

INTRODUCTION

Wilderness (encompassing the Monte Cristo Range), the Glacier Peak Wilderness Area, the Alpine Lakes Wilderness (comprised of the Mt. Stuart Ranges and the Enchantment Lakes), the Mt. Baker Wilderness, and of course, the crown jewel: The North Cascades National Park.

However, additional outposts of these great ranges, such as the peaks east and west of the South Cascade Glacier, and the spires and turrets so characteristic of the Dome Massif, have all been omitted from the National Park. Plans to incorporate these areas into the Park are as tentative as they are overdue. These sharpened heights, green valleys, wildflower-filled meadows, glaciers, waterfalls and lakes require the utmost governmental protection lest they fall prey to private interests. Nonetheless, our menagerie of mountains is like your favorite playlist, but the difference is that peaks, unlike songs, cannot be erased from memory.

This narrative will tell tales of adventure and offer essays on exploration in an admittedly inadequate attempt to impart to the reader the grandeur and drama of these landscapes, bounded by no seas but flowing nonetheless in waves of jagged peaks and vertical spires of snow, ice and rock. It is written not because the words can match the glory of these northernmost ranges in the lower 48 states as much as to impel the adventurer to experience first-hand what this almost-ignored expanse can offer: a mountain tapestry sewing itself into the soul of each wanderer over these lands. Mountains are my opium; when I am in these ranges, I know that I am home.

It's a shame that so few have actually penetrated our nation's most spectacular alpine area or gazed in awe at its rugged topography. Certainly, the Sierras in California have pointed towers but these are few and far between. Banner and Ritter Peaks, just off the John Muir Trail, spring to mind, with meadows and lakelets mimicking the North Cascades, as does the area surrounding The Palisades. In the main, however, what the Sierras offer, especially as you progress to their highest reaches southward, is a sea of sameness, punctuated by rock and grass. In a similar vein, Yellowstone's hot springs and bison are marvels of nature but the mountain worshipper will be disappointed by the lack of any spectacular scenery.

The Grand Canyon (not the deepest gorge in the country - that goes to Hell's Canyon between Oregon and Idaho) is rock and sand, multi-colored and worth one trip, perhaps two, but certainly not more. Even the famed and much publicized Rockies are mostly rounded hills, aged by weather, wind and erosion to the shape of domes, not fangs. True, they feature marvelous gardens of wildflowers but it's only in the Maroon Bells and certain areas close to Long's Peak that they approach the combination of meadow, waterfalls, glaciers and angular peaks so typical of the North Cascades.

Climbing in the Andes features a base camp amidst bunchgrasses but almost no flowers; beyond, you will encounter only snow, ice and rock. On a number of expeditions, we frequently encountered a desert of windblown sand and gravel which stung our eyes and numbed our souls. Indeed, the number of flowering species in South America's mountains is lower by hundreds than in the Cascades. The same may be said of the ranges in Alaska and northern British Columbia. These exalted heights may hold higher summits but within them, one inhabits a world of stone and ice alone, without the mellowing effects of mountain meadows and their calico of wildflowers. The closest one can achieve the brilliance of the Washington's Cascades are certain areas of the Canadian Interior Ranges, the Cirque of the Unclimables and the Bugaboos, but these are many days of travel away.

If you have the money and time, you may travel to the Himalaya for treks and climbs, but there you will again encounter mostly rock and ice, soaring and beautiful at times, especially in the Karakorum Ranges, but, in my opinion, a uniformity nonetheless, bordering on stasis, especially on a month-long trek. Perhaps the Alps come closest to the North Cascades and merit more than a brief foray. These peaks, sharply-defined and glacier-clad, have a civilized allure. Even there, however, amongst the serrated peaks, icy cliffs and parapets, you will most likely be one in a line of trekking tourists, even on the most rugged of routes, staying at a four-star lodge at night with fine-linen

INTRODUCTION

sheets and a parquet-floored dining room, feasting on *haute* cuisine. You will often have to retreat, after a day of climbing, to a village, quaintly European, but saturated with tourist shops. Even the "High Routes" take you through towns and tourist spots, not unpleasant, but definitely the opposite of what we would consider wilderness. Many days are spent hoping to avoid the crowds and the cows with their droppings on your way up most of the peaks.

New Zealand comes close but lacks the wild joy of exploring a route on which you're never certain will succeed, as you must remain on the varied "tracks" to undertake treks in the Southern Island; wildflower species are not as diverse as in the North Cascades and are most frequently shrubs rather than forbs. Meadows are rare. Moreover, in New Zealand, you must spend each night in a predetermined hut, with bed, blankets and a fully-stocked kitchen provided. Expense is a severe constraint there as well. If you have but one chance in a lifetime to travel and summits are your beloved goal, I would recommend Patagonia: surreal, daunting, and otherworldly, a place not easily defined in any human language – you just have to see it. But for many, such trips remain more of an aspiration than a reality. In contrast to these areas, it's the *wildness* of the North Cascades that cannot be matched.

But what of the staggering, sharply-etched peaks shouldering the sides of Norway's fjords jutting in from the Atlantic like watery fingers creeping deeply into the land? Though capped by snow and ice, they form but a single file up-thrusted from the sea's edge and thus lack the depth of the North Cascades, as well as their jumbled diversity. There are simply few mountains behind the mountains. Nor have meadows of wildflowers been fond of such northern latitudes, though the peaks themselves, and their associated rivers and waterfalls merit at least one or two visits for anyone searching for spectacular mountain scenery. I have climbed in all these locations and each has its charms. As a weekend punter, my climbing resumé may be wide but barely an inch thick. Nonetheless, I always welcome a return to Washington's Cascades: for me, the ultimate in geologic and botanic variety and splendor.

At the risk of sounding parochial and even xenophobic, in my opinion only the western Cascades contain a tableau of sharp-toothed spires, glacier-clad giants, mountain meadows colored with the hues of too many species of wildflowers to count, and the waterfalls and deep forests which swell the heart and burst the soul. This alchemy of Nature's primal elements is of greater value than gold. To my eyes, the North Cascades summons up the embodiment of mountain topography combined with the definition of sublime wilderness. Unhappily, this most spectacular mountain treasure is also one of our least-visited and, just as irritating, least publicized as well. When was the last article featuring the North Cascades published in *National Geographic*, *Backpacker*, or *Outdoors* magazines? Before most readers were born. When was it presented as a worthwhile treasure on TV or on any multi-media website? Never.

A recent coffee-table publication by the Smithsonian Institution detailing entire ecosystems on Earth, such as oceans, coastlines, deserts, and mountains, notes ranges on all continents, and even sub-ranges, such as those in Carpathia and Bulgaria, but nary a word or photo of the North Cascades. A recent offering from the Post Office honoring national parks omits the North Cascades. A celebration of the National Parks by National Geographic Books displaying hundreds of photographs devotes entire chapters to many of our parks along with glowing descriptions, but a single line and just one photo of the North Cascades. Ignored nationally, these mountains deserve better as it is they, rather than the written word, which will endure.

Indeed, a contemporary recent edition of the "Great Courses of our National Parks" in a science news magazine mentioned four such parks in California; four in the Rockies; two courses on the Grand Canyon; two on Yellowstone; two on parks in Utah; and one each on the Smoky Mountains and Acadia National Park. This course lumped together the North Cascades with the Olympics (understandable) and Crater Lake in Oregon (strange), evidently ignoring the differences in scenery and flora amongst these three

INTRODUCTION

regions. A second "Great Course", this on geological wonders, devoted chapters to the Grand Canyon, Bryce Canyon, Devil's Tower, and Yellowstone, but nary a word on any American peaks north of the 45th parallel. This national neglect of the North Cascades, an alpine land of crystalline jewels, is utterly damning.

Is this because these peaks lie hidden in the Northwestern corner of our country? Perhaps, but these days, many people travel freely all about the U.S. Is it any farther away from the Eastern Seaboard than the many easier and mostly ersatz attractions of California's multiple theme parks and bus tours of the stars' homes? Not really. Moreover, the North Cascades is within just several hours' drive from the Olympia-Tacoma-Seattle-Everett-Bellingham megalopolis, home to more than five million inhabitants, the vast majority of whom know little to nothing about the glory so close to their homes. Count in my home town of Portland and its satellites extending south to Eugene and north through Vancouver, WA to Bellingham, and there are approximately nine million souls stitched together along the I-5 corridor.

Yet barely a few have experienced the majesty of these wild lands and the freedom of these mountains, while most remain blind to their terrible yet awesome splendor, I hope this book will help them see the value of their beauty in this, our automated age. Our screens, TV's, computers, smart phones, X-boxes, and tablets, all flatten the curves and luscious depths of natural landscapes, at times to our enlightenment, sometimes to our detriment. These mountain ranges permit no traffic jams; no exciting combat or protest exist there; this wilderness has no slums.

Even those who do visit or travel through the highways of these wild lands rarely explore the furthest reaches of the rugged terrain just off these roads. Perhaps they are fended off by tangled underbrush, steep trails, hostile slopes, and the inconvenience of carrying sufficient gear to camp out for one night, let alone a week. Admittedly, there are many who physically cannot make such trips but most can, yet prefer the ease of the modern lifestyle, centered on urban landscapes, electronic devices with their frequently addictive videogames, and adventures on four wheels. They are missing alpine jewels which pierce the Washington sky as strongly as they satisfy the soul of adventure and the absolute beauty of nature unfurled as nowhere else in America.

I realize that much of my bluster about the North Cascades may sound either strident, naïve or even quaint; however, it does rely on my world travels as much as unapologetic chauvinism. I only hope that my occasional hyperbole does not result in too much disfavor for those readers who have differing opinions on the utmost and memorable mountain utopias they hold dear. Arguments can lead to agreements or at least compromises, in which each side leaves the table not entirely in accord but with some small sense of satisfaction. I hope that readers will find this text more affectionate than flamboyant.

Purpose

In this book, I will describe the areas I find of most interest yet also, in my opinion, those most often neglected. I have attempted to avoid the most popular, and hence crowded areas of our ranges. The descriptions run roughly from south to north and then east to west as I find that, although all these lands are worthy of repeated exploration, the most chiseled and brilliant of ranges lie both within the National Park and close to its borders as they sew themselves into the tapestry of your soul. Here, camping on a clear night, the sky is alive with stars and one can sleep with your dreams, then awaken and accomplish them. But even the southern-most trips described herein are filled with acres of flowered meadows and keen-edged peaks of snow, rock and ice, where every crag and void beckon and where mountain vistas are too beautiful for just one trip.

Admittedly, the adventures described herein, and the routes depicted to these summits, will offer no major technical difficulty for the retail-sponsored climbing athletes collecting fees for risking their lives. I am in no position to disparage their heroics; indeed, I, along with the majority of climbers I know, aspire to their astonishing capabilities and accomplishments. But, while we may seem to them (we all probably know a few) poseurs, weekend warriors and merely casual climbers, we all have a niche in this mountainous landscape, and who can measure which among us appreciates, and cares for, these wonder-filled sweeps of majesty more?

We can always aspire to their deeds and hope they can serve as our avatars of the heights and voids within these ranges. The price of love is compromise; the same is true for many of the peaks and routes I'd love to climb but realize they are beyond my competence (or bravery). Thus this tome is undertaken with the typical weekend- to week-long mountain climber in mind, rather than the brave expedition champions for whom autobiographies often culminate their careers. Nonetheless, I suspect that your "average" climber perusing these pages is, like me, consumed by these peaks; they are as much a part of yourself as the air we breathe.

A fluid hierarchy exists among hikers, scramblers and climbers. Too often, it is the climbers who, perhaps secretly, disparage hikers and even us dabblers or those limited to scrambling these peaks, as no more than walkers, not true brave adventurers. Yet who is to say there is a more noble achievement in a first ascent than an amble up a peak such as Kyes in the Monte Cristo's or Alta Peak near Hibox in the Chickamin sub-range? We all differ; every individual's brain and capacity for achieving maximum muscle strength, stamina, and level of coordination contain special attributes and skills others may lack. Those who judge may be conveniently covering up their own muddles and mishaps. At any rate, there exists a fluid distinction among those who venture into the mountains. It may not be courage which distinguishes the hero as much as genetic potential and ample opportunity.

You will not find in this text what the European climbing literature provides in excess: the inner workings of the minds of the climber. There are innumerable texts, mostly Italian, French and British, which try to examine *why* folks climb. Airy philosophies and psychobabble usually follow. Finding mystical meaning in such a self-absorbed endeavor may be replete with dreamy prose but empty in purpose and content. What child doesn't climb a tree just to see if they can surmount it? What youth doesn't rush up a hill, just to see what's on the other side? It's the same curiosity which, combined with a sense of adventure, propels us upwards – always upwards.

We may climb and explore partly to fill the half-empty shells of our ersatz, overcrowded and video-gamed world. While undoubtedly partially true, I believe there is a more realistic motivation as well: Why is it so difficult to merely accept that climbing allows us to connect in spirit with the wilderness; to feel pleased in enhancing our athletic skills; to experience airy heights and spectacular vistas; and, most honestly of all, to accomplish something about which you can feel proud, even if, unlike me, you never boast about your mountain achievements to anyone?

Let's be honest: Climbing combines occasional disappointment but also discovery. It also most often requires a certain tolerance for discomfort. The older one gets, the greater that tolerance becomes. These adventures are arduous; they require exertion but there remains something special about things that are inconvenient. Climbing almost always entails strenuous effort but it also builds a tolerance for hardship and even pain. But on your adventures, you know you made it – or at least gave it your best try. The explorer asks not why, but how. In the words of professional climber Cory Richards, climbing is a self-absorbed process, an "expensive, dangerous recreation [which entails] a certain amount of self-indulgence".

Climbing can be dangerous, though mostly in the general public's estimation. For Washington's Cascades, the most dangerous part of any mountain adventure is the drive back home. Indeed, the most hazardous experience you will ever encounter is to either drive, or be a front seat passenger in, a moving vehicle. Take others to share the driving responsibilities, use caffeine or music if it helps, but, best of all, leave enough daylight to return home unharmed. The safest means to remain intact: Spend an extra night in the wilderness and drive back the next day. Your friends and family will appreciate it.

INTRODUCTION

This is no guidebook; there are plenty of those with specifics on access, elevation gain, etc. Reading any of these or studying the numerous descriptions on a variety of Cascades' websites for the specifics on routes for the same peak (see the bibliography at the end of this text) can create a cacophony of differing opinions, but such variation may be all to the good in providing assistance in averaging out the most feasible route you've chosen. Of crucial relevance for access are the excellent series of trail guides in the *100 Hikes* Series, published by The Mountaineers Press, which will channel your inner mountaineer to the access points described herein.

Even more useful for the active climber, or those who aspire to be, are the three *Cascade Alpine Guides* by the renowned first ascensionist Fred Beckey. He is certainly a hero and should there ever be a climbing pope, he would certainly be entitled to be named a saint. However, occasionally his descriptions are less than crisp or entirely accurate, although I do not wish to tightrope the ill-defined boundary between insight and insult. However, as with the other guidebooks noted in the bibliography, the nature of certain climbs, mainly those more benign, and the gateways to them, contain descriptions filled with jargon varying between the incomprehensible and the inconsequential, being vague or not currently correct.

Nonetheless many of these sources are essential for anyone planning a climb I have not included in these marvelous mountains. These again are, in the main, published by The Mountaineers Books. I do not dismiss these invaluable treasures, but occasionally their accounts are brief to the point of being nebulous, especially on summits far removed from the central spine of the Cascades. This is especially true in the narratives of approaches, often the most tortuous parts of any Cascades climb. This present mini-guide, based on my field notes and tape recordings, is not intended to surpass the Beckey Guides nor the others noted in breadth; it attempts only to capture the essence of our ranges by featuring the less well-known and infrequently-visited meadows and peaks which provide alpine satisfaction absent the hordes of folks concentrated around the more popular landmarks and icons of Washington's Cascades.

Although at times I disagree with Beckey's accounts, there can be no denial that his three volumes are a mandatory read; the present text is merely a minor supplement to his well-researched guides. His accounts of routes and approaches are often admirable but at certain times, they are at best vague. He writes with a clarity more useful than inspired; I'm hopeful the present text will meet both criteria: a guide as well as a paean to these majestic mountains.

It has been most helpful that weather forecasts have become much more accurate than in a past in which they matched predictions about as faultless as those from the Oracle at Delphi. More recently, we have been fortunate in enjoying (most of the time) pleasant outings based on more precise weather information. Nonetheless, as mountain wanderers, we can exercise caution but must expect occasional disruption.

A more complete bibliography will be found at the end of this book, which features the best guidebooks currently available. In addition, websites abound: CascadeClimbers.com and Summitpost.com are most germane. However, they typically consist of a generic "we went there, did that, reached the top, then we descended and went home and it was wonderful". I also take the opposite of the "high point" mentality, in which folks want to claim reaching the highest points in all 50 states, or in all the counties in any particular state, or even all the Himalayan peaks over 6,000 meters. Worthy goals? Perhaps, but not for the mountain-minded. The highest point in Florida, Britton Hill, is in the midst of a cow pasture at 345' elevation.

In counterpoint, these essays, most of them quite brief, are not meant for the pure peak-bagger nor are they mere memories of personal journeys. This is a text more expository than prescriptive. In the main, these essays comprise descriptions of nooks, niches and crannies I've had the joy of visiting, many more than once and often six or seven times, over the past 60 years. Some of these areas, even today, remain largely devoid of mankind's mark. Although the story, among both climbers and fishermen, often exceeds the facts, I've attempted to pass on what I know about these areas in as accurate a manner as possible. They often consist of a brush-choked entry to alpine meadows and far-ranging views and are mostly offered for the weekend scrambler or accidental climber, although some of the routes described require not only caution, but the skills of placing protection and expertise in the mid-5th-class level of climbing.

The peaks I've included will not impress anyone nor add much to any climbing résumé, but are intended for the average weekend climber rather than the elite athlete. Retail-sponsored mountain warriors may view achieving these "gems" as more a hypnotic than a stimulant. Their creed may be to turn the impossible into the achievable. However, my selections are written by, and for, an author with the skills of a middling climber in the hope that others, perhaps as moderately nimble and hearty as I, can value that miracles such as those within these ranges can exist on our planet.

I have not included certain spectacular destinations, such as climbing the great volcanoes of Glacier Peak or Mt. Baker, nor have I written about the anodyne guided tours up Mt. Rainier, a climb more replete with symbolism than substance. The most popular of objectives such as Cascade Pass or certain areas around Snoqualmie Pass, Mts. Baker and Shuksan are omitted, not due to lack of space but because these are so well-frequented, they have almost become a cliché amongst Cascade mountain visitors. They appear to be the embodiment of The *Wizard of Oz*, pretending to be a brilliant magician, when in fact, they are as banal as a paved road up Whitehorse Mountain in the Adirondacks or up Colorado's Pikes Peak. My choices herein are, honestly, quite personal but also, in my opinion, relatively neglected.

Nor have I included the equally striking yet serene Olympic Mountains and National Park just across Puget Sound, although these share, to a lesser extent, the glories of meadows and towers so characteristic of the northern Cascades. (By the way, the exploding costs of now entering, camping, and even parking in the Olympics creates a critically different experience from this spectacular cousin of the relatively inexpensive North Cascades. It is as if its ranges are becoming almost as much an act of commerce as an act of nature.)

At any rate, there is just sufficient room to barely do justice to one range, rather than try to cram into a single text both National Parks and adjacent mountainous regions.

In addition, I've opted to omit the more well-known or famous locations, such as the areas north of Snoqualmie Pass, portions of the regions abutting Cascade and Hannegan Passes and most of the Ptarmigan Traverse peaks. While gorgeous and bountiful hikes, backpacks and peaks abound in these areas, they are so well-known and well-frequented that the majority of Northwest outdoor adventurers need more guidance in these areas than a backpacker needs a heavier load. I think of them as the Costco's of the range, already familiar to hikers, backpackers, scramblers and climbers, who literally have to stand in a line awaiting passage. To quote one of Yogi Berra's famous oxymorons, "People have stopped going there because it's too crowded".

Instead this text aims to introduce both newcomers and Cascades veterans to the more obscure and lesser-travelled options in these, our most rugged and remote landscapes in the lower 48 - *terra incognita* to many of our mountain visitors. Perhaps because they are lesser-known, remote and less familiar, they render mystery and intrigue which is close to magical. One might well quibble that including Bonanza or the West Face Route on Stuart are hardly "hidden areas" in these modern times. Yet, as recently as 2023, we've encountered nary another climbing party on these routes even on glorious-weather summer weekends. The names of some of these peaks may be well known, though little-travelled; others may be anonymous to many Northwest climbers. If you disagree, all the better: We should celebrate dissent as discord sows the seeds of greater knowledge.

You will notice my preference for the open spaces of our mountain meadows rising above the forest floor. Please bear with my penchant for space and views. As with most folks, I appreciate the soothing, yet majestic solitude of our vast, almost omnipresent forests, with their canopies of 250' tall Douglas firs, thick-robed red cedars, shining silver firs, mountain hemlocks, subalpine firs, spruces, and

INTRODUCTION

noble firs. Note especially the Western and subalpine larches east of the Crest; these are actually deciduous trees and turn their soft velvety green needles a brilliant orange before laying down a rug of golden needles as autumn progresses. You can almost see and feel the purifying silence amongst these forest giants so far from human interference.

These woodlands provide a hushed entrance, a soft journey, and a fragrance more balm than costly perfume; they are an anticipation of the marvels waiting above. At times, they hold an eerie silence, often broken by the creaking of boughs bending in the breezes, sounding almost like a baby's gentle first wails. Birds are more plentiful and diverse here as well. They are the musicians of the forest, with the wind providing a percussive backdrop.

Such forests form the definition of wilderness. They are the homes of incredible numbers of animal and floral species and, without them, our mountains would have nothing to soar above, no contrast, no purity of purpose. You may ascend beyond the forests, but you will always, in this range, be able to see the trees. In my mind, however, treks through these giant forests alone would limit you to the floor of this wilderness; you must scale above the towering trees to appreciate the true grandeur of these incredible peaks. As you approach the openings above 4,000', subalpine firs and mountain hemlocks hold sway before yielding to the vistas which open up to provide a fitting climax to most mountain adventures. Many will disagree; it takes a chorus of voices to appreciate differing perspectives. Yet there are many of us who believe that a world without such heights would be a mistake. It is the miracle and mystery of these mountains that makes those of us who love them whole.

As an over-used convention, I will occasionally employ the analogies of battle when describing climbs. Indeed, when thrashing through impenetrable brush, for which these ranges is infamous, or clinging to its fragile walls so often flaked with holds so loose as to toss you off like some insect in the wind, these climbs do seem like warfare. I apologize if anyone is offended, as the successful climber/scrambler does not truly "conquer" a summit. Making it up and down without undue harm is a win of sorts, but it is only because the weather, your competent companions, the textbook guides, and the peak, allowed you those precious achievements. Moreover, in our steel, concrete and silicon world, where most of us exist in a manicured landscape, the mountains are still wild. We never truly "vanquish" a peak. We will all succumb at some point during our brief lifetimes; the mountains will endure for millennia.

Is there really a need for another mountain guidebook? Perhaps not, but I believe, in contrast to most Cascade guidebooks, the present text will not only provide access and route information to overlooked treasures, but also describe the best locations to camp; the flora of our gorgeous and varied meadows; the views from these wonder-filled sites in each specific direction; and a host of summits rarely attempted, with compass directions to identify specific summits to be viewed and identified. You may learn thereby which views are the finest in all directions, north, south, east and west, often from unique perspectives.

Illustrations of suggested routes will be traced on 7½" topographic maps and drawings of approximate courses will accompany these at the beginning of each chapter; an occasional flower drawing of the native alpine flora particular to the area discussed will decorate random pages in most of these essays. I believe that wildflowers are the jewels of our mountain landscapes. Moreover, in contrast to almost all other mountain guides to our ranges, the present book will provide illustrations in color, thus hopefully enlivening your browsing pleasure.

As an aside, it is of note that Rickett's exhaustive compendium of *The Wild Flowers of the United States* comprises six ecosystems: a single volume suffices for each such system; however this botanist required two volumes to cover the flora of the Pacific Northwest. This serves as a testament to the abundant cornucopia and glorious variety of our native wildflowers as compared to every other continental region.

In addition, in an Appendix following the text, I've listed a number of world-class campsites. Many are located on the routes described herein while others occur elsewhere in the Cascades. My hope is that climbers and hikers/backpackers will find these gems, with their exceptional and unimpeded views often amongst wildflower-filled meadows, fulfilling by themselves, whether as respites on a march toward a peak to be climbed or simply as a worthy destination for all who count the mountains as their special refuge.

Environment

While some authors decry the disclosure of their "secret places" so that these do not become overrun, I'm of the opinion that we should strive not to stanch the flow of visitors. The more mountain travelers who access these beautiful spaces, the better we can all appreciate the need to more fully protect our mountainous terrains. The mountains provide a stable point of reference in an otherwise rapidly reeling world. In addition, we hope that more, rather than fewer, outdoor explorers will realize the extent to which the dual scourges of habitat loss and global warming can adversely impact our native flora, fauna and glaciated areas.

We must, however, recognize that much of what we think of as original is, in fact, second or third-growth timber, yet now fortunately preserved. Our world of the wild is mostly delimited these days by humans. The idyllic notion of an untouched wilderness, while enchanting, is an imaginary ideal. From the earliest *homo sapiens* to the crossing of an ice-bound Bering Strait, the primeval world is gone, having given way to the earth's predominant predator: us. Nonetheless, to be silent in the face of this oncoming calamity is to be an accomplice to it. When a tree falls in the forest, everyone hears it, and everyone feels it.

We cannot allow bias to camouflage science. Our country, which gave birth to the idea of untrammeled wilderness, should not be among the first to destroy it. The denial of man-made global warming flies in the face of science; to deny it is simply intrinsically wrong. While popular opinion, abetted by the media, has focused on the loss of tropical forests, about a third of intact forest landscapes are still located in the boreal woodlands of North America, northern Europe and northern Asia. Satellite imagery has revealed a significant decline in these forests, mainly through manufacturing activities, chiefly logging, agriculture and mining. Not much of our world's spaces or species have escaped the impact of human agency.

We are heedlessly destroying many of our planet's ecosystems and crowding out their natural beauty or hunting valuable organisms into history. We have decimated thousands of animal species. They say that domestic and feral cats kill more than one billion birds each year. To find a more predatory species, you only have to look in a mirror. Each photo, seminar or study sounds one more note in the cacophony of this distressing concert. The symphony we know as wilderness might well become this world's swan song.

To avoid this dystopian vision of a lifeless future, governments, policy makers, business leaders and we as citizens must view these changes not with resignation, but with revolt. There is no question that the grim fact of climate change has markedly altered the 4½ billion-year history of our planet; it is now the increasingly rapid *rate of change* that is alarming. It should be expected that a child fears the dark, but it is tragic when adults are afraid of the light. History may well judge the present generation's greatest sin as ignoring the advent of this crisis and doing nothing to prevent it. Surely science and reason must issue an indictment: To not acknowledge a battle is to ensure losing the war.

Indisputably, anthropogenic warming has been compared to a slinky going down a set of stairs – slowly, with many stops and starts; or to minor perturbations causing major changes far from the source, much as a child delivers a wave down a jump-rope with a flick of the wrist at one end. A more profound analogy stems from the seas: Climate change is not unlike a tide, imperceptibly rising yet unavoidable to notice as it reaches its crest. But unlike a tide, global warming will never return to its original position.

Yet strategies to reduce carbon dioxide will depend on more plant life, including trees, grasses, and crops, than our planet currently can provide. Ignorance is no longer an excuse for inaction. However, neither despair nor complacency is warranted. But writing a book by itself cannot rescue this wondrous wilderness, nor can strident voice alone; we need to be more than anti-something. Speak up, get involved, talk with your senator and representative. Climate change has been so frequently noted that we may become inured to its perils. Act now to let your legislators realize that the impact of man-made climate warming on the wild worlds we adore requires out utmost attention.

Guidance and Usage

I have chosen to employ elevations, landmarks, and distances in the text to accompany the routes depicted on the maps and route illustrations rather than GPS positioning. There still exist not a few outdoor enthusiasts who lack GPS devices. In addition, it would be unusual and unwieldy to constantly check positions with a GPS device. Moreover, forest cover often can preclude accurate GPS readings. A GPS device may produce a stew of data, but must be seasoned with the experience of map and compass, as well as an awareness of prominent landmarks. Thus these routes are more sylvan than silicon. In full disclosure I must also admit that a number of these trips were made before GPS positioning became available. At present, these tools are accessible with topographic maps already built into the device or accessible for downloading. Nonetheless, I also believe that the constant checking of your GPS position can drain away some of the adventurous spirit of these trips.

But there also lies a more profound reason to omit GPS readings. Studies at the University of California have demonstrated that constant checking of GPS locations actually siphons attention away from the natural landscape, lowers navigational skills, reduces perception of distance, and results in slower reaction times. I have been on trips in which the leader checked our GPS position over

60 times, this on a clear day! This reliance on a digital crutch can diminish an experience of the outdoors.

Moreover, studies at several universities have demonstrated that individuals trained to chart a course without artificial aides demonstrated heightened activity in the brain's hippocampus (a center for short-term memory and navigational skills). Several of these projects, one in Tokyo and one in a wooded area in the U.S., also showed that reliance on GPS readings led to longer journeys and sometimes directed people into a lake or a barricade; in other words, these readings comprised an algorithmic mirage. Those who were provided with a map and compass demonstrated quicker and more accurate navigation in both urban and forested environments.

Another study, this from a French University, showed that individuals born, reared and remained in a city in which streets were numbered consecutively and spaced in a regular fashion were less likely to successfully navigate their way out of a complicated maze, whereas those raised in cities with streets formed in a haphazard pattern were superior when faced with the same challenge. The researchers' opinion was summed up by stating that "...it might be a good idea to occasionally turn off Google Maps".

I am no Luddite. GPS has saved many anxious hours when caught in a whiteout on a featureless glacier or when entangled in heavy brush with no idea of your position. However, whenever possible (actually most of the time), you will be better served by learning to plot your course by map, compass and landmarks, both before your trip and during it, rather than to rely on GPS readings alone, especially in thick forest, where readings can be unreliable.

Instead, use your eyes like a prism to appreciate your immediate and distant positions. Utilize your smart-phone-enabled "rectangular limb" only when absolutely necessary for safety. And don't allow your batteries to die if you're completely relying on electronics; if you do, and they fail, you may be up a mountain without a map. Several newer guides, listed in the bibliography, can provide GPS

INTRODUCTION

positions for a number of these trips. Unfortunately, several of these published GPS readings have provided conflicting positions, as, for example on Bonanza Peak, where readings would have been most helpful.

While maps and drawings may be instruments of persuasion and even conquest, no dotted line on a map or illustration, no matter which guidebook you choose, can accurately predict your exact route. The diagrams herein provide a holistic overview rather than a granular step-by-step set of instructions. These route illustrations must be viewed as approximations. Snowfields, rockfalls, and gullies change with each passing season. Moreover, reading the multitude of North Cascades Guides, and scanning the ample information available in online accounts, one inevitably will encounter competing narratives. There exist oceans of information which, unfortunately, drain into swamps in the field. No text, nor even close scrutiny of maps and illustrations, can pinpoint every obstacle which will almost certainly be part of most mountain journeys; indeed, often it is just these hurdles, and the ability to overcome them, which excite the true mountaineer.

Moreover, a book such as this cannot predict whatever technological changes may betake our sport in the future: temperature-regulating clothing? More accurate GPS positioning despite forest cover? Drone-assisted guidance? Ever-lighter equipment? In all likelihood, however, the essence of backcountry travel and mountaineering, a spirit of adventure, the stamina and conditioning required to undertake it, and an appreciation of all our wild places, will remain.

Maps and Illustrations

In this text, each chapter contains both a 7½" USGS topographic map with a route and, at times, alternate pathways drawn on it. All chapters will contain, in addition, an illustration depicting a route or, in certain cases, multiple passages, as described in the text. Each map and illustration will depict any relevant road access, where appropriate, in black color. Trails will be marked with a solid red line, while, most importantly, off-trail travel will be denoted by dashed red lines. When a route is out of view, as behind a ridge, that portion will be noted by a dashed blue line, both on the maps and the illustrations. Additional features may mark locations such as potential campsites, avalanche fans, and scree or talus where these are of immediate or crucial importance; these will also be denoted in blue.

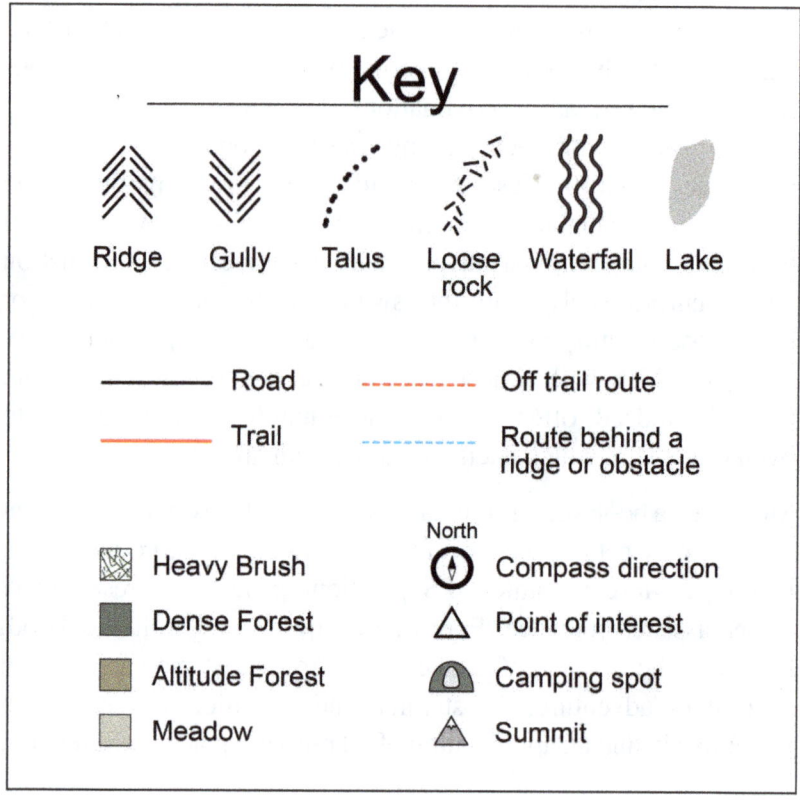

A note of concern is in order here. No off-trail dashed lines can depict with 100% accuracy every twist and turn of a route through dense brush nor even on scree, talus or rock. These, in all guide books, are approximations for several reasons: Conditions change and memories are imperfect. Faced in the field with a map and text, the climber will often be confused about the correct course because there may be no perfect route that avoids all troubles. Common sense and exploration, combined with map, compass, and GPS

INTRODUCTION

readings all help, but a dashed line, whether in Beckey, Nelson and Potterfield, Smoot, or those either listed in the bibliography or herein, are the best approximations of a way forward, not a step-by-step description of a guaranteed passage.

Caution: It cannot be stressed enough that readers should be aware that this book is not a complete climbing or access guide. Its main purpose is to acquaint climbers, scramblers and hikers to mountainous areas of the Washington Cascades that are, in the main, often neglected, overlooked or stand apart from the mainstream of selected regions of the major ranges. Please see the bibliography for references to more complete guides. In addition, adventures in these mountains may require technical experience on rock and ice; the proper equipment in order to travel in these areas; a level of physical fitness appropriate to the areas mentioned; map and compass; compatriots, if possible, who are familiar with the area; as well as a GPS device and the knowledge of how to employ it. Travel through the regions described is difficult and readers should be aware of the dangers inherent in any climb, scramble or hike. This text is not a manual of *how* to climb nor a guide to any techniques required to travel in these realms.

Moreover, guide books, even mine, can seem at times like the aphorisms found in a fortune cookie insert: generic and ambiguous. Careful planning, map-reading, checking about what equipment will be needed, and consulting additional comprehensive guides, would be wise. No line drawn on a map or illustration can take into account every obstacle you may encounter. And please remember, no matter how lofty your level of expertise, you cannot reliably anticipate every consequence within the mountain environment.

Summary

Of course, this is an opinionated piece, and meant to be. No one sees the same rainbow in the same way. Anyway, writing a book about mountains is different than climbing them. And, of course, I am downplaying the charms and spectacles of our other mountain areas, so I hope you can excuse my occasional zest and hyperbole. However, mountain landscapes, for me, require the unique blend of quietly giant forests, the greenest of meadows, a sublime mixture of multi-colored wildflowers, the rush of brooks, the roar of waterfalls, the icy tumble of glaciers, the grand and sharply vertical cliffs, all topped by the sharpest of ranges and summits. The sum of all these elements defines Washington's Cascades. If this book encourages others to go exploring, it will then have achieved its most significant purpose.

I truly believe that if you visit and *explore* these wild lands, you will have to agree that they stand alone as the most majestic yet lovely of all North American ranges, an overlooked paradise, primitive yet approachable. I am not so naïve as to think that none of the adventures I describe suffer from complete obscurity. But this book is not so much a travelogue or a guide as it is a description of the jewels, some hidden, others obvious, but most not so familiar to even the many who have hiked these trails or scaled its up-thrusted peaks. I am hopeful that these descriptions invite you to pursue these pleasures. Better to aim high and fail than to aim low and succeed.

There lie secluded places here, concealed perhaps by distance from a road or by the fabled brush off-trail, yet which hold secret spectacles of far-flung views, sharply angled spires, peaceful flowered meadows, breath-taking waterfalls, and all-around scenery to gladden the mind and satisfy the soul of even the most urbanized traveler – and these occur all in the same place – that is the genius of the ranges just south, then largely to the north, of Rainier. It is a treasure so immense as to feature views far-flung and unique. As I age, recollections of the distant past remain as clear as a flawless diamond, yet yesterday's often seep from my brain. Nonetheless, my memories of the mountains will remain with me until my last breath.

Although this book is personally biased, I hope others will chime in, in their own way, to let us all learn of their treasured and perhaps relatively unknown terrains. The enormity, and severe beauty of

INTRODUCTION

the Cascades is impossible to translate into words alone. You must experience these peaks and valleys, touch their moss and stone, see both their serenity and spectacle for yourself. Yet writing enables knowledge of place and makes possible a pervasive, interactive, and hopefully growing body of knowledge which can be shared and enhanced for future generations. I modestly hope to place my hand on the engine of adventure and, to some small degree, propel it forward. At any rate, the value of this book, of any book, is that it can outlive its author.

So ascend the slope, fight the thorned Devil's club and twisted slide alder, and reach the heathery meadows above, which will provide views burned into your brain. You will not regret the effort endured. Exclamation points were invented for these spectacular views. These green meadows filled with wildflowers, these stone and ice dominions soaring above, and these unforgettable mountains will thrill the heart of all outdoor adventurers. A riot of discoveries awaits. Leave room in your backpack for wonder, and take others with you. Climbing (and driving) alone is not only filled with peril, it is like a one-man birthday party: You don't get any presents you didn't bring yourself. Anyway, this land is too beautiful for just one pair of eyes.

CHAPTER ONE
A Southern Rampart
Mt. Curtis Gilbert
(8,184')

HIDDEN GEMS OF THE WASHINGTON CASCADES

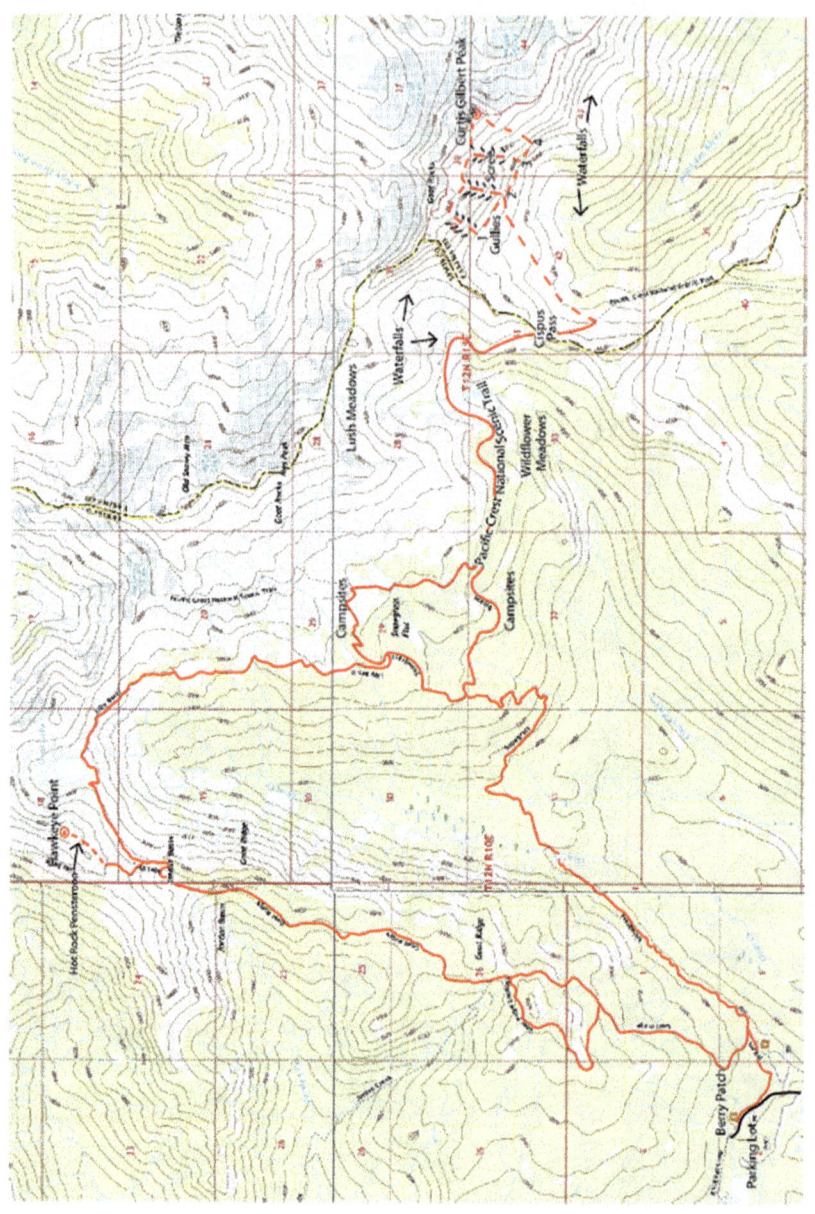

CHAPTER ONE: A SOUTHERN RAMPART

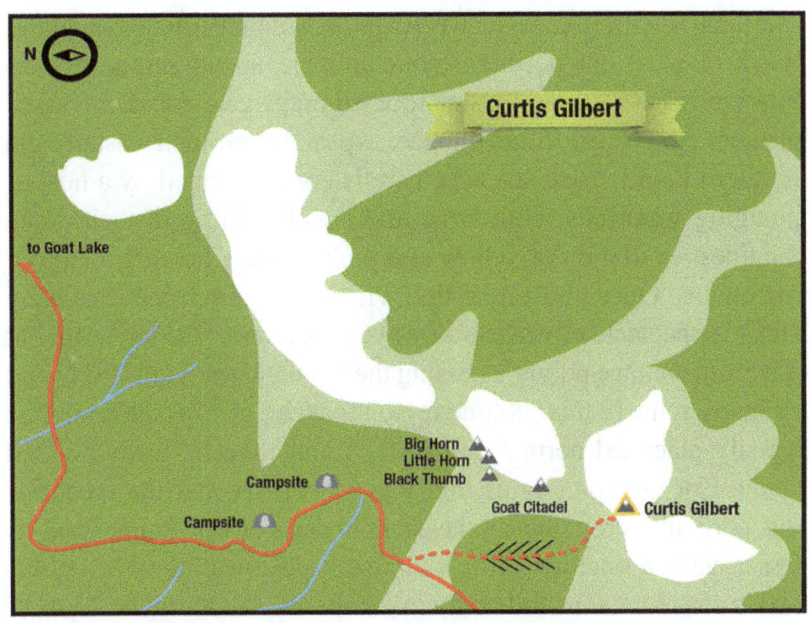

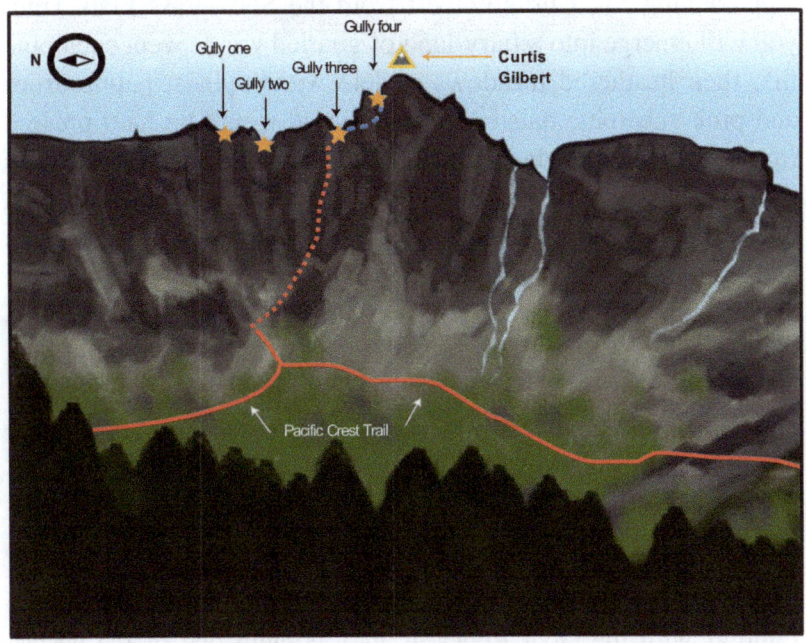

The Goat Rocks, situated between Mts. Adams and Rainier, emulates much of what our northern mountains are about: serene flower-filled meadows topped by saw-toothed crags galore and crevassed glaciers, so typical in our ranges, especially on their eastern and northern flanks. Such splendor here is complemented by a host of plunging waterfalls, both large and small, trailing in their wake the finest exhibition of yellow and pink monkey flowers in all our mountains. Once above tree-line, vistas are unimpeded. Yes, they lack the spectacle of wave after wave of icy spires further north but it is from vantage points accessing the Pacific Crest Trail (PCT) and its many spurs in this sublime region that one can spy, close-in, the heavily glaciated north face of Mt. Adams; the far-away pointed summit of Oregon's pride and joy, Mt. Hood; and the cream of this particular crop, the southeastern aspects of Mt. Rainier and its lesser eastern satellite, Little Tahoma, itself towering over 11,000' above sea level, thus little only in comparison to Rainier's 14,411'.

Approaching Mt. Curtis Gilbert from the Snowgrass Flats Trail, you will emerge into a fairy-land of gnarled wind-swept subalpine firs, then heathered meadows replete with lupines, paintbrushes and pink subalpine daisies. Although you would be hard-pressed to guess it as you glance straight ahead (east), the Goat Rocks Range represents the remnants of four extinct volcanoes. In fact, one can almost imagine its semicircular columns of jagged spines and gentler cones as the remains of an ancient super-volcano's crater, capped by its highest and southern-most distinct peak, Curtis Gilbert. Although first climbed in the late 1890's, this entire area was actually most fully explored by a Portland-based Mazama party in 1934. They were not surprised by its volcanic origins, not only because of its overall architecture but by the rather freely-liberated quality of the rock, as loose and unfettered as that on the many unstable ridges of our other taller volcanoes.

Many novice climbers, with greater aspiration than ability, are familiar with the Goat Rocks as they contain one of the easiest routes to the top of a glaciated summit – Old Snowy. But those with but a trifle more experience can almost as easily ascend the

CHAPTER ONE: A SOUTHERN RAMPART

crowning summit of this charming area - Curtis Gilbert - especially since it often appears on the Mazama Climb Schedule. There is so much more to be gained by climbing this peak however, than bragging rights. Let's begin, for Portland-based climbers, with the fact that, within a 3-hour drive of the city, one can experience the entire ambience of a mini-North Cascades, minus the 6–7-hour trip through Seattle.

One does need to negotiate a long dirt road from U.S. Highway 12 just out of Packwood. But then the fun begins, with a 4-mile hike past bear-grass-filled Snowgrass Flats on Trail 96 (insect repellant mandatory after the bridged crossing of Goat Creek at 2 miles), then right for about another ½ mile to gorgeous campsites rewarding the climber with views not only of all the Goat Rocks, but of Mt. Adams to the south. While there are other equally pleasant camping spots further north along the PCT, which lies just 5–10 minutes above, these take you away from your objective of Curtis Gilbert.

As many of you know, despite being located this far south, this section of the PCT approaches its highest point just north of Old Snowy so it's best to make this trip in late July or August, when the meadows are flower-filled and campsites are snow-free. To climb Curtis Gilbert, best undertaken the day after establishing base camp, proceed south about 1½ miles on the PCT into the luxuriant meadows of Cispus Basin, streaked with lashes of jaw-dropping waterfalls and with one of the most densely populated confections of Northwest flowers to be enjoyed in all the Cascades.

These are partly the result of the 1980 Mt. St. Helens' eruption, which deposited tons of life-giving nutrients and minerals to this area. You might be able to identify not just the familiar blue of broadleaf lupine and the scarlet

Lupine

tall paintbrush, but also the yellows of meadow arnicas and arrow-leaf senecios, as well as the tiny yellow cinquefoils so abundant hereabouts. Constellations of stars are not just the province of the night sky, for here are the prairie stars, starflowers, golden daisies, goldenrods, goldenweeds, wooly sunflowers and gold stars shining as brightly as the lights of Hollywood. And, like a rainbow, everyone sees this assembly of colors in just a slightly different hue.

To reach Curtis Gilbert, trek right (south) on the PCT through these lush meadows as the trail turns from a south-bound course to definitely southeast. As it turns you will begin the off-trail ascent at about 6,160'. Hike up the usual progression of meadow-to-heather-to-scree to a selection of four rock-bound tentacles arching from above, mostly 3rd-class gullies, gleefully ignored in Beckey's Guide. Note, by the way, the shocking hot pink of rock penstemon to your left at the base of gully number 1 (the furthest north); no better display of this plant can be found anywhere else in our Range.

Rock Penstemon

Fortunately, the penstemon also helps in marking an incorrect gully, number one counting from the left. While any of the four class-3 gullies will gain you access to Gilbert's upper reaches, number three is the easiest and, more crucially, the least loose. Please don't encourage more rockfall than is necessary by using a rope. Nonetheless, hard hats are mandatory here, where the glue that's supposed to hold Prius-sized rocks is absent. Note the lichens on the more stable rocks; their eerie patterns conceal the complex life forms of these living organisms, part fungus and part algae.

Once up the gully, drop down a bit and traverse southeast over snow or scree under a jumble of jagged spires and basalt castles with names such as Big Horn, Little Horn and Black Thumb. You could make a dash up one or more of these 4th-class outcrops but this would only deter you from your main goal and establish you as a loose-rock specialist in need of serious therapy. Better to skirt these towers and cross a sandy plain, passing the occasional mop-head of Western Anemone seeds as you head toward the obvious pile of boulders marking the summit.

A rare but beautifully amusing plant can be found here: silky phacelia, with its purple pyramid of multiple flowers adorned with spikes of yellow-tipped stamens. Trudging up the sand and scree, it helps a bit to remember the words of Giorgio Vasari, the biographer of Renaissance painters that "lumps of earth may contain veins of gold". The only gold we found were in the views from the summit, now prominent ahead and attained by a 3rd-class scramble on its northwest side, though many nontechnical variations exist. These are especially rewarding as you can not only gaze to the south for Mts. Adams and Hood but north to the behemoth of Rainier. Such vistas are difficult to measure but impossible to dismiss. Eastward views, though far-reaching, are mainly a smudge of sere hills in Eastern Washington and the naked desert to the horizon beyond.

Back down in camp, consider an alternative route out of this paradise in order to almost circle the square, so to speak. Descend the Bypass Trail back to Snowgrass Flats, then head northeast on Trail 86, which neatly contours under Mts. Ives and Old Snowy to Goat Lake (yes you will almost be guaranteed to see these pesky creatures on the rim above the lake), then up to Goat Ridge to meet Trail 95. Expect torrents of waterfalls on the way, sparkling

Silky Phacelia

Tiling's monkey-flower

and happily accompanied by a kaleidoscope of those yellow (Tiling's) and pink (Lewis') monkey flowers. A herd of elk often frequents this area, possibly trained by the Rangers to magically appear on the weekends, to the delight of hikers and climbers. In fact, in all the trips suggested in this book, none exceed the Goat Rocks in the near-certainty of observing large alpine mammals.

Also, don't fail to take the brief side trail up to **Hawkeye Point (7,431')** for a glorious and even closer view of Rainier and a rare glimpse of a noteworthy and unusual penstemon, the white "hot rock" penstemon, considered most rare anywhere west of our parched eastern deserts. Continue south on the ancient forested rim of the volcano, then descend peacefully to Trail 96, turn right and shortly arrive at the parking lot, dusty and horse-strewn but a better alternative to the trail guides' instructions to start at something mysteriously called "The Berry Patch" (Trail 96A), devoid of berries and filled with even more horse-folk, with attendant poop and flies as thick as cold molasses.

The trip to climb Curtis Gilbert holds many more attractions than mere proximity to Portland and another summit notch on your bedpost. It is the farthest east of Washington's many alpine areas, thus the least exposed to our too-frequent clouds and showers. Moreover, you will experience the pleasures of traversing some of the greenest, most flamboyant meadows in all our mountains, striped with glorious waterfalls and saturated with all the hues of wildflowers one can imagine. In addition, the flora combine the best elements of east and west, with several species inhabiting a narrow longitudinal range; examples include large-flowered collomia and puccoon. It's a long drive from Seattle so don't go alone; you need help with the driving chores. At any rate, this trip is filled with views of our famous volcanoes, all the while climbing in an atmosphere more akin to the giants of the North Cascades than anywhere else within a reasonable distance from our crowded southern Metropolitan areas. In addition, in the Goat Rocks, you might also experience, as I have, being a mere speck within this vast, peaceful wonder of a wilderness, a reasonable distance from home yet so far from the clatter of our urban lives. And remember, like charity, climbing is a gift you can give to yourself.

Hot Rock Penstemon

CHAPTER TWO

Often Better Than Rainier

The Tatoosh Traverse

(5,958'-6,917')

HIDDEN GEMS OF THE WASHINGTON CASCADES

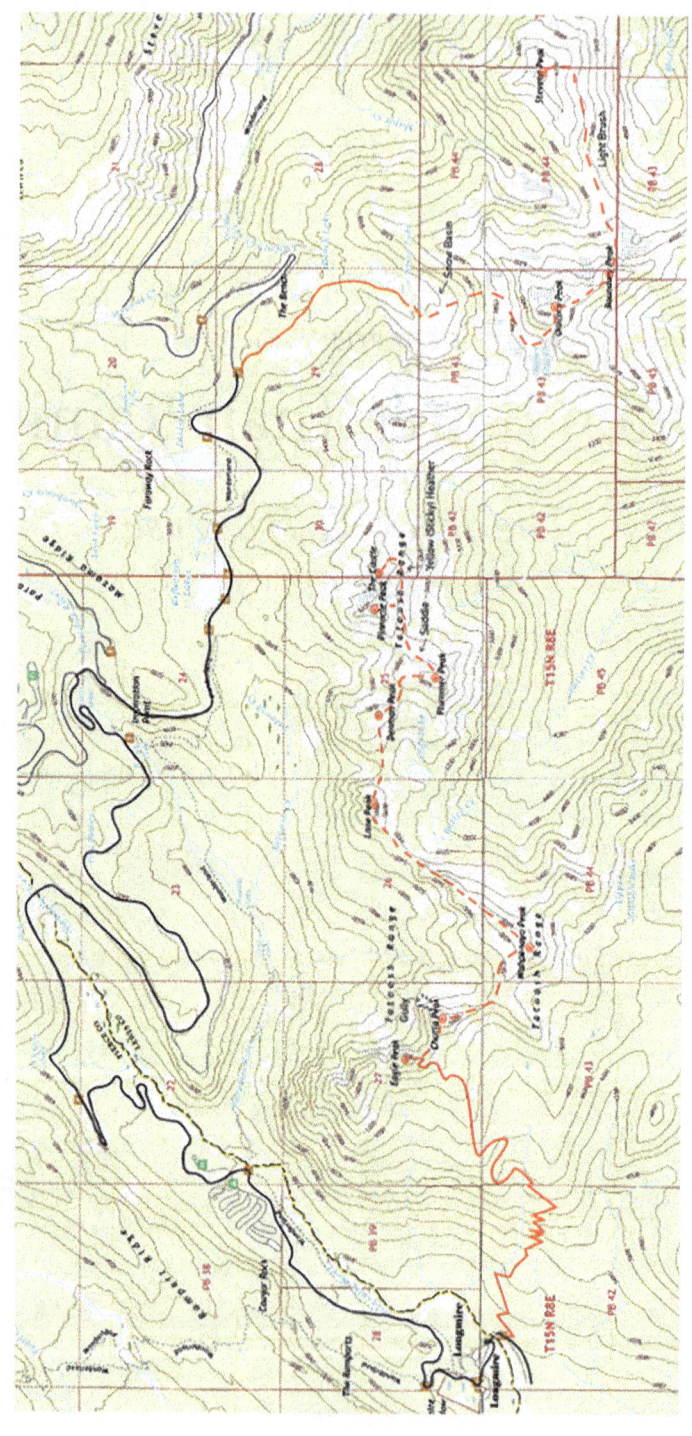

CHAPTER TWO: OFTEN BETTER THAN RAINIER

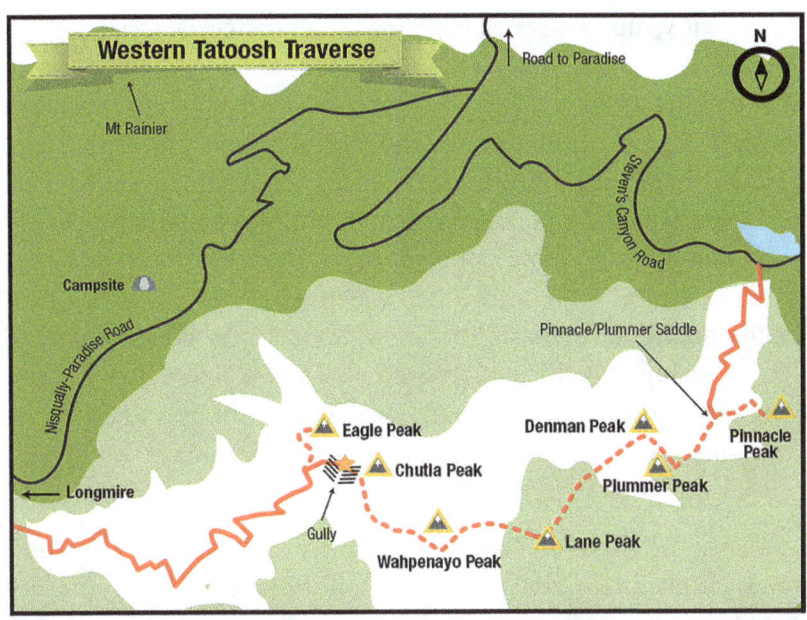

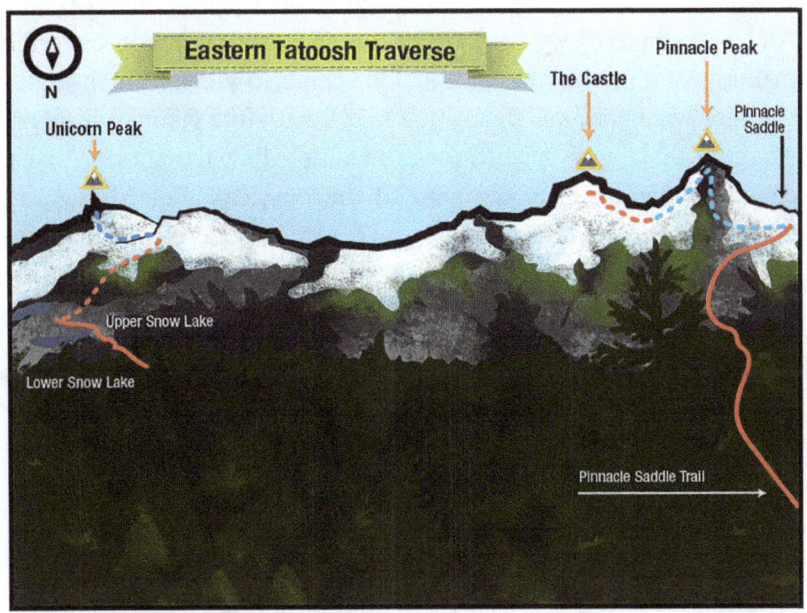

Technically, this compact but jagged sub-range is just south of Mt. Rainier but its similarity to the sharp-toothed peaks north of this hulking behemoth of a volcano render it fit to be included in Washington's peaks of interest and a gem in its own right. Located between Portland and Seattle, it may be considered a bit of a drive from both population centers but, when major hordes are descending on the more popular ranges further north, it provides a dense cluster of worthwhile objectives for the climber and/or the hiking adventurer. Moreover, it offers the added bonus of indescribably magnificent close-up views of Rainier's south face, with the Nisqually Glacier tumbling in a series of crevasses like an arpeggio of downward scales, culminating in a coda of ice blocks, glacial silt-laden streams and waterfalls.

In a sense, Mt. Rainier is the anodyne Everest of the North Cascades: often climbed by barely proficient climbers being led by mostly bored guides. The Tatoosh is different; a less-populated garden of wildflowers and meadows, combined with sharply-defined peaks. Add in a shade of green only the sun can paint and you have the makings of a memorable outing. One can also view, on a spring or summer weekend, the steady stream of erstwhile Rainier climbers slogging their way upward toward Camp Muir, the standard base camp for the climb to the summit the next day. Poised halfway between hype and hope, most will reach the crowded summit with a touch of altitude sickness and fortunately, most are led by competent guides who will ensure their safe descent.

The Tatoosh Range is easily reached by the Longmire-Paradise Road and its continuation onto the Steven's Canyon Road past the turn-off to Paradise. It is comprised of two sections, western and eastern, both of which contain a total of 11 named peaks, the western section beginning with Eagle Peak at its western-most outpost, then continuing with the chunky blocks of Chutla, Wahpenayo, Lane and Plummer Peaks. By taking the Eagle Peak Trail behind the Longmire Resort, the hiker of average scrambling ability (some exposed 3rd-class rock) can access most of these summits in a long day, though with more twists and turns than an afternoon soap opera.

The way, fortunately, is mostly above or at the limit of timberline and can thus be navigated by sight alone, barring any whiteouts. The meadows hereabouts abound with lupine and Indian paintbrush, along with yellow cinquefoil and white Sitka valerian. A more leisurely pace allows appreciation of the flora along with climbing one or two of these summits while enjoying the views north. Even Mt. Adams to the south will be within the scope of your viewfinder or smart-phone camera. But of course, the most lofty views are north to the omnipresence of Rainier.

Eagle Peak (5,958') is a scramble just off the Eagle Peak Trail beginning behind the Longmire Lodge. **Chutla (~6,000')**, stems from a Native American word meaning "rock", appropriate for this chunk of a blocky peak. It can be gained, as can Eagle, from the flowery meadows of the col between these two summits. Chutla holds some excitement for the climber with a tricky traverse and exposure sufficient to turn back the more unbalanced among us. But there is a 3rd-class gully to your left that avoids this venture if you are as challenged as I. Some folks prefer the tiptoe across the balanced but stable 4th-class rock crossing while others appreciate the mere safety of a well-anchored rope. Either way, frankly, most hikers make it safely to the summit. However, please do not trade safety for glory; one scrambler has taken a fatal fall on this tiptoe traverse. If in doubt, take the easier gully to your left. Either way, the summit rewards the scrambler with views of its nearby neighbors as well as Rainier.

Wahpenayo Peak (6,231') can also be reached from the Eagle Peak Trail by traversing below the saddle between Eagle and Chutla on either their south or north sides through mountain hemlocks, subalpine firs and heather. You can glance up at the block that constitutes Chutla's summit as you traverse these easy slopes, then gain the ridge to your right (if approaching from the south), from where a climber's path leads you to the top. Among the western Tatoosh peaks, this summit offers perhaps the finest outlooks as it is several hundred feet higher than its neighbors; the views take in the entire crest of the range, as well as the brooding, snow-clad omnipresence of Rainier to the north.

Continuing southeast of Wahpenayo along the ridge, **Lane Peak (6,015')** is an easy stroll south, up a gentle meadow, and its views of Rainier's glaciated south side leave one wondering how this huge bulk, actually almost a metaphor for a mountain, could exist in the midst of so many lower peaks. Surely plate tectonics, with massive upthrust, could not have elevated it to these heights. We now understand how a volcano can exist even without high altitude neighbors by successive outpourings of magma. We can also imagine how the original inhabitants hereabouts, Native Americans, could have worshipped Rainier as a god; indeed, rising from low footings on all sides, it does convey an impression of being the dwelling place for angels and the Almighty. From Lane's summit, also glance down at tiny Johnson Lake; it lies at Wahpenayo's foot, perhaps in veneration of what lies above.

Denman Peak (6,006') is close by; an enjoyable traverse northeast across meadows replete with blue lupine and flaming red paintbrush accompany you to its summit. Gaze down at Cliff Lake immediately south, and about 750' below Denman's summit, its waters shimmering silver waves in the almost constant breezes on and below these ridges. While surrounded by steep forested slopes, nary a true cliff can be spied.

It is also from Denman (and the eastern Tatoosh peaks described below) that you can most easily spy the torrent of climbers queuing like ants up the snow route towards Camp Muir. The *voie normal* on Rainier reminds one of a Cheesecake Factory, packed and swarming, though with some delicious treats waiting above. I should not denigrate their efforts as, years earlier, I was among them. However, as with ascents of Mt. Everest these days, for a number of inexperienced would-be ascensionists, perhaps prepared by a one-day course and led by talented and patient guides, these crowded routes may infrequently bring disaster as well as success.

As you proceed on the ridge aiming southeast, you will encounter some minor up's and down's, but the traveling is still quite peaceful,

CHAPTER TWO: OFTEN BETTER THAN RAINIER

and the flowers abundant. Look for the small yellow fan-leaf cinquefoil and the rose-purple of the Cascade penstemon.

Continuing southeast on the ridge, or on its north side, you will encounter brief spells of mountain hemlocks, although most of the traveling is above tree-line, with awe-struck views of Rainier's massive southern ice sheets, the largest being the Nisqually Glacier. You will soon arrive just north of the next peak in the Tatoosh lineup - **Plummer**

Cascade Penstemon

(6,370'), with a few sub-alpine firs just at its top partially blocking the view of Rainier. Not to worry – you'll have your fill as you continue on the higher eastern parts of this compact range. The peaks described now are best considered the "eastern Tatoosh",

and are best climbed on a second day in this rugged area. They can easily be accessed from the popular trail beginning shortly past the turn-off to Paradise on the Stevens Canyon Road. This short trail leads in just 1½ switch-backed miles to the col between Pinnacle and Plummer. This saddle is justly as famous as it is crowded due to its easily-gained views of Rainier, close enough it seems you could feel its snow drifting across the highway below to refresh your sweating body.

Subalpine Fir

If you haven't already reached Plummer from the west, you can reach this peak from the saddle. Simply head west on the south side of the meadowed ridge, following a well-marked trail. However, snow lingers here through early August in icy-winter years so an ice ax can be handy for slips down moderately-angled slopes. Its summit, tangled with subalpine firs and boulders, still provides superlative views, especially to the more jagged peaks of this sub-range to its east. Lane can be climbed on the same day as Plummer if you are so inclined (you peak-bagger!) by traversing under Plummer's summit southwest to a point just above a small lake ("Cliff Lake"). From this point, you can scramble west through nicely-flowered meadows featuring three types of heather (red, yellow, and sticky) to attain Lane's top-most point. The effort will be rewarded with spectacular views of the eastern Tatoosh's serrated crests.

Climbers, however, favor these eastern Tatoosh peaks as more of a challenge. Most weekend hikers can attain the first such peak, **Pinnacle (6,562')** from Pinnacle Saddle by traversing northeast from the saddle, then climbing reasonably stable rock to a 3rd-class gully which leads to the top. It's best to follow the lighter-colored rock as you begin the ascent about 500 yards from the saddle, as this bears the mark of the many boots which have chosen the easiest approach. Should climbers be above you, a likely scenario, hard hats would not be out of place. I believe that it is from Pinnacle's lofty summit, though it is not the tallest in the range, that one gains the finest appreciation of the leviathan we call Rainier. Fortunately, these views have no "sell-by" date. Descend carefully; a slip might not be fatal but twisted ankles are not unknown.

Following a climb of Pinnacle, you can also gain bragging rights from the tourists at Longmire and Paradise, as well as from the folks pulling off the highway where the trail begins, to gain a better view. From here (photos mandatory), Pinnacle lives up to its name, jutting into the sky like a sharply angled triangle and appearing appropriately frightening to the uninitiated. In fact, a number of technical but easy 4th- to 5th-class routes dot its west

CHAPTER TWO: OFTEN BETTER THAN RAINIER

face: Look up from the trail as you pass beneath it to appreciate its vertical architecture.

Most climbers combine the next summit to the east with the ascent of Pinnacle. This chunk of rock, called **The Castle (6,440')**, makes up for what it lacks in height by the convoluted approach needed to attain its summit, at least by the easiest means. You must traverse further east along the rock-strewn crest (loose volcanic breccia in some places) from where you climbed Pinnacle, to gain the southeast face of this box of a mountain, where a 50' pitch of tough class-3 scrambling on either its southeast or southwest aspects allows access to its craggy summit. Look at The Castle from the highway, seemingly leaning against Pinnacle they are that close, to see how it got its name.

Next in line, but a fair distance away, stands the crest of the Tatoosh, its highest summit, **Unicorn Peak (6,917')**. From the highway, and from the approach on the Bench/Snow Lakes Trail, about 2 miles east of the Pinnacle Saddle Trail, this peak presents the most striking vertical summit block to be seen throughout the Cascades – a mini-Patagonian daunting spectacle reminiscent indeed of the horn of the mythical beast for which the peak is named. From a variety of locations on the road and the trail, it is well worthy of your best photographs. The short approach trail leads to picturesque lakes that are usually frozen over when ascents in June or July are made on Unicorn. Remember that you are now ascending north-facing slopes.

Above the lakes, a broad-access snow bowl persists through summer. This not only provides access to Unicorn but, throughout the year, is

Sticky Yellow Heather

a favorite of snow boarders and back-country skiers. Take care on this approach to not get in their hasty way! Kick steps up this 20–30-degree slope (ice ax handy) to reach a rocky crest and cross to its more flowery south side. Ascend northeast up heather slopes (the relatively rare sticky yellow mountain heather predominates here) to the south base of the imposing summit tower. It is here that newcomers to climbing may wish to retreat, despite the mantra all leaders use: "It's easier than it looks". The novice's cognitive processes must be overcome and, most often in such situations, personal obligations and group pressure usually conquer dread.

But, on Unicorn, it's true that you should fear not (or only a little) as a gully, variously termed tough 3rd- to easy 4th-class climbing, brings one to the surprisingly broad summit. Some parties rope up for this ascent – it's your choice but you will probably value a cord for the descent. Views will not disappoint. However on top, you're only halfway and it's not smart to celebrate too early at halftime in any game. The descent of the gully looks dangerously easy. Instead of down-climbing it, you really should consider the 50' rappel down the west face preferred by most parties. It's fun if it's not your first rappel as some small portion of it is free-hanging. Glissading down the snow bowl below is an adequate prize to cap off your achievement.

Most folks stop climbing at these most obvious peaks because they are closest to the road and present the most spectacular of appearances. But the true explorer might hazard advancing further southeast to conquer the complete Tatoosh traverse. This will include an attempt on the two remaining Tatoosh gems, first **Boundary Peak** (about **6,450'**) just to the southeast of Unicorn, with unusual views of the entire Tatoosh Range, and finally **Stevens Peak (6,510')**, somewhat isolated about a mile southeast of Unicorn.

One gray day, following a climb of Unicorn, we discussed at length making a run for Stevens Peak, then realized that actions speak more elegantly than words. Thus we rushed toward its summit but reversed the usual "ready, aim, then fire" admonition and instead, were ready and fired before we actually aimed. We descended into the high but somewhat brushy valley between Unicorn and Stevens instead of remaining above tree-line. Shifting patterns of light and clouds passed overhead, leaving streaks of sunlight illuminating the jagged peaks to our south. There, a montane ocean with waves of peaks and ripples of parallel ranges receded into an almost infinite horizon. We followed a rather labyrinthine route up Stevens through a thick mountain hemlock forest, until the trees gave way and we could spy our objective. This vista and the soft light of the sky, urged us on. We ascended directly north (ignoring Beckey here) to the top-most point of this unjustly ignored eastern-most summit in this marvelous sub-range. The ascent presented no technical difficulties. The briars that entangled us on this last traverse were not as sharp as we had feared, and the summit views were the equal of any Tatoosh peak.

Good things come in small packages and this is as true of the Tatoosh, akin to another, not dissimilar range north of here: the Monte Cristo's. Small in comparative stature but compact and rife with opportunity for easy access, the Tatoosh presents ascents for climbers of all calibers, and adds in majestic views of Rainier. Ignoring the Tatoosh would be your loss.

CHAPTER THREE

Lakes and Views East of the Crest

Alta
(6,250')

and Hibox Mountains
(~6,547')

HIDDEN GEMS OF THE WASHINGTON CASCADES

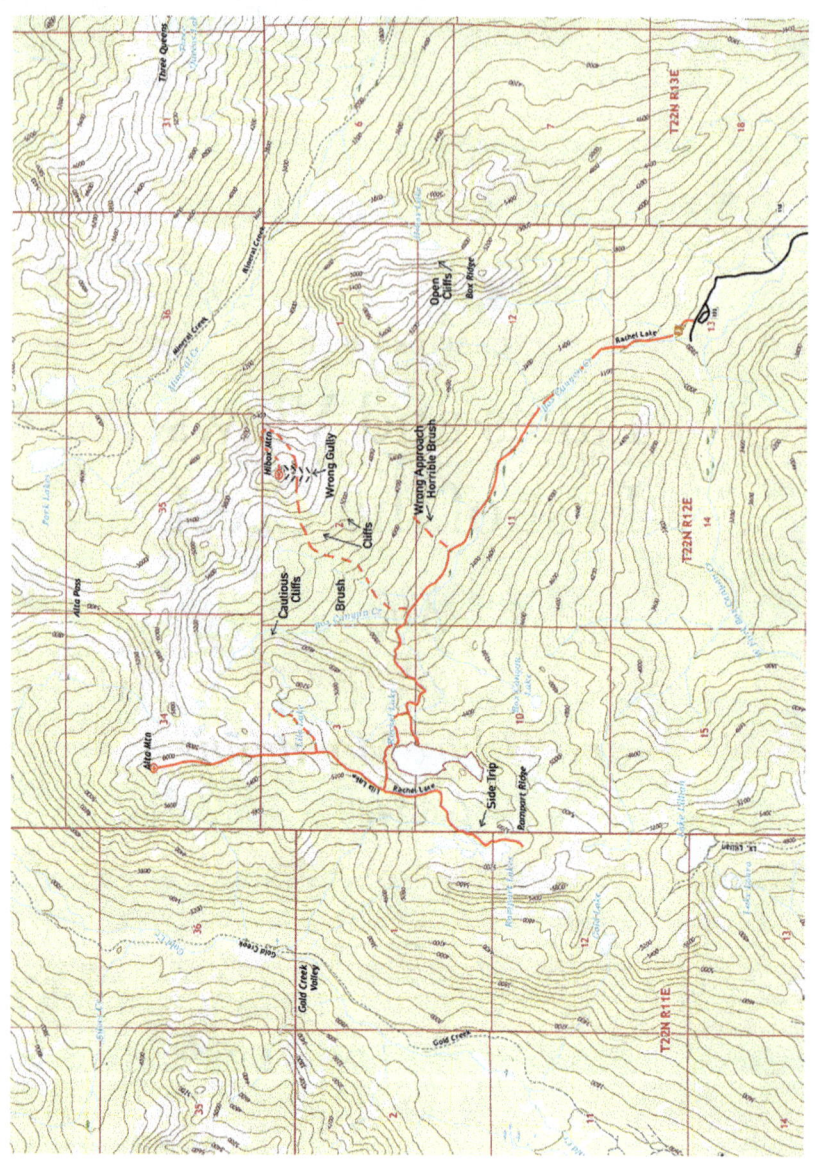

CHAPTER THREE: LAKES AND VIEWS EAST OF THE CREST

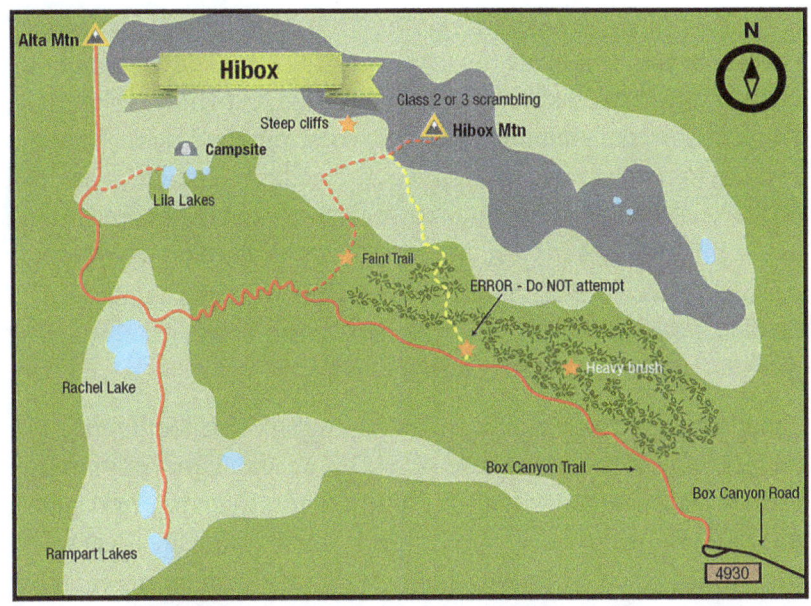

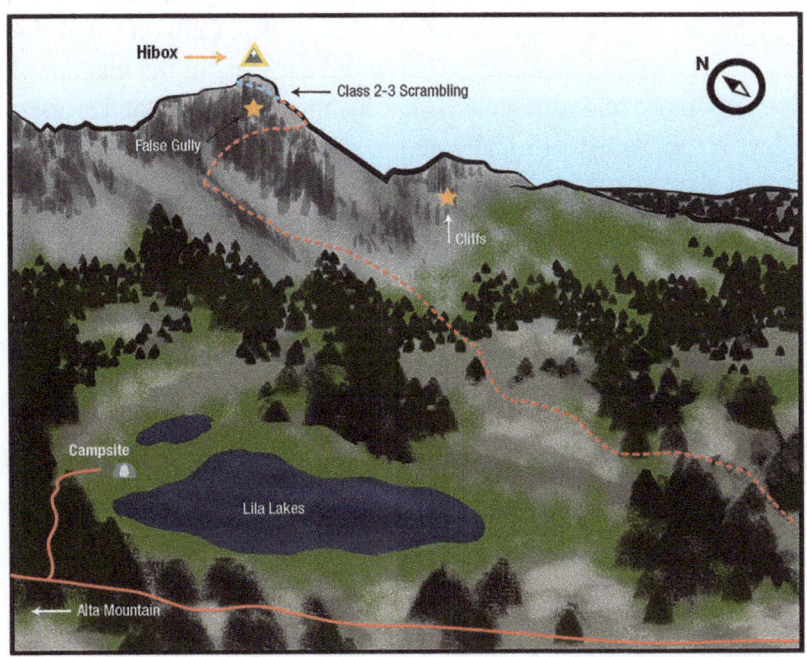

A walk in the sky amidst flowery meadows and lakes with dazzling sunny slashes of light are the many rewards the hiker and scrambler can attain with a modicum of effort on Alta and Hibox. Moreover, you can gain the summits of these two scrambling peaks in about two days and easily get back to your vehicles and town by the end of the second day, although a longer linger rewards as well. Here, you will enjoy not only uncrowded views of the Snoqualmie Pass peaks, but also of Rainier and Glacier Peak. Isolated campsites can be discovered from a lovely and most often lonely lakelet with a premier camping spot at its northern edge.

Take I-90 to exit 62 (Kachess Lake) and drive 5 smooth miles to a major campground at the head of Kachess Lake. Turn left onto Box Canyon Road, usually well-graded. Reach a junction in 4 miles, turn left and drive a scant 0.2 miles to the parking area where the Rachel Lake Trail begins. Although you are driving, then hiking through "Box Canyon", the scenery hereabouts just doesn't seem much canyon-like; it's mostly forest lining Box Canyon Creek and try hard as you may, the appellation of "canyon" in the manner of, let's say those of desert lands, is hardly appropriate. What lies ahead however, is well-worthwhile and requires some flexible planning, as we shall see. Should you complete this trip, however, you will discover more canyon-like scenery beyond.

The Rachel Lake Trail begins, and remains, in deep forest, though brief lookouts to Hibox Mountain and Box Ridge to the northeast are rewarding. Although the trail is rough in spots, steep in others, it is always clear and easily followed. Another bonus is that you won't have to lug any technical metal. If your goal is to climb Hibox, do not allow ambition to trump both common sense and experience by slavishly following Beckey's description about plowing through the densest thickets of brush on this side of the Milky Way Galaxy, unless you are a brush masochist or carry a machete. He suggests prematurely abandoning the trail after several miles to head directly to Hibox's summit. Such a course would leave you ploughing through impenetrable thickets; trying to avoid these, you could attempt to follow one of the many watercourses streaming down

CHAPTER THREE: LAKES AND VIEWS EAST OF THE CREST

from meadows far above but this would require you to fight your way up fatal furrows, weed-choked and boulder-strewn. There is an easier, though less direct, line to its summit; I guarantee it.

Just as the trail markedly steepens and transforms itself into a series of sharp switchbacks, at around 3,700' and about 2½ miles in, look for a faint trail to your right (north). This junction can be easily missed (this comes from my personal incompetence) but is often marked either by a cairn or that standby of all wilderness explorers, fluorescent orange-red surveyor's tape. This trail, sketchy at first, climbs steeply through moderate Douglas fir and western hemlock forest, bypassing a rock wall on your left after about 500' of gain. Straining against this brushy approach will not break you and fortunately the trail becomes clear again until you reach the meadows above tree-line.

Western Hemlock

As you emerge from the timber, it's wise to place surveyor's tape prominently near the last of the branches to mark your way back, thus avoiding the unpleasant experience of bushwhacking, then rappelling over a cliff wall to reach the Rachel Lake Trail on the valley floor. Moderately steep meadows follow, from which the top of Hibox can easily be seen. You may encounter animal, deer or human paths but following one is, in the main, futile as these always seem to peter out just when a good foothold is most needed. Nonetheless, keep aiming just to the right (southeast) of the summit, thus avoiding the need to climb 5th-class cliffs rimming the southern and northeastern walls, which protect the peak's top-most rocks.

Your goal is to aim for the southeastern ridge. When you reach almost to its crest, you may be tempted to simply ascend an

27

innocent-looking gully which appears to lead directly to the top. On my first attempt, as usual, my aspirations exceeded reality. I sniffed opportunity here, but danger lurked. This loose gully steepens sharply at its end, where it merges, in a sinister manner, with the southern cliffs. The linchpin for success is to move to the right of this gully at the base of these stones to gain the ridge via a 3rd-class move through what looks like, but really isn't, a hole underneath boulders. Through this opening you gain the east ridge and an easygoing romp on the peak's north-east side to its crown, the summit of Hibox. While Beckey gives this peak an approximate height of 6,470', the USGS topo 7" series awards it an altitude of 6,547'. I prefer the higher figure.

From this vantage point, all manner of peaks and lakes can be seen. Certainly, Mt. Rainier is both splendid and prominent to the southwest but closer in, you can gaze at peaks seldom admired from this angle and often never seen at all. You will need a map (Green Trails or Pargeter's picture maps are best) to name the unusual and rarely attempted summits to the east. Three Queens stands out immediately, a jumble of talus belying its royal moniker, and beyond, the infrequently visited The Cradle, tough to approach but, once at its foot, easy to climb.

Looking northeast, Chikamin Ridge stands out first, most often dry but sufficiently corrugated to merit your gaze. Try to identify its highest point, appropriately named Chickamin Peak, and to its southeast, the Four Brothers. Directly to your northeast, Mt. Stuart proclaims its dominance over the Enchantments, while to the southwest, the Snoqualmie Ranges rule; see if you can identify Mt. Thompson and, to its north, the perfectly pyramidal spire of Huckleberry Mountain. You and your party will probably be alone, so take care on the descent over steep but tricky meadow where footing is often obscured. Follow a direct line toward the surveyor's tape marking the rude path you followed up.

Depending on your aims, you might easily descend and call it a day, as the ascent solely of Hibox should leave you with sufficient time to return to the parking lot with plenty of summertime light

CHAPTER THREE: LAKES AND VIEWS EAST OF THE CREST

remaining. But further treasures await if you can spare several days or more. If you plan to camp and climb both Alta and Hibox, continue the first day on the Rachel Lake Trail, which climbs steeply up the inevitable switchbacks to attain a saddle, a trail junction, and even better, a view across the expanse of Rachel Lake, a relatively large body of water amongst these uplands. The lake is shouldered by cliffs on its northern, western, and southeastern sides; these are composed of light-colored stone reminiscent of granite, though it's mostly granidiorite. From here, a side trip is in order: A short jaunt left (south) leads in about 30–45 minutes to the first of the Rampart Lakes, a series of pools and waterfalls adorning small basins with most sides surrounded by walls of rock.

These lakes are jewels in this wilderness, each pocketed in its little basin like a diamond in its own setting, with rock walls and meadows filled with subalpine flowers. Note the small-flowered penstemons, with their multiple small purple tubes sticking out in defiance of the many westerly's gusting through the frequent passes hereabouts. Note too the combination of pink subalpine daisies and, here and there, a cut-leaf daisy, mostly a light pink, hiding shyly amongst the frequent rocky overlooks. Blue broad-leaf lupine and tall Indian paintbrush govern this wild dominion, punctuated by the frequent appearance of purple alpine asters.

Tall Indian Paintbrush

The lupines are frequently associated with paintbrushes (we have five paintbrush species common to the North Cascades) for a good reason. No paintbrush can survive without sufficient nitrogen in the soil, yet this very element is lacking in many alpine meadows. The lupines (there are at least six species in these mountains) take nitrogen from the atmosphere and "fix" it into the ground, thereby helping the paintbrushes thrive, like a good neighbor; what the lupine gains in return is uncertain, thereby remaining a potential doctoral thesis for some budding biology student. Much of what we know about the soil in these realms is just beginning to be studied with vigor. We await a future text to explain it all; authors are sorely needed.

Return to Rachel Lake, then turn right to follow a ridge in the sky, actually the south crest of Alta Mountain. Should you ascend to its top, you have only to follow the trail, thus compounding the problem of whether you can claim an ascent of a "real" mountain if a trail led you to its apex. I believe in the affirmative; snow/boot trails usually lead up to Rainier's summit on the easiest routes, while the western sentinel of the North Cascades, Sloan Peak, has a clear path from the glacier to its summit.

The path here from Rachel Lake offers, for its first ½ mile, spectacular views over and down to the lake as its waters can be seen above all but the tallest and thickest of Krumholtz trees. Eventually, you will be truly walking on air: flower-filled meadows, the blooms sewing themselves into the tapestry of the alpine soil and flanking the trail. It seems as if you are walking in slow motion across a Persian rug of varied hues, almost as if there is too much beauty to comprehend in one trip. Particularly prominent are the 2"-tall small-flowered penstemons, with their tiny purple tubes of blossoms shouldering both sides of this open-air trail. The path branches after about ½ mile; take the left branch, which climbs a steepening meadow one mile to the top of Alta Mountain and views as special as those from Hibox, yet without any bushwhacking at all.

Small-flowered Penstemon

CHAPTER THREE: LAKES AND VIEWS EAST OF THE CREST

Imagine a real North Cascades Peak with no brush – it's sort of like eating a gallon of chocolate ice cream without gaining a calorie or an ounce of weight.

Back at that last junction, take the left branch on your return as you're now facing south, or the right branch if you've just arrived from Rachel Lake, and continue a pleasant ridge walk for about a mile until you can see a string of pools, crystal clear and shining like tiny mirrors beckoning you to camp. The trail mostly gives out here but a small path leads about 100' down to these, the Lila Lakes; the largest even has a proper island plopped in its middle. Here, make camp on the north shore on dirt, and while away a lazy afternoon simply appreciating that you are now just inside the Alpine Lakes Wilderness, and the lakes you see or visit are its gems, ornaments much richer and more precious, in my mind, than any man-made jewel. Adding to the charm hereabouts, you and your party, if you have companions, will likely be alone.

But this trip, and the attempt to scale both Alta and Hibox, presents a dilemma. If you first climb Hibox on the way into Alta, what do you do with your heavy backpacking kit? No need to lug it up Hibox, which would be quite a chore. You could hide it in the brush alongside the faint trail junction leading to Hibox's meadows. I prefer to haul the big pack to Lila Lakes on the first day, make camp, then backtrack with light pack to the last junction, where a sharp right will lead you on a clearly defined trail to Alta's summit. Then retrace your steps for an unrushed evening to your camp at Lila Lakes.

The following day, pack out early, leave your overnight stuff hidden well in the brush at the Hibox junction just after descending the steep switchbacks, then ascend Hibox with a light daypack. Back at the junction with the Rachel Lake Trail, find your stuff (yes, I've spent over ½ hour searching for mine) and hike the broad main trail back to the parking lot. This two-day trip accomplishes the best of the two peaks with their views, and the wonder of a plentitude of lakes, some rock-bound, others gleaming in the sun. You just have to feel good on the drive home, tasting what few other North Cascade adventurers have, leaving the Snoqualmie Pass crowds behind (that area always reminds me of a McDonald's) while enjoying the unique pleasures of these mountain and lakeside landscapes. Oh – and be sure to take a friend or two: friendships amplify the good in life.

Note: It is a potentially fatal error (if fatal means not summiting Hibox) to attempt crawling, thrashing and bulling your way through a cocktail of thickets and brush directly from the Rachel Lake Trail before you reach the switchbacks at about 3,700', as Beckey advises. This forest of thickets is emblematic of impenetrable brush. This particular mass of greenery is worse than most I've encountered, especially this far east. Therefore, please heed this Dantean warning, even if it takes a while to locate the faint side path to your right, as described above. Beckey's account of the optimum way to attain Hibox's summit is as baffling to me as an advanced calculus syllabus or the lyrics of a rap song. It may take a while but I'm certain you can find the obscure but visible by-path to your north (right if you're ascending or left if descending) that will lead you, with careful tracking, to the glory of meadows above.

It is an even more fatal error to attempt to climb Hibox from your base camp at Lila Lakes by descending into the valley of Box Creek's headwaters. It may look close and inviting from Lila Lakes and you are probably hardier than I, but only misery awaits. The descent itself is steep and ringed with vertiginous cliffs not apparent from above; the forest and the brush within this hole will fight you as mightily as Sugar Ray. Do yourself a favor and take the path described above off the Rachel Lake Trail; You will thank me a thousand times, or at least once. Follow my mantra: Aim for the heights and avoid the battle up stream-side, gully-filled, brush-laden, avalanche-tracked approaches as much as you are able. Not to worry: There will be plenty more of that in the approaches to the many largely-ignored giants to the north described further along in this text.

CHAPTER FOUR
A Five-fingered Riddle
Lemah Mountain
(7,480')

HIDDEN GEMS OF THE WASHINGTON CASCADES

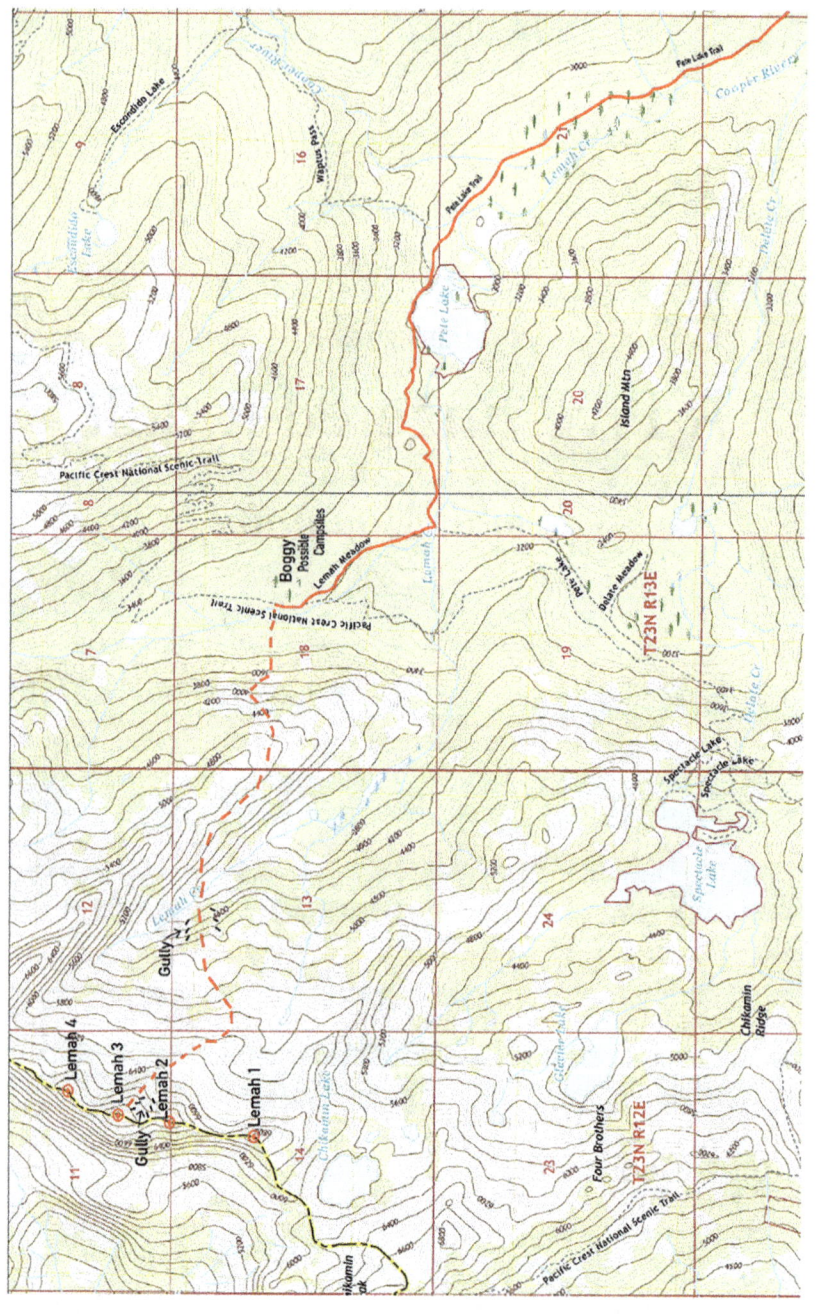

CHAPTER FOUR: A FIVE-FINGERED RIDDLE

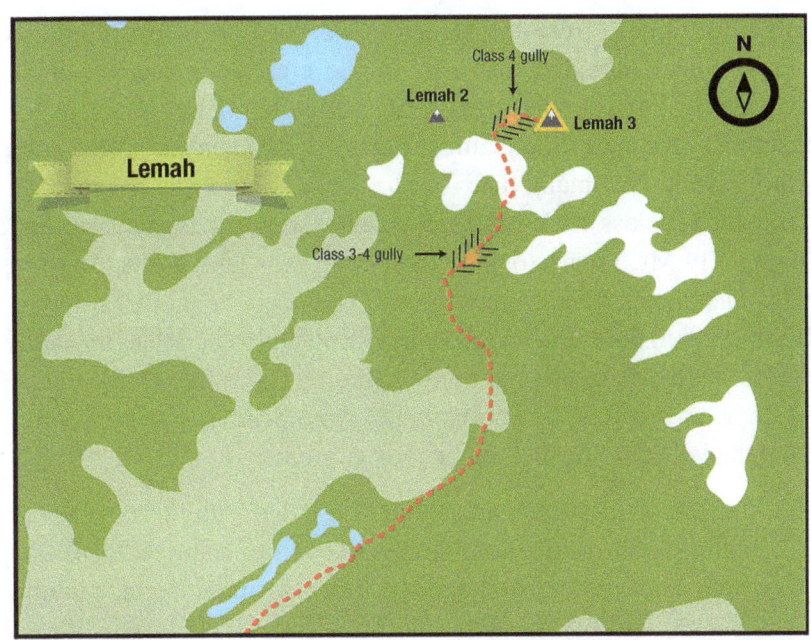

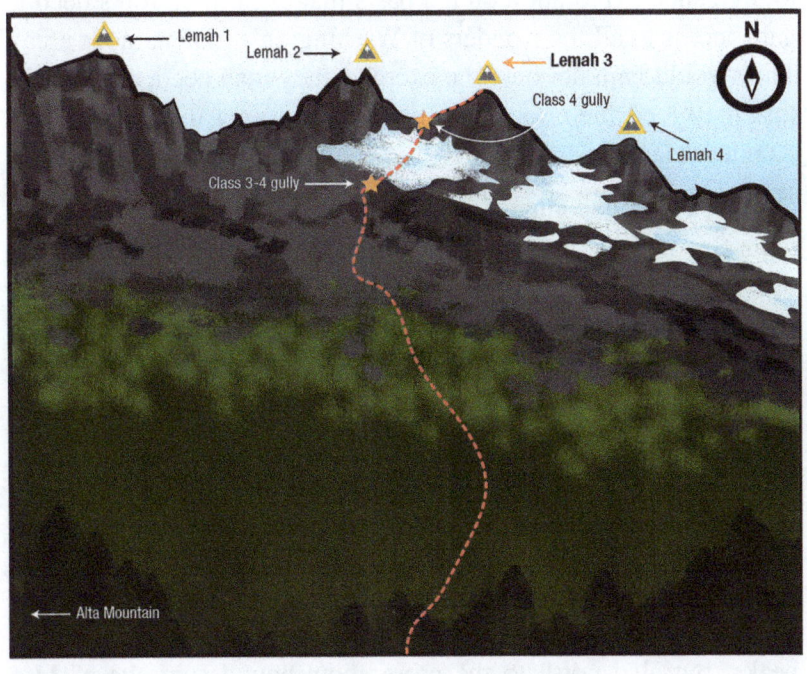

It's a long jump from the Tatoosh range just south of Rainier to the Alpine Lakes area just east of the crest and thus to Lemah Mountain. Some might argue with neglecting some of the major summits north of Snoqualmie Pass, peaks such as The Chair; Snoqualmie Mountain; The Tooth; Guye Peak, with its multiple 3rd- to 5th-class rock routes, unstable though they may be; and especially Mt. Thompson and the pointy pinnacle of Huckleberry. Can this disregard be countenanced? I can only plead that we must limit the length of this narrative but I might also add that, in recent years (really decades), the Snoqualmie Pass peaks and trails have become so crowded (read 60 minutes from Seattle on the Freeway) that they need no further explication from me.

It's the less well-known areas and crags that should be explored in greater depth so as to acquaint, and even popularize, these oft-forgotten summits, trails and campsites described herein. I doubt, in doing so, that they would be overrun by hoards but it is justifiable to urge such exploration on the basis that even more folks need to gain access to all the wonders of Washington's mountainous areas. They would gain not only the exercise they may need, but the awe that may feed their soul and impel them to act to preserve such wondrous lands.

One such area encompasses the summits just north and east of the main Snoqualmie Ranges. Lemah fits this bill perfectly. Since it's the cover child for the third edition of the Spring/Manning *100 Hikes in Washington's Alpine Lakes*, one would think that this multi-summited pinnacle would attract more attention. Although the neighboring Chimney Rock is taller and a more challenging climb, Lemah is both more picturesque, with its five fingers ("Lemah" is Chinook for "hand"), and affords easier access. Part of the Chikamin Group of rocky peaks northeast of Snoqualmie Pass, Lemah and its neighbors include Chikamin Peak and Three Queens, as well as Summit Chief Mountain. This group not only extends southwest for views of the more familiar Snoqualmie Pass peaks, but also north to the more snow-bound summits of Mts. Daniel and Hinman.

CHAPTER FOUR: A FIVE-FINGERED RIDDLE

Access is eased via Interstate 80, then exit 84 to State Highway 903 through the rough mining towns of Roslyn and Ronald to the usually well maintained Cle Elum River Road, then onto the Cooper River Road to Cooper Lake (spectacular views from the lakeshore of Chimney Rock and Lemah), then by the relatively easy 4½ miles of gentle river-bottom Pete's Lake Trail to this forest-bound pond. Continuing on this trail another mile brings the climber to a junction with the Lemah Meadows Trail (#1323B) while another 0.8 fairly untroubled mile on that path leads to the junction with the Pacific Crest Trail (PCT). Just beyond, on your right, Lemah Meadows and camping await.

Unfortunately, for much of the climbing season these meadows are more bog than bivouac, more swamp than shelter. They may be dry by mid-August or they may not. Find the rare patches of dry hillock to settle your tent or try to eke out a spot beneath the trees on your left as you enter the opening. Although these watery bogs prove troublesome to would-be campers, they are hardly fetid or stagnant, being spring-fed continuously throughout the climbing season. There are two compensations here: the magnificent view of Lemah's five primeval and jagged digits to the northwest and the delicious fragrance of the rare bog orchid, its white flowers arrayed along its 2-ft.-tall spike. These botanical gems are as frequent in this meadow as anywhere else in our ranges.

White Bog Orchid

From this spot, Lemah appears to be clothed in robust vertical armor, yet it holds a route to its top largely free of technical difficulties. The actual climb begins from camp early the next morning. It involves scrambling westward up flower-filled meadows and glades of mountain hemlock, across delightful granite boulders to the head of the Lemah Creek Valley, where steeper grades await. Some nontechnical use of hands here and there on patches of sturdy grass and partly-trustable stacks of breccia, a familiar task for Cascades scramblers, brings one to the first climbing objective, a usually snow-filled gully. This chute then leads to the glacial patch beneath the main peak (Lemah 3) and Lemah 2 to its left.

Please feel free to ignore the description in Beckey's *Volume One*; it is as condensed as it is confusing. Smoot's *Climbing Washington's Mountains* is less misleading. The conditions within this gully may determine how eager you are to attack it. Usually snow-filled through early July, in parched summers it may be bare, leading to a class-3–4 scramble on loose boulders (hard hats required!); or it might even be filled with unstable ice by late July through mid-August, the conditions we encountered on our first attempt. Thus our aspirations were tempered by a common foe: lack of time to establish adequate protection. Even if you arrive at this great gully in good condition, a belay here and there might be appreciated by all but the most skilled (or egotistic?) of climbers. Not a few parties have been bedeviled by ice or falling rocks at this point.

On our second attempt, we rejoiced that we had turned our attitudes into action as we scrambled up the bouldery lower gully, loose as a serial thief's morals, to access the upper glacier, now readily gained; while it is relatively free of crevasses, most parties rope up here. The aim is to obtain the notch between Lemah 2 and 3, the main summit, by remaining on the eastern aspect of the slope. The snow generally ends about 500' short of the col but a broad basin beyond, often filled with wildflowers in summer, is a welcome reward.

Nonetheless, another snowfield, then a class-4 gully must be tackled to gain the saddle and the ridge. From this notch, a tsunami of views opens to the north and west, but the best is yet to come. Scramble along the exposed but comfortable northwest ridge-top, favoring the southeast side if necessary, to attain a class 4 step up broken rock to the surprisingly broad summit. I ignored those following me, cursing at my flatulence; after all, it stemmed from the gulps of air I had to inhale in order to keep up and not slow down the party; I simply referred to it as my "wind instrument".

CHAPTER FOUR: A FIVE-FINGERED RIDDLE

All was condoned as we took in the panorama now in full view from the top: the precipitous ramparts of nearby Chimney Rock, the towering pinnacle of Mt. Stuart and the surprisingly snow-laden slopes of Mts. Daniel and Hinman to the north; the sharp towers of the Snoqualmie Peaks troop, including Mts. Thompson and Huckleberry, to the south; the behemoth, Mt. Rainier, looming in the southwestern background; Glacier Peak to the northwest; and the sere plains of eastern Washington. Forget for a while the possible perils of the descent as you luxuriate in the high air and, hopefully, the east-of-crest sunshine.

Even if it's cloudy west of the crest, the views here may actually be enhanced by the typical low fog blanketing the valleys, with the peaks standing tall above. Relax in the knowledge that many parties wisely choose to rappel or top-belay either or both gullies on the descent. It would also be heartening to know you have an extra weekend day in camp, if you've wisely taken a Friday or Monday off. Soaking your feet in chilly Lemah Creek and lounging around in base camp are just rewards after this diverse ascent.

The trek out with full pack is not that steep a descent, so for us elderly ("silver") climbers it's more back-breaking than knee-jarring. When you reach the vehicles, don't rush off without taking another look back over Cooper Lake to the spectacle of Lemah and Chimney Rock towering above the blue-green waters. Camera phones were made for such glorious photos. Also, do not fail to make your first pit stop in the historic mining village of Roslyn, ordering a brew and burger if you like at the corner tavern.

You can sneer at the tourists (Roslyn, and its corner tavern, was where the oddly charming *Northern Exposure* TV show was filmed) and marvel at the decorative Nineteenth Century architecture of the downtown buildings. If you have the time, rummage through the town's dump for forgotten timeworn artifacts of this area's beginnings as a hoped-for, but barely-realized treasure-trove of precious mineral deposits, as transitory as a Hollywood marriage.

With a mere 3 hours from the Seattle megalopolis or a 4½- to 5-hour drive to the trailhead from Portland (well, not as bad as Baker or Shuksan), combined with a relatively benign pack-in, a spectacular, if moist, campsite, varied rock-and-snow climbing, breathtaking and expansive views, and few technical difficulties, Lemah should be on every Northwest climber's agenda. Sure, you won't get as much regard as if you summitted Rainier along with the hordes doing so, but you'll know in your heart and mind the beauties that this oft-neglected north-of-Snoqualmie-Pass area has to offer. And, you'll enjoy the bonus of refreshments at a famous and historic tavern to boot!

CHAPTER FIVE
You can do it: Mt. Stuart
The West Ridge
(9,415')

HIDDEN GEMS OF THE WASHINGTON CASCADES

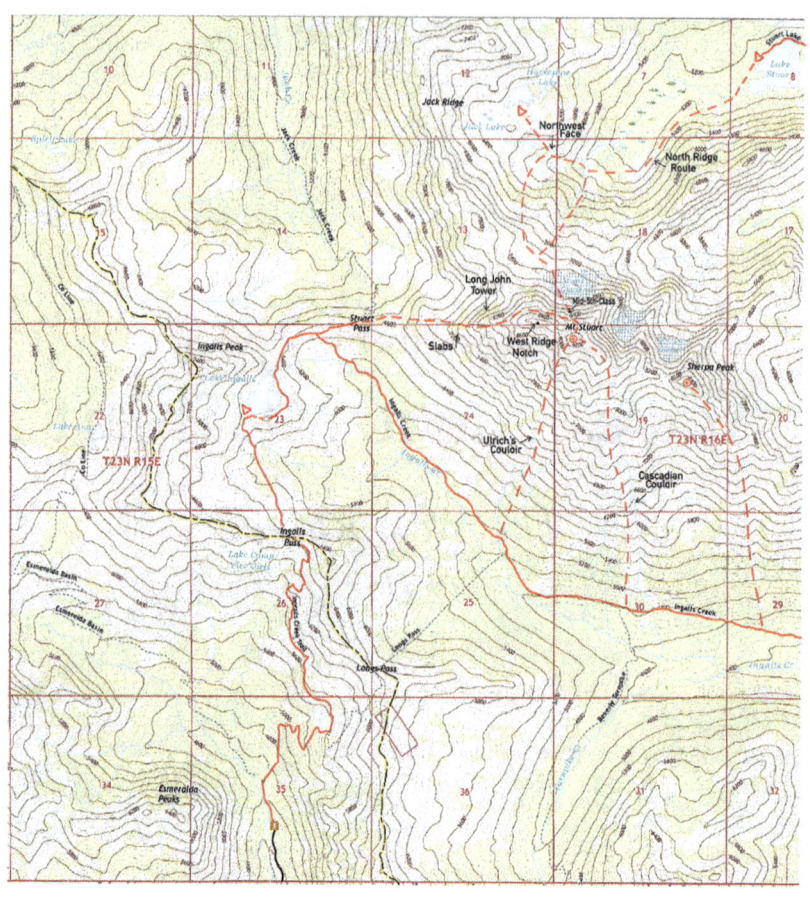

CHAPTER FIVE: YOU CAN DO IT: MT. STUART

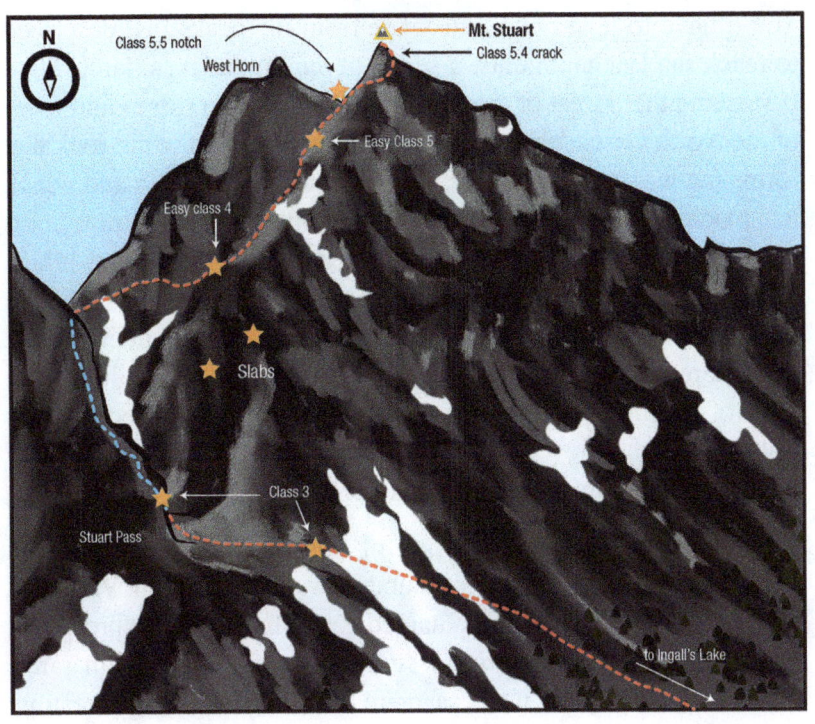

You'd have to leap quite a distance from the peaks just described to reach the Enchantments, a series of summits, lakes, larch-filled basins and that rarest of stone in the basalt/breccia ridges and faces of the North Cascades – granite - pure grey-spotted white rock that forms the wet dreams of rock climbers across the globe and which has made the Enchantment Ranges famous for their grippy holds and 5th-class endeavors. However, even the most novice of hikers can enjoy this area without so much as using their hands to scale anything, while still delighting in this fairyland of mountain basins. Boot steps and wide-awake eyes are all that's required, along with a bit of stamina, to reach this landscape, so well-named, as it is truly one of the most bewitching of realms to be found anywhere amongst the mountains of North America.

You will find a legendary group of boulder basins pocked with magical lakes whose whimsical names reveal their charm: Vivianne, with its sword-like peninsula named Excalibur Rock; Leprechaun; Naiad, from where the craggy summits south of the main range can best be pictured; Rune, a mere pond but a pleasant resting/camping spot; Talisman; Valkyrie; Pixie; Sprite, a lovely color of bluish-green; and the relatively large Titania. But more of this in the next chapters.

Let's suppose that you'd like to impress your friends with a 5th-class route but the west and east ridges of Forbidden look a bit scary and a cursory glance at the vertical walls of Liberty Bell and the Early Winter Spires makes you a bit nauseous. You should really consider what looks like a heroic 5th-class adventure but turns out to be mostly 3rd-to-easy 5th-class climbing: the West Ridge of Mt. Stuart. You will gain a fig-leaf of respectability on this Ridge without the apprehensions of anything exceeding mid-5th-class rock work.

Sure, you've possibly ascended the Cascadian or Uhlrich's couloirs in summitting Stuart the easy ways but the West Ridge is a prize few scramblers, brave as they may be, would attempt. To boast that you've mastered it could gain you some credit among those who've merely scrambled its southern gullies, scanned it through binoculars

CHAPTER FIVE: YOU CAN DO IT: MT. STUART

or seen it in photos, where it appears far more treacherous than it actually turns out to be. Moreover, the Stuart Ranges are often far enough east to avoid the summer sprinkles that sometimes dampen our outdoor plans. Eyeing the West Ridge, do not become discouraged by its sheer angles and vertical walls. Would it take a super-climber to scale this route? Certainly not.

Stuart is a monster of a mountain and its truly technical north face holds anemone-like ice and higher 5th-class rock routes which place them in the province of the elite among us (and which leaves me mostly out of the picture). But the West Ridge only *looks* menacing, its zany and precipitous skyline often more symbolic than substantial. If the technical north face climbs are pouncing leopards and the southern couloirs your lazy housecat napping in the sun, the West Ridge is at least a mountain lion, silent and often hidden, but always lurking and quiet enough to approach the forest visitor within mere feet without her or him noticing its presence.

Some would argue that the West Ridge is hardly an "overlooked, hidden gem", as implied in the title of this book. However, I include it here because it is actually becoming *less* frequently climbed than in the 1990's as well as early in the present century, and for several reasons: First, the vast majority of parties climbing Stuart do so via the southern couloirs noted above; second, an increasingly talented group of alpine athletes are eschewing this "easy" ridge to concentrate on the north faces, with technical ice tools at the ready and the ability to achieve climbs ranking in the higher 5th-class categories. However, the West Ridge Route allows the weekend punter the opportunity to scale a technical climb up Stuart in relative solitude, but always with a competent leader, especially one who is familiar with this route. Though at times entertaining and at others, disturbing, it always remains a challenge well within your grasp. If you're hesitant, do what you think you can't.

My own struggles with the north face routes (North Ridge and Northwest Face) have generally ended badly, my naïve bravery collapsing in proportion to the increase into 5.9 nightmares: a collision between ambition and reality. I speak from desperate experience. Perhaps due to a clerical error, I was allowed onto a climb of the North Ridge. Clumsily following our agile leader on an ascent, I was as nervous as a mink in a fur factory. It had appeared to me that my chances for success on these routes were as likely as detecting gravitational waves from an apple falling to the ground. I had reached my equilibrium of incompetence: For my comfort zone (5.7 and below), these climbs soon went from significant to catastrophic, from fiction to frightening friction. I had leaned the difference between intentions and capabilities. The dangers there were of two dimensions: black ice and loose flakes of rock. Nothing quite illuminates the reality of mortality by facing a 5.9 pitch with scant protection and 250' of runout below.

I was, however, fortunate to follow in the well-placed footsteps of our leaders in those days, though I often regarded them with a mixture of both gratitude and resentment, depending on the technical difficulties encountered at any particular moment. They eased me through what I perceived as an intractable conflict, often with strength combined with sublime poise. Nimble and reassuring, their moves contained an equal amount of subtlety and rigor. They always seemed so blasé about what I considered life-threatening circumstances. For me, strict attention was always required; indifference could lay the tracks upon which failure could easily travel. I must admit to having taken two plunging falls on several ultimately successful attempts, ably protected by a belay from above by the assistant leader. I could only mutter the two weakest words in the English Language: "I'm sorry".

American Bistort

At one point, our leader proposed I lead a 5.9 pitch; me leading 5.9 is equivalent to trying to imagine a new color. On the summit, I was proud but not anxious to repeat such routes for years thereafter. My success on such technical challenges owed more to the leaders' skills than my humble fumbling. I viewed even a single success more as a miracle than a pattern.

But the West Ridge offers a more feasible approach. To reach this route, proceed about 5 miles past Cle Elum on I-90, then exit onto Highway 970 and travel about 6 miles to the Teanaway Road. Next you must endure 23 miles on this at-times rough byway to its end and the beginning of the Ingalls Lake Trail. This gem travels woods at first, with the tallest firs and spruces seeming to scratch the sky. But soon the trail emerges into glorious flower-filled meadows, traverses Ingall's Pass, then drops you into a basin filled with the shimmering turquoise waters of Ingall's Lake.

A campsite here not only offers towering views of the southwestern aspect of Stuart's granite faces and gullies, but a chance at a chilly dip if you're so inclined and have better circulation than I. Unfortunately, from this perspective, it looked as feasible for me to ascend this sharp-fanged Ridge as I could steal a star from the sky. More happily, flowers abound, including tall purple Cascade Asters; blue lupines; scarlet paintbrushes; white American bistort and Sitka valerian; and 1–2' tall partridgefoot, sending a spike of tiny white flowers skyward. A nicer place to camp amongst these eastern outposts of the North Cascades would be hard to find. At evening tide, mystical vibrations almost seem to whisper across the waters, urging you to accept the challenge of a technical ascent the next day.

Sitka Valerian

From here, do not despair if the West Ridge appears frighteningly jagged (which it is) as you need to keep in mind its saving grace: It, and all of Stuart, are composed not of the tottering black basalt and gneiss so loose it sometimes feels like you're trying to climb an overhanging sand dune, but of bright white granite, solid as... well, a rock.

I was delirious with joy that we had a leader, a well-known female climber, who was cautious and not flashy, and who had scaled the ridge several times in the past. I was both a bit embarrassed, but secretly smug, all the more so because she had named me as assistant leader after the real assistant bailed. To begin, proceed along the eastern shore of the lake and ascend north to Stuart Pass and the start of the actual climbing route eastward. Nothing too difficult here at first; just some gratifying 3rd-class scrambling at the speed of thought, and this amongst giant blocks which pleasantly do not move much when you hold onto them. However, the Ridge narrows (why do they always do that?) but easy escapes north or south provide decent holds, with occasional 4th-class moves required to keep you alert.

There are the usual grassy slopes and ledges, which eventually lead around a corner to a stupendous sight: Long John Tower, at about 8,700'. Its name may come from some ancient pirate and its shape resembles more a hedgehog standing on its back feet than a tottering turret, although it does accentuate the feeling that you are in the midst of seriously rocky terrain. Note the lichens, plentiful on these granite rocks. They appear to thrive in just two dimensions, flattened against the rock, their colors grey to red to green. Their apparent simplicity belies their complexities: They consist of both fungi and algae, both nurturing the other in symbiotic friendship. The green one is usually called the "map lichen", and indeed, its verdure is an equal to any topo map's grass-green to my eyes.

Fortunately, the way here is clear: Keep traversing east, crossing ridges and those persistent gullies, occasionally leaving the Ridge proper when the crest itself seems too menacing, until you achieve the West Ridge Notch. At this point, the least fearsome course is to stay on the Ridge's south side for about 60 ft. until you can re-gain the crest itself. Here I suggested what appeared to be an easy crossing; lucky for me our leader, Becca, had little taste for compromise and brooked no dissent. Later I learned that my choice would have led us

CHAPTER FIVE: YOU CAN DO IT: MT. STUART

into severe 5th-class territory. Fortunately, Becca, both patient and prudent, chose a direct course, despite my tendency for careering to and fro. The traverse and short ascent required more delicacy than power. This section took me longer than the last 2 minutes of a close NBA game, with more timeouts and fouls (rests) than action. Our leader feigned indifference to my whining as we set up solid belays, which quieted my insecurities. Ashamed, as assistant leader I had all the charisma of a phone directory.

From this spot, one may encounter easy 5th-class holds on rock with Velcro-like solid foot and hand placements, until a series of ledges brings the climber to one last lie-back in a crack system and then, thankfully, the bungalow-sized elusive target: the summit blocks. Here, offering thanks to the rock gods and treats for the leader, the entire panoply of the Alpine Lakes Wilderness splays out at your feet.

Directly to the south lie Colchuck and Dragontail, separated by the Colchuck Glacier. Mt. Rainier hovers, menacing, beyond. Then, across Aasgard Pass, Little Annapurna, Mt. Temple and McClellan Peak can be seen. Unfortunately, the ragged pinnacles of the Cashmere Crags and the Rat Creek Group, with names such as The Hook, Crocodile Fang, The Blockhouse, and the Dragon Teeth, all beloved of rock wall heroes, are partly hidden further south. Nonetheless, to your southeast, Sherpa, Argonaut, and Colchuck Balanced Rock come into view (it really is barely balanced – until the next earthquake).

Look to the north for a view of Glacier Peak, and northwest to the snowy mantles of Mts. Daniel and Hinman, while again to the north, Bonanza comes into view. Further north, the glacier-clad giants of the North Cascades are a bit too distant to identify but one stands tall in the far and hazy northwestern distance: Mt. Baker. Don't neglect the views across the Enchantment plateau as well, dotted with lakes, ponds, and tarns abutting the white granite stones and flowery meadows of this bewitching land, all capped off by the alpine larches, their needles so lime-green in summer yet so deeply orange in fall.

Descent is often down the Cascadian or Uhlrich's Couloirs but this entails a steep climb back to the Lake. It is possible, however, to find adequate rappel stations so as to reverse your course down the West Ridge and avoid any unnecessary ascending (one of the foundations upon which my own climbing career has been built). Unfortunately, packing up after base camp, there is about 500' of gain to Ingall's Pass. Some of my companions were a bit grumpy on the way out but, strangely, I seemed drunk with joy at having completed an exposed mid-5th-class ascent but, at least at the summit, I remembered that I needed to sober up quickly for the numerous downclimbing and rappelling ahead.

The trek up, then out, is usually accomplished without too much pain. So try this jewel of an alpine ascent, quite within the capabilities of the average 4th- to easy 5th-class climber, yet one which will test your skills as well as sharpen your appetite for even tougher routes in the future. Now, whenever you look back at Stuart, visible from so many of our other great peaks and the unchallenged emperor of Washington's Alpine Lakes, you can justifiably boast about climbing a "really tough technical route" and be almost honest about it. Just hope your audience is either in such a state of blissful ignorance that facts about Stuart's challenges are irrelevant or that they are so inebriated it wouldn't matter much anyway.

CHAPTER SIX

Shaking the Dragon's Tail

Colchuck

(8,705')

and Dragontail Peaks

(8,840')

HIDDEN GEMS OF THE WASHINGTON CASCADES

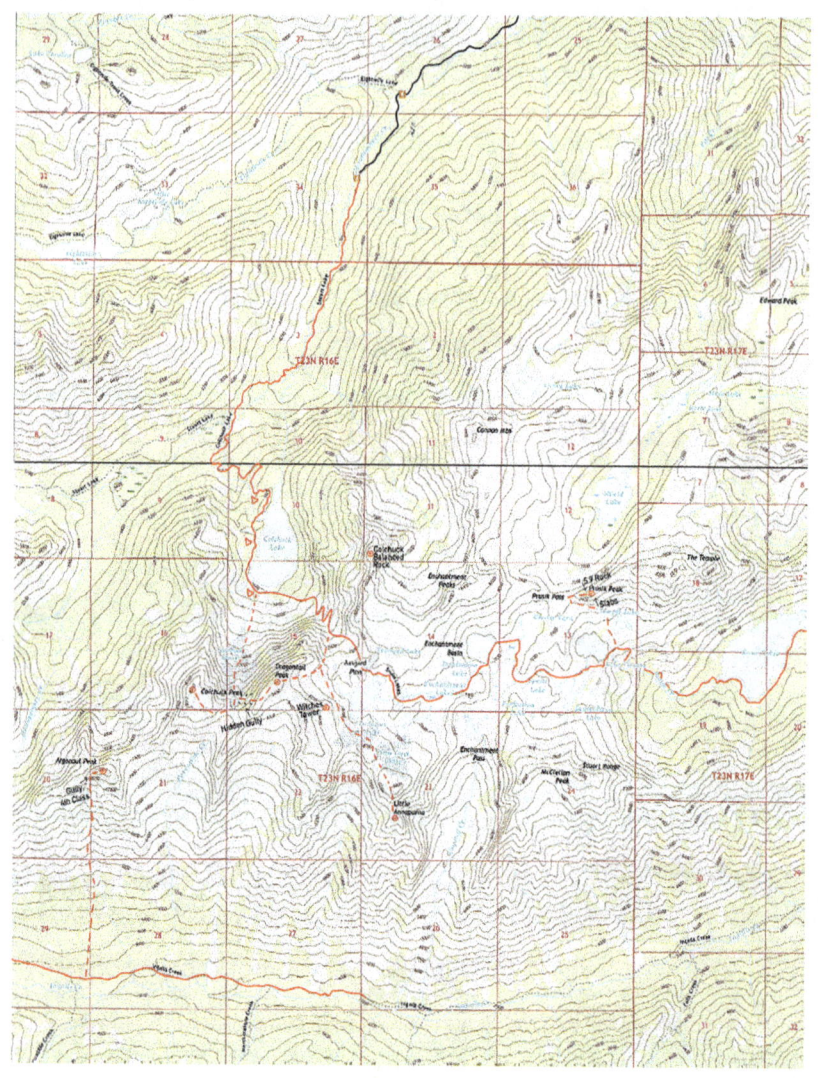

CHAPTER SIX: SHAKING THE DRAGON'S TAIL

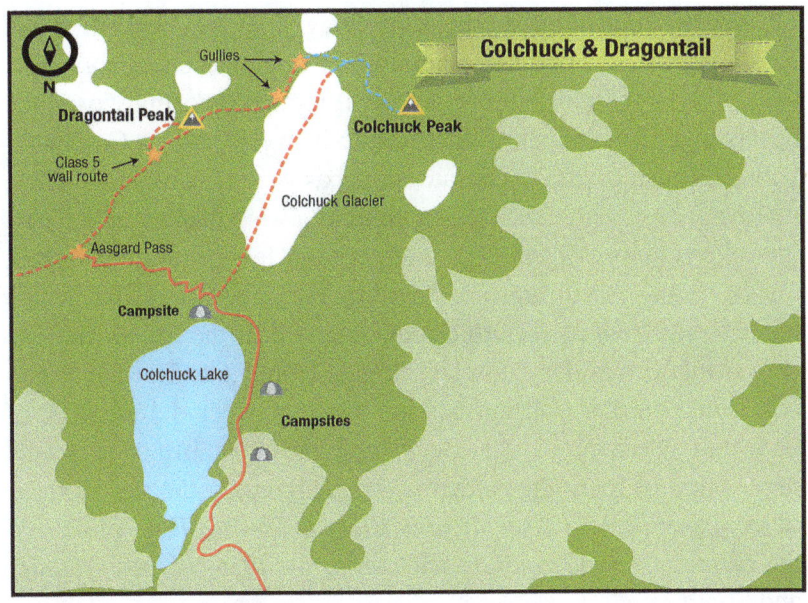

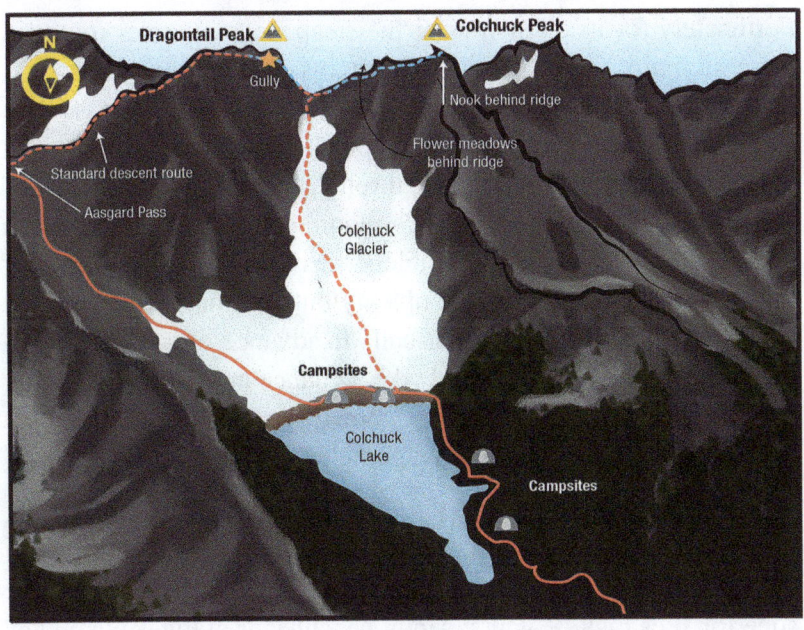

Of all the Enchantments, perhaps Dragontail has witnessed the most technical rock climbs, undoubtedly due to its sheer northwest face, made even more impressive as it looms imposingly over the mildly angled Colchuck Glacier just to its west. Many a Colchuck-bound climber of only moderate skills has gazed in awe at this face, realizing, as have I, that it poses more of a wish than a reality. This unbroken granite wall also has counterparts, less commonly visited, on the peak's north and northeastern faces, although the peak's name stems from its teetering rock towers near the true summit as seen from Aasgard Pass. Pitches ranging from 5.6 to 5.11 have been completed on this wall but perhaps the most accurate measure of its formidable nature is that Beckey devotes 10 entire pages to the description of its multi-graded routes, surpassing the descriptions of any other peak in his *Columbia River to Stevens Pass* version of the *Cascade Alpine Guides*, aside from the titans of Mts. Rainier and Stuart.

Fortunately for us dilettantes of the steep, several easier routes to these summits exist. One usually begins with a 4-mile trek on a decent, though occasionally steep, trail to Colchuk Lake, a base camp rendered scenic by the jutting pinnacles of improbably poised rock walls and minarets peering through the lush green needles of the larches. Just below the lake, a required stop in August enables you to sample the luscious thimbleberries thriving in a prime patch of sun. Camps at the Lake are aplenty but you must register at the Leavenworth Ranger Station, usually in advance, and often early in the spring, although you could take a chance at the few remaining vacancies mid-week by simply showing up at the Station that morning – I wouldn't hazard the gamble.

You can put down in clutches of firs nearly lakeside, with views through the trees across to Colchuck Balanced Rock along with the lofty towers encircling it. However, arrive early enough and superior sites may be yours: sandy beachheads at the south end of the Lake itself, with unobstructed views of the Aasgard Pass peaks and down valley to Cannon and Cashmere Mountains rising above the entire blue-green expanse of Colchuck Lake, the largest body of water in all the Alpine Lakes Wilderness. A few clouds and peaks reflecting off the lake embellish the alpine ambience.

One goal, quite feasible for the semi-experienced but glacier-equipped climber, is to conquer **Colchuck Peak**, a relatively easy ascent up the Colchuck Glacier. The climb up was a continuous lesson in why this upland and its surrounding heights are called the Enchantments. To our left the vertical granite walls of Dragontail Peak soar 1,500' toward the sky; below, the pearlescent blue-green waters of Colchuck Lake simmer in the sun; in the distance to the north, serrated and notched ridges and summits stretch seemingly to Canada. On our ascent, we watched the superior rock warriors on the fearsome eastern wall of Dragontail inching their Yosemite-like way up this vertical parapet. Crack climbers will risk their reputations (and more) on these steep barriers. Fans of faster-paced sports would find this as exciting as watching a chess match or someone else's kids play T-ball, unless you know what you are looking for.

But those of us somewhat familiar with the vertical challenges of wall climbing were enthralled by these stone masters slowly and carefully inching their belayed way up the sheer 90-degree wall. Unfortunately, my name and the words "5.9 class" are only found in the same sentence ending with the word "failure"; their talk of cordelettes and cam sizes were, for me, akin to watching a foreign movie without subtitles.

In contrast, once over the glacier, the class-3 scramble up the south side of Colchuck is a pleasant exercise, the climber's path shouldered by lupine, paintbrush, partridgefoot (check the leaves for how it got its name), purple asters and daises along with the more rare alpine jewels of silky phacelia and a variety of recondite but colorful white and golden alpine draba's.

Patridgefoot

55

Back at the col there may be time for an ambitious climber to scale **Dragontail** from the west. Search for an obvious rocky gully with loose class-3-4 climbing, which soon turns a bit steeper.

Although pleasantly uncertain of what lay ahead on our attempt in this gully, a bit of loose class 4 failed to sap our unearned confidence. We found that as long as you respect the stones and, importantly, test each hold, you will be fine. The gully (hard hats required) topped out on a serrated ridge perched above the Lost Plateau, a wonderland of tottering spires above twinkling lakes with King Arthur-type names such as Sprite and Viviane, Gnome Tarn, and Troll Sink. Colchuck Balanced Rock and the unlikely boulder perched unsteadily atop Sherpa Peak dominate the view to the north but to the west, Argonaut, Colchuck and the abrupt north walls of Mt. Stuart, emperor of the Enchantments, glisten.

But exactly where is the top of Dragontail? Three bouldery pinnacles crest the ridge. On our climb, while I was too cheap to have invested in an altimeter watch, I consulted the tattered shreds of my topo but the lines were too close, at least for my aged eyes, to discern much of anything. My partner, David, declared, somewhat mysteriously, "I'll let you know". Taking out his half-full water bottle, David lined up the other two of our three apparent summits. He next eyed each through his horizontally held flask and determined that, indeed, we were on the highest point.

"You can't tell which is the highest point with that crazy technique", I protested but, as usual, David remained unperturbed. I am chagrinned to report that, in subsequent trips up Dragontail, David was correct. The topmost of these crazily tilted towers is the northeast one but several to its south would also make excellent viewpoints and are of almost equal height. You could climb each one but that, in my mind, would be a triumph of technique over purpose.

The trip down that makes the most sense is to simply down-climb rickety but easily-angled rock to reach the snow slope to the east of the summit and happily glissade to Aasgard Pass, then down the steep but well-marked trail to your home away from home –

CHAPTER SIX: SHAKING THE DRAGON'S TAIL

your base camp at Colchuck Lake. Unfortunately for us, we had left some gear at the Colcuck-Dragontail col, so we had to carefully navigate our way back, climbing down the gully, then descending the glacier to the lake. We were late, having planned only the Colchuck summit, but it was a moon-filled descent and at nightfall, the glacier's reflections obviated our need for headlamps. It was an eerie but wonderful experience to view the Enchantments, their peaks sharply defined against the dusky sky, its pools reflecting the moonlight like the spooky gaze of a prowling cat, with shards of light illuminating our way.

If you are the type of climber who believes there are winds of change but it's your job to change the winds, then by all means tackle the steep technical routes of Dragontail's west and north faces. You can scale these walls but descent thereafter is a necessity. Rappelling the routes is standard but you still must descend the northern-most part of the Colchuck Glacier. Many such hard men and women bring only rock shoes for the technical climbing but, after rappelling from the top, a scant few such rock stars slip and slide down what would have been an effortless descent with boots and crampons. A small number have even tragically perished on these rock-shoe descents. It is remarkably ironic that these wall artists achieve such technically severe rock climbs, but they must presciently tailor their descent to the icy environment soon confronting them; after all, the ratchet of courage turns in only one direction.

So climb Dragontail either from Aasgard Pass then up the easy snow slope to its east, or go for the gully route on which we succeeded. What these routes lack in technical difficulties, they compensate with their views. We had hoped that our "hidden gully" up Dragontail's northwestern flank constituted a first ascent. Unfortunately, our enthusiasm was exterminated by finding a Cliff Bar wrapper halfway up "our" gully.

CHAPTER SEVEN
Slicing the Washington Sky
Prusik Peak
(~8,000')

HIDDEN GEMS OF THE WASHINGTON CASCADES

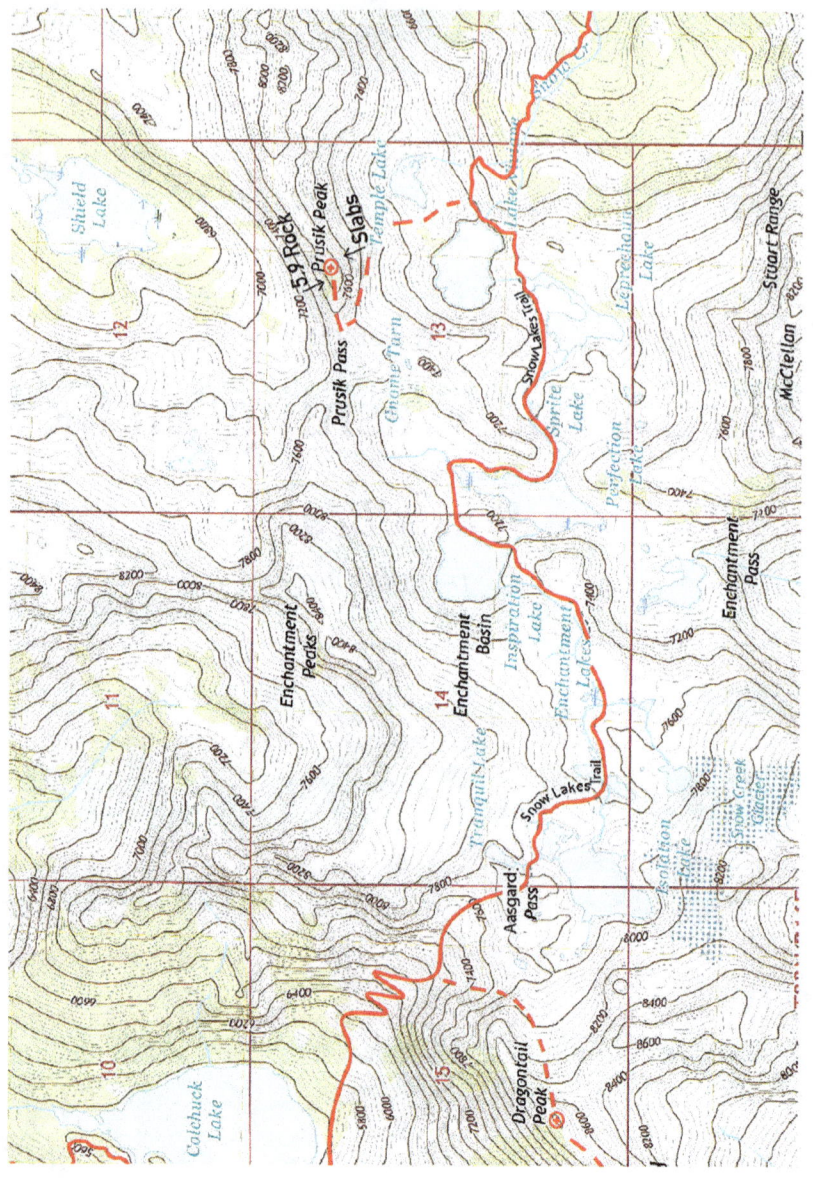

CHAPTER SEVEN: SLICING THE WASHINGTON SKY

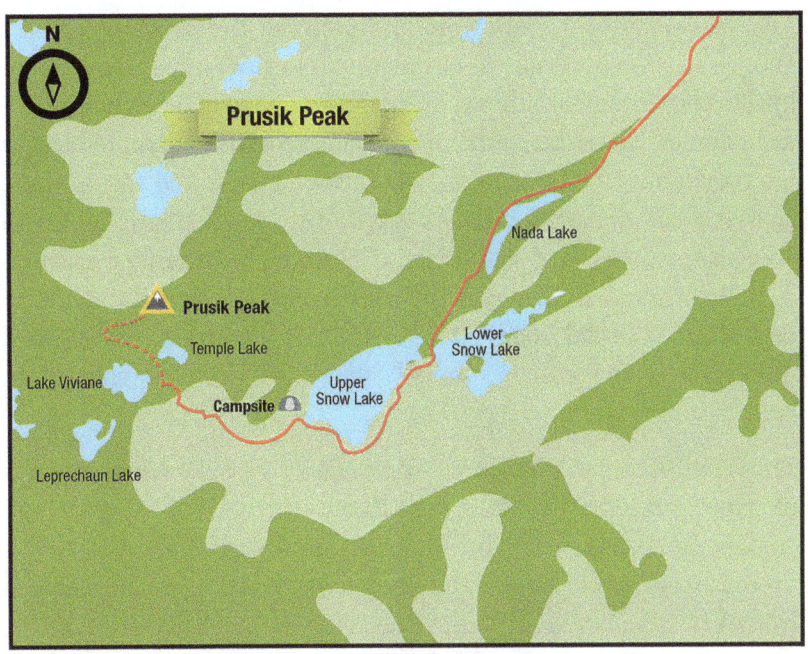

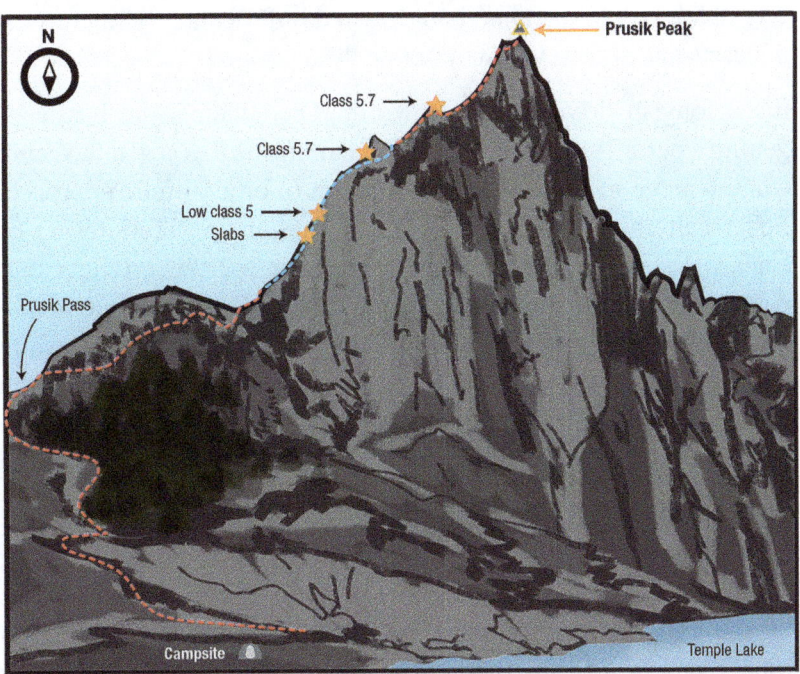

The white knife of jutting granite piercing the Washington sky known as Prusik Peak is familiar to Northwest climbers more by its photographs than by its real-life image. One would have to imagine that some quirk of tectonic up-thrust, combined with the inevitable erosion of less stable rock, has created this granitic near-vertical spear, its flanks appearing so precipitous as to abolish any thought of scaling them. Because of its remote location in the well-named Enchantment Basin, and because it cannot be seen from any road, many climbers, hikers, and backpackers have missed the good fortune to actually see Prusik Peak for real, a sight not easily forgotten.

Those without the chance to approach this peak, whether from the Colchuck Lake-Aasgard Pass Route or from Snow Lakes, can content themselves with the numerous photos of its famous visage on the many guide books and calendars crowding retail shelves. However, whether you climb Prusik or simply choose to see it up close as you wander the land of the Enchantments, with its crystal lakes, white granite boulders and improbable slicing turrets, minarets and spires, you will not be disappointed.

It's a longish drive to Leavenworth. Then there's the hassle of getting a permit to even enter the Enchantments if you want to camp – and believe me, you will after either a 6- or a 10-mile approach. Folks call the Leavenworth Ranger Station (509-548-6977) or enter a lottery online months in advance for the privilege. Of course, summer weekends are prime time but even mid-weeks are often full in summer and, surprisingly, so are the autumn days in late September through mid-October. It is in fall that the larch needles have turned orange and drop like golden shards on the freshly fallen snow.

Many shoulder-season Enchantment visitors will remember crunching through the newly-fallen snow, the frozen crystals giving off their own special light. Repeated visits here are never boring; they seem to also be frozen in your memory and grow better with time, like a Stradivarius violin or a fine Bordeaux wine. Whatever the season or approach, however, you will have to share the trails

CHAPTER SEVEN: SLICING THE WASHINGTON SKY

with tripod-carrying photographers anxious to enshrine their fame on Prussik, which, along with Mt. Shuksan, has become the most photogenic and hence most photographed of the peaks in our range.

I prefer the somewhat gentler Snow Lakes approach as opposed to the scramble with heavy packs over Aasgard Pass but either approach carries the benefits of lakes, views, and flower-filled meadows. On a recent trip following a fire, not uncommon in these parts, the weathered bark lay bare in spots, painting a varnished reddish-orange tinge, especially unmasked after a brief shower. Above the upper Snow Lake (actually a reservoir), the path steepens and cairns sometimes mark the way, but you finally reach the Upper Enchantment Basin.

The meandering trail across the Upper Enchantments takes you around wryly-named pools and lakes such as Valkyrie, Leprechaun, Troll, Pixie and Sprite. The first lake you encounter from the Snow Lakes approach is Lake Viviane at 6,785' and from here Prusik Peak is first visible, though not in its famous spire-like form. Turn right off the main path on a faint trail above the Lake, however, gain a few hundred feet to Temple Lake, and you will see Prusik's pinnacle in all its bright white granitic glory, a sight for the sore eyes of Cascade climbers inured to the dark-gray unbridled basalt and gneiss to the west of the Enchantments. Its sheer verticality is daunting and engendered fear in my brain, which soon metastasized to my stomach and other organs unmentionable in such a text. My thought was that, at 5'8", I had about as much chance of summitting this thing as I had of becoming a power forward in the NBA.

Nonetheless, we ambled up the climbers' path, now well-worn, which traverses the west side of the Lake, then ventures to the south side of Prusik. The tread continues a bit to the beginning of the most popular route up the peak, and, not surprisingly the easiest and my favored route to its jagged summit. Now is the time to put to rest the factoid that most climbers believe about Prusik: that it was named when the first ascensionists lassoed its sharp summit, then prusiked to the top.

In fact, Fred Beckey and Art Holben accomplished the first ascent, the East Route, in 1948 and Holben did lasso something near the top but it was not the actual summit, which is more like a clump of chopping blocks than a kitchen knife. They probably lassoed a pinnacle on the eastern edge of a left-leaning tower, then made an easy 40-foot traverse to the true apex. Their climb required aid and several pitches of 5.8 climbing, though on clean granite. This myth thus has both the merit and the drawback of now being impossible to verify, lost in the memories of the original ascent team.

The climb of the original ascent on this blade of rock was anything but quotidian. Today's standard route, the West Ridge, is much simpler, though it still challenges my athletic mediocrity. First continue on the climber's path to the start of the west ridge. There is no need to progress west to Prusik Pass as the standard route can begin just east of the pass and thus is more direct. Here easy slabs to the east lead to low 5th-class climbing on blocks of granite. Many climbers have their favorite and efficient manner of rock climbing; mine is not among them. I struggled to reconcile my goal of reaching the top with the requisite skill as being fundamentally contradictory.

Nonetheless, airy class-5.4 to 5.7 moves were fortunately solid enough, despite my teetering inadequacies combined with a fear of crashing on the rocks below. In an alternate universe (or perhaps the moon?), I would have flowed up the pitches but here on Earth I scuffled and jousted at the rock. At many points, the moves here required delicate footwork rather than brute strength. Thus I was more than happy to finally reach the ridge proper (though not yet the summit) and enjoy the expansive and airy views of all the Enchantment peaks and lakes, from Stuart in the west through to Colchuck, Dragontail, Little Annapurna, Sherpa, Argonaut and McClellan Peaks to the south and west. Among other unprintable thoughts, I realized that, for me, the old 5.7 was the new 5.15.

An additional delight was the appearance of the relatively rare Sitka mistmaidens, peeking out from almost vertical rock crevices. With scalloped leaves and a 3" stem, their diminutive five-petalled white flowers grow mainly off vertical walls wet and often dripping from snowfields above. Despite some clouds drifting in on our ascent, the horizon rising and falling with the vagaries of the wind, these castellated summits, softened somewhat by the mistmaidens, traced as jagged an expanse as can be found anywhere in this wilderness area.

After contemplating this vast panorama from the ridge, follow a series of granite friction slabs, fun if protected but hazardous rope-less. The most difficult pitch awaits, an exposed but protectable traverse around a horn (5.7), followed by exposed and tenuous tip-toes across ledges on the north face, then a lie-back up a corner to a 4th-class chimney. This, happily, leads to a scramble up the top-most blocks. Do not expect to gain a sharp blade at top despite the photos of a knife-like summit. The actual top-most point is more a jumble of blocks than a clean-edged sword.

Sitka Mistmadens

Sometimes, the views from far away are more spectacular then up close. Nonetheless, these summit views from Prusik are truly spectacular, except for those prone to vertigo: The snow-clad peaks of the Cascades are visible to the north and of course, Rainier to the southwest. Bonanza stands to the north while Glacier Peak and the Dome massif can be spotted to the north-west. Descent is fortunately prearranged by thoughtful folks who had bolted and otherwise protected the rappels down either the north or southwest faces.

For the more adventurous climber for whom risk is an invitation, a number of routes up to 5.11 exist, which I will not be testing. But for the truly skilled and vertically hard-wired, it may be that difficulty resides in their DNA. Gazing up at the more technical routes, particularly on the west and southern aspects of Prusik, we weekend adventurers realized that these routes form more of a fantasy than a reality. We could at least be vicarious avatars to the professional-grade climbers who dare these great deeds. By scaling Prusik via the route described above, you can finally equate something dreamed with something actually accomplished. But beware the weather report. Cloistered this far east, incoming storms are not easily seen nor anticipated; clouds here can become overly excited, leading to a wind-whipped summit epic under angry skies. In such conditions, views may vanish faster than a hacked credit card account.

Regardless of how you approach Prusik, whether to climb, backpack or just to stare at it for a day, you can say you've at least seen the actual peak rather than its image, though both are spectacular. Even should you not aspire (interestingly from the Latin *to breath upon...to hope to attain*) to climb Prusik or bring your cowboy rope to lasso something, you will not be disillusioned; they call it the Enchantments for a reason: The peaks, gardens and lakes will bewitch you as much as the lasso- and King-Arthur-myths which have lent their names to this most charming of destinations. Go and see this textured landscape – it is truly paradise found.

Finally, peering up at Prusik or down and around the Enchantment Basin forces one to wonder at the geologic forces which thrust up and honed these majestic peaks over millennia. Rocks from afar colliding with our planet, then forced deep within the earth, only to be thrust upwards by tectonic forces into these jagged shapes would make a great show if viewed in super fast motion. Unfortunately, we cannot fast-forward geologic time on our smart phones or VCR's. Understanding the science of tectonic uplift enriches the experience but even without such knowledge, the sheer majesty of this display forces us to recognize there are miracles of deep time we can never witness within our own brief existence.

CHAPTER EIGHT

Only Lesser in Altitude than in Alpine Experience

The Lesser Enchantments

HIDDEN GEMS OF THE WASHINGTON CASCADES

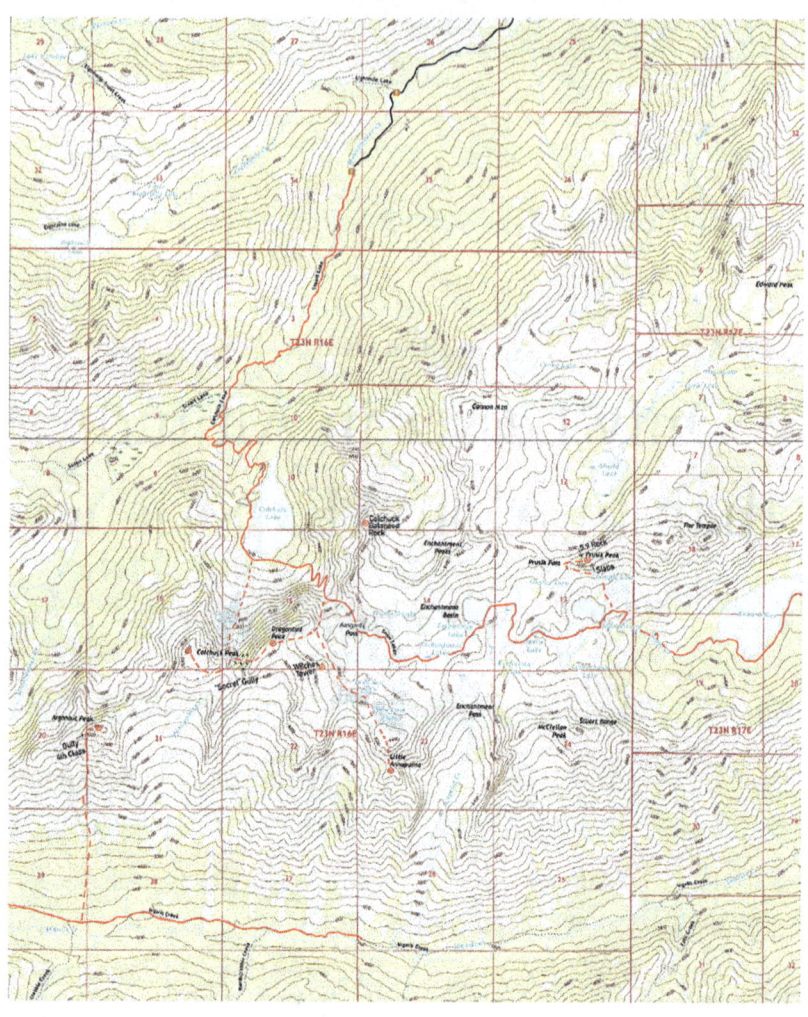

CHAPTER EIGHT: ONLY LESSER IN ALTITUDE THAN IN ALPINE EXPERIENCE

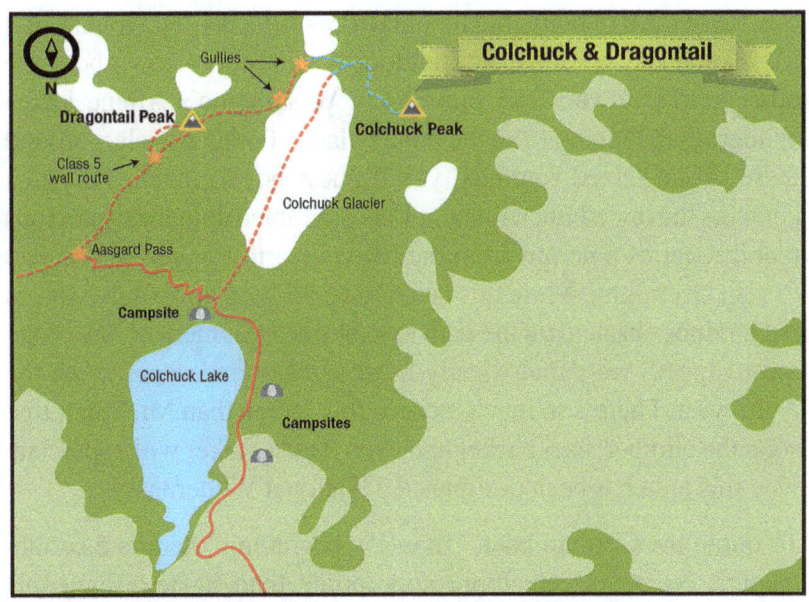

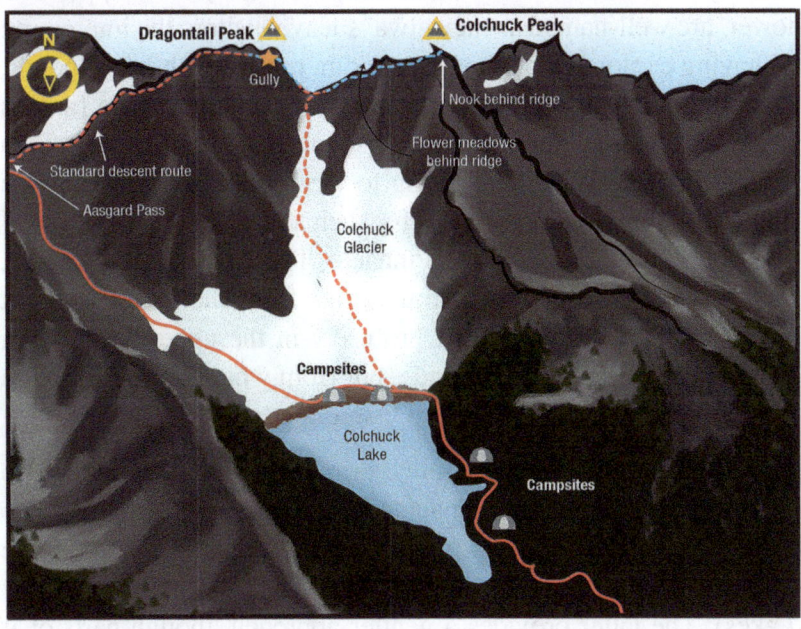

Yes there's Mt. Stuart, Ingall's and Prusik Peaks, Dragontail and Mt. Colchuck, but do many outdoor adventurers know about the other granite towers and summits in Washington's Alpine Lakes Wilderness? Judging from the relative lack of other travelers around these oft-neglected summits, you'd guess not so much. This area contains the famed Enchantment Lakes, a fabled domain so precious that it requires a permit from the Leavenworth Ranger Station just to visit overnight. While this is a hassle, all who do so agree this is but a minor obstacle on the path to sublime enjoyment of one of the most rugged, yet paradoxically most serene, landscapes in all the Northwest. There's so much more to this region than Mt. Stuart that soon the climber, backpacker and even the day hiker will appreciate why this area has been designated a National Wilderness.

To quote the German poet, "In every beginning, there is a certain magic". No words are more appropriate than in describing this journey. For starters, the Enchantment Basins, both upper and lower, are well-named as they always leave visitors the impression of having explored a mythical kingdom, replete with lakes, ponds, waterfalls, flowery meadows, heathered benches, and the famous deciduous alpine larch trees whose needles fade to a golden orange in the fall before floating to the ground. Jagged summits abound, with names appropriate for such a magical setting: Cynical Pinnacle, Flake Tower, Pogo Pinnacle, The Boxtop, The Candle, and Razorback Spire. Rock routes rise from the lower basin at Snow Lakes and bloom most profusely in the upper basin, from which many climbs can be made, but from which there still exists untrammeled pinnacles awaiting first ascents.

For climbing or backpacking, two prime choices for a gateway to this enchanted region both emanate from roads out of Leavenworth: the Colchuck Lake Trail (4½ miles) or the longer but more scenic Snow Creek (also called Snow Lakes) Trail (6¾ miles to Snow Lakes). The latter provides a gentler approach, though parts of it have been marred by recent fires. Still, the burnished orange bark exposed on the many firs and Lodgepole Pines add a glistening note, belying the description of a dry-stick forest. Fortunately,

CHAPTER EIGHT: ONLY LESSER IN ALTITUDE THAN IN ALPINE EXPERIENCE

unlike people, when trees die, they remain upright. Permits are usually only available for mid-week or off-season forays. However, for high-summer weekends, and in the glorious autumn season from mid-September to late October, reserve early or expect an uncertain lottery.

It is in the fall that the arrow-straight alpine larches turn golden orange. Their bejeweled needles fall and rest lightly upon the chiseled crystals of early snowflakes dappling the frozen ground.

An early autumn morning can appear as a dimly-lit photograph with a gossamer of frost. It is also then that you will have to fight off the many professional photographers anxious to make their mark with artsy shots of gold on white, backed by the persistent spires of the Enchantment Range. Until the fourth season evicts them, you might best go mid-week, and bring your warmest belongings for protection from the omnipresent night-time chill.

Alpine Larch

Fortunately, campsites are abundant at Colchuck Lake (5,570') and at Snow Lakes (5,415'), and above on the Enchantment Plateau itself. From Colchuck Lake, a rough and tough 2,500' vertical scramble in just ¾ mile over the famed Aasgard Pass is best left for the following day - my recommendation, considering that gravity has always been my enemy, and gravity has almost always won. On this jagged up-thrust, once achieved, diverse and scattered turquoise jewels of shimmering water bear whimsical fairy-tale names: Lake Vivienne, with its sword-like Excalibur Rock; and ponds and tarns called Talisman, Valkyrie, Leprechaun, Naiad, Sprite, Dryad, Pixie and Troll. Astride these two approaches is the saddle of the previously-mentioned Aasgard Pass (7,800'), a renowned viewpoint above which soars the vertical granite walls of

Dragontail Peak (8,840') capped by its lopsided maze of frightfully jagged towers. Underneath, a bounty of blossoms creates carpets of color, as if a crazed artist had spilled cans of blue, purple, red and yellow across a matted backdrop of green.

There is enough here to satisfy the backpacker for at least a week of exploration. Here lie secret tarns, east-side wildflowers (over 150 species have been identified in summer), heathered meadows colored red and white, the remarkable rock needles of Dragontail, the improbable spires of **Colchuck Balanced Rock (8,200')**, the sharp-edged and neatly-cleft granite sword of **Prusik Peak (~8,000')**, **Witch's Tower (8,520')**, **Jaberwocky Towers (6,840')**, **Rosebud Spire (7,700')**, **Sherpa (8,605')** and **Argonaut Peaks (8,453')**. Climbers could easily spend many summers trying to achieve all the technical routes (some as yet unclimbed) but even first-time scramblers and novice mountaineers will discover sufficient delight for endless visits to this rugged wonderland.

Technical climbs, up to 5.11, can be found on the massive west-facing solid granite wall of Dragontail Peak; nonetheless, most routes on this wall are rated mid-5th class to 5.8. All these begin either at Colchuck Lake or near Aasgard Pass. However, the Northwest Face Route is mostly a 3rd- and 4th class scramble up a loose gully (if I did it…well, you know), while the East Route is, in the main, a clomp on snow to a westward turn onto 3rd class rock. Colchuck Balanced Rock is a 3rd-class scramble through tangled underbrush from the eponymous lake, though the final (unbalanced) boulder problem requires protection; it is usually not climbed – the views are just as spectacular from beneath it. Peer over the brink if you dare, down to the azure Colchuck Lake, the (usually) blue sky, and the white-to-grey speckled stones and green meadows of Aasgard Pass.

Despite its fierce name, **Little Annapurna (8,448')** turns out to be less than Himalayan. From Aasgard Pass, one simply climbs moderate-angle snow to its shining cone of a summit. Likewise, **Witch's Tower**, near the pass, is neither haunted nor, on its southwest aspect, much of a tower. Scramble talus and 3rd-class

CHAPTER EIGHT: ONLY LESSER IN ALTITUDE THAN IN ALPINE EXPERIENCE

boulders to its top for incredible views southeast down the Snow Creek Valley, with its multitude of brilliant jeweled lakes and, with binoculars, scan northeast for high-tech rock artists across the valley attempting to draw a line up the precipitous routes on Snow Creek Wall.

For the more adventurous, a different approach to this area, familiar to most Stuart climbers, is to hike the trails from the end of the North Fork Teanaway River Road, over Long's or Ingall's Passes, then descend to the Ingall's Creek floor. **Sherpa Peak (8,605')** can be ascended from this valley as it lies just east of Stuart. On its oddly-shaped summit is another example of a curious balanced boulder visible from the valley below. Although the romantically-inclined believe these spooky rocks were left behind by some mischievous giant, glacial deposition during the last Ice Age is a more likely explanation. Sherpa's South Route begins at the valley's base just downstream from the beginnings of the Stuart routes, then traverses east-side (light) brush to an open basin on the peak's southeastern slope. It then ascends a broad gulley just east of the summit. One then follows an obvious ledge and chimney system (class 4) to the top. Once there, you can more closely examine how car-sized boulders can sustain such precarious perches.

Just east of Sherpa lies **Argonaut Peak (8,453')**, a rock-strewn citadel with what appears to be a strange box-shaped summit. From the Ingall's Creek Trail, ascend moderate brush on the south flank to a gully (hard hats!) that provides access to the easy summit ridge (3rd- and 4th-class). On one outing, we were already in the Ingall's Creek Valley on an extended outing so our ambitious eyes turned to Argonaut. However, between inspiration and completion lies the tough part, replete with perspiration.

On our first try, our course veered from confusion to chaos as we had wandered into an adjacent crack on the north face (5.6). At this point, our leader, much more skilled in rock-craft than I, fell ill and asked me, the assistant (and reluctant) leader to assume control. Feigning courage, I was an unlikely inspiration, in all likelihood conveying uncertainty more than confidence. On 5th-class rock, I felt inept, like I could ruin even the sleeves on a vest. This could well have turned into a tragedy of errors, but blissfully unclear of the way, skepticism overcame hope. Glad that we had brought additional protection, we struggled to the summit's boulders. We then ruefully eyed the preferred 4th-class gully we had missed, just to our right. It then occurred to me that leadership without foresight is like a ship without a sail.

Other climbs and scrambles are available on **The Temple (8,292')**, **Enchantment Peaks (~8,200')** and **Cashmere Mountain (7,533')**. By car-camping at DeRoux Campground, two miles before the end of the North Fork Teanaway River Road, one can scramble both **Esmeralda Peaks (6,480')** and **Hawkins Mountain (7,160')**. Both feature views from Stuart to the snow-clad giants beyond and further north.

Whether day-hiking, backpacking, scrambling or climbing, the Enchantments offer an entirely different perspective than our usual west-side forays. The rock is both more solid yet its hues brighter and more varied; the flowers are a slightly different breed; and the landscape is drier and less snowbound, yet strangely dotted with more lakes than out west. If you choose to attend this concert of delight, I believe the optimum season might be in late autumn, when snow on the ground is painted golden with the orange needles of the many subalpine larches. The deciduous shrubs may be mostly bare, their naked limbs outstretched like skeletons praying to the heavens above, but also making it easier for you to spy the magnificent scenery all around.

Go too late, and you might be disappointed as, by the onset of wintry conditions, the golden needles have disappeared. Best to wait until next spring; under snows, these trails will rest. Surely, spring and summer will return, and bring a pause to the ever-present clouds and gloom of a Northwest winter. The drive may be a bother but not to the seasoned wilderness traveler, and the weather is almost always superior to that further west. Try these lesser Enchantment peaks and you'll become a believer: That "lesser" is simply different.

CHAPTER NINE
A Prize South of Route 2
Malachite Peak
(6,261')

HIDDEN GEMS OF THE WASHINGTON CASCADES

CHAPTER NINE: A PRIZE SOUTH OF ROUTE 2

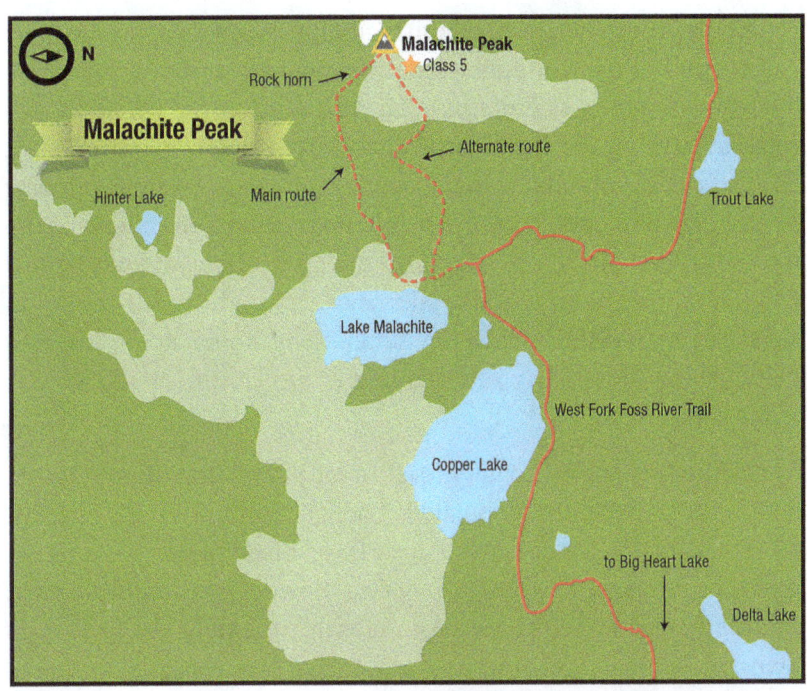

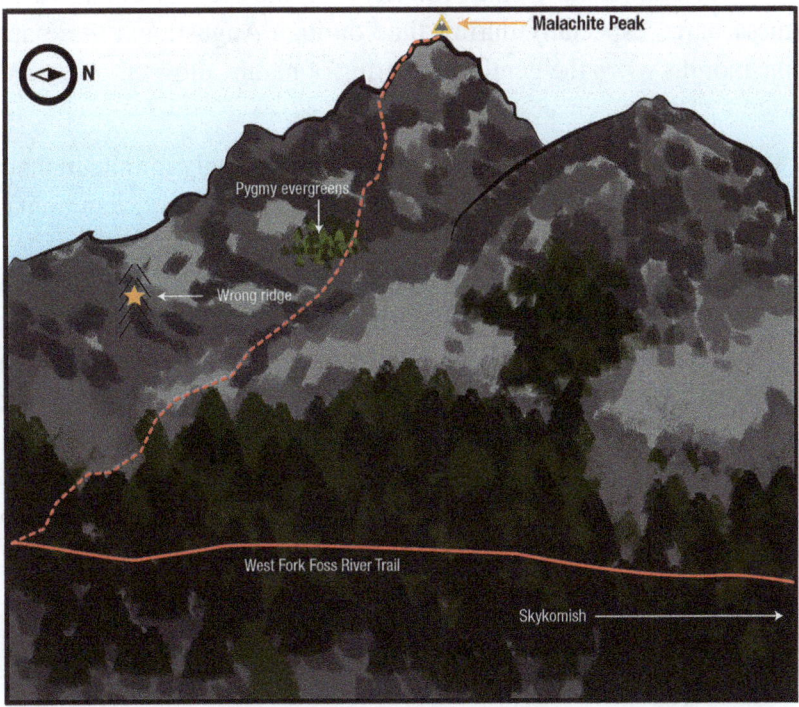

Lake lovers and those who cherish granite spears amidst waterfalls and rugged cliffs will appreciate the approach to Malachite Peak almost as much as gaining its pointed summit. Invisible from any road, even from the heavily travelled Foss River dirt tracks, most climbers and scramblers have never laid eyes on this unfairly neglected spire, but it is to their remiss. From its approach up the West Fork of the Foss River to the apex of its summit, there's enough mountain tarn, pond, lake, meadow and overall beauty to satisfy every North Cascade day scrambler/climber, not to mention the very real possibility of fresh lake trout for dinner should you make camp.

Malachite lies approximately level in latitude to the more famous, and more frequently populated Enchantments and Mt. Stuart. However, its longitude may as well be as distant from them as the moon in terms of its forests, meadow flowers and, unfortunately, its weather patterns. These more closely resemble the Olympics than the sunnier east-side trips described elsewhere in this text. Nonetheless, friendly skies for days on end are not unknown in these parts, especially during June through August, and these are the months when the gentle simmering of nature allows flowers and views to be at their best.

And what views they are: glittering lakes seemingly infinite in their sheer number and variety, with names like Chetwoot, Panorama, Otter, Angeline, Big Heart, Copper, Malachite and Trout. They form a veritable necklace of sun-streaked waters feeding the hungry West Fork of the Foss River. Moreover, they rival the more famous chains of bejeweled lakes best seen from La Bohn Gap to the southwest or the more popular Enchantment Lakes, girdling the high meadows in the midst of Stuart and Colchuck Peaks due east. These lakes dwell within a cluster of rarely climbed summits, such as Bald Eagle, Silver Eagle and Wild Goat Peaks; Iron Cap Mountain; the charmingly-named Camp Robber Peak; Tourmaline Peak; and the tallest of this cluster, Big Snow Mountain (6,680').

Begin this journey by exiting Highway 2 south onto the well-maintained Foss River Road #68, about 2 miles east of the village of

CHAPTER NINE: A PRIZE SOUTH OF ROUTE 2

Skykomish (good burgers and fries at the Inn right off the highway in town). Pass the East Fork Road at 2 miles and continue on to the deteriorating West Fork River Road, then turn right and ride the washing board excuse for an access track 2 miles to its end at about 7 miles from US 2. Most vehicles can accomplish the rough ride without too much bottom thumping.

The trail plunges into second- and third-growth forest but it's a nicely shaded walk nonetheless, especially appreciated on a hot summer's day. You can hear the West Fork continuously plunging over rocky steps in the distance but access to the river itself is limited due to much bushwhacking. No need to worry; there's plenty of potable water from side streams, at least until mid-August and also after passing Trout Lake at 2,000' and 1½ miles (where most fishermen end their journey, perhaps because of its nomenclature as much as the presence of more fish than any other of these lakes). The trail here is wide and easy as it gains altitude at a relaxed angle. In about another 2 miles, watch for a side trail, unmarked, and more of a climber's path than the boulevard you first traveled.

This root-strewn and rocky track gains altitude at a more arduous angle, though the trip to Malachite Lake is a brief ½ mile. Note the many Star Flowers and Bunchberry flowers strewn about the forest floor. These white blossoms have no need to invest energy in producing color, being easily seen and smelled by pollinating insects amidst the darkened surroundings in these woodlands. The bunchberry is also called Canadian dogwood and is a close relative of the dogwood trees seen in low forests and, in cultivated and colorful form, decorating city lawns and thoroughfares. Its petals are actually modified leaves called bracts; the actual flowers are tiny and are located in the center of each bloom.

Bunchberry

You are soon rewarded by the blue-green waters of Lake Malachite at 3½ miles from road-end, and at about the 4,000' level. Well-named after its bejeweled moniker, this polished gem sits in a gorgeous basin girdled by sharply carved cliffs which can function as a canyon-walled echo chamber. Campsites are few but a water and snack break are surely in order.

Beckey's descriptions of the off-trail route from the lake are nebulous at best. Although the country hereabouts is somewhat open, we still managed to find ourselves in the shoes of the philosopher Nasreddin. This Arabian wise man lost his precious wedding ring and was found outside looking for it in his yard. Perplexed, his wife asked why he was looking outside when he surely had lost it indoors that morning, to which Nasreddin replied, "Because the light's better out here."

After some fumbling around on a ridge we thought would reach the summit we realized that we had strayed too far to the south Descending (I hate that), we next curved west around the north shore of the lake, then ascended a lightly timbered slope due west. At around 5,000', avoid going too far south into a meadow and timbered gully. Instead stick to the northeast slopes at an ever-steepening angle and aim for a clutch of stunted mountain hemlocks (Beckey uses colorful language in describing these as "pygmy evergreens"). From here, the last of the thin forest, climb grassy meadow, which eventually gives way at about 5,900' to blocky but relatively stable talus.

Mountain Hemlock

Now, you could aim directly for the rocky summit but cliffs intervene. Instead, bear slightly left (west) to a saddle just south of the bouldery summit. Gingerly, head north around a rock horn, rated as class 3; however, with exposure, it might be useful to

CHAPTER NINE: A PRIZE SOUTH OF ROUTE 2

protect this pitch, even though it is the sole step requiring anything but hands and feet, heart and lungs. From this point, you are on a ridge southwest of the true summit. Follow this ridge north, level at times, yet with a few step-up boulders forming a stable scaffolding by which to surmount the upper part of the ridge's top. Near the summit, a few class-3 moves over huge boulders brings one to the top. An alternative route heads due north from the lake to the northeast ridge but ends up requiring protection on cliff bands just southeast of the summit.

From Malachite's apex, views are widespread and unfamiliar to even the most well-travelled North Cascade voyager. Who amongst us could identify peaks hidden from viewpoints more popular both east and west? Use one of those picture maps sold in ranger stations and small grocery stores or a 7.5" or 15" series of topo's to try to identify peaks rarely seen and, especially to the south, little-visited: mountains with names such as Iron Cap Mountain, Davis Peak, Terrace Mountain, La Bohn Peak and the well-named Dip Top Peak. Big Snow glistens white to the south with its icy mantle. Further to the south lie the Snoqualmie Pass peaks, often crowded with hikers, backpackers, and PCT endurance athletes.

This mini-range comprises the southern-most of the more angular summits north of Mt. Rainier. Yes, Rainier can be seen, hiding its bulk in the southern distance, but turn to the east to view the snow-clad massifs of Mts. Daniel and Hinman and, to their south, Bear's Breast, Little Big Chief, Summit Chief, and the crowning tower of this compact range, Chimney Rock. This blocky tower with near vertical faces on all sides carries a distinction, along with Nooksack Tower on the ridge leading east from Mt. Shuksan; Forbidden Peak; and Mt. Slesse, just beyond the Canadian border: Each has no easy non-technical route to its top. To the north lie the snow-domed giants of the North Cascades beckoning all to test their slopes, but, from this vantage point, each is difficult to identify except Glacier Peak in the northeastern distance.

While the views of summits near and far from this lookout are plentiful and most unusual, the prospect below from whence you came equals or surpasses that from the top itself. From this vantage point you can truly appreciate the gem-like chain of lakes forming the headwaters of the West Fork of Foss River. Blue-green Tourmaline, Copper and Malachite Lakes lie far below while deep blue Little Heart, Angeline, Delta and tiny Trout Lakes provide complementary hues. It would be a shame, barring urgent tasks, not to tarry and establish a base camp at one of these lakes or the numerous unnamed tarns along the main West Fork Trail. Try to time your visit to early or late in the climbing season to avoid our tiny friends, the black flies and mosquitoes. Good sites off the vegetation can be found, especially at Trout and Copper Lakes. Why rush back to civilization when you could take a cool night's rest at one of these gems?

For those who never met a mountain they didn't want to climb, open country leads to some of the "lost" peaks to Malachite's south. Of interest are the relatively untouched summits of **Wild Goat Peak (6,305'), Bald Eagle Peak (6,259')**, and **Silver Eagle Peak (6,241')**. All can be reached from campsites at Big Heart Lake (the most scenic) and Chetwoot Lake (limited but passable), and all are scrambles absent any need for technical equipment. Unfortunately, the intriguingly named **Dip Top Peak (7,291')**, with a curious saddle between its two horn-like summits, must be reached from points further east proximate to the approaches to the Mt. Daniel region.

So be the first on your block, village or even city, to summit Malachite or its neighbors, and you will not only gain plaudits for your exploits but most certainly will be asked what and where Malachite Peak is. No need to keep the secret; others will only rarely follow. And bring along some friends; a sense of shared destiny can only enlighten this lake-laden and rarely-visited mountain expanse.

CHAPTER TEN

Mines, Mountains and Alpenglow

The Monte Cristo Range
(~5,480'–7,172')

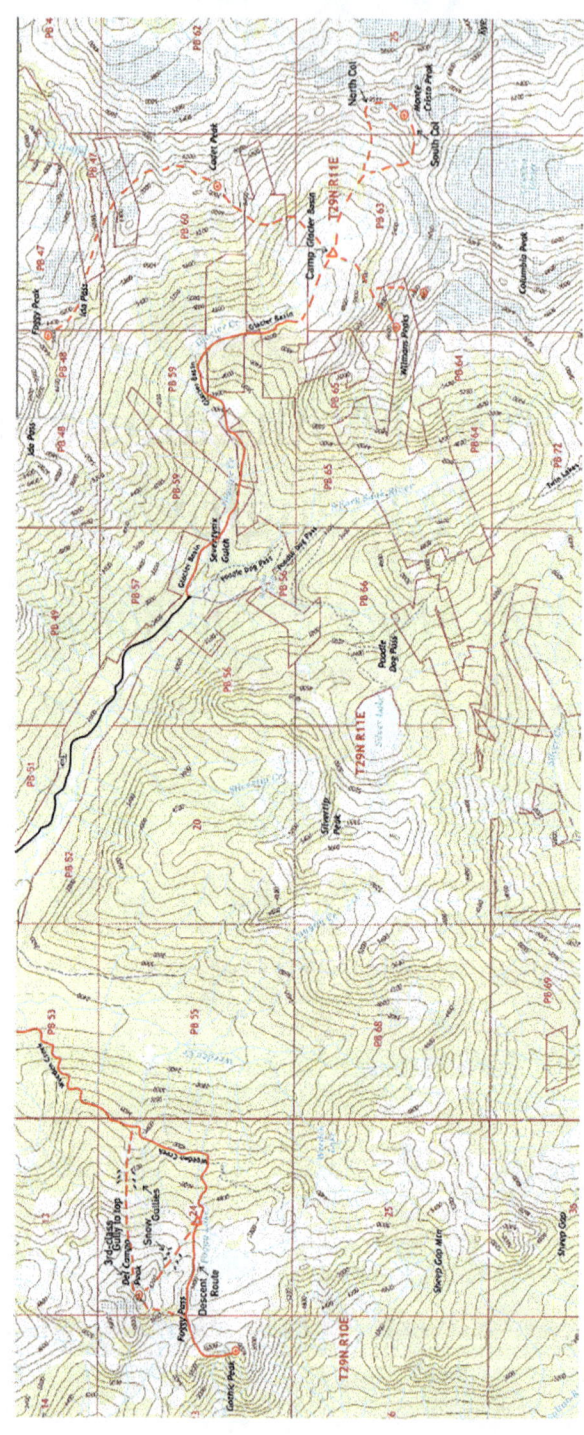

CHAPTER TEN: MINES, MOUNTAINS AND ALPENGLOW

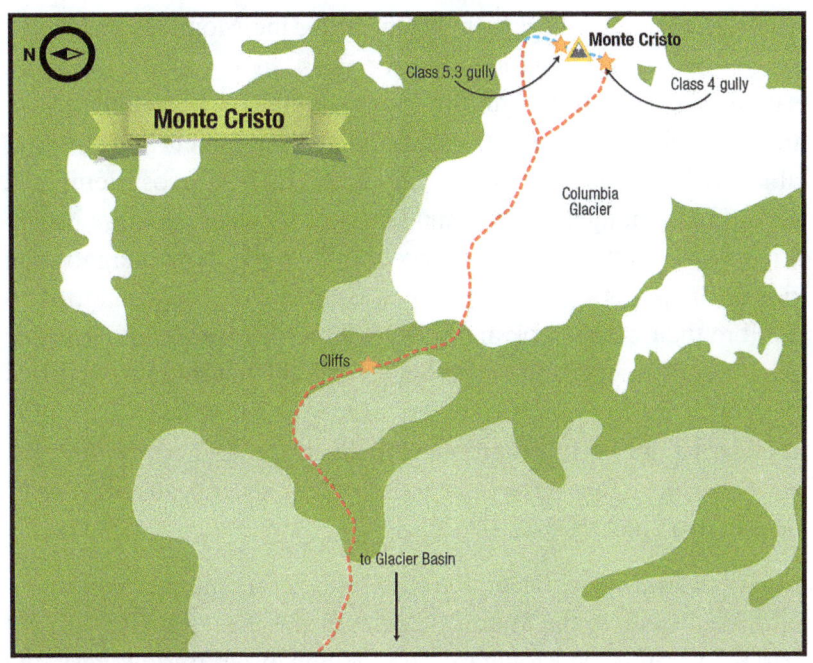

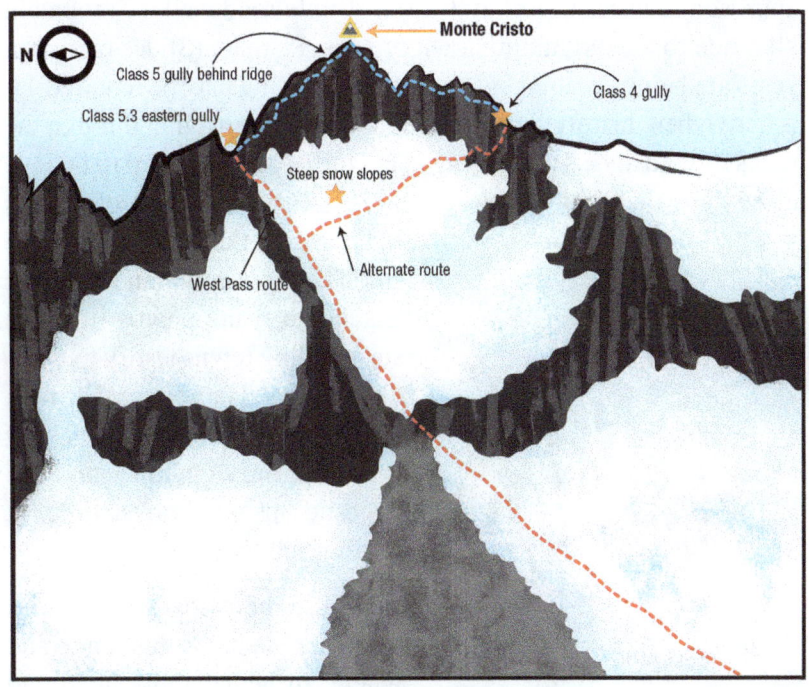

Although compact in length and breadth, the Monte Cristo's, just southwest of Washington's Glacier Peak area, contain sufficient saw-toothed peaks and jutting towers, glaciers, waterfalls, lakes, trails and climbing routes to satisfy hikers, scramblers and climbers alike. It is reminiscent of the Olympics in both ecosystems and elevation, although this is a land bounded by no seas. These Monte Cristo's lose nothing to their more northern and larger neighboring ranges in terms of rugged beauty and endless opportunities to explore their every nook and void. A three-day weekend is best for the time-challenged; an entire season could be spent exploring this delightful range, which rivals in beauty the better-known alpine regions to the north. There are too many peaks here to describe each one, but a few stand out either for their sheer beauty or ease of access (read lack of brush).

One of the most popular approaches, whether for hiking, camping or climbing, leads to the famous Glacier Basin. Leaving Highway 92 (from Everett – the Mountain Loop Highway) at Barlow Pass, the approach requires a slightly tedious 4-mile road walk or mountain bike ride to the old mining town of Monte Cristo. (Slides in distant years are being repaired but some bike-carrying may be required.) It is here where history buffs will luxuriate in rummaging through the relics of gold and silver mining in centuries past. It's hard to believe these days that this was once the site where thousands of miners lived and worked and where once stood hotels, saloons and brothels. Black and white photos from the surrounding towns testify to those distant days. The contrast between the rusted relics surrounding this once-thriving town and the majestic peaks surrounding it could not be sharper.

It is also here that views open up to the giants of this range and where an actual trail, steep and

Alpine Aster

rough, leads in another 2½ miles to a heaven of rushing creeks, waterfalls, a carpet of alpine flowers, and glacier views furring the colored meadows. I think of these networks of brooks, streams and waterfalls as the veins of the mountains. Above, towering spires of breccias, diorite and, surprisingly, sandstone, require neck-bending to take it all in. Just to the south lie the Wilman's Spires, rising as steeply as church steeples, while the view to the east is of Monte Cristo Peak itself. Scrambles here include a day-trip up **Cadet Peak (7,186')**, to the north of the basin. To gain its worthwhile summit, push north through sand and the most unusual of Cascades rarities - light brush - to a climber's path through pleasant heather, then to a 3rd-class scramble to the top and far-reaching views.

Back in the basin, take a few days and nights to enjoy the surroundings, with plentiful wanderings here to discover unknown alpine flowers and surprisingly sparkling creeks. Plentiful red and white heathers abound, along with blue lupine; both red and white Indian paintbrushes (the same species – only the color is different); towering purple Cascade asters; and pink alpine asters and daisies. Spend enough time to appreciate this rugged yet peaceful beauty and contemplate, if your skills allow, the many ascents for another day, either technical or scrambling, all of which emanate from this glorious bowl of a basin.

Cascade Aster

Perhaps best of all, in the evening under hopeful skies streaked with salmon, watch the reddish light creep up as alpenglow slowly ascends the snow-clad west face of Monte Cristo Peak itself. At night, far from any urban glow, trace the Milky Way, magical and moonstruck, to contemplate how insignificant we are in the broad scope of the universe: reflections which offer perhaps the best cure for human arrogance.

Cadet is topographically the eastern culmination of the **Pride of the Mountains Range (6.600'–6,880')**. Hubris may be appropriate here, as this well-named chain throws up impressive rocky crags as often as politicians promise prizes they can never deliver. First come **The Cadets (6,800'–7,040')**, some of which apparently, according to sources from Beckey to The Mountaineers and the extensive archives of Portland's Mazamas, have never been climbed. Viewed from a distance, they would appear to require the roughshod rigmarole of technical bushwhacking skills and endurance. It also appears they would need at least 4th-class skills but loose rock (is there any other kind hereabouts?) await the unprepared. It is probably safe to say that more people have walked on the surface of the moon than have attained many of these rock-ribbed stony summits, some of which even bear names.

Foggy Peak (6,810') follows along this Pride of the Mountains Range but brush and cliffs from Glacier Basin make the ascent an adventure. After a gap, through which flows Elliott Creek, a second unjustly ignored sub-range, **Addison Ridge (6,480'–6,799')**, continues northeast. Its highest summit is the southern-most point of the **Gemini Peaks (6,799')**. The approach (when one is attempted – it is rarely tested) originates from just east of the old town of Monte Cristo, and soon encounters slide alder and vine maple, apparently inseparable twins thwarting many an attempt. Other intractable greenery, along with cliffs and all whatnot, is needed to reach the crest. Here, 4th-class scrambling brings one to a summit so infrequently visited that its summit register (an old tin can with a single piece of paper within) recorded the names of just three parties, the last dated 2019.

Slide Alder

For those open to more challenging climbing but less bushwhacking adventures, **Wilman's Spires (~6,100')**, east of the basin,

CHAPTER TEN: MINES, MOUNTAINS AND ALPENGLOW

offer towers, spires and horns so precariously perched, they seem ready to tumble with the slightest breeze. For those who cannot abide a pinnacle or tower without wanting to scale it, these offer low-to mid-5th-class climbing out of Glacier Basin on relatively solid holds. There is even a rock pinnacle called **"The Count of Monte Cristo" (4,800')**, on the southwest ridge of **East Wilman's Spire, (6,120')**. **East Wilman's Peak, (6,880')** is the tallest of this mini-range of maxi-sharpness. It lies at the northwest end of the massif and remained unclimbed until 1970.

Vine Maple

The approaches to East Wilman's Peak are not from the basin, but from the south, up the '76 Creek Trail to a gully and stream which lead to scree and boulders but no technical difficulties in climbing to the summit. Grand views abound, especially of the Monte Cristo Group from a different perspective, along with the tottering towers of the Wilman's Group, the entire extent of Addison Ridge and the Cadets. Looking down, one can sense the beauty of Glacier Basin, a serene interlude amongst the stormy symphony of these rugged ranges.

Perhaps a grander project from the basin is to ascend **Monte Cristo Peak (7,136')** itself. Head east through heather, then talus, to reach permanent snow on the west face, then ascend at a 30–40-degree angle (crampons helpful here) to a notch in the ridge north of the summit. Cross to the east side to a high offshoot of the Pride Glacier and head south for the summit.

Unfortunately, the description in Beckey is about as clear as a Federal Reserve report and as informative as a post-game NFL interview. This partly results, however, from glacier shrinkage. Now (summer of 2021) there is a 20' moat protecting a final 40-foot tall blank headwall after crossing the shrund below the summit. But most every wall can be breached. Find a low 5th-class gully just to your right; I grappled up a crack system, creating a caricature of a rock climber. Up to this point, I believed I had an embarrassment of riches, but here, I encountered simply embarrassment. To be honest, my feeble attempt failed, leaving me to congratulate those in the party above who had summitted. My more nimble companions flowed up this pitch, which led to easier 3rd-class scrambling to the peak's uppermost boulders.

In retrospect, however, I came to realize that it's the struggle itself that may matter as much as the success. You are accomplishing something even more valuable than those who climb these pitches with apparent ease: They climb every pitch with grace but in your struggle, you have already succeeded by trying your best. You have to practice the easy things, not...well, you know. You have reached and even exceeded your limits and there is no place to go now but upwards, as it is the effort that is as valuable as an eventual triumph.

I finally reached Monte Cristo's apex via a variation from the basin (the West Face Route), which climbs steep snow southeast to a loose pass to the south of the peak, then ambles up a knife-edge ridge (we mounted it *au cheval*) to a reddish gully. My leader scowled at my sniveling, refusing protection on the exposed ridge. Others in the party deftly scaled the crest while I played the role of the man who murdered his parents, then asked the judge for leniency as I was thus an orphan. No pity for the clumsy. In the event, the climbing turned from easy 5th- class to 3rd rapidly. The ridge angles right to a slanting ledge until it reaches a 4th-class crack which leads to easier bouldering at the apex.

A second well-traveled route approaches a different sub-range within the Monte Cristo's. It also leaves from Barlow Pass but exits right (south) from the road after about one mile onto the rather abrupt 3-mile Weden Creek Trail. This track gains 3,000' but passes many eye-filling waterfalls and leads one into Gothic Basin, another idyllic spot, this graced by a lake (Foggy Lake on the topo but also called Crater Lake, about 5,200') amidst the flowers, boulders

CHAPTER TEN: MINES, MOUNTAINS AND ALPENGLOW

and marmots. From this spot, an easy scramble takes you to non-technical **Del Campo Peak (6,610')** by ascending due northeast, then circling to its north side to climb a wide 3rd-class gully on shockingly stable rock.

One could also reach Del Campo's summit early in the summer by leaving the trail at about 4,000', or about ½ mile later at 4,700' and take a more direct line to Del Campo's summit by climbing 25-30-degree snow slopes to just southeast of the summit block, then circling to its north side to ascend the gully mentioned above. Should time allow, scramble across Del Campo's south ridge down to Foggy Pass (about 5,700'), then to **Gothic Peak (6,213')**, jutting above the lake. A hardy subalpine fir may block a direct line but escape to the west or traverse the stout tree's limbs to achieve the blocky top. Both peaks feature views exceeding the climbing effort required.

A third, and favorite, scrambling route departs Highway 92 17.7 miles past the Verlot Visitors Center to the Sunrise Mine Road, #4065. Drive 2.3 miles to road end, then ascend The Sunrise Mine Trail; it first crosses the South Fork of the Stillaguamish River (take care - it is often swift and wide until mid-July), then rises steeply 2½ miles to Headlee Pass. Snow often lingers in the northwest-facing basin of this trail until August. The last 500' are composed of insane switchbacks etched into the shale. A climber's path then leads across scree to tiny Vesper Lake. From here, a scramble over car-size boulders advances one to the top of **Vesper Peak (6,214')**. This easy ascent belies Vesper's sheer north face, replete with mid- to high 5th-class routes. From this summit, one can scramble the ridge east to **Sperry Peak (6,120')**, high above the diminutive lake in the basin below. Sperry also has precipitous north and east faces featuring extreme rock climbing.

The Monte Cristo's hold so many other peaks in such a dense area that there is no space to headline them all. Stellar projects include ascents of **Columbia Peak (7,172')**; **Kyes Peak (7,280')**, the tallest of this tightly-packed range; or sharp-topped **Silvertip Peak (6,140')**. Any of these can be reached by the average mountaineer within a long weekend. A more accurate guide to this range than Beckey is the ancient but still accurate *Monte Cristo Area: A Complete Outdoor Guide*, published in 1977 by Northwest Press (currently out of print but still available in outdoor bookshops in Seattle and Portland but sadly not online).

If this is unavailable, Beckey's *Cascade Alpine Guide 2* (green cover) will suffice along with the latest edition of the *100 Hikes Guide to Washington's Glacier Peak Region* by Ira Spring and Harvey Manning. The 7½" series of topo maps, rather than the Green Trails versions, also offer much support. In many of the adventures noted above, GPS assistance will provide reassurance inasmuch as this rugged range lies far west of the crest and thus subject to frequent overcast skies, winds and precipitation. These can be hostile slopes subject to the unbending commands of wicked weather. Just as an incoming tide washes away the creations of sandcastle architects, an incoming storm can wipe out the mountain plans of even the most daunting of high-country explorers.

N.B.: This entire area features deeply-cleft basins which hold snow later in summer than in many other regions. Call the Verlot Ranger Station (if open) at 360-691-7791 or the Darrington Station at 360-436-1155 or 360-452-4501 to check.

Regardless, the Monte Cristo's are a relatively easy drive away and beauty almost always trumps distance. Combine painless access with spectacular mountain scenery and you have a perfect getaway. There is thus no excuse for the city-bound mountaineer to not pay a visit to these rugged ranges, so close in distance, yet so distinct in the majesty of their slopes, streams and meadows.

CHAPTER ELEVEN

The Matterhorn of the Cascades

Sloan Peak
(7,835')

HIDDEN GEMS OF THE WASHINGTON CASCADES

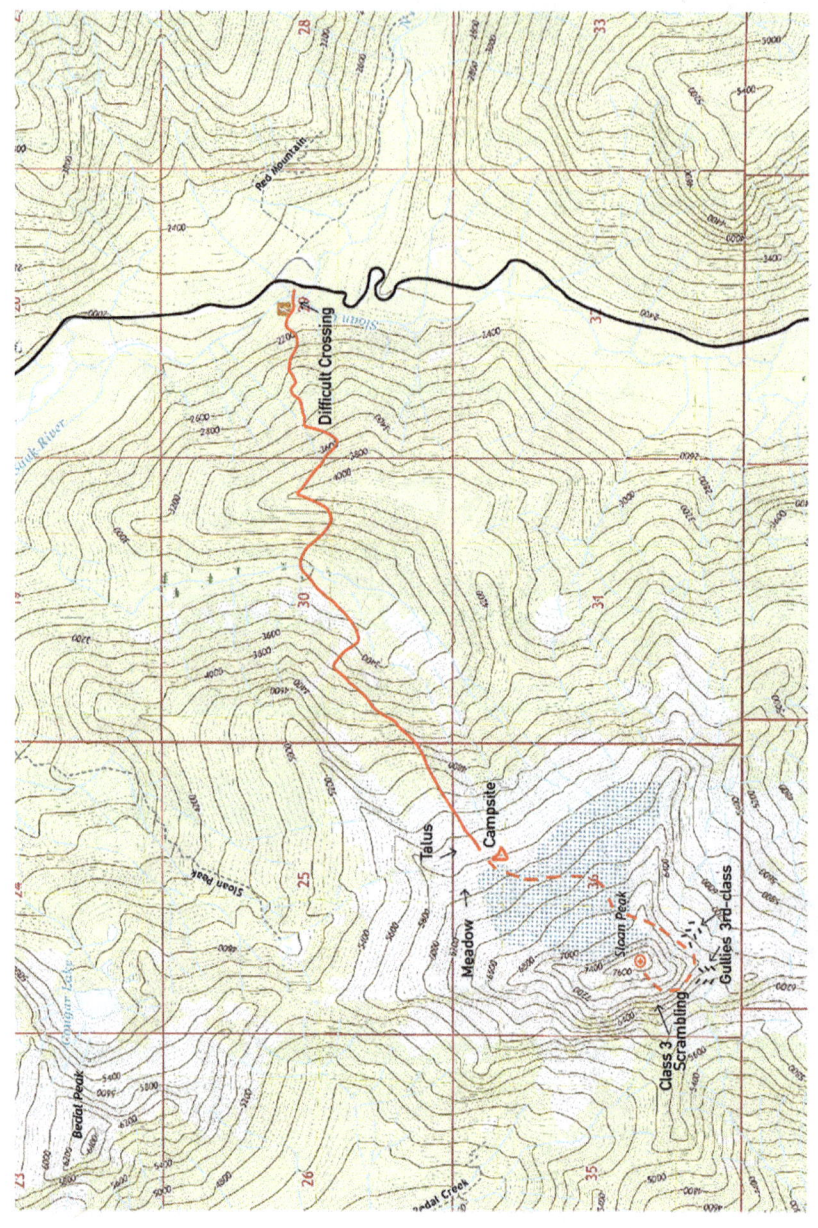

CHAPTER ELEVEN: THE MATTERHORN OF THE CASCADES

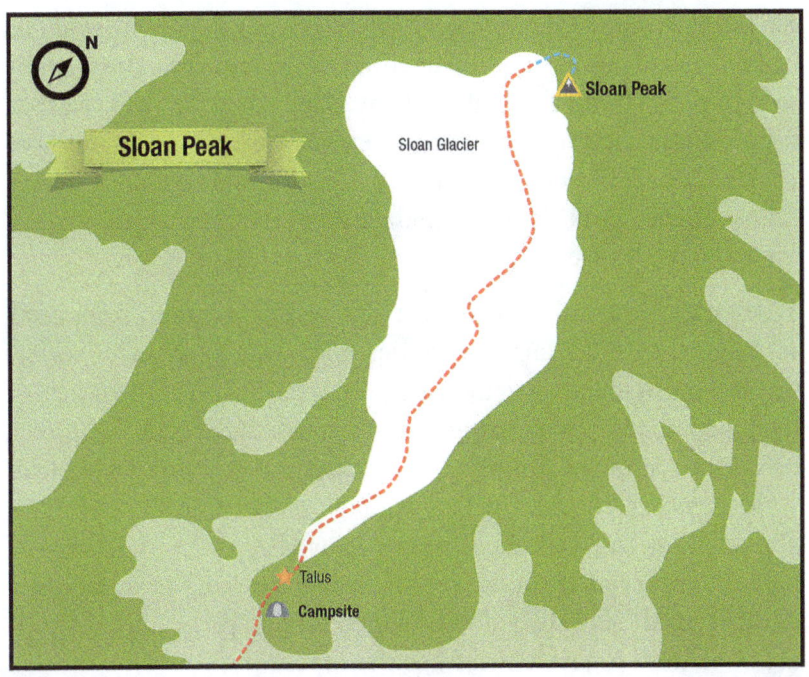

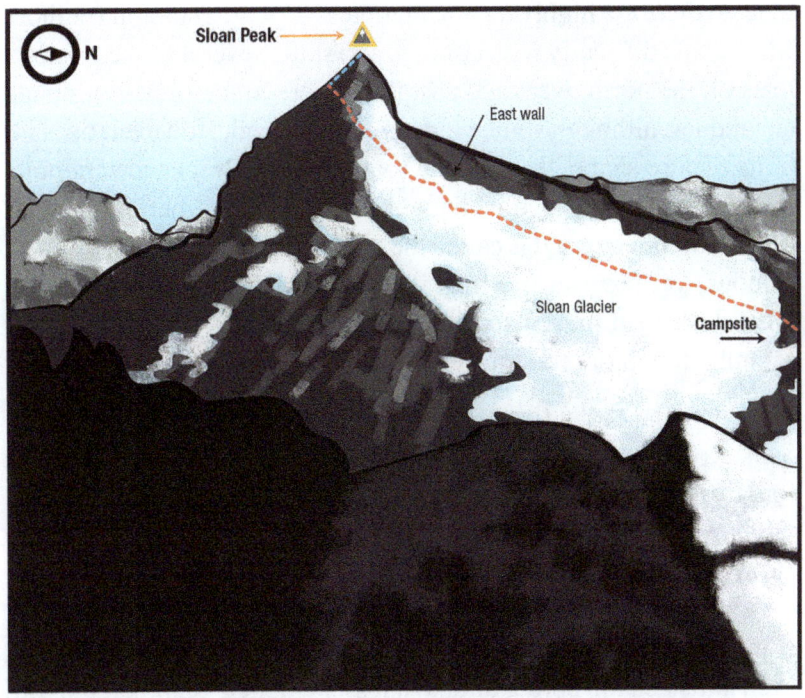

Sentinel of the southwestern Cascades, Sloan stands in splendid isolation and bears the distinction of being the most easily recognized summit from almost any other Cascade peak west of the crest (and from several eastern ones as well). This "Matterhorn of the Cascades" does indeed bear a distinct resemblance to that famous Swiss peak, its north and eastern faces as sharply vertical as any in the Range.

When mountaineers achieve most any western summit, from north of Rainier to the Canadian border, they can most easily orient themselves in identifying the vast sea of peaks around them by first facing south and recognizing the distinctive sheer walls of Sloan, its curious almost lopsided shape defining the western border of what climbers consider the beginnings of the true Cascades. Its abrupt north and east faces, when viewed from most roadways, make it appear as if Sloan would require the skills of a nerveless climber, an artist of the void, for whom soaring perpendicular walls are invitations to tackle these hostile slopes.

Indeed, there are highly technical routes to Sloan's summit for those who equate difficulty with courage and skill. Several of these knotty lines on the north, west and east faces were first climbed using aid techniques, although some have now been freed. However, because of its bizarre shape, there is one route even the weekend scrambler can accomplish, though its name betrays the asymmetric nature of Sloan's architecture: It is called the "Corkscrew Route", convoluted, sinuous, yet precise. It winds its way around the various vertical obstacles Sloan presents yet somehow manages to land the adroit scrambler, without too much fuss, onto its coveted summit.

First, take the Sloan Creek Road to its end at the North Fork of the Sauk River, where the sole potential difficulty emerges. One must ford this turgid stream, here really more a river than a creek. Indeed, the North Fork here exceeds the Main Fork in width, especially at prime run-off season, which appears to coincide with climbing season all too frequently. Many parties schedule fall for their attempts as the North Fork is more easily forded then. However, even at its peak in spring and, to a lesser extent in summer, the ford

CHAPTER ELEVEN: THE MATTERHORN OF THE CASCADES

can be managed by locating the widest part of the torrent, loosening backpack straps, and using trekking poles.

Not a few climbers bring an old pair of sneakers or, if you don't mind the icy current, flip-flops. These can be stashed at the other side of the crossing but hide them well; vandals hereabouts are not unknown. You might also try to locate a supposed log crossing 50 yards upstream but, as can happen when trying to follow the advice of Fred Beckey's Cascade Alpine Guide, Number 2 – the green one (which is usually dead-on for technical routes), here the author is intensely verbal yet profoundly unclear about how and where to regain what is an obvious trail just across the river.

Once safely across, this sometimes-steep path winds its way through first- and second-growth forest, up to a world-class campsite in an almost-level heathered meadow, with unparalleled views across the Sauk River valley to the colossal massif of Glacier Peak, so close it seems you can almost taste its snows. Campsites abound but try not to trample the fragile greenery and subtle beauty of this parkland, carpeted with blankets of alpine meadow flowers. Use instead the sandy sites already barren. It may appear that heather is indestructible but a few nights of sleeping on top of this seemingly hardy shrub can assassinate it forever.

Cusick's Speedwell

Floral alpine jewels abound here, including the rare 2-ft. tall yellow soft arnica; tall crimson Indian paintbrush; tiny white spikes of the ubiquitous partridgefoot; and the small delicate Cusick's speedwell, as deeply purple as any royal's robe. Although the views outward are prodigious from here, look up as well to the severely angled eastern wall; its perpendicular angle would even make coffee nervous, although several mid-5th class routes have succeeded here. Like me, be thankful you are not attempting that precipice the next day. Nightfall may put a brake on this gorgeous excess, but watch, as evening advances, the pink of alpenglow stealing up the western flanks of Glacier Peak, as fine a show as any special effects a Hollywood studio might produce.

Hoping for a welcoming sky the next day, climbers first proceed from the heather up and over a crumbly ridge, then descend to embrace the mildly-angled Sloan Glacier (rope up, please and take crampons after early summer). Climb it heading south to its uppermost point just under the forbidding wall of the east face. For those of us who resist these highly angled walls and are content to simply bag one more summit and covet its views, a boot track now exists from this uppermost southern reach of the glacier to a 3rd class gully, luckily with solid holds so rare in these ranges. Proceed first across a heather shelf at its top, then ascend boulders to a second easy gully, solid as the first, and you will end up at the western ridge, where a scramble leads to the topmost stones. You have essentially wound yourself around the summit, from north to south via the eastern Sloan Glacier, thus squaring the circle: hence the "Corkscrew" moniker.

Because light travels in a straight line, the obverse of the fact that Sloan can be seen from so many of the Cascade peaks means its magisterial views encompass all those summits from which it can itself be seen. The most striking view is to the east, directly across the Sauk drainage to the colossus of Glacier Peak. To the south, Whitehorse and Whitechuck can be spotted along with many of the tightly-clustered Monte Cristo's. You can argue which is which as you peer northeast to the Dome group; then north to the improbably-angled Buckindy Crags and gentle Snowking to their north, followed by Colonial and Snowfield; and on to those utmost of our northern giants, Baker and Shuksan, gleaming white in the hazy distance.

The confidence of more serious climbers can be tested on several routes up Sloan's western face (class 5.4), as well as the northwest buttress (class 5.8), part of which forms the distinctive "Matterhorn" appearance. The north ridge (low class 5) can be gained from the saddle between Sloan and its northern sibling, **Bedal Peak (6,554')**.

CHAPTER ELEVEN: THE MATTERHORN OF THE CASCADES

In fact, Bedal is a fine objective in itself. To gain its top, first traverse north at around 4,000' from the Sloan Peak Trail through timber, then meadow, to reach the northeast ridge, where scrambling blocky boulders brings one to a summit lost in the shadow of its more famous neighbor to the south, but sharing with it the same far-reaching views.

Sloan's north ridge is classified by Beckey as easy class 5 (an oxymoron in my opinion), but, from most reports, one should anticipate low- to mid-5th-class roped climbing on the loose ridge itself. The southeast face has been noted to have mid-5th-class routes with shockingly solid holds, but the true test-piece for the hardened climber is the east face direct. Although it begins from the same glacier as the "Corkscrew Route", it then veers off into a series of wicked and awkward blocks which lead to overhanging gullies marked by the omnipresence of chock-stones. This route was accomplished first in 1967 and rated as Grade IV, class 5.8 and A4. The first successful party required aid, but this tortuous route subsequently has gone free, though the exact line taken may have differed a bit from the first ascent.

However you gain Sloan's pointy summit, whether by normal means or the extraordinarily steep technical climbs of its famous walls, be prepared for views which will be seared into your memory in the best of ways. No finer nor more unusual viewpoint can be gained so easily in all our mountains south of Darrington.

CHAPTER TWELVE
A Gem Neglected
Mount Chaval
(7,127')

HIDDEN GEMS OF THE WASHINGTON CASCADES

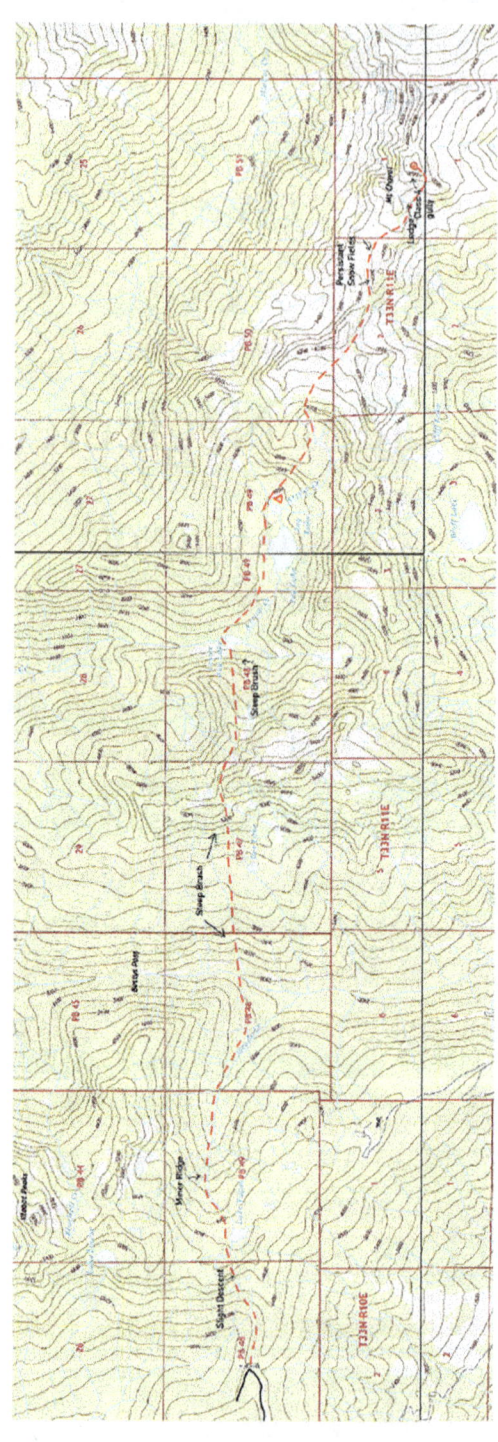

CHAPTER TWELVE: A GEM NEGLECTED

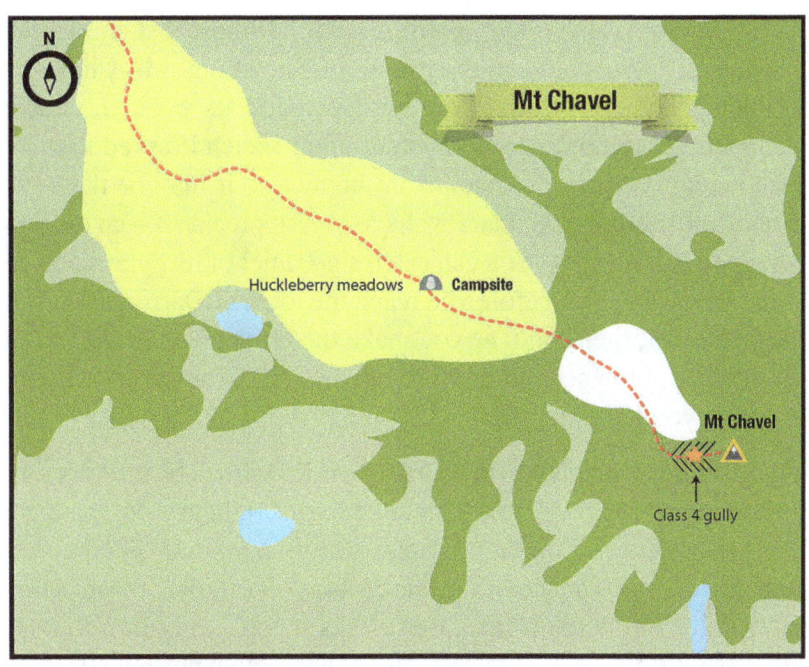

What on earth, and where, is Mt. Chaval? Almost lost amidst the clusters of snow-clad summits south of Snowking, Mt. Chaval is oft-neglected yet rich in eye-filling splendor. Its pointed, almost symmetrical summit is what a child might sketch if asked to draw a mountain. Mostly obscured from highways, it may be the most beautifully abrupt peak that few have ever appreciated – an enigma wrapped in a mystery. You can catch a glimmer of its pyramid from State Route 530 just before you reach the town of Darrington off to the northeast, then again as you make the 90-degree turn left from the middle of town, continuing on Highway 530 for the first several miles as you travel north.

Approaching Darrington, of course one is first struck by the towering north face of Whitehorse Mountain on your right as you approach the town. With its rocky pinnacles (the true summit lies beyond and is less spectacular), and cascading waterfalls off perpetual snowfields on its north face, most folks would justly turn to their right (south) to gawk at this seeming behemoth's north wall. In so doing, they would miss the pyramid of Chaval to the northeast.

However, should you ignore the lesser-known peaks such as Chaval, you are at risk of foregoing the pleasure of treading relatively untrammeled land and conquering far-flung views from unique perspectives. When we reached its summit in 2012, there were but three other names in the ragged summit register. (None was Beckey.) I dare say that fewer climbers have achieved this summit than have walked in outer space. Yet its rugged character and its stunning summit profile beg for many more visitors. The climb itself, while precipitous at points, is really just a class 3-4-pitch up a gully after traversing mildly angled snow slopes, but the approach, well, that may be the tough part, as is so true among many of our Northwest's peaks.

Chaval is the predominant peak in the equally-unknown area of the inscrutable Illabot Range, favored in the past more by loggers than climbers. Fortunately, this area is now protected but the logging roads remain, although they rarely lead one easily into the rugged landscapes we mountaineers cherish. We took Highway 530 past

CHAPTER TWELVE: A GEM NEGLECTED

Darrington, then drove the Illabot Road 16, just off the Highway, then Road 1610 northeast to a point where it turns due north.

From here, Beckey's approach descriptions are more of a bromide than a benefit. He recommends a more northerly route off the Tenas Creek Road, then a bushwhack to Boulder Lake, but from our usually cursory glance at the topo's, we believed this pathway would entail even more altitude loss, steeper climbing, and more mileage through the brush than the more direct route described below. Web posts do, rarely, mention Chaval, their directions more often baffling than clarifying. Ever anxious to avoid as many obstacles as possible, yet unencumbered by an excess of advanced planning, we opted for the more southerly route. As it turns out much of the time, lacking foresight was always one of our attributes.

Climbing can begin with a notion, followed by study and preparation, but it often can end with a measure of both audacity and chaos. Chaval proved the latter; dread crept in as we approached this unknown emptiness of green and brown. At first glance at this distant peak from the logging road, I felt we were lost even before we began, as sure to summit it as it would be to separate us from our shadows. Undeterred by lack of forethought and knowledge, we plowed through the usual west-side brush. Possessing the navigational skills of a houseplant, I meekly followed. I kept thinking that climbing was supposed to be a non-contact sport.

Devil's Club

We considered Eddie, our leading brush-beater, bulky and with a boxer's broad nose, sort of the Tonya Harding of climbers: graceful in spots yet ruthless in others. Yet even his pace slowed to that of a snail; I felt like a beaver in a trap snapped shut by impenetrable vegetation: Salmonberry, white rhododendron, and Devil's club almost prevented progress. It proved impossible to tame the brush, so we suffered this green scaffolding, hoping energy bars could fuel our slug-like progress; unfortunately, at most they only allowed a tortoise-like uphill slog.

Nonetheless, several younger compatriots began advancing well beyond my feeble pace; although I knew their packs were weightier than mine, they seemed to me to be carrying nothing but air. Thrashing through brush is not glamorous – but it is vital. After what seemed like days (it was only 5 hours on the clock), we then emerged onto an ill-defined ridge above Lake Tupso and remained high on that ridge paralleling Grade Creek in the distance to our south. The way was not only thick with brush but, at times, steep as well. I tried to internalize a meditative assertion of the Dalai Lama that pain exists by which to measure pleasure; it wasn't working.

Persistence, however, often trumps ability. Eddie, built like a block of concrete, chuckled in bemused patience at my sluggish pace. At times abrasive, Eddie was less bluff and bluster, more hearty, cheerful yet plain-spoken; his greatest asset, and the one we treasured most, was his utmost persistence and optimism, grating at times but mostly propitious. Turning northeast a bit to avoid steep cliffs, well-hidden at first by the thick brush, we descended a bit to pass Lower (3,453'), then Upper Jug Lake, at about 3,950'. Noises in the forest below us gave us pause; was it a mountain lion or a bear?

Not so lucky – it was simply the most dangerous animal in the wilderness, *homo sapiens*, a straggling member of our own bedraggled party. (Embarrassing but true: the women in our group were more in front than many of our "stronger" males.) Finally, we followed Jug Creek for about a mile before heading uphill to just northeast of the Upper Lake. Blessedly, just above the lake to the northeast, we encountered heather and meadow nirvana. Suddenly, the cacophony of the undergrowth was drowned out by the melodies of wildflowers, open skies and far-reaching alpine views.

Our blissful evenings at a campsite around 4,500' were graced with the densest concentration of subalpine huckleberry (*Vaccinium deliciosum* – honestly, that's its Latin scientific name) south of Mt. Baker. By the time we were finished picking, scarfing, and collecting

CHAPTER TWELVE: A GEM NEGLECTED

these low-lying juicy specimens, our hands, lips and tongues were as blue as the summer sky east of Lake Chelan, and this stain didn't wear off for a number of days. We must have been a sight in the Darrington Café after we arrived back at our vehicles. By the way, no matter what your mom, friends and partners tell you, there is no scientific distinction between huckleberries and blueberries. They are all in the genus *Vaccinium*, and all are members of the Heath Family, as are all azaleas and rhododendrons.

Subalpine Huckleberry

But we had endured the brush in order to climb Chaval so the following morning, after blueberries with a smidge of oatmeal, we began our trek directly eastward toward the peak. Although Chaval has three summits, no one could mistake its crowning pyramid, the western-most of its craggy peaks. Rarely attempted, its middle summit (about 6,950') is but a pile of rocks but it does have a sharply-defined southeast wall; to my knowledge (admittedly limited), this has never been attempted. An east peak (about 7,050') rises at an acute angle on its northwestern aspect and resembles, from some perspectives, a mini-Chaval. There are no written accounts of its ascent, although it does not look like any technical marvels would be required to gain its summit.

We bypassed a fearsome looking cliff just to the east of Upper Jug Lake on its more gentle south flank. We next headed first south then southeast, avoiding cliffs to our west, then encountering a snowfield traversing Chaval's northwest face at a moderate angle (ice ax probably best here but crampons, even in late summer, not usually obligatory). This led to a reasonably stable ledge bearing from left (north) to right (south) but deviated from Beckey's description. (Has he really ever climbed this? His name was absent from the summit register, an unusual absence amongst these Cascade peaks.)

We found a 4th-class gully bisecting the west face, which set our masterful leader's hands on fire as he rapidly flowed with deft maneuvers to the top, cordless. Although being the least agile of the group, I appreciated a rope. On the descent, while more talented climbers scrambled down, I proved an encumbrance for which a rappel provided the only cure. Extraordinary views abounded from this vertical perch: Glacier Peak's northwest face dominates to the south, but the Buckindy Crags (see next chapter), also unfairly neglected, rise to the east in frightening array, an assemblage of crumbly turrets, spires, obelisks, and leaning towers at improbable vertical angles that few explorers have ever seen, much less attempted. Their reddish tinge makes their appearance all the more other-worldly and their overall visage can only be described as whatever the opposite of delicacy is.

To the north, the mass of Snowking and its eastern outpost, Mutchler Peak, dominate, with even their southern slopes robed in snowy mantles throughout the summer. Beyond, the experienced North Cascader can discern Eldorado, fronted by the varied pinnacles of TeeBone Ridge, and the Cascade Pass Peaks jutting above Mutchler. To their west lie Snowfield, Colonial, and a barely visible Pinnacle Peak, beckoning visitors along the Highway 20 corridor. To boot, a necklace of jade green lakes sparkles amongst the greenery, including Crater, Chaval and Cliff Lakes, plus an unnamed gem just to the summit's southeast.

Chaval has been climbed from its south but this requires the staunchest of stomachs to tolerate a two-day approach through a tangled mass of brush from Tenas Road. This route climbs past Hurricane Peak and eventually ends up in the blueberry meadows we reached in a day with less brush-beating. A northwest route via Jug Lake appears passable but again gains the same base camp.

For the climber who commands confidence on these often-loose stones, a technical approach up the north ridge might seem appealing. Much of this route is simple scrambling over agreeable heather with the same approach as for the easier west route described above. However, following the ledge system to its northern-most point

CHAPTER TWELVE: A GEM NEGLECTED

leads the climber to the ridge, where tricky 4th-class ridge-running soon ends at a huge gendarme blocking easy progress. Here, follow slabs to a ledge and a jam crack (rated 5.7 by the first party) to advance to a roof, where turning the corner to the west leads to easier ground and the snow slopes progressing to the summit. Some of this climbing appears to require the scalpel rather than the knife. While Beckey describes the rock as generally solid, on our attempt at this route, we found that the real world is not often as kind.

In a way, some folks would prefer that this expanse, encompassing the Buckindy Crags, the Illabots and Chaval, remains untrodden and as pristine as possible. They welcome a paradise largely unexplored, despite, or because of, its formidable brushy defenses guarding the steeper, rocky and snowy terrain. Yet this is what the true mountaineer craves, a paradise largely unpenetrated.

But is this protectionism an elitist manner of thought? I believe that the received wisdom of isolation and protectionism is based on naked assumptions clothed in fine theoretical robes. There should, I believe, lie a deeper honesty here: I would invite alpine explorers, scramblers, climbers and backpackers into this wild and untamed wilderness, so as to better appreciate what the Washington Cascades offer, beyond the teeming peaks most have already ascended - and to also cherish the reasons it must remain protected. In fact, that is the premise upon which this text is based.

CHAPTER THIRTEEN

It's All in the Approach

Mount Buckindy
(7,320')

HIDDEN GEMS OF THE WASHINGTON CASCADES

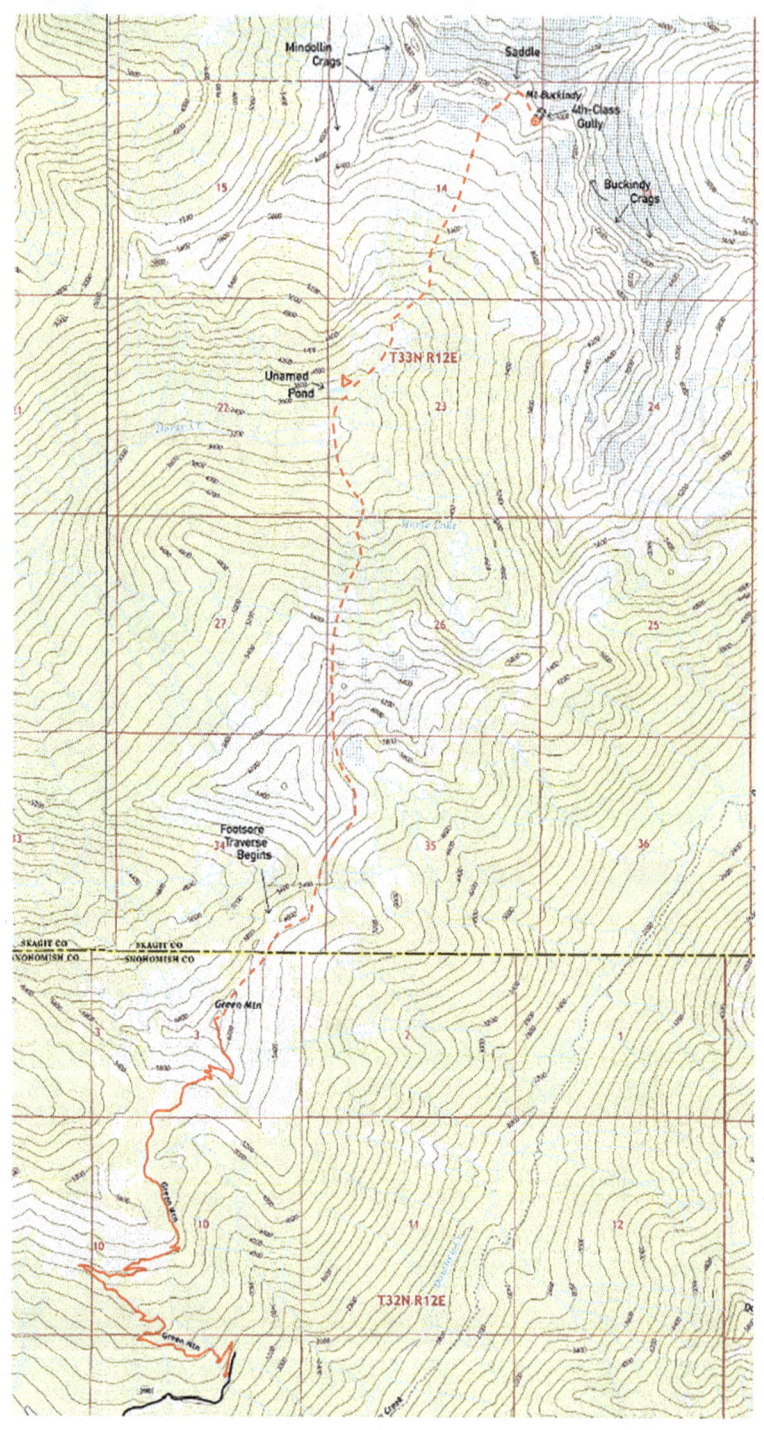

CHAPTER THIRTEEN: IT'S ALL IN THE APPROACH

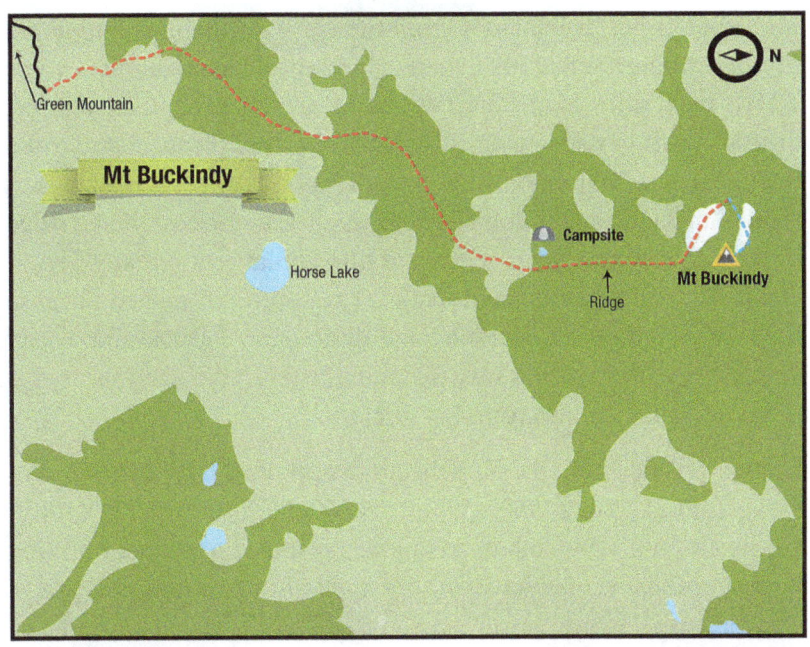

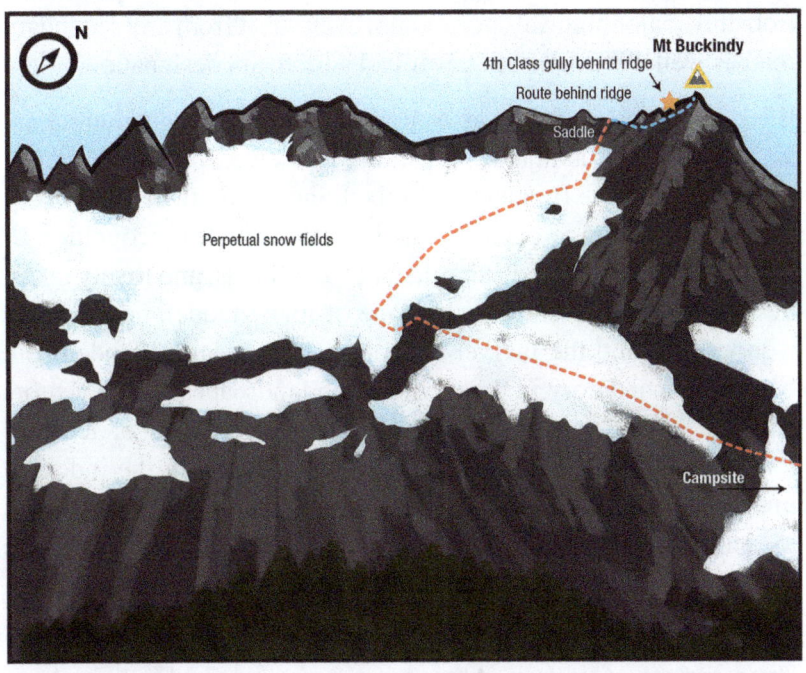

Some peaks get their names from the Native American languages first describing them: think Sahale, Shuksan and Snoqualmie. Others derive their titles from, what looks to human eyes, their shapes, at least from certain perspectives. Within this plentiful group lie the numerous "pyramids", "pinnacles", and "towers". However, a more mundane appellation has been applied to the castellated ridge of leaning crags, skeletal spires and tilted pillars comprising Mount Buckindy and its associated Crags. They were all named because they lie at the crest separating the drainages of Buck and Kindy Creeks; not a very clever way to nominate this red-tinged sub-range of razor-sharp steeples for most of eternity.

But we're stuck with the nomenclature approved by some Board of Geographical Names whose members may have been fed up with all the jigsaw and saw-teeth appellations presented to it and, hurrying home for dinner, may have simply applied this so non-descriptive title because they had never viewed Buckindy's jagged appearance. In fact, very few people really have, as this range is not only invisible from any major highway, you cannot even see it from any secondary road as well. "Wilderness" never had a more apt designation.

Buckindy is as secretive as a mountain lion, yet its summits are as sharp as that animal's fangs. When viewed up close, as, for example, from the frequently climbed Snowking, their complexity seems to discourage exploration. The trouble with recognition of this spectacle of tattered summits, meadow-lands, and lovely lakes, lies with its inaccessibility, the bane of many hidden gems in this wonderland, and the marvel that many conservation-minded folk believe is mandatory in preserving such landscapes. Yet if visitors take care while wandering through this wonderland of tectonic forces and subsequent erosion, they may leave with the indelible image of a wilderness unspoiled, and may repel any future attempts to annihilate it. Hopefully, we climbers, scramblers and hikers should set the example and leave with only a sunburn and boot-prints to mark our passing.

Hype springs eternal, so when we approached Buckindy early in this century, we knew we were in for a tedious voyage, but what we

CHAPTER THIRTEEN: IT'S ALL IN THE APPROACH

encountered made even the access to the famed Pickets (see later) seem almost tame in comparison. In retrospect, the sparks of this pretentious plan were fueled by the tinderbox of hubris. Certainly, the beginnings didn't faze us as we tread our way up the Green Mountain Trail off the Suiattle River and Green Mountain Roads to attempt what is known as the South Route.

You can even tag the summit of Green, with its fine views of Glacier Peak and a view east to the Dome massif beyond. But the approach to Buckindy really begins about 300' shy of Green's summit. From here, do not believe Beckey's reassuring notes about "a scenic alpine trek....", or "a goat path ". This passage will require deft footing as opposed to a delicate pilgrimage. Do not be fooled by the open slopes ahead just off the Green Mountain Trail; they may appear willing but vegetation here will prove more of a curse than a blessing.

It is possible to stay high, at around the 5,900' level, but this, a "foot-sore" traverse, made even me, a wildflower enthusiast, curse the corn lilies which crowd these slopes. Apparently, other, stouter climbers in our party were perfectly happy – perhaps they had "feets" of strength. We encountered what seemed like a conveyor belt of these 3-5' tall slippery plants and thus were never certain, with each step, whether a slide would occur. The flora, permanently wet from ocean breezes, was as slithery as a greased politician and I as slow as a three-legged mule. The travelling was similar to riding on a bicycle: If we stopped, we would simply topple over. We soon learned that aspiration minus perspiration would lead to desperation.

Corn Lily

Thus we constantly had to ask ourselves what mattered most: our problems or our pride? I tried to keep mindful of the saying that living fully is accepting suffering but somehow aphorisms were of no particular help. We stumbled across acre after acre of this mini-forest without ever actually seeing bare ground, so thick was the greenery. Some folk use crampons on similar slopes to assure better adhesion but this would truly have harmed the vegetation. Even though we cursed the lilies, we were still careful to not slice them up with our climbing steel. In the end, however, this traverse actually proved more of an irritant than an insurmountable obstacle.

Hours of such traversing led us through several saddles, one of which seemed to lead down to Horse Lake. But by this time, we had passed most of the difficulties of the traverse and had gained the ridge, where white heather and purple small-flowered penstemon eased the way. Finally we could at least see where our feet were landing. Not wanting to lose precious elevation, we continued on or just east of the ridge and at the next col, spied a pond, not apparently on either Beckey's normally accurate diagrams nor, surprisingly on the 7½" topographic map series; it resided just to the west of the ridge and only 100' down from it. Although just a seasonal tarn really, it provided a grateful camp spot for our worn-down crew, with bare level ground at last. Tents, supper and sleep quickly followed.

We began our adventure early the next morning under agitated skies, the mist successfully hiding our anxieties in this infrequently-explored universe. Regaining the ridge, plowing through brush, and negotiating peace with bouldery 3rd-class rock, we advanced toward our barely visible objective. The teetering towers to our northwest leaned in every direction, some seeming to be of another dimension altogether, defying the laws of gravity. The topmost summit of all these pinnacles was clear but we were equally impressed with the crags on the eastern rim. These, the actual crest of Buckindy Ridge, resembled the rotting teeth of a giant old man who had never seen a dentist. It appeared as if that same Patagonian giant had taken a hacksaw and drill to create this beautifully tortured landscape.

Reddish in hue, these towers had not been named by the first party to visit this area in 1963 but subsequently were traversed by a party in

CHAPTER THIRTEEN: IT'S ALL IN THE APPROACH

1972, a relatively recent timeframe to be so anointed. Seemingly on the point of collapse, the Buckindy Range of towers, so fragile yet sharp in their appearance, seemed, at closer and closer approaches, to confirm Mandelbrot's conception of a fractal universe, becoming increasingly complex while repeating their overall spiky contours at smaller and smaller scales. We wondered whether it was gremlins or phantoms who had named and scaled these tottering peaks? It seems possible as they now bear whimsical names from west to east derived from the original *Lord of the Rings* saga, such as Caradhras, Orthank, Dol Goldur, the Sword Pinnacles, Dol Amroth, and to the northwest the Mindolluin Crags. We were at a loss to pinpoint which was which among this mountain mayhem, as each lumpy lopsided spire merged in our addled minds into an array of castles, turrets and belfries so complex we wondered if they could ever be separated into named summits.

The 1972 party was partially successful in reaching a few of the highest points of several of these pristine pinnacles, which appeared to us to have had crowns applied by a giant dentist due to capstones perched precariously on top of some of their teetering spires. Many were so slender, they looked as if a stiff breeze could knock them asunder. We believed we were truly seeing the bare bones of the earth as we passed by. The 1972 party, and an earlier one in 1969, had made the ascents of all the named crags but, in reality, there are intermittent fangs and incisors not tall enough to merit an appellation, but seemed to us barely approachable and probably still virgin.

Indeed, the first ascensionists reported rock as rotten as a crooked used car dealer. Their ratings ran the gamut from easy scrambling to class 5.5 climbing on crumbling gneiss and granidiorite. Holds seemed to peel off in their gloved hands as easily as politicians lie. Many of these towers, after a few "first ascents", have been discarded into obliteration, like antique over-grown trails disappearing in the fading light. We deemed ourselves lucky that we were only attempting the tallest of these towers, Buckindy itself, said to bear solid enough holds to allow even a weekender like myself to enjoy a trip up to its summit.

Once the ridge ran out, we traversed a permanent snowfield in a southern-facing bowl to reach the saddle between the Mindolluin Crags and, to the northeast, Buckindy itself. Reassuringly blocky, at first the final ascent of the summit pyramid involved rotating around to its north side then up a 4th class loose gully; here, I did not allow pretense to trump fear and requested a belay from my more capable companions above. Once up this chute, easy scrambling around slabs and ledges led to the summit. Finally, intent became reality. In 1995, there were four party names in the summit register (none were Beckey) but the first was that of the 1969 group (Allen Smith and Dean Wilson); they apparently achieved the first recorded ascent.

From the summit, views south to the apex of Chaval, then east to Glacier Peak and the Dome-Sentinel group, were all outstanding, as were the southern aspects of Snowking, Mutchler and the Cascade Pass Peaks, along with the saw-teeth of Teebone Ridge, culminating in the glaciered slopes of Eldorado. To our immediate southeast stood the pointy pillars of the Buckindy Crags themselves. Hazy in the far northern distance, but no less impressive, stood the bulwarks of Mts. Baker and Shuksan. No more unique panorama of these western-most outposts of the middle Cascades can be had from any comparable viewpoint. After absorbing these matchless sights, my abilities, slim at best, widened to a chasm; thus I was happy to rappel the gully, though my more limber teammates descending it frowned on my clumsiness.

Lack of easy access combined with the absence of views from a road, have rendered Buckindy a marvelous mystery to most climbers and back-country explorers. What a shame that such an outstanding region of crag, lake, and meadow remains virtually unknown to outdoor enthusiasts, especially as it lies within 60 miles of a megalopolis of over five million inhabitants. Perhaps one day, such mysterious and obscure ranges will be overrun by mountaineers, hikers and backpackers; I doubt it though in our lifetime of fascination with electronic devices and urban landscapes. Maybe that's for the best. Such a point of view may be a relief for some readers yet a disappointment for others. But I cannot help

CHAPTER THIRTEEN: IT'S ALL IN THE APPROACH

but wonder if some visiting adventurers wouldn't dream of this fractured yet magnificent vista, with scenes that are now seared into their souls, and thereafter work hard to preserve it.

CHAPTER FOURTEEN
For the Matchless Views
Buck Mountain
(8,573')

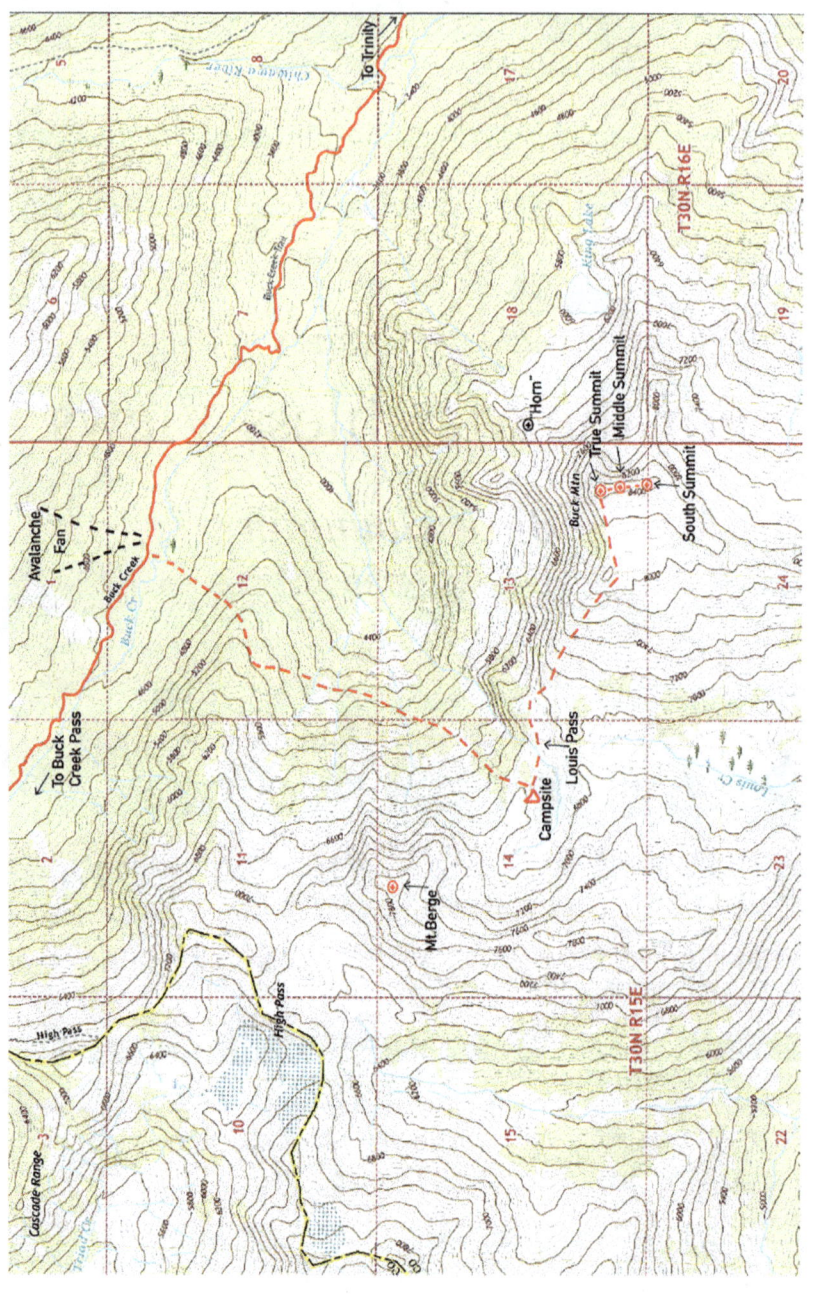

CHAPTER FOURTEEN: FOR THE MATCHLESS VIEWS

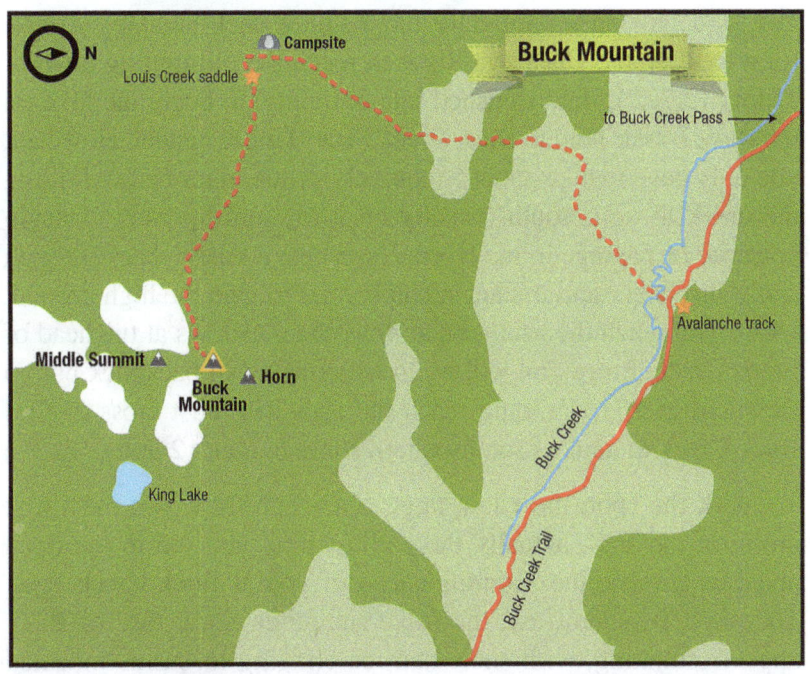

Yes, you will have to endure the 23-mile back-breaking excuse for a road up the Chiwawa River to reach the old mining town of Trinity (2,772'), now vanished into antiquity, to begin the hike on the Buck Creek Trail to Buck Creek Pass, 9 miles distant. However, you only have to hike about 5 relatively gentle miles before fording the creek to your south (usually on a log jam upriver) to begin your rite of passage in the North Cascades: a bush-whack through spiky shrubbery and mutant subalpine firs to gain the high ground, where you reach the heather and flowered meadows at the head of Louis Creek. Since you will be shouldering a full backpack but no technical gear, you should reach the spot you must cross or ford Buck Creek to gain its southwestern shore in about 2 hours.

To mark the spot, there is a large avalanche track you must first cross on the trail, actually the earliest time you are in the open and can glimpse the summits ahead of you at Buck Creek Pass. To your left (southwest) the triple-summited north face of Buck appears stunning, with snow and ice clinging to basins indented onto its face like icy pockmarks, and waterfalls streaming down its precipitous slopes like massive tears from a forested stony giant. The summit itself cannot really be seen from this vantage point; it lies beyond the horn of rock jutting out of the peak's northern reaches. Many a scrambler may have posed the question, perhaps silently to themselves: "We're supposed to climb that?"

Cross Buck Creek just at the end of the avalanche track, at about 4,300'. If early in the season, try to find a log jam up-river; by August, a ford or stone-hopping may be feasible. Although Beckey's green *Alpine Guide 2* promises "minor brush and small trees", be prepared for some abject misery in bushwhacking to gain a minor spur descending from Mt. Berge, due west. Try to stay on top of the spur to avoid deep ravines cradling icy streams and choked with brush.

Though Beckey suggests that you can follow game trails and a rude path on top of the spur, we failed miserably to locate any tracks, animal or human. Right, left, ahead and behind us was all brush-filled Hell. Other sources, chiefly on the internet, were as inscrutable

CHAPTER FOURTEEN: FOR THE MATCHLESS VIEWS

as a Mac tablet trying to fool a Turing test. We should have known: Brush here is as predictable as a rainy December day in Seattle or a summer weather forecast for San Diego: sunny and 72 degrees.

Once atop the spur, however, the going got a bit easier; aim in a southwestern direction but avoid going too far south as cliffs there guard this old giant's northern flanks. As the spur gives way, it is best to angle southwest toward a col between Mts. Berge and Buck, which you can see through the dense under-curtain of salmonberry, white rhododendron, and other diverse shrubbery evolved, so it seems, to thwart climbers' attempts to reach any objective.

The brush is unavoidable, and often we felt corralled by tentacles of greenery, a nightmare of the most sinister of plants, alive and reaching out to ensnare the climber. (Why can't those geniuses inventing lightweight gear and thermal electronic jackets devise clothing which lubricates our progress through this stuff?) Our spirits sank as deeply as the greenery we encountered. Unlike Prometheus of Greek legend, I would be unable to regenerate my torn tissues for weeks thereafter. However, staying on minor ridges and aiming for the saddle will prove the most facile means of travel. On our first climb, we made slow and uneven progress through a garrison of stunted thick-trunked subalpine firs. In my own attempt at escape, I became imprisoned in an Alcatraz of knarly firs and had to plan my egress only with the use of my ice ax. I imagined a troop of future climbers finding my prehistoric skeleton, ax raised in a last attempt to free myself from this tree-barred tomb.

Yet adversity creates opportunity; with slow progress you will gain the anteroom of fewer trees just before you reach the open meadows at around 5,900'. You are now able to spy more obviously the objective for this first day: the saddle between Berge and Buck. Here, pleasant but steep meadows feature the 1-2' tall spires of white partridgefoot; 3' tall Sitka valerian; and American bistort, the latter earning the nickname of bottle brush because of its spike-like clusters of flowers at the ends of its stalks. Pink and purple daisies and asters combine with blue lupines, crimson paintbrushes, yellow shrubby and fan-leaf cinquefoils to carpet this alpine parkland

Fan-Leaf Cinquefoil

as you labor up this outdoor garden, the equal of any found in our urban landscapes. You will finally reach the saddle, the low point between Berge and Buck at around 6,800', and the headwaters of Louis Creek, flowing down the opposite (southwestern) slopes of Buck into Napeequa Valley. This basin, flower-filled and with barren flat spots to camp, gains your first day's objective, and delivers you at the foot of Buck's rocky trio of summits.

This marvelous glen, saddle as Beckey described it, is indeed, lined with a "thin fence of larch" (the alpine species) on its northeastern slope, but largely, the col itself is free of trees. A few sub-alpine firs and hemlocks dot the landscape but are too sparse to thwart views out to the Buck Creek Pass peaks of Mts. Cloudy and North Star. Beyond, to the east, Glacier Peak soars, its many eastern-facing glaciers in resplendent view, only tarnished a bit by the outlines of Mts. Berge and Cleator. Brahma Peak is due south but is hidden by Buck's western and southern reaches. Make camp on sod bereft of flora, and enjoy, after a well-deserved rest, an amble south or north for even more distant views of Clark and Ten-peak Mountains to your southwest and Fortress and Chiwawa Peaks due north.

From this vantage point, you could, if you have the energy (we certainly didn't) meander down east-northeast on deceivingly gentle ground, to catch a view of an enigma: King Lake. You can view the lake by descending heathered meadows about 500', but beware of straying too far as you will soon encounter cliffs descending to the lake, something you definitely not wish to do. King Lake sits in its own diminutive basin, somewhat of an anomaly on such a steep northern slope.

Climb day should begin by hiking the broad west ridge of Buck, first in meadows, then on either snow or talus depending on season.

CHAPTER FOURTEEN: FOR THE MATCHLESS VIEWS

Your major difficulty will be determining which of Buck's three summits is truly the highest point. Received opinions and Beckey list Buck's apex as 8,528', and describes the climbing goal as the middle of Buck's three peaks, at this same elevation. However, he acknowledges that the north summit's elevation might be slightly higher at 8,573'. Confusion here is as thick as the brush; the 7" topo, however, confirms the north summit as the highest at 8,528'.

To add to the confusion, the Green Trails map lists the north peak as the top-most point at 8,573'. Whichever, it appears from near the three top-most points that the northern-most bundle of rocks is the highest; our GPS and altimeters split the difference at 8,550'. A south summit can easily be reached along the southern ridge; its height appears to be about 8,500'. To reach the true north summit, scramble the middle peak first over stable boulders, then traverse just below its western ridge to ascend 3rd-class rock to its apex. This peak is not the jutting northern horn so prominently seen from the trail; from the true, northern summit, you can look downward to spy that rock horn, and be glad that you don't have to traverse the technical knife-like ledges and ramps to reach it. There may be souls who are up to that challenge, but most of us respect the laws of gravity to tempt such a hazardous undertaking.

Views now truly open up: First to catch your eye will probably be an unobstructed view of Glacier Peak's eastern face, with the Cool and Chocolate Glaciers standing proud. Extending east from the Gendine and Honeycomb Glaciers is a snow-bound ridge encompassing the Dakobed Range, with the Kololo Towers thrusting up from a uniform mantle of snow, like soldiers guarding the ice. Next in line to the east stand the abrupt slopes of Tenpeak, not often climbed because of its arduous approach. The Moth and Butterfly Glaciers clothe the northern slopes of Challangin Peak while the Pilz, Richardson and Walrus Glaciers protect the northern flanks of Clark Mountain.

It would be rewarding to learn about the etymology of the names these ice-rivers bear, but even the obsessively studious Fred Beckey has not much to say about their derivation, even in his "notes" section. The Chocolate Glacier may have that tasty name due to its dusty appearance but there is already a "Dusty Glacier" on the peak's northern flank. Others, such as the Moth and Butterfly Glaciers could be named after their shapes, though I've never been able to appreciate any insects' silhouettes when viewing Glacier's southeastern slopes.

To the southeast, Mt. Stuart stands tall in the distance, lording it over the other Enchantment peaks and beyond, the lesser-known and untrammeled Chickamin Range. The northeastern view encompasses Maude, Seven-Fingered Jack and Mt. Fernow, while due north, the Dome massif dominates, with the well-named Spire Point standing out in stark relief. Beyond, the brooding hulk of Bonanza cannot be mistaken. Chiwawa, Fortress and Dumbell [sic] Mountains can be spied across the Chiwawa River drainage to your north. The views to the south are dominated by the snowy mantles of Mts. Daniel and Hinman, partially concealing the Snoqualmie Pass peaks beyond. The southeastern shoulder of Glacier Peak hides most of the Monte Cristo's but a few can be singled out in the hazy distance. Try not to gaze too long north into the valley of Buck Creek; it might remind you of the brushy descent to come this day or the next.

Hopefully, you will be able to relax back at camp and descend the following day. It's a shame that, for most of us however, the clock and calendar rule our lives, so a same-day descent may be necessary. This adventure exposes the scrambling Cascader to the essence of the North Cascades, with trail, then a bushwhack, a steep ascent topped by some confusion about where the true summit lies, then crowned by a scramble to learn the truth, followed by the ultimate success of gaining the top before waging war on the brushy descent. It is perhaps a bit too metaphorical, but Buck may mimic the worthwhile struggles in life we all must surmount to reach our goals. Or, from a more prosaic point of view, maybe it's just another tough-to-reach mountain top we can bag and brag about. Whichever, Buck stands tall, at least in my memory, as encapsulating the North Cascades' experience to a perfect tee.

CHAPTER FIFTEEN

Poor Spelling but Great Mountaineering

Dumbell Mountain
(8,421')

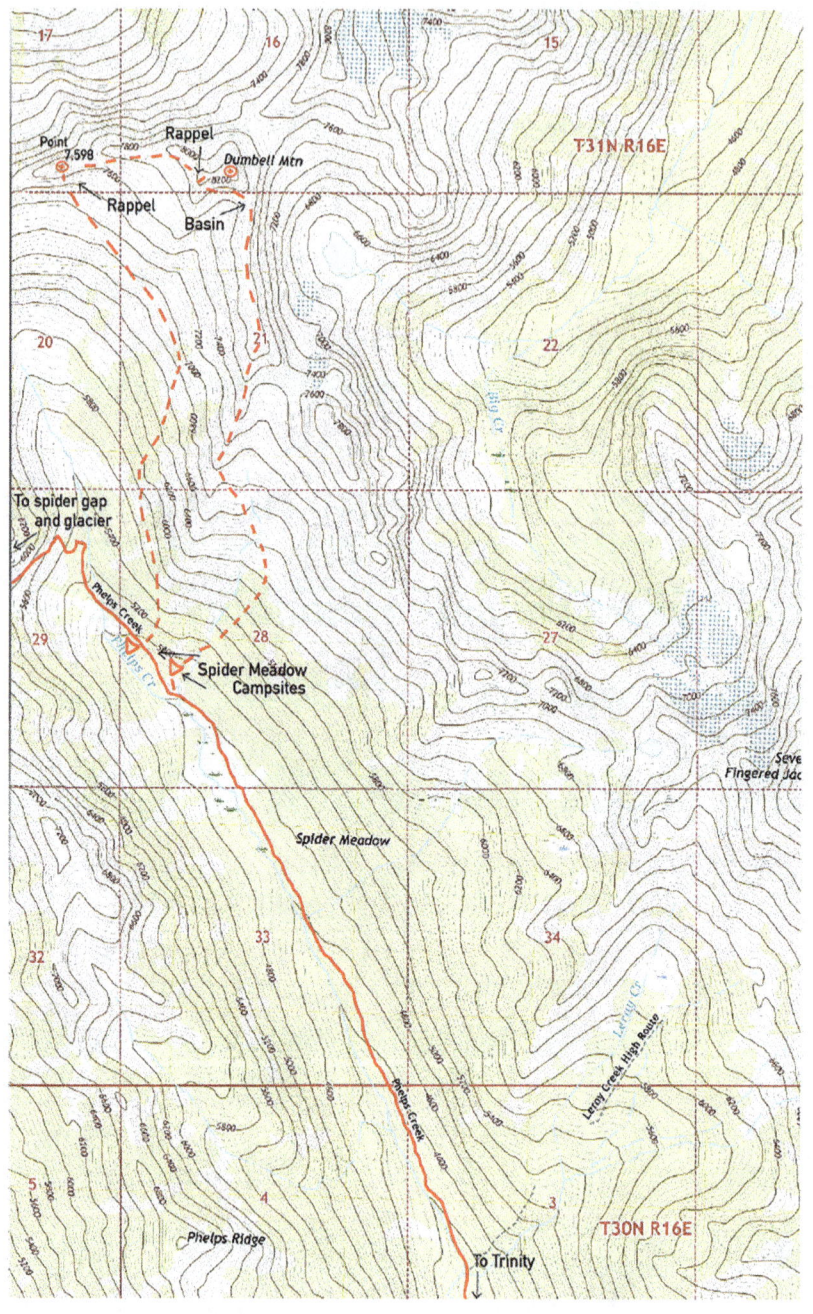

CHAPTER FIFTEEN: POOR SPELLING BUT GREAT MOUNTAINEERING

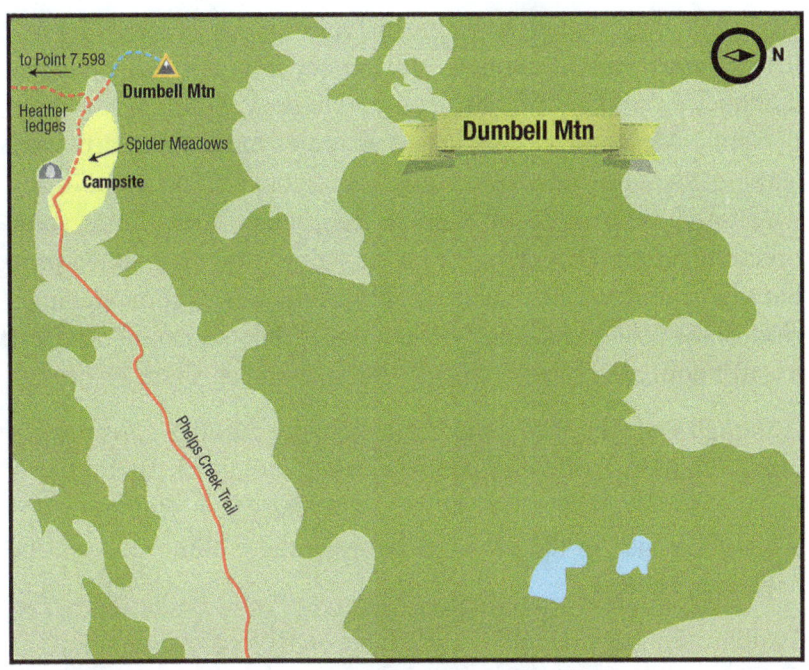

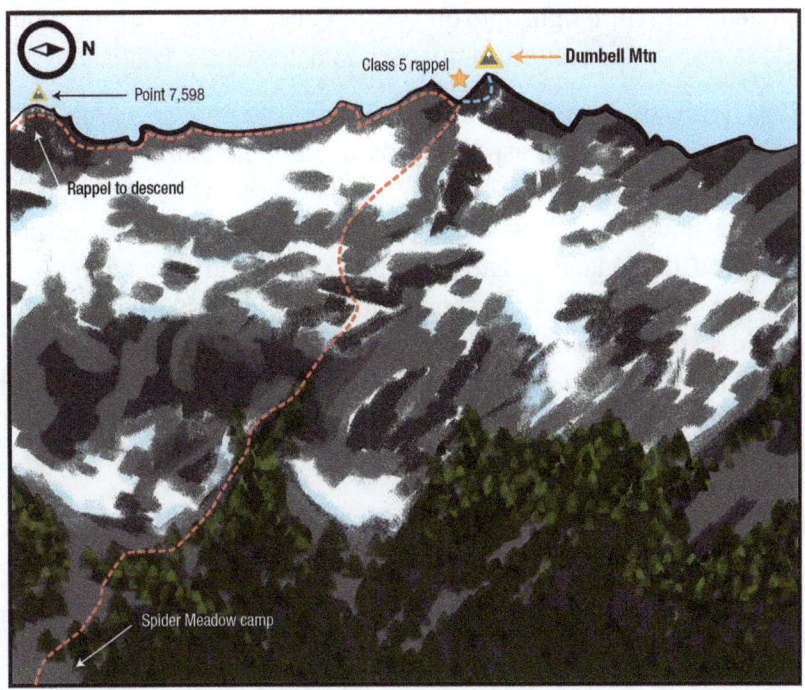

Who and why would someone name a peak "Dumbell? First, it's not even spelled correctly. ("Dumbbell" is correct, but some dumbbell left off a "b".) Moreover, this peak, sitting at the head of Spider Meadow, with its kaleidoscope of multi-colored flowers and breathtaking views of surrounding mountains, does not in any way resemble a piece of exercise equipment. True, from some obscure northern aspect, one could imagine a twin-summited peak but this strains the imagination. Perhaps the appellation stemmed from some near-sighted early explorers as the mountain does have a lower northeastern peak (8,260') but a dumbbell shape? Not.

Although Dumbell forms the head of Spider Meadows, its peak is rarely climbed, though it is quite accessible. Since I've climbed it twice, you can readily see the bar is set fairy low. But there was a big difference in the 25 years between these climbs, as will be explained below.

To approach this peak, drive the Chiwawa River Road for about 23 miles (usually in passable condition even without a high clearance vehicle), then turn right onto the Phelps Creek Road #6211 for about 2½ bumpy miles to its terminus at the Phelps Creek Trailhead.

It is perfectly reasonable to be discouraged by the number of vehicles parked here, especially on a brilliant summer weekend, but many parties will be heading up the Carne Mountain Trail at ½ mile in, or the Leroy Creek Trail at 3½ miles (see the Seven-Fingered Jack/Maude Chapter), while others will be attempting a traverse across Spider Gap and Spider Glacier (what must be the world's slimmest and gradually inclined of permanent ice-fields), down to the Chiwawa drainage, thus completing a loop. Others will be intent on climbing Red Mountain or Chiwawa, but truth be told (a rarity among us climbers), Dumbell holds superior views.

For you hardy climbers, Spider Meadow, about ⅓rd of a mile beyond 5 miles, holds reasonable approaches to Chiwawa and Fortress peaks. Along the trail in the lightly shaded meadow are pockets of mountain hemlocks which provide ideal camping spots at about 4,750' elevation. Dumbell looks rather lumpy at this point,

CHAPTER FIFTEEN: POOR SPELLING BUT GREAT MOUNTAINEERING

and, dare I say, uninspiring? Not to worry; the meadow and the views from Dumbell's summit will compensate.

On one of our approaches years ago, the faulty weather kindled anxiety as well as hope. (Happily, meteorologists' forecasts are more accurate these days.) It had rained that morning and cloud patterns raced across a furrowed sky. Since I had refused to replace my original Gore-Tex jacket in many years (one of the original test models, I'm sure), it proved as watertight as a teabag. While mountain rain can be fierce, it is more often like walking through a cloud. We had to remind ourselves that where the sun always shines, there's a desert below. Gossamer veils sheathed the greenery like fine embroidery, but the mist was brightened by a rainbow as the sun emerged and we rejoiced as we reached the pastures of Spider Meadow. Here, a confetti of color seemed to have showered down from above.

Monkshood

The first breaches in the forest feature a 3' tall plant with tiny white flowers all in a flat cluster at top. This is Sitka valerian. Further on, lupine begins in earnest, while once in the midst of this glorious alpine parkland, tall purple Cascade asters vie for attention with leafy asters; deep purple monkshood is present, sort of an inverted delphinium, which prefers moist settings, as does tall yellow arrow-leaf groundsel. In shorter grasses further along, subalpine buttercup features yellow waxy petals while

Subalpine Buttercup

fan-leaf cinquefoil, also with five yellow petals, can be distinguished by its flat non-shiny notched petals.

There lies a large campsite at the beginning of the meadow in the last clump of hemlocks at 5¼ miles; other sheltered campsites exist at the farthest reaches of this floral wonderland in another ½ mile. Streamlets, all comprising the headwaters of Phelps Creek, drain throughout the summer from the snows clasping Dumbell's flanks. By all means, use the established campsites on duff, not flora. Plenty will be found after an adequate search. What a wonder-filled spot to spend an evening: Although you could start early, climb Dumbell and hustle out in a single day, there's too much to see and wonder at for such a hasty exit.

From your camp the next morning, note that Dumbell has two prominent peaks (though it still doesn't much resemble a dumbbell), with the northeast peak the shorter of the two. Your goal is to unfortunately leave the foot-happy heathers of the meadow at around 5,150' and aim north-northeast, first across talus, then easy heather benches and boulders, followed by scree, avoiding the steep southeast buttress on the peak's western side. There is a minor cliff amidst stunted subalpine firs and mountain hemlocks between 6,900' and 7,550' but this can be also bypassed on its western flank.

Aim for the south ridge, just above to your east, which brings you to a basin at about 7,800'. You should enter this southwestern basin, from where a saunter up to the saddle should present no technical difficulties. Then easily gain the saddle between the true summit and the shorter, but taller-appearing, Southwestern Peak (~8,390'). The western ridge could be climbed but it appears to require 5th-class protection. Instead, drop 50' to a permanent snowfield, then traverse at the 8,350' level across the gently-angled snow to gain the western ridge at the spot where it appears directly beneath the summit. Easy boulder-work up to the ridge brings you to the top-most point.

At least this was the description in the 1980's. Two decades later, when we approached the saddle and gazed, bewildered, at the

CHAPTER FIFTEEN: POOR SPELLING BUT GREAT MOUNTAINEERING

snowfield below, we were amazed to see that it had retreated at least 90', leaving an almost blank vertical wall to descend (for comparison, see the Monte Cristo Chapter). We rappelled to the snowfield without much thought about getting back up it on our return – my common mistake. On that return, I stared at the wall we had rappelled down with a quasi-Biblical sense of retribution. I feared that this wall was as tricky for me to solve as it was easy for the leader, David, to scale, as he waltzed up the sheer cliff, cheerfully expecting me to follow. Dave, upon whose probity I had always relied, seemed a tad irritated at my hesitancy to follow, but I had no other choice. After all, I had a belay from above.

Still, I felt like a man with a fork in a world of soup. I waited for about 20 heartbeats, cursing Dave, before following, though truth be known, I needed three trials and much tension, both in my mind as well as from the rope, to re-gain the saddle, thus achieving a triumph of weak technique over ultimate purpose. Even following a 5.9 pitch represented an accomplishment of sorts for me, though in reality I had, early on in my climbing career, set a singularly low bar. The descent, nonetheless, was pleasant thereafter.

Why bother? Well, conditions may have changed but warming continues so you'll have to go just to see. Trip reports in CascadeClimbers.com are sparse, perhaps because it's really not that cool to say you've climbed Dumbell and then have to misspell it in addition. But the views – oh the views! Staggering to say the least. Dumbell sits at the head of two massive valleys: Phelps and Chiwawa. To the immediate southwest, above Red Mountain (it really is iron-red) sits Chiwawa and Fortress, then the Buck Creek Pass peaks, while beyond, the views of Glacier Peak's southeastern flanks are as unobstructed as they are unforgettable.

Buck Peak stands sharply due south. To the immediate west is the mysterious and rarely frequented **Greenwood Mountain (8,415')**, tough to approach but a symmetrical pyramid dominating the view from Holden Village. Though Beckey describes an approach by first climbing Dumbell, he fails to mention the daunting task of initially losing 1,000' of altitude, then, with what appears from the view and the map, several class-5 pitches at around 7,800' before attaining his "walk along a broad ridge".

Views to the north aren't half-bad either. Foremost is Bonanza, its southern glaciers in full regalia and its complicated collection of summit teeth in unabridged view. Copper Peak is due east, while to the south lie Fernow, Seven-Fingered Jack and Maude. To the southwest, just over Buck Creek Pass, the spires and turrets of the Dome Massif bear witness to the ravages of upthrust followed by erosion and glaciation, carving and chiseling away the softer rock to reveal the fangs and arêtes left for us to wonder about and admire. Deep below, the turgid rumblings of what must be a thousand waterfalls drain off these higher snows, carving steep-walled valleys on their courses down to the named rivers at these mountains' feet.

Your descent, aside from the wall mentioned above, should be pleasant enough and a walk out the tranquil Phelps Creek Trail should pose few problems. But another course might be considered once you've attained Dumbell's summit: **Point 7,598**, a sub-summit of Dumbell just north of Spider Gap. This is a prominent and angular pyramid, impressive and enticing in appearance from Spider Meadow. This pinnacle could be gained from Dumbell's summit (with protection for a few mid-class-5 pitches) by a long traverse along its western ridge, which turns abruptly south after running roughshod over a minor hump at 7,825', then simply walking the remainder of the ridge south.

On my first climb of Dumbell, my partners, rigid with intent, "suggested" (insisted) we try this alternative, despite my pitiful moaning in protest. These aces of ascent were not prone to ignore every bump and pinnacle in view. Speaking fatigue and lack of skill failed miserably. In this binary moment, my compatriots seemed to always believe not to try would represent the biggest failure of all. To paraphrase Shakespeare, I learned to "tempt not the desperate climber". Though I offered my companions a less technical descent, which would simply have us follow the broad and pleasant ridge to Spider Gap, then amble down the climber's

CHAPTER FIFTEEN: POOR SPELLING BUT GREAT MOUNTAINEERING

path to reach Spider Meadow, they would have none of it. The price of both love and climbing is compromise so I followed with my usual sense of foreboding, recognizing that shared goals do not always equal shared motivations. I was snarling when I should have been charming. In retrospect, many climbs, and particularly many routes may represent a compromise; no one side walks away completely satisfied.

We proceeded over rough terrain, protecting the odd 5th-class moves to reach the **Point's** summit. At times where the ridge steepened and exposure was paramount in my mind, I suppose I resembled a caricature of a climber, arm-wrestling my way up like a sloth on stilts, where the others were nonchalantly waltzing up the rock. I distinctly recall passages where I was seared on the grill of reality. Anyway, as we reached the **Point's** apex, I pointed out to my confederates, mostly out of spite, that views were much the same as from Dumbell. We next rappelled south directly off the summit, then descended pleasant heather and some blocky talus to reach the meadows. Though I often complain, I owe a debt of gratitude to my partners (many of them Mountaineers or Mazamas) for their patience in the face of my clumsiness. (However, I do hold the distinction of being the oldest clumsy mountain climber still alive.)

The pleasures of Dumbell belie its name. Moreover, when it's rainy or even if the sky west of the crest is simply tortured, Dumbell may be mostly in the clear. Yet with a fortuitous forecast, walking in to Spider Meadow while in the final gasps of a late morning sprinkling, one can appreciate the all-too-frequent drip, drip, drip of these Cascades. One secret is to touch the rain and marvel at the sky-water that renders these forests and meadows so lush. The dampness helps to value the infinity of soft sounds amid the benediction of a gentle rain you hope will soon be but a memory.

CHAPTER SIXTEEN

Two for the Effort of One

Cloudy Peak

(7,915')

and North Star Mountain

(8,096')

HIDDEN GEMS OF THE WASHINGTON CASCADES

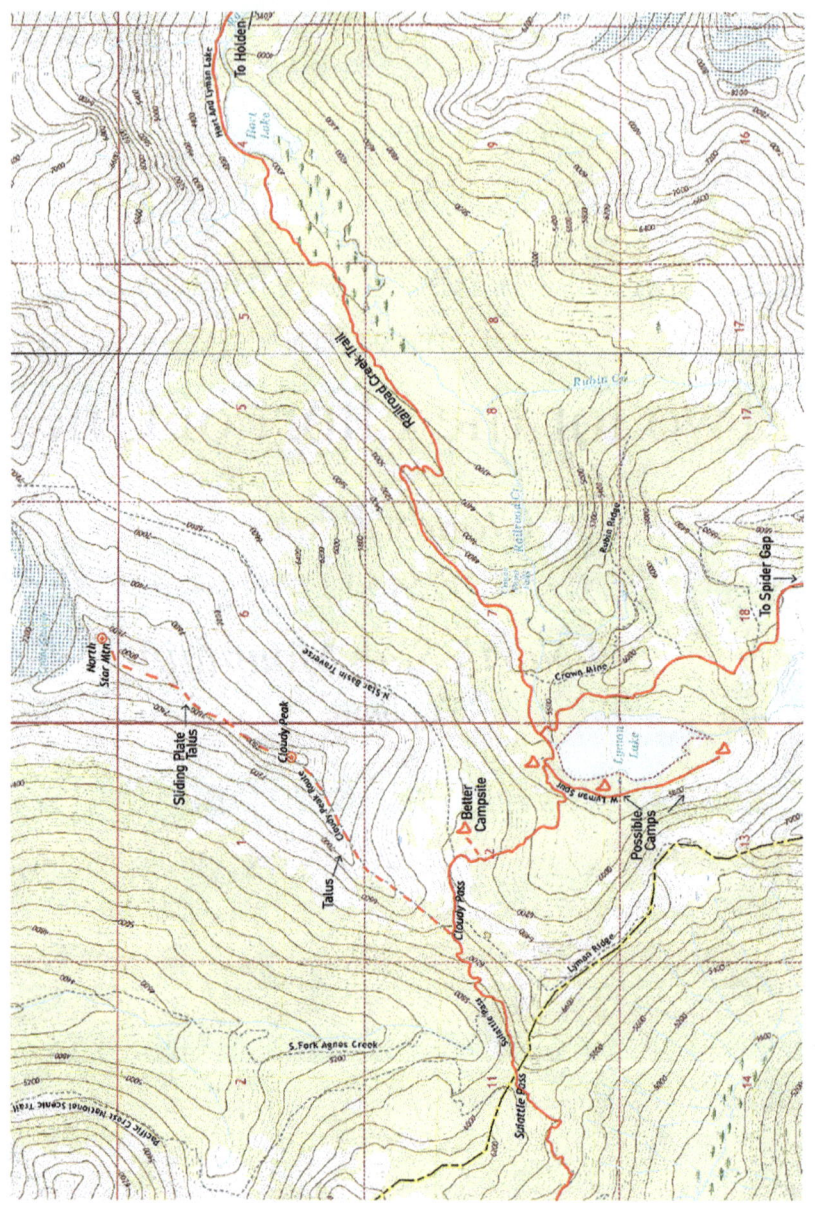

CHAPTER SIXTEEN: TWO FOR THE EFFORT OF ONE

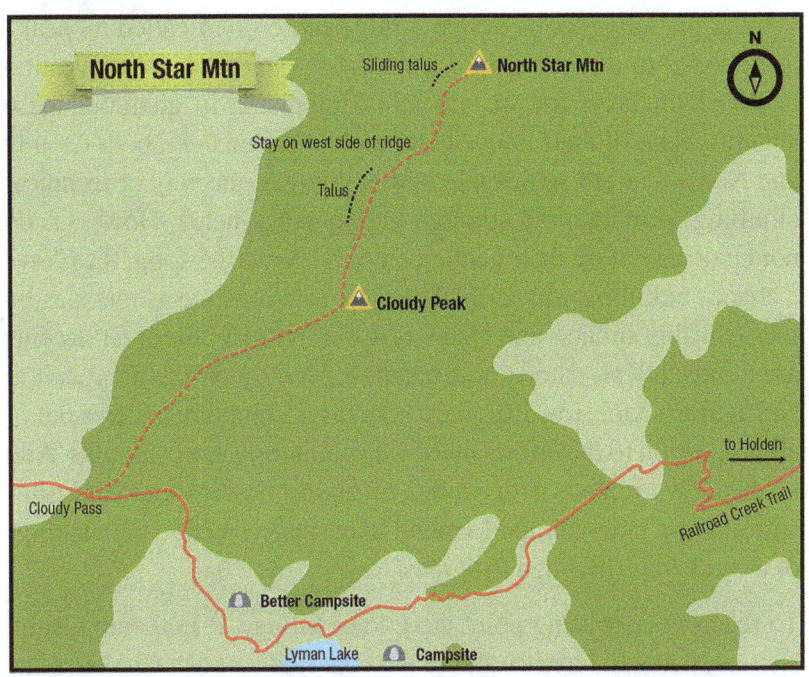

Why is the tallest point above a ridge more often called a "peak" as opposed to a "mountain"? This is too philosophical a question to dwell on here, for we are more interested in attaining these summits than in their nomenclature. And fortunately, both Cloudy and North Star are achievable with nothing in the way of technical climbing gear required (though hiking poles help). However, do not be deceived by their gentle contours: As in the song, they have a chance at killing you softly, but not with your face as much as by their shifting dinner-size plates of loose rock. While their ascents are nontechnical, care is best taken, especially on the approach to North Star's top. However, they both offer voluptuous views out of all proportion to the efforts involved in attaining their summits. Add in meadows replete with armies of alpine flowers and campsites surrounding jade-colored Lyman Lakes, and you have the makings of a weekend trip tough to surpass.

To reach your starting point at Holden Village, a Lutheran Camp/Retreat, you will have to endure the boat ride up Lake Chelan to the Lucerne Landing (see chapter 18 for a more complete description), then, even worse, the 11-mile bump and grind in the Lutheran-occupied bus and the occasional strains of 1940's-era outbursts of song from your fellow travelers. Once, we were even "raided" by a band posing as ersatz cowboys, halting the bus and demanding "loot" (in mid-western accents), much to the amusement of their Lutheran brethren. If you can tolerate this part of your multi-faceted journey, you will encounter nothing else you can't handle beyond Holden. Despite my unduly sardonic comments, Holden, and the Lutherans who vacation there all summer, are quite a pleasant bunch; they will even offer you an inexpensive lunch and promise to pray for your safe return. I appreciated those invitations as I could use all the help I could get.

Since it probably won't take that long to reach your base camp, you should really stroll around Holden, view the massive tailings which have reduced Copper Mountain, to your immediate south, to a Swiss-cheese hill, more tunnel than earth and rock. All the copper and whatever the miners were hoping to find is now pretty

CHAPTER SIXTEEN: TWO FOR THE EFFORT OF ONE

much exhausted. Interpretive signs along the way help to explain the genesis and workings of the various mines and form an unusual, but interesting, way of beginning a climb. Oh, and don't forget the bakery as you begin the trek up the dusty Railroad Creek Road; their cinnamon rolls are no larger than Cinnabon's but just as tasty (thus bad for you but OK before and after a climb).

It's difficult to imagine now, but Holden and the Railroad Creek Road comprised the epicenter of a vast mining operation in the late 19th and early 20th Centuries. Gold and silver were constantly on the minds of those financing these remote operations, which rivaled those at Monte Cristo to the south. Cabins, a cog rail tread, and a rudimentary railroad were all built up to Hart Lake, and even beyond at Lyman Lakes, 4½ miles in. But despite the toil and dreams of the bosses and crews, only copper and molybdenum were ever extracted in commercially valuable quantities.

You begin by walking up the west-bound road, beginning at around 3,450', which soon turns to trail, mostly river-bottom gentle, though several steep pitches and some talus-hopping do offer entertainment, especially before and following the Hart Lake turn-off. Although campsites are available at Hart Lake, press on to gain, at 4½ miles, the first of the Lyman Lakes chain.

A note of caution, however: The Railroad Creek Trail sits in the trough of a valley famed for its winter avalanches. Go too early (June or even early July), and you may encounter not only accumulations of snow to contend with, but worse, uncut logs to leap, or in my case, crawl over. Much brush can impede travel so try to leave Holden with sufficient time to make it to Lyman Lakes before sundown. I would advise you to leave the blissful Lutheran Camp no later than 2 PM.

Note the yellow 2' tall daisy-like flowers of mountain arnica, yielding some color to the browns and greens of the forest floor. Breaches in the woodland cover soon give way to openings within the first several miles. Compare Sitka valerian, with flat white compound-flowered heads, to American bistort, with a conical

Mountain Arnica

mop that looks like its other name – bottle-brush. Lupines are out along with their frequent companions, Indian paintbrushes. The Pea Family lupines actually inhale nitrogen from the atmosphere (well, technically that's not completely accurate but close enough – it's the bacteria on the lupines' roots that do the dirty work), then implant it into the ground, enriching the soil and thus allowing the paintbrushes, which requite nitrogen but cannot manufacture it themselves, to thrive.

Even if you're tired at Hart Lake, push on to Lyman Lakes, where campsites off vegetation abound. Depending on snow conditions and season, you may encounter the first of this lake chain at 4¼ miles, though camping here is marshy. Proceed to the largest of the lakes, the second one in, at 5,600', where its northern shore offers good sites. Even better, try to keep pushing upward on the Railroad Creek Trail.

Within 600' above the lake, a rarely-used campsite to your right exists at about 6,200', with easy access to a creek. This site offers four advantages: fewer bugs, better views of the entire chain of lakes, less elevation to gain on climb day, and a lower risk of bears eager to munch on *your* munchies. While the bears hereabouts have been mentioned in a number of publications, I've yet to see any sign of them. You should take precautions by hanging your food. These bears are not in the least interested in attacking you; they hunger after human food. From the experiences of many, they seem particularly fond of cookies and potato chips. Snackers beware.

The green tint of Lyman Lakes is due to their origins at the copper-rich rocks beneath the Lyman Glacier, a relatively large one at its terminus, which, at around 5,600', is lower than most in these ranges. At one time in the past, perhaps the 1950's, this glacier

CHAPTER SIXTEEN: TWO FOR THE EFFORT OF ONE

extended all the way north to the snout of the largest of these lakes; icebergs were not uncommon throughout the summer. These days of global warming have had an immense effect on glacial retreat here; it's often a good hour's walk to reach the ice these days.

No need to explore if you'd rather appreciate the immediate surroundings. Moisture-loving plants abound around the lakes, including subalpine buttercup, often emerging right through the snowbanks it inhabits, its warmth actually melting the snow to allow it to flourish; elephant head, with big ears and a fair-sized trunk; bird's beak lousewort, burgundy and coiled at top; and the rare bog orchid, a ghostly white throughout, but with a delightful fragrance. On higher ground, yellow fan-leaf cinquefoil, purple subalpine asters, and purplish cut-leaf daisies thrive.

Cut-leaf Daisy

From either camp, the next day follow the ever-steepening switchbacked trail up to Cloudy Pass, ill-named by early explorers angry at Mother Nature's maddening skies. Since the main purpose of gaining the pass and these two peaks is the incredible views, one hopes you had scoped out the increasingly accurate weather reports (unavailable to the earliest adventurers) and chosen the best of azure skies for this endeavor. After all, let's face it: it's the views and experience you're seeking. Boasting that you climbed Cloudy and North Star will gain you little glory in adding them to your climbing résumé.

Nonetheless, these vistas, even from the pass, are among the best of all the Cascade saddles. Surrounded by a silent audience of alpine flowers, it's not a bad place to rest your pack and shoulders, even though it's a day pack, so no complaining here. Just sit and stare. Because I'm a flower nerd, I cannot bring myself (as you've probably noticed with some irritability) not to point out certain alpine species so well-represented here. No scrambler should fail to appreciate their delicate beauty and, perhaps, to sometimes learn their names. To my mind, wildflowers are the jewels of the wilderness.

Mountain goldenrod sends up spikes of tiny yellow daisy-like flowers in compound heads, often amidst the talus; subalpine daisies show a blush of pink on their ray flowers, all surrounding a golden center, also composed of multiple disk flowers; mountain arnica looks like an oversized yellow daisy; while wooly pussytoes really does resemble the upturned paw of your typical housecat; rock, or cliff penstemon, showers splashes of insanely intense rose-purple blooms as tubes coloring the alpine rocks in showy fashion; the related, but more subdued, small-flowered penstemon is common, with deep purple tubes pollinated by hummingbirds and bees; pink and yellow monkey flowers trace the frequent stream courses flowing down from snow banks off the pass; red and white paintbrushes live in happy confluence with both broad-leaf and spurred lupines; and, to top it off, multi-colored phlox carpets the meadows in shades of pastel blue, rose and white.

Both red and white heathers dominate the floral landscape as you begin the ascent from the pass; these are frequently accompanied by partridgefoot, a small spike of yellowish-white flowers sticking up above its bird-like cleft leaves; spreading (alpine) stonecrop can be found on the tops of sunny rocks, colored yellow or red (to protect it from exposure to ultraviolet rays) and often in a circular pattern - these seemingly thrive on top of pure rock, sans soil – its roots sneaking down the tiniest of crevices while its cactus-like leaves collect and hoard the infrequent rain throughout a Cascade summer. Higher up, spiky phacelia, with purple flowers and

Spreading (Alpine) Stonecrop

CHAPTER SIXTEEN: TWO FOR THE EFFORT OF ONE

orange stamens protruding beyond its petals is often accompanied by Sitka mistmaidens, especially where tiny rivulets can collect the moisture this plant demands. By the way, it is incredulous to most Northwestern travelers that the most severe stress these alpine jewels endure is drought during the summer!

Should you wish to extend your expedition, you could move camp, conceivably conquer Cloudy and North Star with light packs, move on to Suiattle Pass, then follow goat and boot-built paths west to the more famous Miner's Ridge and the icon of Image Lake, surely the most celebrated and photographed body of water hereabouts, with a perfect reflection of Glacier Peak's northeastern facets, diamond-clear and perpetually snow-bound. But more of this later.

From the pass, a climber's path leads north, then northeast, following the broad ridge toward Cloudy's rocky summit, perhaps a 1½-to-2-hour jaunt up talus and flakes which have the nasty habit of sliding about where you think they shouldn't. Beware the northwestern cliffs and there should be no problem. Do not, by all means, take the time to discover Beckey's "sandy ledge" to the east; it is either a fiction or represents my frequent inept attempts to follow the master of the Cascades. Just as I avoided to detail the view from the pass, I'll defer to North Star for a complete description of the vista from Cloudy's summit as it is essentially the same, though even more far-reaching. Tip-toe down the low-gradient ridge north of its top to the saddle between these two peaks, then follow the ridge north to North Star.

Ever notice that the descriptions in climbing guides make little mention of actual conditions on these "easy" peaks? I have. To actually climb North Star no technical equipment is needed; nonetheless a strong set of poles, stout boots, and very strong ankles help. The ridge actually becomes thinner as you climb, then rudely ends in a vertical wall. This could be surmounted directly by employing your 4th-class skills on rock as loose as a size 40 dress on a runway model, but I preferred to avoid this unpleasantness and deferred to the west side of the ridge at about the 7,800' level. Here, you can contour around the western fringe of the summits (there are two; the true top is the one furthest north) until an easy passage, though over loose dinner-sized plates of unsteady rock, lead to the broad, view-filled summit.

The views are heavenly. Just as they say that an atheist hearing Handel's Messiah will leave the concert hall a Christian, these views make me question, but only for a moment, my scientific agnosticism. Foremost, to the southeast, human eyes cannot help but marvel at the northeastern slopes of Glacier Peak. Pick out the four most prominent glaciers: From the south, first comes the Chocolate Glacier, a tasty sheet of flowing ice; next, to its north and separated from it by a jutting tower of rock called Dusty Wedge, the North Guardian Glacier sits just above the rarely attempted satellite summit of Glacier Peak, named Gamma Peak. Numerous sheer waterfalls off these icy reaches form the headwaters of Dusty Creek in well-named Multicolor Canyon. Next to your right (west) flows the heavily crevassed Dusty Glacier itself, with the Ermine Glacier just to its west. Draining Glacier's northern slopes are the Vista and Ptarmigan ice sheets, just visible above their intervening rock barricades.

But look in any direction for less snowy but no less opulent vistas. There is no end to the satisfaction of these ranges: To your immediate north Bonanza competes with Glacier, with its spectacular show of the Isella and Mary Green Glaciers sheathing its southern slopes and guarding its complex array of spires and pinnacles. These often confuse even the most accomplished North Cascader in identifying with certainty the actual summit (it's out of sight from here). The Dome Massif dominates the northwestern view, with Agness, Gunsight and Sinister Peaks protecting Dome itself, but allowing a peek at Spire Point just to its west. To your east, Fernow, Seven-Fingered Jack and Maude stand in stately procession, while due south, Fortress and Chiwawa present steep profiles belying their relatively uncomplicated routes of ascent. Far below, the jade/copper-green of the Lyman Lakes chain sparkles; you can almost imagine the recession of the Lyman Glacier up-valley leading east to Spider Pass.

CHAPTER SIXTEEN: TWO FOR THE EFFORT OF ONE

Allow plenty of time to relax and appreciate the full scope of this viewpoint, one of the best you'll have of the northern aspects of Glacier Peak and surely the closest you will come to Bonanza without actually scaling its heights. You'll have time to saunter back to camp, pack up and out, but to where? You'll probably arrive at Holden too late to catch the bus in time to grab the last boat out of Lucerne. And don't anticipate a highly appreciative audience back at Holden, where we thought any applause must have been one-handed. These folk have seen too many climbing parties to show much admiration.

Not to worry. The blessed folks at this village will serve you dinner if you wish (beats freeze-dried), make up a cabin for you with towels, sheets, and then provide a customary breakfast the next morning, all for a pittance which you know will be contributed to a good cause. Yes, you might have to endure an evening of gospel stories and Lawrence Welk songs, but at least you'll have reassured the Lutherans that their prayers (and yours) have been answered in a most marvelous, if not miraculous, manner.

CHAPTER SEVENTEEN

From Heaven's Own Campsite

Mts. Maude
(9,082')

and Seven-Fingered Jack
(9,100')

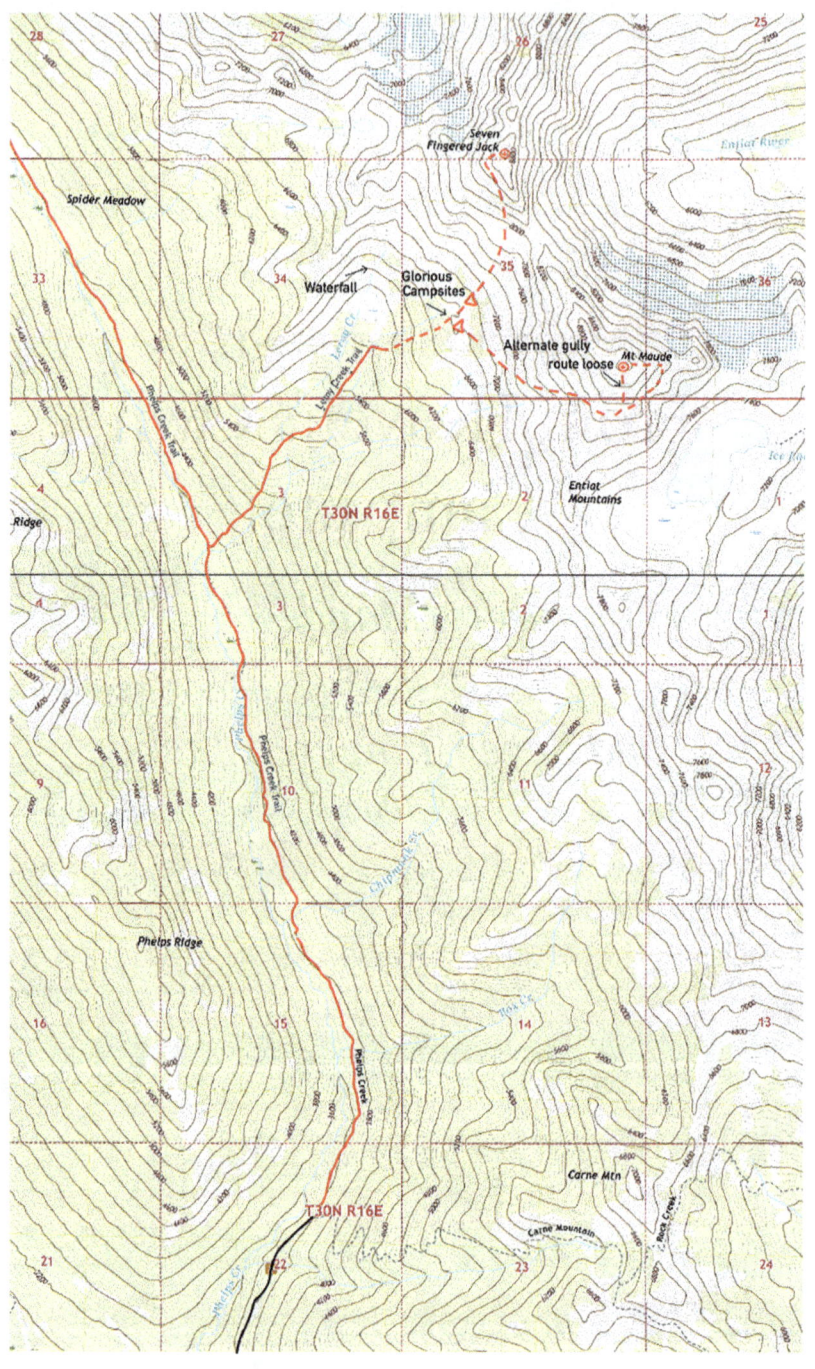

CHAPTER SEVENTEEN: FROM HEAVEN'S OWN CAMPSITE

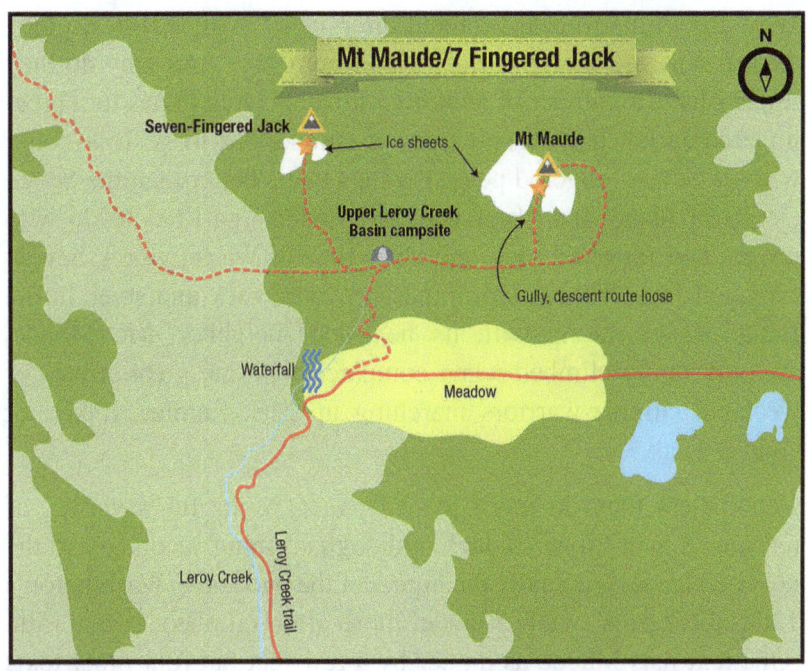

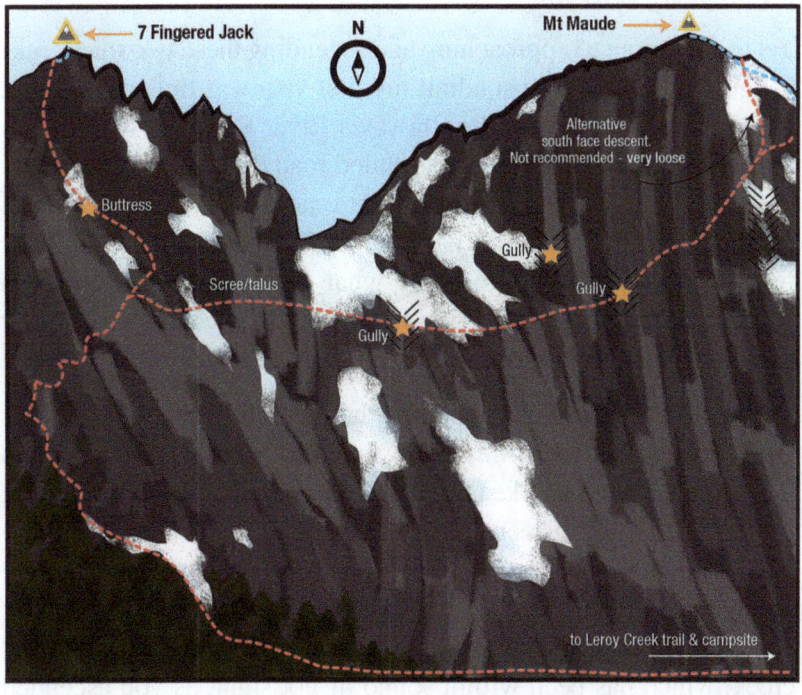

153

Why are so many peaks named after Jack? Which Jack do they mean? Why are they most often odd numbers? And why do they usually have a number of abnormal fingers? Oregon has its Three-fingered Jack while Washington, of course, has to go four better with its Seven-Fingered peak. Perhaps that's better than the Seven Devils of Idaho. It's likely that the "fingers" part has to do with towers and fangs of rock and so it is with Washington's Seven-Fingered Jack. This tottering mass of loose rock and scree in the Entiat Range, along with its next-door neighbor, Mt. Maude, are only rarely climbed when compared with the great armies of weekend climber-warriors marching up Mts. Rainier, Baker, or Glacier Peak.

Nonetheless they do merit more frequent visits for a variety of reasons: Seven-Fingered Jack, although seeming secondary to the hulk of Maude, is actually the higher of the two and is Washington's 12th tallest peak, while Maude, more often climbed, is the 15th. (One text lists Maude as higher by a few feet but four other texts are probably correct).

Yet there's more to approaching and ascending these two than peak-bagging (although I must admit my first visit was thus motivated). After a 23-mile drive on the Chiwawa River Road off Washington State's Route 2 (follow the convoluted road directions in the many trail and climb manuals), take a right onto the Phelps Creek Road another 2½ miles or so to Phelps Creek Trailhead. Plan on at least two days, maybe three, to enjoy what you will discover to be a world-class campsite; lingering here is a lazy pleasure no climber should neglect to forego.

To get there, proceed up the gentle Phelps Creek Trail about 3 miles (why do texts differ so much on mileage? Some say 2.5, others 3.2 – to me it seemed like the latter), then turn right and head north up the increasingly steep Leroy Creek Trail about 3 miles to the bewitching charm of lower Leroy Basin, 6,000'. The path largely surrenders to the floral elements in a meadow marked by a rushing waterfall on your left, representing just one of many in this busy creek, which has been within sound, if not sight, as you ascended

CHAPTER SEVENTEEN: FROM HEAVEN'S OWN CAMPSITE

from the Phelps Creek Trail. Cross the creek heading east, then immediately watch for a climber's path to your left which ascends north, steeply at times, through scant timber at around 6,100'. Although this is the dry side of the range, there is almost always running water at the head of Leroy Creek, but no easy access on the way up, so carry plenty of H_2O as you labor up the track.

You emerge above tree-line to upper Leroy Creek Basin: campsite paradise. There are few richer spots to camp than in this treasure-filled basin, with flat spots atop alpine fir-and subalpine larch-clad hillocks among swaths of both yellow and pink monkey flowers rimming the creek. With the stillness of these partly wooded dells, you can experience the pleasant sensation of feeling tiny in the hold of giant powers.

Most folks are inclined to call it a day and retire to admire the far-ranging views of massive Mt. Fernow next door to the northeast; the sharp-edged spires of the Enchantments further east; the soaring snow dome of Glacier Peak to the south, seeming to float like a white apparition above the wildest corners of the Glacier Peak Wilderness; and summits rarely attempted, even by grizzled North Cascades veterans – peaks southeast such as Mts. David and Bandit, plus Sopa Peak, as well as the better-known brooding hulks of Bonanza and Stuart, and the snows of Chiwawa and Fortress Peaks above Spider and Buck Creek Passes.

Camp for the afternoon or climb if you have the energy (and remaining daylight). The trek to either peak makes for an interesting afternoon, and there will be minimal misery mixed with the majesty of ascent. Seven-Fingered Jack is usually the first peak tackled. I still count a variable number of fingers on this natural whimsy, but the point is to head north from base camp to the col between Maude and Jack, then ascend northwest directly up scree or snow toward a faint buttress. Do not take any of the gullies to your right; they appear easy at first but end in vertical 50–100-ft. splintering walls invisible from below and represent a wish based on a hunch, a poor policy amidst falling stone.

The buttress reaches a saddle where a multitude of fingers confronts you. Which is the highest? Some climbers simply ascend the one that looks most pleasant but the true summit is the leaning spire farthest north, so keep going due east; the toughest moves require only scrambling skills, mild-mannered class 3 – a relief to many neophyte alpinists if a disappointment to others: those mountain warriors and artists of the void who never see a technical line without wishing to scale it. I am as likely to attempt one of these north face routes about as often as your barber says you don't need a haircut. Do not attempt those daunting northern faces if unprepared; a general practitioner would not be fit to perform neurosurgery.

Maude can be gained the following day. Its southwest route consists of a traverse east on a sometimes climbers' path, with some mildly unpleasant gully ups and downs, to the southwest ridge, where an easy scramble over talus, scree (ugh!), then pleasant flower-strewn meadows, provide a view-filled amble to the top.

Far-reaching dioramas now open up to the northwest from either summit, with forests, valleys and watercourses amidst the giants of the North Cascades, including Baker, Shuksan, the chiseled incisors of the Pickets, and the regal snow ridges of Eldorado, as well as the wind-scoured and often sere corrugated hills to the east. A bonus is the view down to the northeast at the twin Ice Lakes, where floating icebergs may be seen throughout the summer. After soaking in the view, you could descend the south face directly via a gully for variety but this is hard-hat country amidst inconveniently-placed blocks of unstable basalt, schist, granidorite and dacite. I honestly cannot always unerringly distinguish which mineral is which. I just recall that they're all loose.

Maude is also famous for its forbidding north face, where a gaggle of rough ice climbers, hoping for a sustained spell of frigid weather in winter or early spring, can embrace the ice and attempt Grade III routes marked by 50–70-degree angles and the need to have sturdy front-point crampons and twin axes. The ridges enclosing these ice pitches are made of different bones than those on the peak's southern aspects. Of interest is that these glaciers on the north face of Maude

CHAPTER SEVENTEEN: FROM HEAVEN'S OWN CAMPSITE

have receded even in our own recent memory and a northeast-facing pocket glacier on Seven-Fingered Jack, mentioned in Beckey, has now completely disappeared. It is as likely that I would succeed on any of these routes as you will profit from investing in Argentinian bonds.

One needs no further proof of man's destructive effect on this once glorious scene; hikers, climbers and all outdoor adventurers are in a perfect

Alpine Hulsea

position to demonstrate courage in the face of ignorance and combat the attack on anthropogenic climate-change deniers. However, we must do so with the caution that, in impugning unawareness or lack of scientific understanding, we may create more resistance than affirmation. Often, an accusation is met with even more robust resistance.

Along the way up both peaks, rare alpine flowers lighten your efforts. The purple ball of a flower with yellow stamens protruding like knitting needles is spiky phacelia, a relative of the waterleafs familiar to all who trek the low Cascade forests in spring. Those gardens of yellow daisies are comprised of the golden, or subalpine, daisy. You may even spot the rare alpine hulsea, with a multitude of yellow daisy-

Spreading (Alpine) Stonecrop

like blossoms emerging from deeply in-cut leaves. It appears more commonly to the south on alpine lava beds; this marks its northernmost range. Lily-white spikes of partridgefoot are omnipresent along with spreading (or alpine) stonecrop. This prize is a species in the *Sedum* family, which includes cactus-like leaves and whose relatives are well-known to gardeners almost everywhere, including the *Sempervirens* species of urban gardens (commonly known as "chicks and hens") and the jade plant, so abundantly potted near indoor windows in many family homes and businesses.

Another rest that evening back in camp is clearly in order, especially given the long drive back on dusty logging roads. In this lofty perch after dusk, far from the urban light-free night sky, gaze across the heavens as meteors, comets and manufactured satellites chase each other across the inky blackness; trace the outlines of the Milky Way, and try to identify the constellations, all of which the vast majority of our city-bound citizens will unfortunately never witness. Best to pack out the next morning, following a well-earned intermission of sleep and breakfast. While most North Cascades climbs are subject to the unbending commands of the weather, these eastside peaks almost always guarantee runs of sunny days and cloudless nights throughout the summer and well into fall - all the more reason to make the long drive. By all means consider visiting these alpine jewels, well within the range of the novice climber; your memories will thank you.

CHAPTER EIGHTEEN
An Enigma Resolved
Bonanza Peak
(9,511')

HIDDEN GEMS OF THE WASHINGTON CASCADES

CHAPTER EIGHTEEN: AN ENIGMA RESOLVED

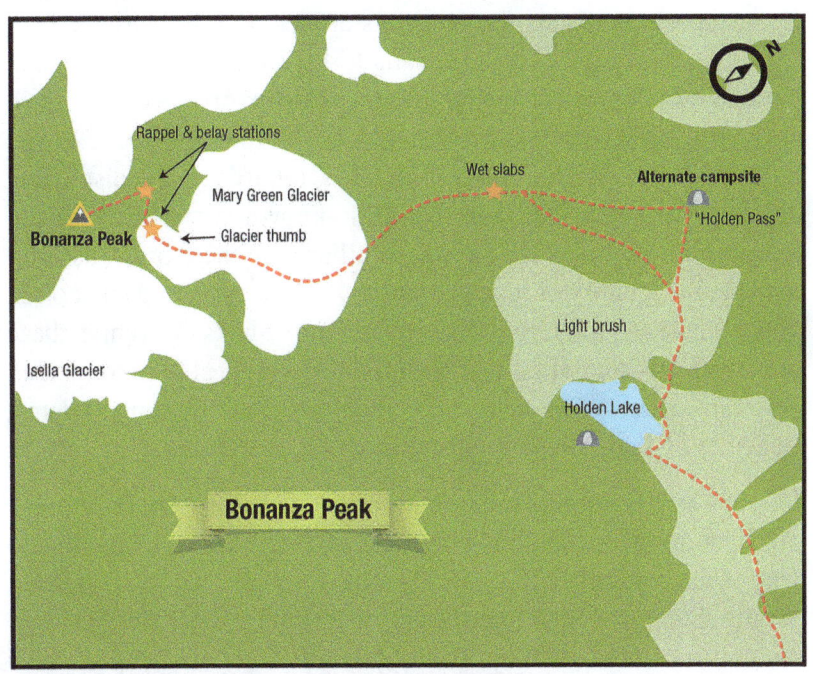

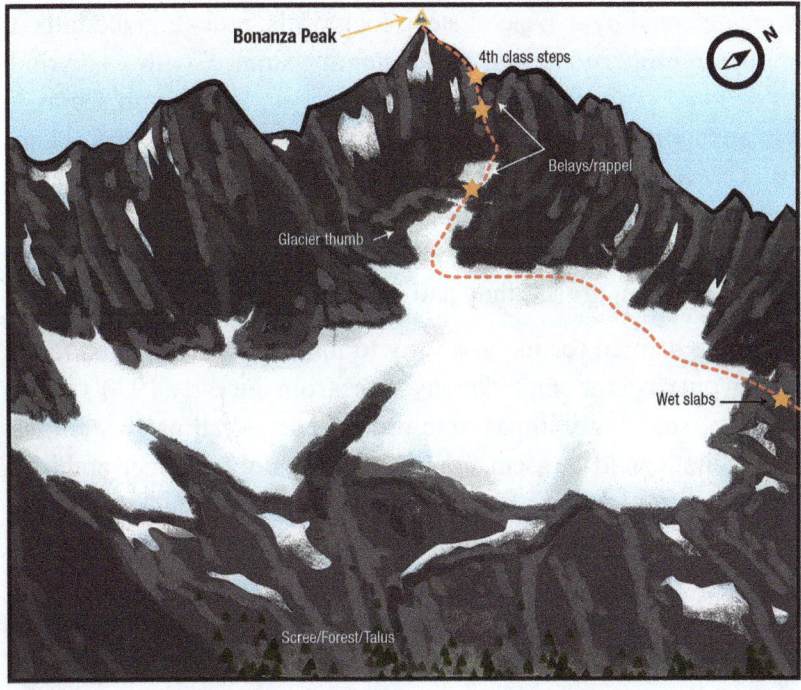

Bonanza stands in singular and sinister isolation. Its massive bulk is like a guard dog who never fails to bark loudly. With complex webs of ridges, glaciers and rock faces, it also involves a complicated approach, involving first a boat, then a bus, then a hike, followed by technical, often unstable rock, thus rebuffing and dispiriting climbers for years. Yet there is a little-known accomplishment in reaching its summit. Ask anyone familiar with the North Cascades to name the identity of its highest non-volcanic peak and most often you will hear replies of "Mt. Stuart" or "Shuksan".While these peaks are spectacular in their own right, the highest point on which you can stand, aside from Mts. Rainier, Little Tahoma, Adams, Baker and Glacier Peak - volcanoes all - is Bonanza.

Relative neglect of this imposing mammoth stems from its earliest, but frustrating, encounters with route-finding puzzles compounded with the complexity of its summit towers. It was labeled "North Star" on early topo maps when the Forest Service was assigning names, although the true North Star is a heap of talus and rubble to its west. The initial attempts on the real Bonanza were defeated by a maze of steep rock walls, rock- and ice-falls of immense proportions, and its sinister appearance, with a labyrinth of serrated pinnacles on its multiple ridges. Here, truth seems to have evaporated. These fearsome features, combined with problems of access, frank terror at encountering the shark-like teeth of the peak's crests, and the topographic mix-up of names, all combined to convince early miners and explorers to claim they had conquered Bonanza when, in fact, they had merely walked up North Star.

Bonanza, named for its proximity to mining claims (which failed to pan out), was attempted many times from the early 1930's but its maze of seemingly impassable routes repelled all early attempts. These first would-be ascensionists unfortunately divorced ambition from reality. However, eager climbers from the Mountaineers and the Portland-based Mazamas, along with private party endeavors, provided valuable information, particularly about the Mary Green Glacier approach, now considered the easiest route to the top. Sometimes, disappointment, exploration, and success all eventually merge.

CHAPTER EIGHTEEN: AN ENIGMA RESOLVED

Those scouting parties, as so often happens, prepared the way for the final triumph. Bonanza's summit was successfully reached in 1937 by a small party, including Joe Leuthold of Mt. Hood fame. Since the 1970's a number of successful ascents have occurred, yet the peak is a complicated and dangerous enigma, one to be attempted, even by its "easiest" route, under stable high-pressure weather conditions. Wind, snow and rain at any time of year could whip up something nasty on this, one of our most knotty of all peaks in the range. To aggravate this conundrum, wicked oncoming weather may not be obvious this far east, as intervening peaks to the west of Bonanza can hide Zephyrus, the Greek god for the western wind (and derivation of the English word "zephyr").

With a favorable forecast, you must begin your tangled journey at the boat dock in the vacation town of Chelan. Try to reserve ahead to the logically-named Lake Chelan Boat Company as tourists often occupy most of the space on the fastest of boats (40 minutes); the slower one could take hours to reach the Holden Landing. This dock is also known for some reason as Lucerne, despite the absence of any village, Swiss-like or not, at this location. You could also drive an extra 17 paved miles to Fields Point on the western side of Lake Chelan to pick up the fast boat there, perhaps saving 30 minutes or so overall. In addition, the crowds are less constricting at Fields Point.

Remember that you must take everything you will require for the next several days, all hopefully ensconced in your largest backpack. From Lucerne, prepare to take a rickety school bus up the 11-mile one-hour ride on the bumpy dirt road to the village of Holden itself. Less troubling than the washboarded drive may be the Lutherans themselves, who now own the village and are known to break out in song with annoying but jovial ditties from the 1940's all the way up to the village; many will vacation there for weeks each summer. Set in the midst of ancient mining activity, the detritus of the mines is astonishing, with tailings much taller than several NBA centers standing on top of each other.

Ancient mining equipment is, to this day, still all strewn about the place, yet Holden remains both a summer retreat and a starting point for many trails and climbs, as well as a tourist attraction. This mountain township itself would seem an anomaly in such a vast wilderness. But human's lust for silver and gold often demolishes our wildest of lands. Indeed, Copper Mountain, just to the south, is riddled with so many mining tunnels, it's a marvel it hasn't collapsed upon itself.

Holden Village, purchased by the Lutheran Church (for $1.00 they say), is not an unpleasant sight. Its cheery log bungalows, cabins and mess halls lend a sort of buoyant aura to this seemingly misplaced island of civilization in the midst of the Chelan wilderness. Try to arrive around noon; the Lutherans know no strangers and you will be invited to an almost-free lunch before you start your trek. The Lutherans unanimously say they will pray for your safe return from the climb, sort of like the Buddhist rituals in the Himalayas, but without the prayer flags, white scarves and yak dung. Should you, God forbid, perish on the peak, rest assured your name will be inscribed on the side of the village's Town Hall, accompanied with the lurid ringing of the church's bell.

Take in some of the sights and signs punctuating the village itself before embarking west up the very road the bus used, but stop after a few minutes' walk at the Bakery, where fresh cinnamon rolls will ease your journey to Holden Lake at 5,276'. The road ends in ¾ mile and there begins the actual trail, here called the Railroad Creek Trail. Another ¾ mile's walk brings you to the junction with the Holden Lake Trail. Take this right-hand turn and climb steeply on this rough but clearly marked pathway to the gem of Holden Lake, surrounded by steep forested slopes on its northern, western and eastern sides.

Alpine larches punctuate these forests, turning golden in fall. Picturesque campsites abound, though many sturdy parties, perhaps cheered on by the cinnamon rolls, ascend the steep northern forest to campsites at "Holden Pass", an unofficial name but a conspicuous gap between Martin Peak to the east and Bonanza itself. Camping here is unpleasant for large parties but two to three tent-sites will prove comfortable.

CHAPTER EIGHTEEN: AN ENIGMA RESOLVED

The climb of the Mary Green Glacier route should begin quite early the following day as unknowable difficulties lie ahead. We raced the sunrise, stumbling over stunted vegetation from the pass. I was less than lucent as we plodded upward, lost in fearful contemplation of Bonanza's reputation. Route flexibility here is feasible until you reach the 6,500' level. The way, at first seemingly obvious but eventually profoundly convoluted, begins here with a lateral traverse westward from a notch through scrub to a series of waterfall- and glacier-scrubbed tonalite, a whitish rock masquerading as granite. Glacial scratch marks are obvious here.

Alpine Larch

One of many cruxes is encountered at these crossings westward, which occur at about the 7,000' to 7,500' level. Here, you must traverse across the sloping 30-degree angled rock which, unluckily, contains the melt-water of the glacier above. All summer, you will be essentially delicately dancing with wet boots across a slope from which, should you fall, your name may well be inscribed in the Holden Village Town Hall as the Lutherans evidently did not pray hard enough for your soul. More solid protection here other than prayer is sparse. Protection can be found as some parties try to place a fixed rope at each end of the three most hazardous spots; many simply skip across these thin waterfalls with hope as their guardian. Spotting opportunity in a crisis, I discovered a thin horizontal crack about 50' below the usual point of traverses and made it across rope-less.

You now progress to the Mary Green Glacier itself after a few 4th-class moves up enormous boulders. The glacier is gently angled at first but you must aim for the prominent "thumb" marking its highest point and adorning the eastern slope. This thumb is far steeper than the glacial walk across the Mary Green so protection is advised. Crampons and ropes are often essential anyway, as Bonanza's glaciers are famous for hidden crevasses. While most Cascade glaciers are in retreat, this thumb appears like an ice sheet in reverse, always present and threatening. After mid-summer, however, its main barrier may be a huge bergschrund near its upper-most section. From this icy stub, accessing the rock beyond may prove difficult in late summer, when a substantial moat blocks further progress for the unprepared.

Silky Phacelia

Once across, 4th-class rock moves up a series of loose gullies (follow the belay loops) may prove difficult to protect due to the inconvenience of down-sloping rock. Your burden is eased somewhat by the comical spikes of silky phacelia, clinging to crevices in the gray rock. It throws up 1' tall stems topped by a pincushion of purple, with orange spikes (its stamens) protruding all about. It is one of the delights almost completely limited to the Cascade Ranges, extending to the Coast and Interior Ranges of British Columbia.

Here, a series of seemingly small decisions could lead to trouble. My climb-mates, more skilled at route-finding, probably grew weary of my expressions of doubt, which were really whimpering's of quacking cowardice. I tried to lie to myself and our party, noting that it takes courage to admit you're afraid, but that was not accepted well by the more skilled among us. At any rate, you can use the loops for belay anchors; these are usually in place on out-jutting horns but test these first. Many are frayed from overuse, overwintering and exposure to the sun. Others seem to have been so frequently used and re-tied that they appeared to be of Gordian complexity. Test, test, test.

CHAPTER EIGHTEEN: AN ENIGMA RESOLVED

Your object is to reach the northeast ridge while still alive and ambulatory. You can see what you think is the summit amongst a series of stony canines and incisors but the true summit lies just beyond, at the southern-most reaches of these jagged obstacles. But if you've come this far, the ridge is negotiable by bypassing the most acute of these towers generally on their eastern side. A jaunt over 3rd-class minor crags brings you to Bonanza's summit. The actual top is marked by a register and by extensive views of a majority of North Cascade peaks east of the crest, along with the large volcanoes, the Dome mini-chain, and Baker and Shuksan to the north. To the immediate southwest lie the Enchantments, with Mt. Stuart barely peeking above the other summits and ridges in the Enchantments– or is Stuart simply jealous that it is but a mere three rope-lengths shorter than Bonanza?

While the views are worth the effort, don't tarry too long; unfortunately, the descent may take as long as the climb itself, what with the need to set up multiple rappels and the protection needed to cross the glacier after its been sitting in the sun all day. In addition, you must re-traverse the awkward down-sloping rock, now wrought with actual waterfalls as sun-loosened snow up top has been melting while you were concentrating on staying alive further up. Always fighting the tyranny of time, it's best to head back to your campsite as rapidly as possible under these sometimes tiresome, tedious, and oft-times precipitous conditions. Set a reasonable turn-around time, generally in summer around 2–3 PM, lest you encounter westerly baleful winds and storms, sneaking up largely unnoticed behind western slopes.

You also probably should walk the three miles back to the Lutheran haven of Holden from the Lake, but if you do, you will be forced to spend the night at an overcrowded campground just west of town. Better to pay for a bunk in one of the rustic lodges (the fee is always quite reasonable). The busses rarely make late afternoon or evening runs back to the landing at the Lake and, even if they did, no boat will pick you up until the next morning anyway unless you've made private (and more expensive) arrangements. Do not expect too much excitement; the audience in Holden has become inured to returning climbers so don't expect a hero's welcome.

Bus and boat, then escaping the annoying optimism of the Lutherans, are small burdens in exchange for a successful ascent of Bonanza as you will reap more than celebration, copper or gold: the satisfaction of attaining the highest, and one of the most complex of non-volcanic summits in the North Cascades.

There are certainly more technically difficult routes on this massif as well. The Soviets visited in 1975 and succeeded on the north face of the southwest peak, rating it a Grade V at 5.9. The south ridge was climbed in 1956 and can be partly viewed from high elevations on the Mary Green route. It has seen the fewest of repeat ascents, even though it was rated no higher than Grade III, low 5th-class, but with extreme exposure. Loose rock and debris cascading off the walls above the Company Glacier made the ascent harrowing. The east side has seen a few additional ascents, but the loose rock has repulsed many parties.

More accessible for the hardened North Cascader is the Company Glacier Route; you can glance over at it from the Mary Green approach. It's as fearsome as it looks, though it had been climbed as early as 1937. Full rock and ice gear are mandatory. An alternative might be the south face, rated at Grade II and 5.5 but, following an aborted attempt, I don't believe the rating (actually, I always imagine this figure is an underestimate after feeble attempts above 5.7). On Bonanza, grading an ascent is hazardous, mostly due to loose rock and lack of adequate perches to place actual, rather than virtual, protection. It might best be left to those who successfully camouflage fear with courage. We can share vicariously in their bravery and optimism. Moreover, unclimbed and even unattempted routes still exist on Bonanza's northern and northeastern walls. The more aspiring rock and ice athletes could add a brick or two on these precipitous parapets from which climbing careers can be built. Because the many routes on Bonanza's north and eastern faces remain unclimbed, perhaps its greatest mysteries are those which remain unsolved.

CHAPTER EIGHTEEN: AN ENIGMA RESOLVED

More popular now than in prior years, the Mary Green route may see a number of parties on a clement weekend. It represents a fusion of the quotidian (cars, boats, hordes of tourists, a civilized township, and a stroll up a dusty road) with the sublime: a climb with spectacular views and challenges sufficient to keep even the skilled route-finder sharp as the fangs surrounding its summit. Also, watch for falling rock if a party is above you. Even this route should be avoided if skies are charred and winds fierce. The massif stands sufficiently tall above timberline that it suffers the worst of any weather from east or west. Nature revels in the quirky delights of her strength. If forecasts are uncertain, stay home. Bonanza's wind-whipped summit is not worth your name being inscribed on the Holden Village Town Hall nor the tragic sound of the town church's peal.

CHAPTER NINETEEN

Infrequently Explored, Some Peaks with No Recorded Ascents

Peaks of the South Cascade Glacier
(7,188'– 8,261')

HIDDEN GEMS OF THE WASHINGTON CASCADES

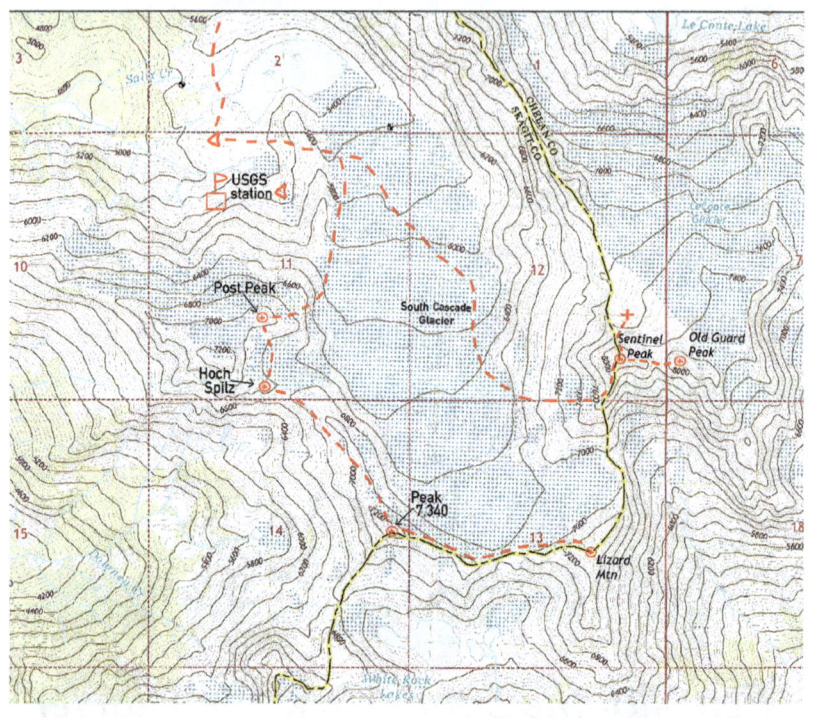

CHAPTER NINETEEN: PEAKS OF THE SOUTH CASCADE GLACIER

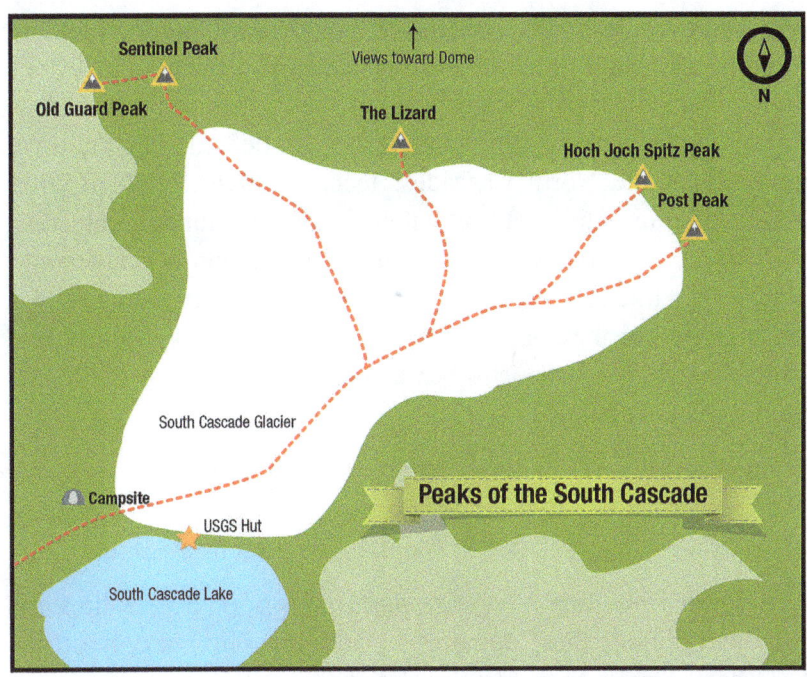

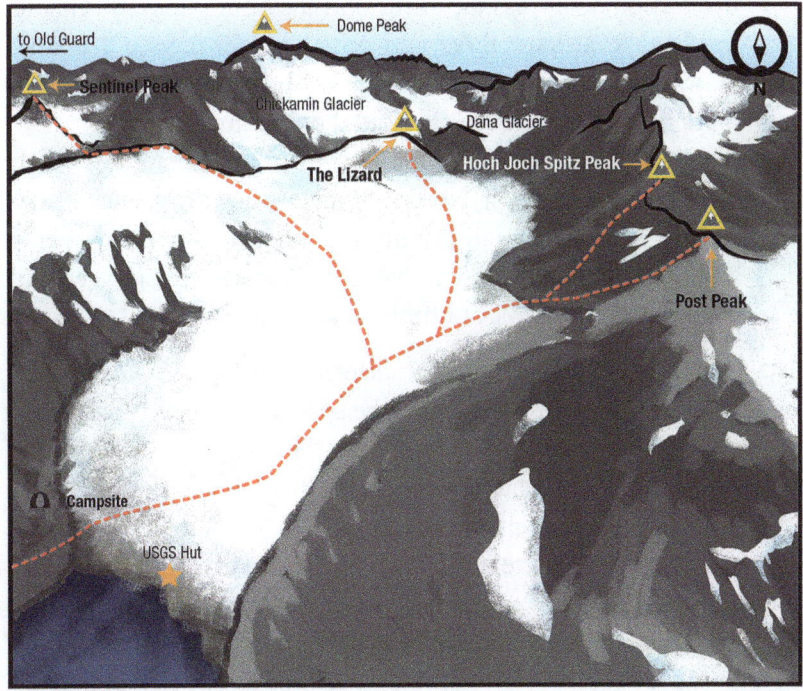

Wouldn't you like to be the first on your block, neighborhood, or even Megalopolis, to climb such peaks as The Lizard, Hoch Joch Spitz, and Post Peak? Never heard of these? Never came close to them? That's because they lie secluded and defended by the usual suspects of the North Cascades: technical brush; sodden paths masquerading as trails, all of which disappear at random intervals; invisibility from many roads and major trails; and by guidebooks who would like to keep these scenic spaces as covert and secluded as possible lest they be overrun by hordes of hikers, backpackers and climbers. Yet the climber's creed is to venture forth into territories unknown.

Therefore, my preference would be to enable those hardy enough (or sufficiently foolish, depending on your point of view) to undertake the journeys described in this chapter. The reasons are three:

- There is minimal to no risk that armies of outdoor enthusiasts will trample these domains because they are not only off the beaten track, there *is* no track to begin with.
- In addition, to access the climbs off the South Cascade Glacier would take at least three and possibly four days. Of course, many climbers would readily give up a few days off work, but there lies a third excuse to avoid these realms:
- None of the peaks you will climb from the glacier are barely recognizable to most North Cascade climbers because they are not particularly tall nor are they that difficult to climb. In addition, they will thus probably remain infrequently visited, even during the peak of climbing season.

However, should you enter this paradise of almost overlooked glaciers and peaks, you will not soon forget the spectacle and surprises which lay in store. Quixotic and exceptional, this area, just south of the National Park, is fortunately protected by the Glacier Peak National Wilderness. It is difficult to reckon why a National Wilderness is much more heavily protected than a National Park but it may have something to do with a park being a place partially devoted to recreation; a wilderness is supposed to be just that – as it was in its natural state, with no roads nor man-made intrusions except trails.

CHAPTER NINETEEN: PEAKS OF THE SOUTH CASCADE GLACIER

This maxim is too often ignored but you can still find dedicated rangers sawing huge blown-down logs across a trail with a two-man hacksaw; electric battery-operated saws are believed by some, perhaps with cult-like worship of the wild, to be too much of a manufactured product, and too noisy to employ in such hallowed ground. Good exercise and good to see that some folks still adhere to the original goals of preservation, at least to a reasonable degree.

Unexpectedly however, in the midst of one of the wildest places you can access in the lower 48, you will still come upon civilization where you'd least expect it: The U.S. Geological Service has constructed a station (more of a hut, really) at the base of the South Cascade Glacier, which has been in retreat since the Station first measured its terminal moraine in 1957. At that time, the hut was placed near the rubble signaling the terminus of the glacier proper, but significant warming has now created a gap of ¼ mile between the glacial terminus and the Station. Nonetheless, research during the summer is still carried out there as this glacier is one of the longest in the range; numerous gauges are in place to monitor not only global warming but to help predict water flow vital to plant and animal life downstream.

I was fortunate at the hut to speak with Erin Whorton, M.S., of the U.S. Geological Survey, who explained that water flow and snowpack are continuously monitored as downstream, reservoirs and agricultural use are dependent on this glacier's outflow. Indeed, the South Cascade River, emanating from the picturesque copper-green moraine lake at the Glacier's base, forms the majority of water that eventually flows into the principal artery of the Cascade River, technically known as its North Fork. If occupied by scientists when you visit, they will be happy (well, perhaps just patient) to explain their projects in this rugged location.

But there is a big "if". A four-wheel drive vehicle with adequate ground clearance combined with judicious route-finding with map and compass or GPS will definitely be of assistance in gaining the glacier. First, you must take a right turn (south) off the main Cascade River Road (#1500) onto Road #1590. This "road" lies just past the

Mineral Park Campground, about 16½ miles from Marblemount. Note: *The 100 Hikes, Washington's Glacier Peak Region* by Spring and Manning misnames this last campground as "the Mineral Creek Campground". The road had been blocked by blowdown for a number of years from 1990 through the early years of this century but is now passable with high-clearance vehicles for about 1½ miles, where a small parking area, usually devoid of cars, brings you to the South Cascade River Trail, #769, about 1,600' in elevation.

In about ½ mile, the main trail branches left and, although it is unmaintained, it can be followed with some bushwhacking by sticking to the river's edge. It will lead you to the terminus of the Middle Cascade Glacier; therefore, you should not be tempted to follow it. If you do, you will be forlornly abandoned in a hole, a nice valley to admire first-growth timber (mostly alders and hemlocks) but from which any reasonable person would be hard-pressed to make any but the most technically difficult, cliff-ridden and brushy ascents. It might be feasible to reach the summit of Spider Mountain from here but not without encountering what-all in terms of prickly flora and corn lily traverses, all of which may leave you with stinging scratches and severely deformed ankles. Best to leave Spider to the routes made achievable from the Ptarmigan Traverse east of this peak.

White Rhododendron

At this same ½ mile point, the trail that proceeds straight ahead may look promising, and indeed it is the route to the peaks you *can* climb, all without much technical metal, although crampons and ice ax are necessary. Yet as is so often the case, the path soon becomes a boot-beaten boulevard entangled in white rhododendron, sticky currant, salmonberry and Devil's club, and soon, in about one mile, surrenders entirely to the shrubbery. Your best bet is to follow the river in heavier timber about 200–300 yards on the north side of the South Fork, but in late summer, walking directly in the river's path, hopefully on occasional gravel bars, seems feasible.

Hooded Ladies' Tresses

There are, however, delights in store; the bushwhacking becomes less fearsome as you progress uphill and soon you can see the huge South Cascade Glacier, one of the largest in the range and one whose terminus still lies lower than most of our other large glaciers because of ridgeline shading effects. Other charms are the many species within the Orchid and Lily Families to be found and identified, especially the fragrant snow-white bog orchids thriving in the ever-present swamps, and a garden of hooded ladies' tresses, whose white flowers are arranged in a spiral down its stem; these are especially abundant at around 5,100' in a damp part of the trek, just as the trees give way to the views of the Glacier. In no other spot that I've encountered in 60 years of climbing in the North Cascades have I spied more of these enchanted floral gems. Their Latin species name (*Spiranthes romanzoffiana*) honors the Russian Count Romanzoff, an 18th Century explorer and amateur botanist.

Your goal is to attain the morainal lake, named on maps, of course, as "South Cascade Lake" at about 5,292' elevation. Although it lies at the former terminal moraine of the glacier, where camping would be uncomfortable at best, campsites are available in flatter terrain on the southeastern side of the lake, hollowed out by the scientists, or in the meadows above the lake on its southern side. Expect to see icebergs floating in this shaded glade, where sunshine, even on bluebird days, is more valuable than gold. It is astonishing, even though you know it will be there, to see the retreat of the Glacier in recent years.

From these campsites, you can view the entire sweep of the Glacier, angling southeast and shouldered by jagged peaks and spires on both its east and west sides, many of them bearing the unfair ignominy of remaining anonymous and some which possibly have remained virginal to this day. It is to these that you should turn your attention in the days which follow. Visit the hut and talk with any scientists hovering about (you can identify them as the males all have beards and all the women have tattered stringy shorts – some stereotypes are really true). Gaze at sunset on this magnificent panorama of glacial ice, shards of icebergs in the green lake, pinnacles on high, and stars unseen by your city-bound friends. You are safe in this glorious basin, and secure with the realization that very few have preceded you, even to this day.

But if it's your aim to climb, there's more to accomplish than you may realize. Depending on your goal, you can plod up the glacier on its east or west side. On the east lie the more well-known peaks of Sentinel and Old Guard, while the west side holds an opportunity to climb/scramble even lesser-known terrain. By doing so, you may summit a line of serrated peaks and points that even the well-educated North Cascades veteran may never have visited.

I imagine that all these summits have been reached but records of several of these points are nonexistent; they may still be untouched. Moreover, they all lack registers on their tops, a testament to the infrequency of summit guests. The glacier is of moderate angle and, depending on time of year, most parties fail to rope up. This may prove to be a fatal choice as the glacier can be heavily crevassed. Still, by adhering to its sides, one can be reasonably safe, as the crevasses which do form are mainly in the middle, as is typical of these gently sloped frozen rivers. Anyway, the peaks of scrambling interest lie to the west and east, except for one at the very head of the glacier.

Proceeding up the west side, there are a number of apparently sharp spires whose climbing histories remain unknown. You may try your luck on these, though the rock is a mess of crumbling granidiorite and composited stone as easily loosened as a disintegrating stack of marbles. There is no record of ascents but I'm certain these prominent steeples have been climbed, though no climbing guide lists them as distinct summits. It appears that some technical pitches

CHAPTER NINETEEN: PEAKS OF THE SOUTH CASCADE GLACIER

would be encountered, although the lack of adequate crannies, chimneys or gullies would make protection thorny at best. The first named peak of interest lies to the south of these tottering towers. Beckey has christened it **Post Peak (7,188')**, to honor Austin Post, an early productive and creative explorer of these ranges. Post has no officially sanctioned name and most topo maps fail to bestow one but it has a prominent summit well above the western reach of ice on the glacier.

Approach it from the glacier's western fringe at about ¾ mile up, at the 6,600' level. Begin this nontechnical ascent from the high point of the snowy basin which points a finger towards the summit. This actually forms the highest and northern-most point on the blocky ridge which borders the glacier at about 6,800' elevation. Aim for a snow saddle just south of this summit, then tackle the loose talus on Post's west side to arrive at the top in about one or two hours' time from the lake.

Post may have no officially-approved title but the views, especially to the south, are as unexpected as they are spectacular. When ensconced in the glacier's hollow, one is essentially in a frozen valley. But by scaling Post, you gain the first views of what lies to its southwest: the incredible north face of Dome shining in the sun, whose rays glance off the Spire, Dana and Chikamin Glaciers like shards of pure white light. Each is heavily crevassed and sheds, in their terminal moraines, enormous icy blocks, the remains of towering seracs from above. These now litter their lowest slopes like so many ice cubes in the bottom of a colossal cocktail. That so much ice could remain frozen is a wonder this far south in the Range, but the northern exposure of the Dome Peak massif shields these slopes from the sun just long enough to allow a buildup of snow each year. Thankfully, thus far, global warming has not seemed to subdue this spectacle.

From Post, **Hoch Joch Spitz (7,360')** is a matter of another mile or so up the glacier, but beware of western cliffs plunging off into the Downey Creek Valley. Its name may have an origin of which someone is aware but it remains unclear to me. Nomenclature aside, its summit can be attained by aiming at the highest point on the ridge south of Post Peak. Here lies a col to its north, from which an easy class-3 scramble leads southwest to its blocky top. This summit, actually in most years a mere nunataq, pokes its rocky top out from the earthen and stony substrate which lies hidden under the snows. Its views match those from Post, but on its top, you are even closer to the panorama of the Dome massif's north face.

Marching further up the glacier, you can also summit a peak which actually is nameless. In Beckey, it's called **Peak 7,340**. It forms the southern-most high point off the western shoulder of the glacier and actually looks like a mountain. It has a pointed summit which rises above the ice sheet and requires another 1¼ mile slog up the snow to reach its top-most rocky crest. Ascend moderately steep (30-degree) ice and snow, then blocky chunks of rock on its north aspect to attain the summit. Even better views of the north face of Dome dominate the scene, but you also can see the aptly-named twin-topped Gunsight Peak to Dome's east, and, presiding over these southern views, Glacier Peak to the south. Well down below, the shimmering White Rock Lakes gleam; campsites from here on the Ptarmigan Traverse allow National Geographic-quality views of the Dome massif. Also, turn to look north and see how far you've come from South Cascade Lake.

While all three of these peaks can be climbed in a day, don't stop there as the best of the west lies ahead, at the very apex of the glacier: **The Lizard (7,400')** and its twin summits. These may have appeared to someone like a reptile, although to me, the resemblance is pure imagination sprung from the brain of a feverish early explorer. At any rate, if you've come this far, there's no reason *not* to scale The Lizard. You begin at the head of the glacier and clamber over blocks of somewhat loose rock to reach its western summit, then argue over whether that is the actual top. You can ramble to the notch between these two high points to the eastern summit but it makes little difference. From either one, the other looks higher and the topo's don't much help. Anyway, in such a snow-bound wilderness, the true difference between fact and fiction

CHAPTER NINETEEN: PEAKS OF THE SOUTH CASCADE GLACIER

can be easily ignored; the numbers may not matter as much as the journey itself.

From this viewpoint, you have an unrestricted panorama of the north faces and pinnacles guarding the summits of the entire Dome range, all draped with Himalayan-like ice. These include not only the heavily crevassed glaciers of crystalline snow mentioned above, but Dome's spires to its west, with names to strike fear into the souls of scramblers and climbers alike: Hydramatic Spire appears as a needle to Dome's immediate west, followed eastward to the steeples of Overdrive and Dynaflow Towers, and culminating in Spire Point, with the Spire Glacier to its northwest.

To the east of Dome, twin-topped Gunsight, Sinister (a name to repel most climbers), and Agnes Mountain shine against the hopefully blue sky, while to the north, the giants of the Ptarmigan Traverse stand proud, especially Spider and Formidable. Even the peaks south of Cascade Pass, like Magic and Mixup Mountains can be glimpsed. Look down as well at the tiny tarns guarding the White Rock Lakes, from which the most imposing photos of Dome itself populate the slick coffee table books of the Cascades. There is no finer viewpoint of the peaks, lakes, waterfalls and forested valleys to the south than from this perch at the very origin of the South Cascade Glacier, about as otherworldly to the human eye as it gets.

Should you, the next day, or the first climbing day if you are restricted in time, wish to scale the slopes to the east of the glacier, you can gain two better-known and more popular peaks, familiar because of their proximity to the famous Ptarmigan Traverse on their eastern sides. These are sometimes climbed by ambitious and vigorous Traverse parties on their way past Dome.

The first, and most easily accessed from the eastern shoulder of the glacier, is **Sentinel Peak (8,261')**. You can tell from its altitude that it requires more climbing than the peaks forming the glacier's western crest. It is easily sighted as the most prominent summit on the glacier's eastern fringe. From the upper reaches of the glacier, ascend in a northerly direction over talus, snow and occasional welcome bursts of heather, to greet the southwestern aspect of Sentinel's southern slopes. From about 7,100', you meet the main rock forming the southwest ridge and face. This might appear menacing but actually it holds the key to a scrambling ascent to the top. Good holds on surprisingly solid rock make this 3rd-class route enjoyable for the average scrambler.

From the summit, views are even more prolific than from the Lizard as you can now follow much of the Ptarmigan Traverse from its genesis at Cascade Pass through Magic and Mixup Peaks to Old Guard and Le Conte. To your northwest, the brooding hulk of Johannesburg menaces, and even north beyond, Sahale and Boston Peaks come into view along with the tips of Forbidden and Eldorado as well.

An additional bonus is the view down to Yang Yang Lakes (don't ask), actually a series of lakelets late in summer, and another slightly larger body of water to its south: Le Conte Lake. You can also glean a jagged ridge of spiky needles heading east to LeConte Mountain called the Sprenger Spires. Their ascents are rated as "easy 5th-class rock" but to me, they look unapproachable, though a route from the South Cascade Glacier has been achieved after a long day of protected climbing on disintegrating rock.

If you've accomplished Sentinel, another peak close by and accessible to all scramblers lies in wait for the peak-bagger: **Old Guard (8,240')**. It forms the eastern-most extension of a sharp ridge between it and Sentinel. The Le Conte Glacier clings precipitously from its northern flank. The first ascents were made from the west, then the southeast, but were deemed tricky due to brush and route-finding as they originate deep in forested valleys. Nonetheless, early explorers in these river basins reached the Le Conte Glacier, from which easy scrambling led to the summit.

However, from the South Cascade Glacier, the easiest route (and thus the one I prefer), is to down-climb 3rd-class fairly stable rock from Sentinel to the gap between Sentinel and Old Guard, then descend 300' to reach the Le Conte Glacier. Though Beckey

CHAPTER NINETEEN: PEAKS OF THE SOUTH CASCADE GLACIER

recommends a rappel into the bergschrund, then a tippy-toe across the head of the Le Conte Glacier, in many years due to glacial shrinkage it is possible to work around the 'schrund on rock with nicely sized handholds to gain Old Guard's south face, from where class-3 rock makes for a pleasant jaunt to the top.

While the views from Old Guard are essentially the same as from Sentinel, one can actually spy more of the Ptarmigan Traverse Route from this summit. Moreover, you've gained another peak to add to your climbing résumé. Approaches from the east or directly from tricky gullies lower on the South Cascade Glacier have been mooted, but they appear to encounter rugged cliffy terrain, falling rock and steeper ice and snow. Besides, Sentinel and Old Guard are only about one hour apart, so you may as well climb both; it's a long day's outing but feasible for the average party.

A few stout parties have made the ascent of **Le Conte Mountain (7,762')** from the South Cascade Glacier but this would entail discerning which of many gullies doesn't end in a high 5th-class wall. You could make a long traverse to gain the Le Conte Glacier through a gap south of Sentinel, then a steep icy ascent, then 3rd-class rock to Le Conte's actual base, from which easy rock leads to the top. This appears feasible for a strong party starting early in the morning, but this venture would seem to be a lengthy exercise. Le Conte is most easily accessed from Yang Yang Lakes on the Ptarmigan Traverse by ascending the mountain's eastern flanks.

From base camp, it will take another day to follow the South Cascade River down the valley and then to locate the largely overgrown South Fork Trail, but your trip to this wilderness has provided views both mighty and unique. Indeed, it appears that they have been shared by only a handful of groups in the past. Only those who have dared such arduous journeys can achieve such splendid rewards. True, these routes and peaks are becoming more popular but it is likely that you will meet no other climbing parties on your exploits here, in the midst of some of the wildest, least-travelled terrain in all the North Cascades – and perhaps be educated by a geologist along the way.

CHAPTER TWENTY

Imposing but not Unclimbable

Mt. Formidable
(8,325')

HIDDEN GEMS OF THE WASHINGTON CASCADES

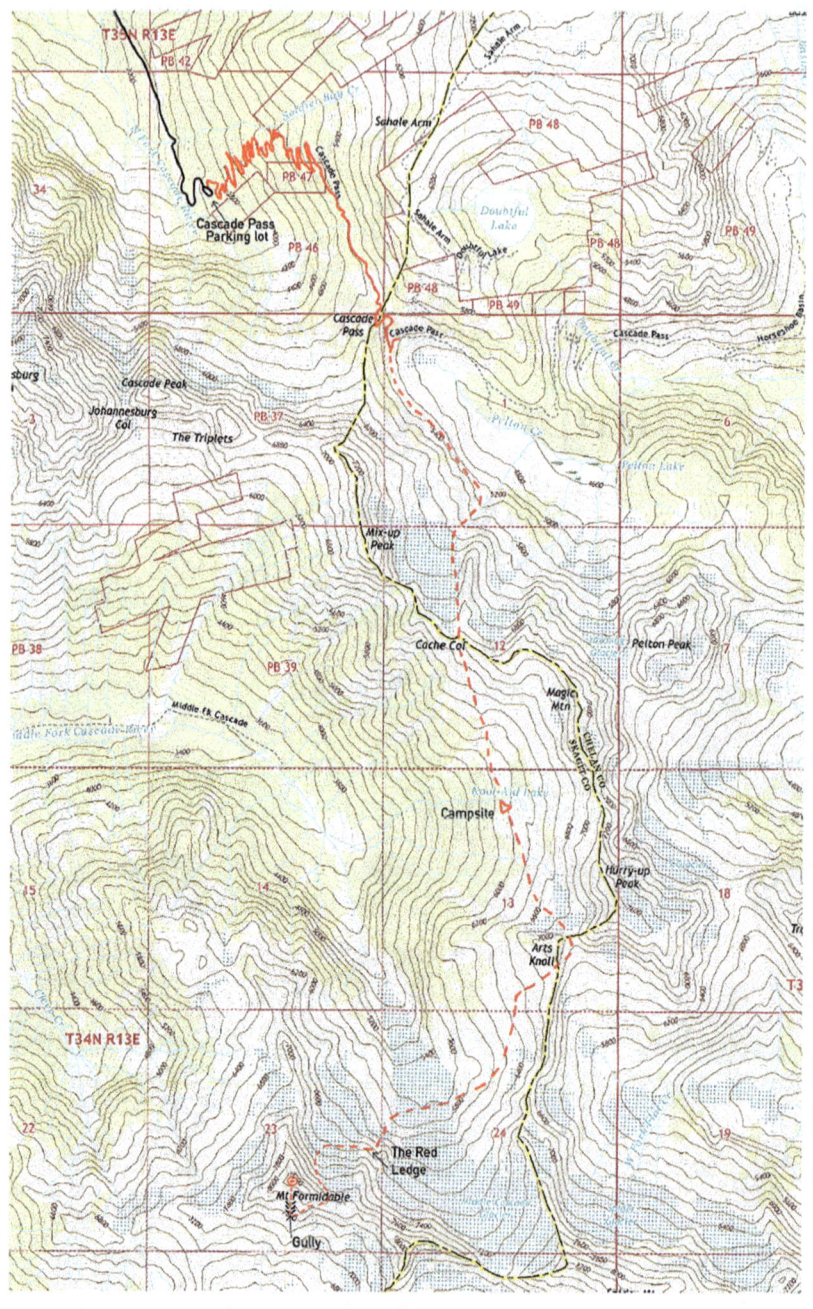

CHAPTER TWENTY: IMPOSING BUT NOT UNCLIMBABLE

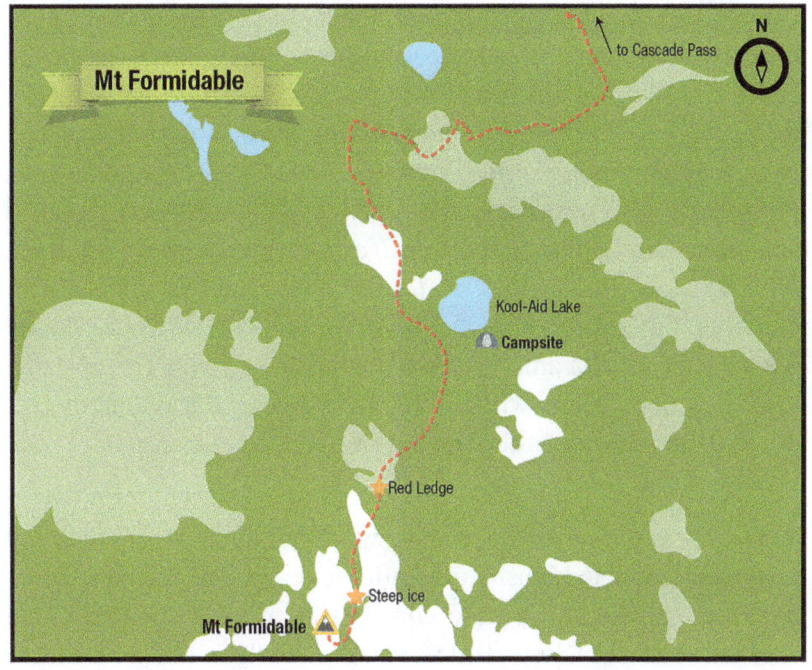

One of the original North Cascades explorers, Herman Ulrichs, conceived the name of this peak in his 1934 explorations of the North and Middle branches of the Cascade River, stating "I suggest the name 'Mt. Formidable' as expressing the quality of this peak." Now a semi-popular climb from the fabled Ptarmigan Traverse, Formidable also poses a modest challenge to Northwest climbers as a three-day outing, its north ridge route a reasonable scramble on 3rd-to-low-5th-class rock after some occasionally steep glacier climbing, but mostly on moderate snow and ice. For those who do not have the time or ambition to accomplish the entire Traverse, the route described below will accomplish a weekend's ascent, though not without some careful planning lest you encounter greater peril than required.

While you could make the mistake we did of approaching the peak up the untrammeled brush of the Middle Fork of the Cascade River to reach the Middle Cascade Glacier (described in Beckey as an alternative to the North Ridge Route), surely a more agreeable beginning would be the familiar yet spectacular 3.7 mile trail to Cascade Pass. Here, the views are special, particularly west to Eldorado, its summit clothed in crystalline white and featuring its sharply-shaped snow-bound north ridge, which most parties must scale to reach its summit.

To the south lie multi-summited Johannesburg; then to its east, The Triplets, which actually spear the sky with three well-defined peaks. Next door, find Cascade Peak. Further south, the Ptarmigan Traverse peaks of Magic and Mixup almost hide the shy north face of Formidable, whose summit can be glimpsed from the pass. To the north, Sahale stands out, concealing the acutely angled thumb of Boston Peak to its north. These familiar Cascade Pass peaks are like a fine aged vintage port; despite repeated visits, they prove to be delicious hosts which enrich us further with the passing of time.

Prepare, however, to have company, even on a weekday and even under petulant skies. The parking area at the Cascade Pass trailhead often seems more crowded than that of a Costco on a winter's weekend. More hikers have tread the 3½-mile switch-backed

CHAPTER TWENTY: IMPOSING BUT NOT UNCLIMBABLE

thoroughfare to Cascade Pass, mistakenly called a trail, than moths drawn to a light bulb. You may take in the crowd-pleasing views, perhaps overly smug in the knowledge that even more glorious sights and off-trail travel plus actual climbing is in your future.

Indeed, a pecking order has unfortunately arisen between hikers and climbers, the latter regarding the former as less adventurous, less capable, less gifted, or less fearless than those who dare to ascend these mighty mountains. Yet nothing could be further from the truth.

I have known, and tried to keep up with, many folks who prefer to hike rather than climb. There may, however, be excellent reasons for their inclination not to climb, including lack of experience; having no training in the ropes and hardware of climbing; no interest thereof; lack of a mentor or leader among hiking friends; or simply wishing to enjoy the outdoors from the safety of a trail. Being a hiker rather than a climber may not be due to timidity but instead may be more about choice and circumstance. We all started as hikers and we all should take delight and value the allure of these majestic views, either from a trail or from the heights of a mountain. In fact, it may be from lower tracts that these mighty giants of the North Cascades yield the finest of spectacles. Think of the views from an airplane flying over a mountain range; it is only from its lowest path that these peaks clothe themselves in their loveliest wardrobes.

Caution: This route is closest to Beckey's "Southeast Route", which appears to be the one preferred by Ptarmigan Traverse parties; it remains higher, and does not approach the Formidable-Spider col. While I propose the longer, but technically less difficult Southeast Route, our adventurous leader eventually proved that her choice, described below, would save time. In the event, we adopted a fudge of a compromise that, by its nature, left no one totally satisfied but eventually worked to all our benefit. To some, it is dauntingly complex, but most non-Traverse parties will find it more direct. While it does encounter the infamous "Red Ledge", it continues to climb on either loose 3rd-to-4th class rubble or, depending on season, steep ice or snow. It continues up a gully on, then above, the Middle Cascade Glacier, but the ascent up this eastern gully can include treacherous black ice or low 5th-class rock, though mostly with stable holds. Following this line will take strength and precision; even with both, it is not without risks.

I have taken this approach twice under varying conditions. From my early perspective, the route I propose here appeared quite straightforward; this sanguine outlook proved myopic. It is not as simple or easy technically as Beckey's "Southeast Route" (which really has little to do with the southern fortress of the mountain) but it is more direct, saves time and is quite feasible for parties comfortable with steep glacier travel and low 5th-class climbing.

If your goal is to combine a climb of Formidable with that of Spider, either in a one- to two-day outing, stick with Beckey's accurate instructions under his "Southeast Route" description. However, if you are content with climbing Formidable alone from Cascade Pass, I believe the route suggested below, while beyond a scramble, will in the long run save time for a pleasant one-to-two-day foray into one of the Ptarmigan Traverse's most mind-bending scenery. Was our plan reckless or resolute? We saw it as neither: an opportunity as much as a threat.

From the pass, eye-filling but almost too popular a spot, proceed southeast on the well-worn passage up the Mix-up Arm to the Cache Glacier (usually absent crevasses) and ascend gently to Cache Col. In doing so, you are essentially trekking the northern genesis of the famed Ptarmigan Traverse. Next, after luxuriating in the views south to Magic, Mix-up, Spider and LeConte Peaks and north to Sahale and Boston, descend about 500' to the charmed tarn of Kool-Aid Lake (named by the obviously parched first traverse party) at 6,120'. Views out to Dome from this spot are both precious and mighty at the same time. Dome's north face, with its

Tall Indian Paintbrush

CHAPTER TWENTY: IMPOSING BUT NOT UNCLIMBABLE

Dana and Chickamin Glaciers, predominates, but Spire Point, Sentinel and Old Guard stand proud against the hopefully welcoming sky.

Here, camp just above the lake on benches at one of the world-class base camps of the North Cascades, these around 6,130'. See if you can identify the two species of crimson Indian paintbrush. The taller species has leaves that taper to points, while the harsh paintbrush has a more bristly stem and upper leaves which end in a three-pronged terminus.

Those tiny yellow flowers are usually fan-leaved cinquefoil; while the other small yellow flowers which color these divine meadows near the lake and its streams are subalpine buttercups, often spouting blossoms when late spring snow still covers these meadows. Indeed, it is the heat generated by the plant itself that melts away its snowy surroundings.

Harsh Indian Paintbrush

By the way, you can tell the difference between all buttercups and cinquefoils as the buttercups shine brightly with their waxy sheen, and their petals are never notched; the cinquefoil's petals are flat, without glitter and are almost always slightly cleft in two. Small white spikes betray partridgefoot, obligatory in the alpine meadowlands of the Cascades.

Fortunately for those of us who shudder at anything over 5.7, the views from here to Formidable's north and northeast faces only *appear* to present problems which are... well, formidable. Viewed from this spot, your future might seem easier to embrace if it were not so difficult to grasp. But rest well, for the next day's climb, while time-consuming and

Patridgefoot

complex, is more benign that it appears. It begins on the heather and grass slopes above the lake but remains at first at about the 6,200' level. You will be following Beckey's "North Ridge Route" but only as an approximation.

You next continue south but ascend gently at first to the base of a bluff, bypassing Art's Knoll on its east side and arriving at a menacing-looking cliff forming Formidable's northeastern face. Here, a previously-hidden ledge ("The Red Ledge," more gray than red), is airily exposed but quite broad ("broad-as-a-sidewalk"- that never reassured me much). Many parties place some protection here. It's not too difficult a crossing but its exposure can make some climbers as nervous as a guilty burglar in a police line-up. Interesting how, on a climb, time moves in an elastic fashion, slowing down at the trickiest pitches, speeding up on more friendly ground.

This moderate ascent ends in some talus and then a flowery meadow at 6,700'. Ascend briefly to the edge of the Middle Cascade Glacier just above its awe-inspiring icefall, then climb its 30-to-40-degree slopes, avoiding any late-season crevasses, to the saddle just east of what appears to be the main col. This ascent can be harrowing for those unaccustomed to steep ice and double-ax technique, particularly late in summer when stone-cold ice replaces snow. Corded climbing with judicious placement of ice screws is mandatory here unless your name is Alex Honnold. Climb this headwall to reach one of the many Formidable-Art's Knoll saddles, at 7,400'.

From the col, descend a few hundred feet (always disheartening), then climb the ridge for several hundred feet. You must down-climb again, this time to the west, to reach the Formidable Glacier decorating the peak's northeastern face. Then ascend gently southeast, passing two bouldery gullies to the main spur plummeting south from the summit. Do not attempt to climb the spur (as we mistakenly did on our first approach) as it consists of un-protectable rock the consistency of beach sand. Instead cross over the spur to the third gully descending southeast and climb this also-loose but sounder chute (class 3–4 – helmets imperative)

CHAPTER TWENTY: IMPOSING BUT NOT UNCLIMBABLE

to a permanent snowfield facing south-southwest, then turn right to gain a saddle on the ridge proper. This route avoids the usual attempts to reach the Spider-Formidable col; more direct yet only slightly more difficult, it is preferred unless your (worthy) goal is to conquer Spider as well.

The majority of climbing on this ridge consists of boulder hopping, however with unsettling exposure frequently encountered; belays at several points (rated at about 5.0) would come in handy for the weekend climber. When problems arise, as they often do, take to the west side of this ridge, where holds are both more conspicuous and stable. From about the 7,900' level, however, it's a 3rd-class scramble to the top-most jumble of boulders.

From here there are too many peaks to name but the view south is noteworthy, with all the Ptarmigan Traverse Peaks, the impressive north walls of Dome defended by the tremendously glaciated ice of the Dana and Chickamin Glaciers, and Glacier Peak itself hulking in the distance. Look north to the start of the Ptarmigan Traverse and sudden slopes heading east and out to the thirsty and lonely hills of eastern Washington. You can also see the northern tip of Lake Chelan to the southeast. To the northwest, Mt. Baker stands white and proud while on a clear day, Glacier Peak rules the southeastern skyline.

Moss Campion

Closer inspection around the summit reveals a miniature gardenland of purple spiky phacelia; crystal white Sitka mistmaiden, seemingly blooming directly off its rock-bound substrate and with neatly scalloped leaves hiding bashfully in the crevices and damp gullies just beneath the summit; and the familiar moss campion, plastered against angled rock faces, masquerading as moss with its pad of tiny leaves and rose-purple flowers standing out from its yellow-green cushioned base.

One would hope you are attempting this climb under friendly skies. Sudden storms out of the oceanic west can sneak up unseen at first, partially hidden by the bulk of Johannesburg. While modern-day forecasts have usually proven accurate, they cannot pinpoint what weather will bless or haunt you in these regions and its many small ecosystems. Skies and clouds can become incensed quickly; thus the climber must remove emotion from reality. A retreat from this wind-whipped summit or its north ridge, so exposed to the elements, is no failure. Success can only be ensured when everyone returns to base camp in a somewhat healthy, though enervated, manner.

Most parties camp a second night at Kool-Aid Lake (we certainly did after both of our ascents). At the lake, you can appreciate the black alpine sedge in the meadows encircling the shore, while farther from the waters, find the reddish seed-heads of leather-leaf saxifrage; light violet wandering daisy; and the deep-burgundy sparsely-flowered blooms of bird's-beak lousewort, with its finely dissected leaves. The next day includes the inevitable trek back to the SUV's which reign at the Cascade Pass parking lot.

Black Alpine Sedge

This ascent really should be a three-day outing as the drive back to the Seattle or Portland area is at least four to seven hours in duration and fraught with more danger than the climb itself. You will be exhausted after the lengthy and icy dance out. We all know someone who fell asleep at the wheel, coffee and music notwithstanding. There are no belays on I-5. Nonetheless, Formidable makes a fine 3–4-day destination if you are searching for an accessible and relatively feasible climb in the Cascade Pass area, notable not only for its sheer walls and snowy environs but for its relative ease of access (read lack of brush) and the magnificent views from its summit.

CHAPTER TWENTY: IMPOSING BUT NOT UNCLIMBABLE

Moreover, you will likely be the sole party in the area attempting the ascent. A few adventurous Ptarmigan Traverse through-hikers may try the south or southwest routes but these would hamper progress on the Traverse by several days. Best to go in mid-to-late-summer for the flowers, but crampons and ice ax plus some rock pro is advised in any season. While its imposing form and terrifying walls may be formidable, the way to its summit would have impressed Mr. Ulrichs as quite reasonable indeed.

CHAPTER TWENTY-ONE

The Panorama Prevails

Mount Buckner
(9,192')

CHAPTER TWENTY-ONE: THE PANORAMA PREVAILS

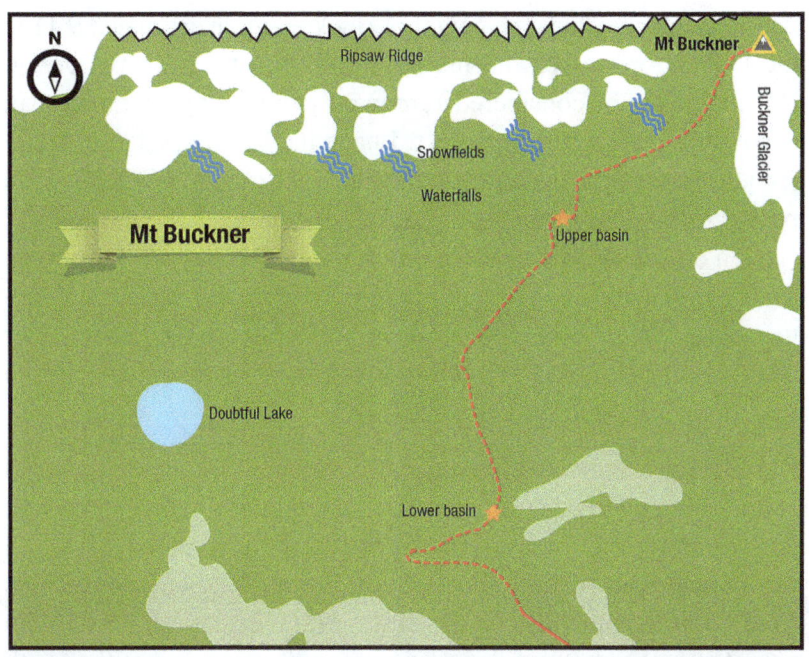

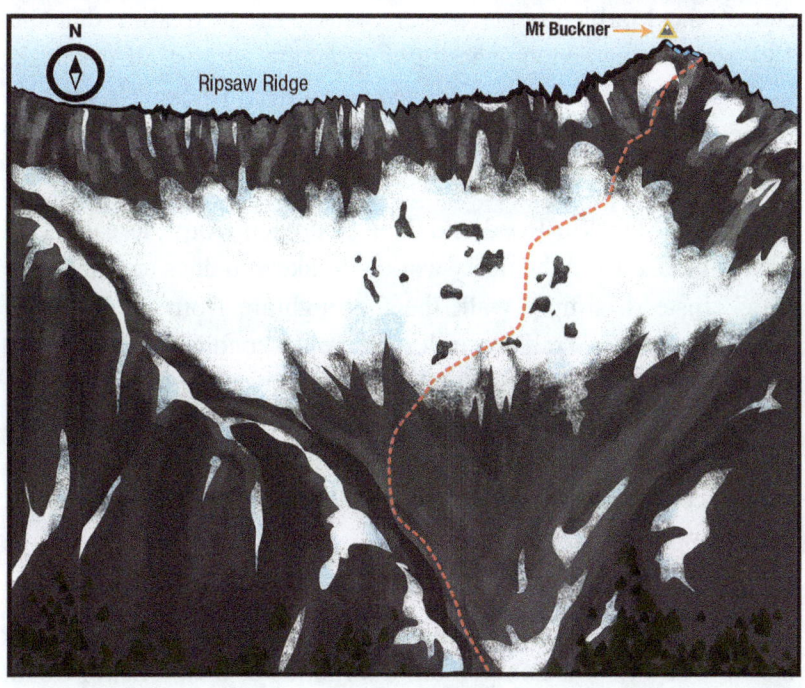

199

Although Beckey lists the height of Buckner as an estimated 9,114', the USGS topo gives the higher elevation, one I always prefer. Buckner could be considered a frequently-climbed peak rather than a feature in a *Hidden Gems* text. I have included it because, while it could be regarded as one of the commonly-climbed Cascade Pass peaks, in fact, it is often overlooked on the west by the Sahale/Boston crowd, or by those heading south on the popular Ptarmigan Traverse. It could even be a jumping-off site for those brave enough to tackle Goode or Logan (whose north-facing Banded Glacier could also be included – a senior Mountaineer member led us up its first direct ascent in the early 1970's).

But Buckner (named after an early miner – what isn't?) holds charms enough to warrant more attention than it's usually received. Its summit register, replaced in the early 2000's, signaled just seven other successful parties, although a number of subsequent ascents have been documented online since. Nonetheless, all those who view the color photo of the slim horizontal panorama at the south end of the Marblemount Ranger Station should realize that this 180-degree view, encompassing and naming almost all the peaks in the North Cascades, was indeed taken from Buckner's summit. In fact, if it's far-flung views you're after, you could do little better than make this class-3 ascent.

Ignore the Stehekin Road and Trail approach from the east. This road is blocked and the dusty walk will take you days to reach base camp. Instead, simply walk the thoroughfare from the west via the Cascade Pass Trail 3½ miles before descending past the entry to what used to be the base camp for Buckner climbs: Horseshoe Basin. Just as with Cascade Pass, too many humans trampled the greenery and camping is justifiably forbidden in this, the most magnificent of basins (see below) in all our range. You will enter it tomorrow on climb day.

To camp for the night, walk another downhill mile to Basin Creek Camp, or, if that's full, as is often the case, trek another mile and a half to Cottonwood Camp, the old terminus of the Stehekin Road. Yes, you will have to ascend these miles the next day but with just a day pack sans technical gear. Note the numerous Sitka mountain ash trees as you descend from the Pass.

Depending on the season, they may bear small white flowers but these tend to be short-lived. Most folks only notice these shrub-like trees, usually about 5–10' tall, in fruit, usually about mid-July through August, when their intense scarlet berries are favored by bears. (Humans find them unpleasant at best and disgusting at worst.) On climb day, pack up to re-climb the trail to its junction with the Horseshoe Basin Trail, now on your right, not regularly maintained, but its single mile to the first full glimpse of this glorious Basin is easily navigated.

Sitka Mountain Ash

Whatever your goal, once deeper in this magnificent basin it is the view upwards that astonishes. Gaze toward the cirque headed by the Sahale and Davenport Glaciers. First, note the pyramidal Boston Peak, with its northern outpost of Sharkfin Tower, then look past the jagged incisors of Ripsaw Ridge, and around to the permanent ice fields fronting the western faces of Buckner and Booker Peaks. Furious waterfalls scour these walls, emptying their streams in cascades plunging thousands of feet, almost too numerous to count. In no other range aside from Aasgard Sound in New Zealand, have I witnessed such a torrential sight. I've counted eleven major cataracts and several more minor streaks, all emptying into the Stehekin River on its course to Lake Chelan. In late June through mid-August, one must shout to be heard above the pleasing din of this liquid barrage, painting the walls wet, where water is the main artist.

Once fully in, at about 1½ miles, look east to spot the Southeast Route, the easiest pathway to the top. This point is at about 4,800'. Take note of the numerous and enormous marmots, eager to steal whatever you've sweated in; relax, as they're vegetarians, disinterested in your Clif or Lara bars. Of even greater import, it is best to ignore Beckey's *Green Guide's* advice to ascend all the way to the Black Warrior Mine; this will only produce the anguish of a dense fog of brush, peppered with a few class-5 cliffs thrown in for sport. You will not find the "old cable" he mentions; it, along with most of the ancient mining equipment, has been wrenched free and carted off, perhaps by the marmots to fortify their underground condominiums.

Instead of ascending all the way to the mine, at about 100 yards before the trail steepens to the old mineshaft, bear northeast through lighter brush, though still largely opaque, utilizing the many slide alder, vine maple and Cascade mountain ash trees as handholds to pull yourself up the steepening slopes. Through the service of the shrubbery and your own efforts, you will, after about 750' of this haul, arrive at an armistice with the brush and find yourself in a second open basin at around 6,500'.

Small-flowered Paintbrush

Although we have dragged our full packs to camp in this area once, there was scant water and even less level ground. Best to camp in the official sites mentioned above. This upper basin is filled with alpine wildflowers. The paintbrushes here are named small-flowered Indian paintbrush and are more often a dull white, rather than crimson red.

You're now above timberline and the views keep on looming larger with each boot-step forward. Just keep tooling away, aiming for Buckner's south ridge and you'll be fine. This ridge of movable gneiss might be guarded by snow early in the season, but the gentle 30-degree angle should prove no problem; if so, you can always move to your south, where the going is less steeply inclined.

CHAPTER TWENTY-ONE: THE PANORAMA PREVAILS

Once you've achieved the ridge, head north; you can spy the twin summits of Buckner; the first one you encounter, the Southwest Peak, is estimated as several feet higher than its northeast twin. Whichever you stand on, the other will most assuredly look taller. Now for those panoramas. As you twirl about, you really can spot almost all the major summits of the North Cascades, barring the Enchantments and the snag-toothed ridges and towers north of Baker and Shuksan. These views are not only all-encompassing but stunning as well. Even Glacier Peak and the distant Dome area summits are in view, while the Olympics appear above the distant Seattle/Everett haze. You've earned a big lunch and, even better, a perch which no mountaineer could distain, even though you took the easy way up.

For the hardened North Cascader, the North Face of Buckner features 45–60-degree ice on the Buckner Glacier (now shrunk to two distinct arms minus the snow connection of cooler years past). Such routes may be plausible for some mountain athletes, rootless vagabonds of rock and ice, but hardly practical for the weekend scrambler. You must begin that journey from Boston Basin, thus ensuring much up-and-down traversing, but with the immense benefit of crossing directly beneath Ripsaw Ridge, its saw-teeth tottering close above as you try to concentrate on the massive Boston Glacier crossing. Snow flukes, crampons, ice screws and twin axes were surely appreciated on our attempt. Our leader tolerated my clumsy and sluggish pace. Russ was always exciting but fortunately not excitable. He sometimes moved, I reckoned, faster than coal plants are closing in the Pacific Northwest. Happily, no rock protection is necessary as you wind up either at the very top, or close to it on the south ridge.

A similar approach was taken in 1967 by climbing an ice couloir leading almost to the Northeast Summit. The East Ridge and Southeast Ridge and Face have seen several attempts, many of which were successful. One must begin both from near or at the lovely but distant Park Creek Pass, straddling the Chelan/Skagit County line. Both climbs should be rated Grade III due to the extremely unstable rock beneath your boots – rock shoes would be worthless here. Parties have reported class 4- to easy class-5 conditions, with difficulty, as one would expect, of placing adequate protection. Our parties placed prudence ahead of pride in not attempting such stone-bound challenges.

The Southeast Face was first conquered by a 1987 party, who reported a mixed alpine route starting from near Park Creek Pass. Their party encountered mostly class-3 loose shale but with some ice patches mixed in with the obligatory heather benches. Above the heather, they headed for class-3 slabs, then ascended the southern arm of the Buckner Glacier to reach a ledge (class 4), from where they described a class-3 solid "staircase" to the summit, exposed but "of pure joy". I somehow must have missed that state of rapture on a more recent unsuccessful attempt to trace their route.

It is also possible to reach the South Ridge Route from the Park Creek Pass Trail about ¼ mile below the pass itself by ascending the south arm of the Buckner Glacier to the South Ridge. From the first party's description, it is difficult to discern much of a difference between this route and the Southeast Face Route described above. On several sorties from near Park Creek Pass, our own group encountered steep heather, slabs, then 45-degree black ice (in August) to attain the Southwest Summit.

Regardless of route chosen, a climb of Buckner represents the heart and soul of the North Cascades: brush, old mining equipment, heather benches, greedy marmots, flowered meadows, steep snow and ice, all culminating in a panoramic view made justly famous not only in Marblemount's Ranger Station, but in countless grocery stores, gas stations, other ranger stations, and even an odd post office if you can find one. It occupies my climbing room wall as not only a reminder of the majesty this range commands but as a call, a signal, to get out of the office and go climbing. Just beware of those piggish marmots.

CHAPTER TWENTY-TWO
A Dance with the Devil
Teebone Ridge
(6,985'–7065')

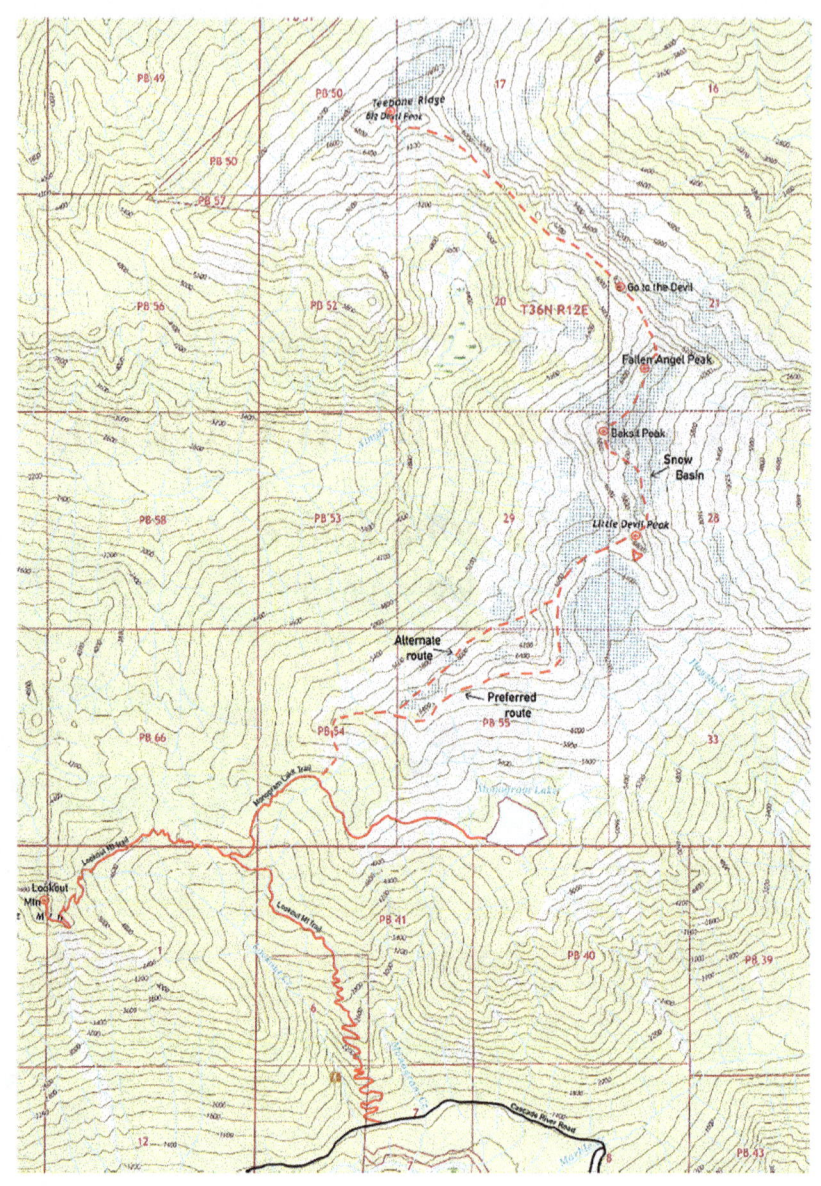

CHAPTER TWENTY-TWO: A DANCE WITH THE DEVIL

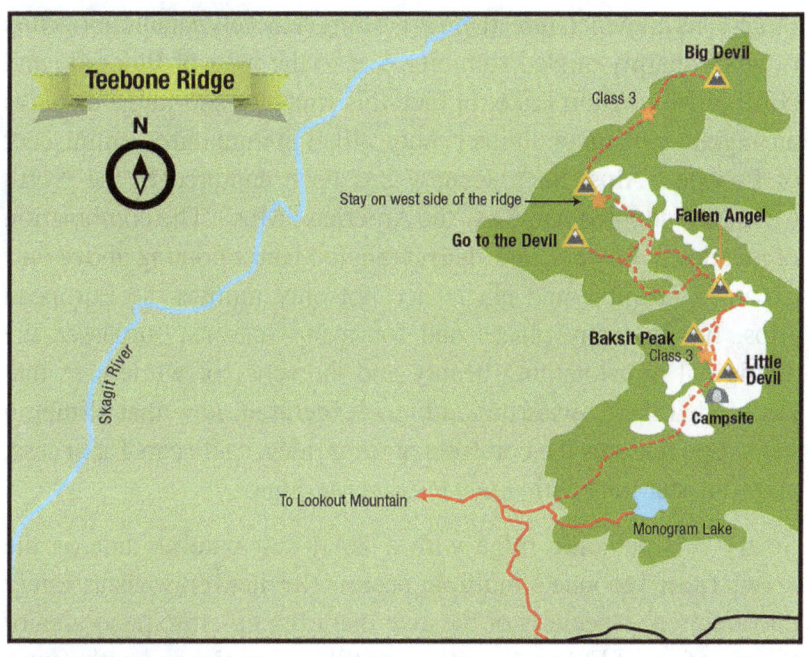

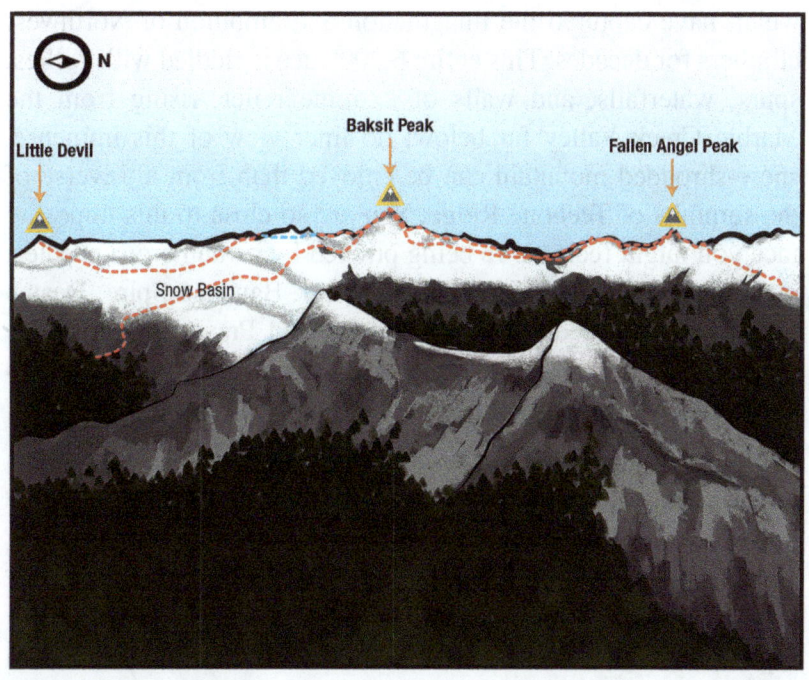

Despite its nomenclature, there is nothing remotely satanic about this ridge of sharply-angled summits, just to the west of Eldorado and north of Monogram Lake. In fact, this ruptured sub-range displays an angelic *tableau* of alpine beauty, albeit in miniature, reminiscent of Europe's Alps. Such scenery has been captured in the North Cascades' adopted name as "the American Alps". The combination of meadows, flowers, and sharply-angled peaks floating above vast expanses of snow and glacial ice not only mimics the European Alps, but in many places and for many reasons, surpasses the aboriginal in astounding beauty and the sense of wilderness that has eluded their Swiss/Italian/French brethren, now that climbing in Europe features the comforts of train rides, cable cars for access, and four-star inns with *haute cuisine* for dinner.

So try this demonic ridge with a devil-may-care attitude as the views from Teebone's multiple peaks offer heavenly vistas rarely encountered, especially of the awe-inspiring up-close panorama of the west face of Eldorado, with its needles of gneiss and with names which have captured the imagination and ambition of Northwest climbers for decades. This entire 6,200' face is riddled with gullies, spurs, waterfalls, and walls of extreme relief, rising from the Marble Creek Valley far below; no finer view of this immense, snow-shrouded mountain can be enjoyed than from a traverse of the summits of Teebone Ridge. You are so close to this imposing face you might feel you're being pricked by its numerous needles, including Flower Tower, Oliphant Tower, Bandana Spire, Dean's Spire, Dorado Needle, Marble Needle, and Praying Mantis. The famed Triad, though more to the east, can be identified leading up to the glaciated summit of Eldorado itself.

Bring binoculars for tracing the various routes up Eldorado's western wall, all extremely technical. Teebone will offer one of the most spectacular views in all the Cascades and the approach, and climbs of its various summits do not require vast amounts of heavy hardware. Some stout parties have made the traverse without roped protection, but I would recommend a 9-mm 60-meter cord and a few chocks or cams for the easy 5th-class moves on climb

CHAPTER TWENTY-TWO: A DANCE WITH THE DEVIL

day, along with crampons and ice ax, recommended in any season. By the way, in my first solo attempt, although I was successful in scaling all the named peaks except Big Devil, on my second night camped below Little Devil, a storm whipped up a wind howling as loudly as the Devil himself might roar; it was so fierce I thought it might even sweep away the Lowly Lord himself.

My subsequent attempts were, fortunately, better informed by improved forecasting. To begin, drive 6½ miles up the Cascade River Road to several small pull-outs on the south side of the roadway. Across the road, to the north, locate the beginning of the Lookout Mountain/Monogram Lake Trail, #743. Your pack may be heavy, though you should try this route with a friend or two to share equipment, as the trail is steep in spots. Regularly maintained, the Teebone Ridge and Monogram Lake Trails hug the southern boundary of the National Park. At about 3 miles on the path, there is a T-junction and here you must make a choice. The trail to the left leads to Lookout Mountain, though at times blow-down makes following it a chore, depending on maintenance from the Park Service. While you would think the views from Lookout would be panoramic, and indeed they are, they cannot compare should you choose to turn right here and begin to follow the trail to Monogram Lake.

Please ignore Beckey's imperative to descend to the hellish bug-infested Lake. It is Hades incarnate. There are no views, though plenty of campsites. But why lose altitude? The Lake is at 4,800' but by the time you proceed on the trail, you will have to lose about 300' to descend to it. Anyway, to climb up to the ridge from the Lake, you would have to ascend slippery corn lily and heather slopes to gain the first named summit of Teebone Ridge, Little Devil, at almost 7,000' itself. Instead, aim higher: After about ¼ mile on the trail, traverse off the level trail northwest into the meadows at about a 30-degree angle, aiming for the ridge itself.

Amongst the many alpine flowers adorning these meadows, note the alpine asters, with lance-like basal leaves and purple flowers, partially easing your way. You must next cross a wide gully at about 6,020' but the going, while all off-trail, is not difficult. You can stay high on the ridge leading to Little Devil or, bear due east and contour around Point 6844, then head north to hit the ridge at 6,600'; the latter is easier going and, therefore my preferred course. Depending on season, you will encounter mildly-angled snow near the top of the ridge, although by late July, the southern exposure here has pretty much melted it away. As you approach the Ridge, the panorama opens up of Eldorado's western face, but the best is yet to come.

Cling to the southern crest of the ridge as close as you can, stepping off to the south if ice has accumulated near the ridge's top. Watch for cornices off the north side, though I've never encountered one here. The alternative route lies just northeast of the ridge but steep ice can be encountered there. Either way, look back to acutely angled but anonymous peaks to your south and southwest. What the devil are these? They lie at an altitude of approximately 6,400' to 6,800'. You can climb them if you really want to stake a claim to climbing every peak on this ridge of wonders. However, you would be reversing your route if your goal is the Devils themselves.

It makes more sense to continue on a northeastern rising slope to the base of Little Devil, about 2 miles northeast of where you left the Monogram Lake Trail. You can view the serene lake at all points on this traverse, relatively straightforward and light on brush, but corn lilies occasionally make the footing tricky, especially with heavy pack. However, there's hardly the need for GPS positioning if the weather is clear, as it should be; you will be exposed on this ridge to weather from the northwest so I would recommend this traverse only if you can afford three days at the minimum and can avoid chaotic skies, precipitation, and cloud-obscured loss of views.

Rosy Spirea

CHAPTER TWENTY-TWO: A DANCE WITH THE DEVIL

Just at the base of Little Devil, a cleared area sufficiently large enough for several tents, provides marvelous views of Eldorado and, to the south over Monogram Lake, the peaks of Hidden Lake and the Cascade Pass area, including Johannesburg and Cascade Peaks. Spotted saxifrage comprises most of the flora here, along with thrashes of subalpine spirea, though corn lily, taller than corn in a regular cornfield predominated the ascent from the trail. The sharp profiles of Forbidden, Boston, Torment and Despair are partially shielded by Eldorado, but what a screen it is.

Spotted Saxifrage

Without leaving camp, Eldorado's west face, luminous and sparkling, stands proud against the hopefully sparkling sky. This level spot of real estate is most often all yours; I have never encountered a party there, though if occupied, another potential campsite exists further to the northeast. The strange part of this campsite is that it is almost on the top of Little Devil itself. One could ascend the southeastern slope in the evening after dinner if you're anxious to bag peaks. A mere stroll over 2nd-to-3rd-class boulders up its southeastern aspect might take all of 15 to 30 minutes. If this be Devil's country, then let all Hell break loose!

But what this site holds in terms of level sandy ground and eye-filling views, it lacks in running water. You could descend 300' to a small stream, then lug your shmoo or water bag back up this steep slope but a superior idea is to simply return a few 100' along the ridge and allow the melting water off the omnipresent ice on its north face drip into your water bags. This may take some time but the visits I've made to this stunning spot have always seen icy water practically cascading into whatever receptacle I had available. At worst, you can always scoop snow from the ridge's northwestern side but caution is advised in descending the icy snow lingering in this basin. Whichever route you choose to gain essential hydration, the effort is well rewarded by the opulent views and the opportunity to climb, the next day, an assortment of peaks and ever-broadening views from this rarely-visited province within the National Park.

On climb day, begin early if your objective is to traverse the ridge in its entirety. (Many parties avoid the last summit, Big Devil, as this involves a 1½-mile traverse, partly through brush and forest, bypassing some cliffy terrain.) Start first by scaling **Little Devil (6,985')**, then dropping a short 300' into the snow basin facing northeast. Traverse the snow basin as high as you dare to capture **Baksit Peak (6,960')**, also known as the **"Middle Devil"**, which lies about ¼ mile north of Little Devil. This is an evil looking peak, actually with a double summit, the northern-most apex being the tallest.

Continue to traverse in the usually snow-filled basin, ascending slightly until you can readily identify Baksit as there are a number of sharp aiguilles between it and Little Devil. You may have a devil of a time identifying which point is tallest. The highest summit here should stand out as the tallest peak north of Little Devil. Cross the main ridge itself to the peak's west side, then scramble loose but easy 3rd-class rock to its top.

In distinction to Little Devil, look hard as you may, there will be no summit register, a testament to this seldom-visited mountain along this splendid ridge. The views expand a bit more now, as the Cascade Pass peaks are more visible, along with Triumph and Despair. Forbidden's eastern and western ridges denote a nice counterpoint to the symphony of darkest green forest and the turbulent waterfalls plunging into the deep valley of Marble Creek below.

From Baksit, in about an hour's traverse ½ mile north though the snow basin (keep on its eastern aspect) lies **Fallen Angel Peak (6,840')**, the next obvious keen-edged pinnacle on this ridge. To believe Beckey, who is usually correct about these chronologies, it wasn't successfully climbed until 1982. Stay southwest until you

CHAPTER TWENTY-TWO: A DANCE WITH THE DEVIL

can ascend permanent snow to the peak's southern aspect. Climb about 50 feet on relatively solid easy 5th-class hand- and foot-holds to reach a gully just to the east of the top.

The few folks who have accomplished this climb have told me they succeeded without protection by ascending the "correct gully", but which one? Thus I followed alone but as they say, the devil is in the details. I scrambled several routes leading nowhere except to Hades before locating a stony couloir which allowed access to the summit boulders. All the way, I wished for some perlon from above. But does Heaven exist in these hellish realms?

Either rappel or down-climb the same way from whence you came, avoiding the northern and western facets unless you are prepared to free-rappel or descend upper 5th-class stone and ice. Braver adventurers than I could test these routes, as yet to my knowledge, un-scaled. A crag, just to the Angel's northwest, called **"Go to the Devil"** (about **6,247'**– I disagree with Beckey's elevations here; the topo is more reliable) has fallen, in 1966, via a short low 5th-class route on its western face.

A decision must now be reached: whether to complete the traverse to Big Devil or to return to camp, well-satisfied that you have made one of the scarce ascents of these sharp-edged blades puncturing the Washington sky. The other option is to traverse on to the baddest devil of them all, **Big Devil Peak (7,065')**. On a subsequent trip, our party elected to continue, despite my self-anointed role as devil's advocate, expressing concern about a congregation of approaching clouds on the horizon and reminding our crew that Hell hath no fury like a stranded climbing party in the North Cascades wilderness. In the main, however, the choice to continue to the Big Devil himself should be dictated by time, weather, and group ability rather than a devilish attitude.

I would estimate that the tricky traverse northwest to Big Devil would consume about 1½–2 hours, even though it is but a mere ¾ mile away and the climb is non-technical. However, the way is often brushy as the easiest route lies on the western fringe of the ridge, and you also must negotiate several gullies and lose, then regain, about 400'. Though I hold no divine origins of the Bible, in these hellish and tiresome realms, I was reminded of the Biblical passage which urges us to "Put on the whole armor of God, that you may be able to stand against the wiles of the devil...for we wrestle not against flesh and blood... but against the rulers of the darkness of this world."

On this western aspect, darkness (in the form of timber) actually intrudes at about the 6,300' level, though it is not overly brushy. If you chose a reasonable turn-around time, perhaps by mid-afternoon, you could figure on achieving this rarely visited summit and make it back to camp while still light, given summer's longer hours, but no later than 3 PM nor in worsening weather. But beware: The devils you know may not be sufficient.

Should you decide to go to the ultimate devil, remember that this peak is guarded not by steep rock but by something more frightening. It lives up to its name by being not only the tallest of the range but by a convoluted approach requiring excellent navigational skills, as on the approach, the top is not always visible. You must trend in a generally northeast direction, staying fairly close to the eastern edge of the ridge's crest. The summit, approached by any other angle than its southwestern face, will soon bring heartache and trouble. A number of cliffs block other routes but by any passage, a number of up-then-down gullies must be managed. Adhere to the ridge's eastern fringe, then traverse beneath a series of spines called **"The Six Hellions"** (about **6,700'**).

Try to avoid plunging too low into the mountain hemlocks. You should arrive at the last gully, and now you are truly between the devil and the deep blue sea (or at least the Pacific). This point is described in Beckey's diagram as a "10-foot-wide notch". The summit, clearly in view, is now a scramble over loose but easy 3rd-class rock to the top-most point. You will now have achieved what few who've come before you appreciated: views of Biblical proportions despite the infernal appellations. These can only be described as heavenly as you will be rewarded with a different

CHAPTER TWENTY-TWO: A DANCE WITH THE DEVIL

perspective than from any other points on the ridge, or indeed within the entire western Range.

And what a view faces you now: Eldorado's western face still lords it over the Marble Creek Valley but that drainage now seems far removed as you are essentially looking over the junction of the Skagit and Cascade Rivers. Peer over, if you dare, to the astonishing waterfall-streaked precipice of Big Devil's north face and recall Beckey's unique directions to reach Big Devil's summit via its north face: "From the North Cascades Highway [Route 20], *raft* across the river." [emphasis mine]. One could imagine early explorers building a raft out of the now-protected Douglas Firs, then attempting to avoid being swirled westward trying to cross this maelstrom. These faces have been climbed but we weekend amateurs will have to be satisfied that more brawny and vigorous folk, who are not only more skillful and courageous, but more tolerant of discomfort than most of us, have persisted against these obstacles. Perhaps for them, the path may lay more inward than outward bound.

Big Devil's Summit cannot be seen directly from the North Cascades Highway but it can be viewed from the Marblemount Ranger Station. Should you look south while travelling between Marblemount and Newhalem, you can appreciate the diabolical complexity of the enormous 6,000' north face, with its many runnels, icy barriers and plentiful waterfalls, complete with water-streaked shining rock, slick as a silvery mirror, jealously guarding this approach. Few parties have succeeded on it: A northwestern route was climbed in 2 days by a 1963 party and the northeast ridge vanquished in 1964, which also required a bivouac. Technical difficulties were not mentioned but Beckey concludes, with typical understatement, that "This is a long and strenuous route". Once, on top of Big Devil, we witnessed a party of three professional climbers emerge, late in the day, from their three-day battle with the north face. As we absorbed their story, we stood as respectful witnesses to the hellish ravages they had endured. "Hell hath no fury…"

Nonetheless, the southern route I described is feasible and doesn't require any technical climbing. And what views there are from this vantage point! Besides an oblique and novel view of Eldorado to the east, Colonial and Snowfield loom to the north across the mysterious and brush-filled valleys of Haystack and Newhalem Creeks, their sides shrouded by the huge McAllister Glacier. Its handmaidens, Pinnacle Peak and Paul Bunyan's Stump, complete this snowy silhouette. Look further north, just to the west of this sub-range, to gaze in admiration at the North Cascade's most iconic range – The Pickets, spearing and thrusting their rock and ice-bound summits into the sky, and well-protected by the steepest of walls and glaciers in the continental United States. Triumph, with its famous step along its southern ridge and Despair to its north can be spotted by the knowledgeable party.

However bewitching they are, don't fail to appreciate the views eastward: Just north of Eldorado, Dorado Needle lives up to its jaw-boned name, while further to the northeast, Klawatti and Austera Peaks stand in regal and snow-bound array, while between them, scan the vertical canines and incisors colorfully named Tepah Towers, Tillie's Towers, Piltdown Tower, Chaco Tower, and the Klawatti Klaws. Amongst these pinnacles stand sharply angled spires and steeples too numerous to name; they scratch the skyline in jagged disbelief. This ridge, angling north from Eldorado, ends in the rarely attempted Primus and Tricouni Peaks. Approaches to both involve tremendous courage in facing the worst technical brush the Cascades seems to enjoy in thwarting aspiring climbers.

While the bulk of Eldorado partially obscures the views of Forbidden, vistas to the east beyond Hidden Lake Peak's lookout reveal an incomprehensible spiny, knife-like crest, including the tops of Forbidden and Mt. Logan, and the beginnings of Ragged Ridge (binoculars here would help). To the south, clear views open up along the Teebone Ridge you've just navigated, and beyond, Snowking hogs the spectacle, along with its glittering lakes at the foot of this snowy giant. Considering these views, one recalls the flawed theory that we use just 10% of our brains (which, neurologically, is pure fiction) but up here, on the heights of the Devils, we can at last use 100% of our hearts.

There are actually points along Teebone Ridge, unnamed but clearly visible to the northeast, including **The Trapezoid** (or **"Last Devil"**, about **7,000'** tall). However, it's best not to linger too long in an attempt to claim the entire ridge as you may have a devil of a time getting back before dark. Despite the views and the wish to fully cherish these sublime surroundings, the trip back to a camp at the base of Little Devil could lie hours away. A typical party of weekend climbers/scramblers will spend at least 3–4 hours on the trip back, even without climbing any of the peaks on the ridge. Seldom visited and rarely traversed in it is entirety, Teebone may be named after the infernal underworld and its nether regions, but those who hike, scramble and climb these ridges and peaks will have reached, in my opinion, quite the opposite: a true yet overlooked heavenly paradise.

CHAPTER TWENTY-THREE

Spine of the North Cascades

Backbone Ridge
(7,040'–8,040')

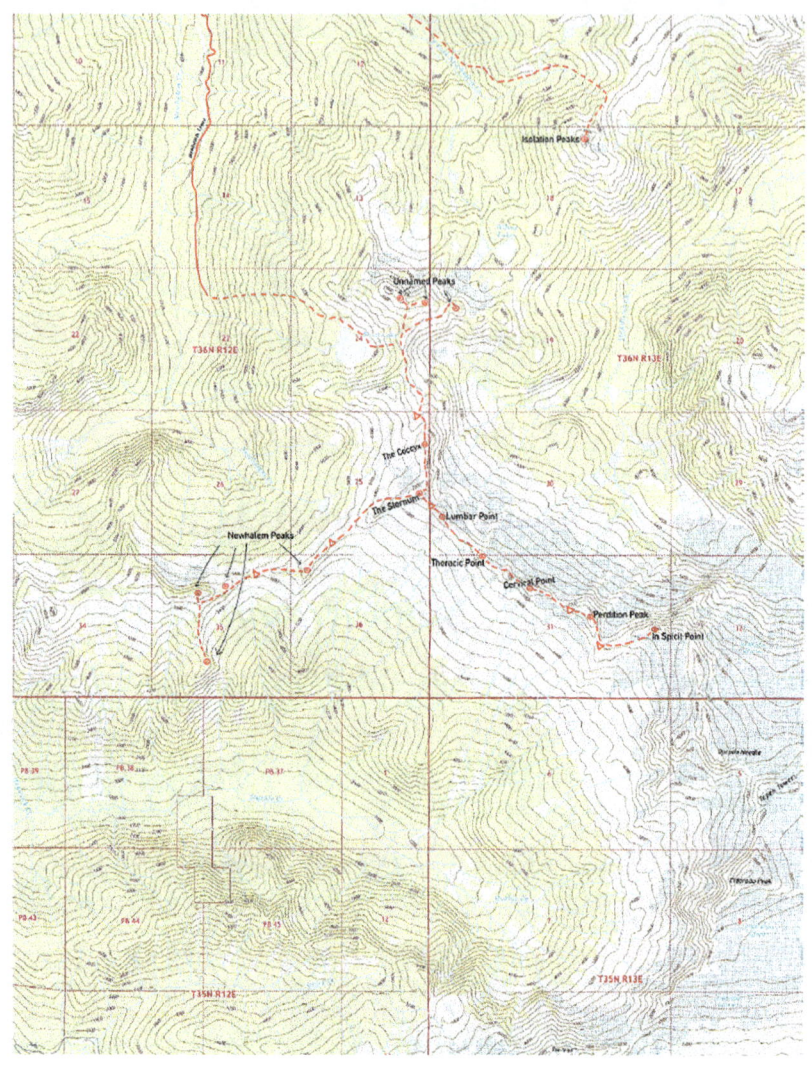

CHAPTER TWENTY-THREE: SPINE OF THE NORTH CASCADES

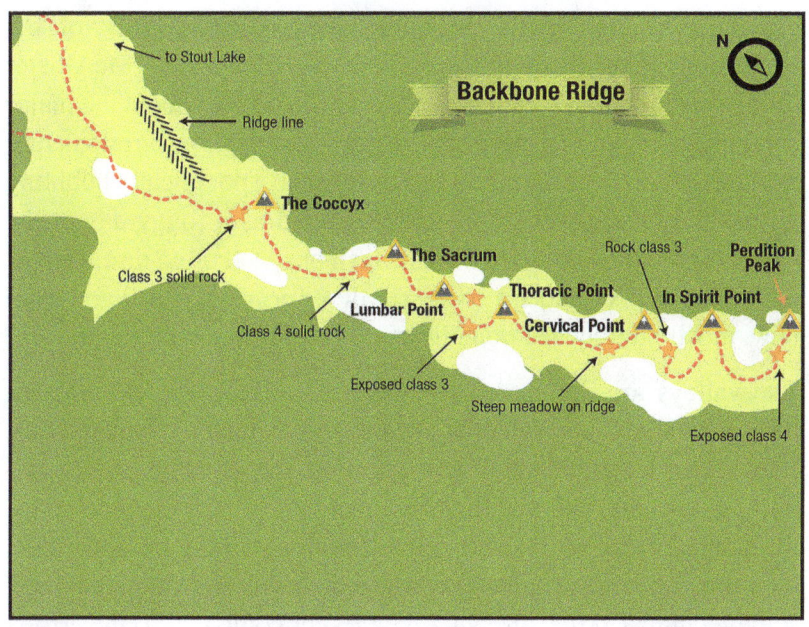

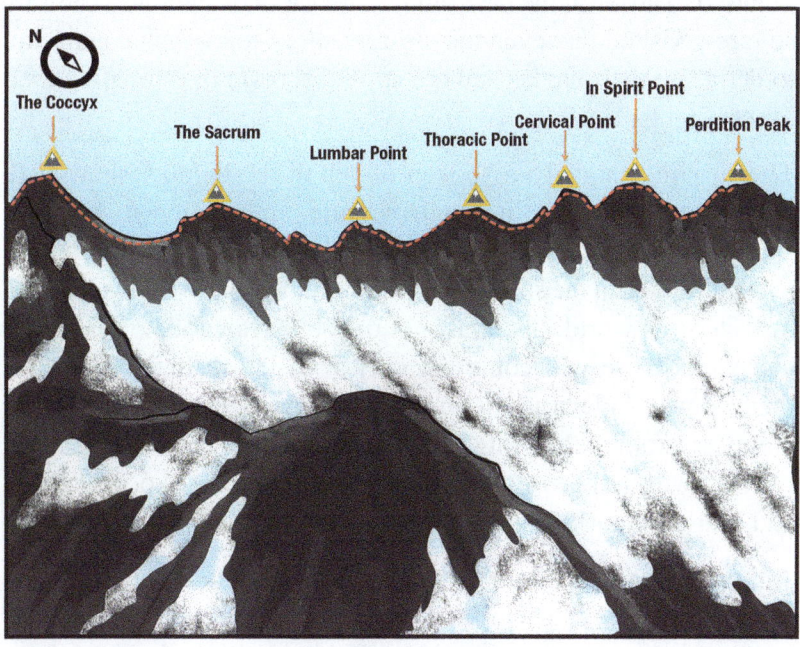

221

The toothed and bristly peaks between the East Fork of the Newhalem River (sometimes spelled "Nehalem") and McAllister Creek must seem like mere parentheses in volumes about the major and better-known regions of the North Cascades. Descriptions lurk in odd corners of the literature and on the web, sporadically bubbling up but then fading away; they are as lucid as a foggy day at the Coast, as reliable as a used Volkswagen bus, and often disappear as quickly as a pika under a rock. Yet they form a serrated and even now, mostly untouched domain worthy of further exploration.

The valleys are dominated by noble and silver firs and western hemlocks; they are ruled by bears and cougars. Human bootprints have hardly made a dent into this, the most hostile, brush-glutted enigma within the National Park. Those who have challenged these approaches give testimony to the arduous treks into this emerald jungle; the peaks themselves, while requiring some technical skills, are but a mere jaunt compared to the efforts required to arrive at the base of these needle-like summits. They are so rarely visited that even the most recent of topographic maps fail to delineate their names and are still inaccurate in estimating their exact heights.

Those with whom I've spoken about their attempts show both elation and dejection in equal measure. In addition to my own feeble attempts to reach these realms, I share their frayed appearance and yet rejoice in the small but meaningful lessons we have learned. To enter this world, one must not dabble in fantasies of views far and wide; these will come but only with the realization that the dreaded west-side brush has prevented some of the world's leading climbers from attempting to penetrate these regions (personal contacts with Jeff Lowe, John Roper, Ed Bolton, the Skoog brothers, and Mark Twight).

Although Beckey defines the Ridge as just the peaks on the acute alpine crest trending northwest between Marble and McAllister basins, I believe the true "backbone" should also include the sharp summits surmounting the valleys separating the East Fork of the Newhalem River and the McAllister Creek drainage as well. These

CHAPTER TWENTY-THREE: SPINE OF THE NORTH CASCADES

Marble Creek and Newhalem towers, also described in Beckey, are worthy of attempts by those whose bravery has morphed from an attraction to an unadulterated obsession. Courage in the face of brush this thick can be considered mad but those few who have surmounted these summits will have breathtaking views and tales to tell which amaze even the most experienced of climbers.

We should begin, in these accounts, from north to south, although the ranges I will describe emanate from western and eastern points as well depending upon manner of approach. Indeed, many of these peaks lie just east or west of another sub-range, rendering latitude a poor substitute for accurate GPS readings and should encourage good use of 7½" topo's and compass. Our first range of summits is that of Beckey's "Backbone Ridge", trending northwest between Marble and McAllister Creeks. It is so named because of its rather regularly spaced top-most points, somewhat resembling a spinal column, though one with severe scoliosis.

This Ridge can be considered a northwestern extension of the spectacular towers from Dorado Needle in the south. Perdition Peak (7,675') can be envisioned as the springboard from which these bony summits arise. Nevertheless, the 7½" topo map fails to award the peak a name, merely denoting it by its elevation. It can, however, be found on Pargeter's picture map, although that diagrammatic chart, helpful in identifying peaks, cannot be trusted for cross-country travel.

The "easiest" route to this blissful mountain nirvana begins by driving south as far as you dare on the Newhalem Creek Road; this passage is not regularly maintained. Therefore, if entering this jungle from the north, you might find the "road" has deteriorated into a trail after about 2½ miles. Elevation gain is to be expected as you will usually begin walking at low footings, about 1,300'; it sort of feels like you're starting from the Danakil Depression as, from this point, you must hike another 5 steepening miles to reach Stout Lake (about 5,220'), so named perhaps because it takes a hardy hiker to gain its shores.

Fishermen use this trail but they are not carrying the essentials you will require for an extended expedition lasting at least 3 days and possibly more, including some hardware for easy 5th-class climbing accompanied by the additional thrill of merciless exposure. From road-end, the sometimes path brings you, in about 3 hours, to the Lake. Here, buggy campsites can be found. However, I recommend that you try to attain a superior campsite on the Ridge itself the same day, though another 1,000' must be gained through west-side brush best described as tangled thickets as evil as a green nether world.

If you have the strength to carry on, try to head east/south-east to gain the ridge emanating from Eldorado's northwestern extension, due southeast of the lake. It's a tough slog and, during our trip, it seemed as if the gears of our progress were often monkey-wrenched. Though we were unstoppable, we were not prepared to be invincible. Soon, we began to feel like slaves to the greenery, as if a green vortex threatened to suck us back to the lake. At times, I was about as successful at beating back the greenery as I was in trying to bake a chocolate souffle' without it collapsing. It seemed like a cul-de-sac of misery. (My therapist says it's important to talk about these things.)

The wretched shrubbery impeded our efforts but it also added fuel to the fire of our eventual success as, at around 6,100', the terrain opened up and both views and campsites were located just before the ridge on a few level sites, or on the ridge itself in saddles between peaks at around 6,200'. Each col could be considered the cartilaginous discs separating these equally-spaced vertebrae. The crest, especially on its western flanks, provided relatively open-ground and bug-free travel on the Backbone, which now required the surgeon's knife of route-finding rather than the construction worker's

Rosy Spirea

CHAPTER TWENTY-THREE: SPINE OF THE NORTH CASCADES

bludgeon in order to beat the brush. Finally, success arrived only by the combination of struggle and time.

Views here are magnificent, though the travel is up and down. Sulfur buckwheat and thrashes of rosy (subalpine) spirea eased the way. (Many wildflowers have multiple common names; hence scientists utilize Latin designations to keep everyone organized and happy.) The route is occasionally steepest on its northeastern aspect, from which both cliffs and unnamed pocket glaciers originate (Beckey honors them with the names of "Backbone" and "Perdition Glaciers"). These feed into McAllister Creek from its numerous tributaries. Glance down at the vertiginous northeastern faces to marvel at the McAllister Valley, so brush-choked that it appears impossible to negotiate.

Sulfur Buckwheat

Yet a few souls have actually approached this mess called a valley by beginning their arduous trek from a camp on the Thunder Creek Trail at 7½ miles, then undertaking the precipitous brush and cliffs of the McAllister drainage. From this point, access to the pocket glaciers can be climbed to reach Backbone Ridge. Even though the route to this spine from Stout Lake is treacherous enough, the McAllister approach is even worse and will certainly occupy a stalwart party several days of struggle; it has been accomplished by those who equate suffering with success.

The reasons to ascend this ridge are both personal (achievement and bragging rights) but aesthetic as well. The views from the ridge and especially from its high points described below are outstanding. Up close, the entire northwestern aspect of massive Eldorado comes into proximate relief, its glittering glaciers easily identified, especially the McAllister ice sheet, while hints of the Inspiration

Glacier can be spied as well. This panorama encompasses a continuous blanket of ice and snow to your immediate southeast. The Devils are to your west, while to the south lie Snowking and the rarely attempted Sonny Boy Peaks. To your southeast, past Austera and Klawatti Peaks lie Tillies Towers, as sharply defined a serrated crest as any in the Cascades, finally topped off by the pinnacle of Primus Peak.

Look beyond as well, for an unobstructed view of the Cascade Pass Peaks, including Torment and Despair, their very names signaling the hazards they present to would-be climbers. Sahale and Boston poke their heads above the vastness of the green valleys and spectacular waterfalls of Thunder Creek. In the eastern distance, Logan and Goode can be spotted while to the north, Colonial and Snowfield command the most immediate attention. Even further north Baker and Shuksan shine in white splendor, thus completing a 360-degree perspective unrivalled south of Cascade Pass. By all and any means, challenge the brush and the steep valley sides; you will probably not return to this spot, so take in the splendor from this spinal column and yes, use your smart phone camera if you must. For me, the images from these peaks and points will never be deleted from my anatomical mother board.

Although you can climb most of these vertebrae both from north-to-south and south-to-north directions, it makes more sense to list them beginning from their northwestern reaches if you are entering this rarely visited range from the Stout Lake approach. Therefore, proceeding from tail to neck, the first peak to conquer is **The Coccyx (7,280')**, a tailbone about one mile distant from the easiest point on the ridge, where you can camp, at about 6,600', and gaze down at Stout Lake. From the northwest, The Coccyx appears sharply pointed, but the actual ascent can be made rope-less.

Aim in a southeasterly direction from your camp just north of the ridge; the peak can then be climbed from its northeastern ridge by angling south to the head of the small glaciers mentioned above, then a scramble on class-2–3 rock to the blocky summit. The southeast ridge can be climbed in fairly easy fashion but involves

CHAPTER TWENTY-THREE: SPINE OF THE NORTH CASCADES

an extra detour if your plan is to ascend all the named peaks on the ridge in a single (very long) day. A glance east and down reveals a plunging cliff face, thus reassuring you that, despite the difficulties, you have succeeded on the most reasonable route.

If the ridge in its entirety is indeed your goal, proceed down the southeast crest (some exposure here but no technical difficulties) to a small saddle and glance up at your next objective, **The Sacrum (7,148')**, not really shaped like one anatomically but at least it fits the bony analogy. It lies about ¼ of a mile southwest of The Coccyx and can be vanquished by its western face on solid class 3-4 rock. **Lumbar Point (7,040')** is your next goal, though many "senior" climbers, such as myself, would prefer not to mention the word "lumbar" too frequently.

Although Beckey endorses a route from the summit's northeast ridge, a more direct route also can be negotiated from the col between Lumbar Point and The Sacrum, utilizing 3rd-to-4th-class solid holds; technical equipment is not required for either route, unless someone in your party, or even you as leader, consider exposure sufficient grounds for protection. I was overjoyed that my lead climber had fixed protection on this crest, which turns quickly to a face route necessitating testing holds and searching diligently for the most solid ones available.

Thoracic Point, (7,175') - (I've added 5 feet to Beckey's estimate based on GPS, altimeter and squinting glances at the topo lines on the 7½" series map) lies about ¼ mile southeast of Lumbar Point, and continues the anatomical nomenclature. We circled the topmost point to gain the southeast ridge, easier than its northwestern counterpart, as the rock on the latter looked wobbly, although it could have been we who were tremulous. Either route is classed as "3", but we encountered 4th-class loose rubble as we descended southeast, finally rappelling the southwestern face. Being a physician, I was determined to reach **Cervical Point, (7,360')**, the last of the Backbone's anatomical analogies. It was a scramble from its col between it and Thoracic Point on its north side, with occasional snow but mostly grassy meadow and easy rock.

Having completed the anatomy of the spine, we were not fully finished as several peak-like points could be seen further southeast. The first of these is named **In Spirit Point (7,480')**. This peak is actually an extension northwest from Tepeh Towers and Dorado Needle. Circle west to its southern aspect to avoid steep cliffs on its eastern slope which faces the McAllister Glacier. Some all-season ice can make this crossing treacherous but crampons are helpful. By all means, avoid the precipitous northeastern slopes, where an arm of the McAllister Glacier combines with near-vertical cliffs plunging with alarming speed toward an unhappy ending in the valley's greenery.

You can gain access to In Spirit from its more neighborly southwestern side, (rather than from the southeastern face endorsed by Beckey). Scramble meadows, then non-technical rock to pleasantly access the summit. The views are stupendous but don't tarry too long if your goal is to reach the very southernmost points on Backbone Ridge and return to camp without the bivouac we endured. The tallest peak anchoring this entire spine is named **Perdition Peak (7,675')** and its views, particularly out to Eldorado's northwestern facets and angles bring you face to face with the terrifying towers and needles that you can only appreciate from this viewpoint. Perdition is well-named as the term can be taken to mean a state of final spiritual ruin. The best way (and possibly the only way for me) is to keep to the western side of the ridge, bypassing several cliffy spots, to reach Perdition's west ridge, from which a 4th-class exposed climb on relatively solid rock leads to the summit.

Protection for all but the most skilled and sure-footed climbers is mandatory. You are now only about 1½ miles from Dorado Needle and in full view of the many towers that extend north from the bulk of Eldorado. Several have no record of ascent while others, such as Early Morning Spire and Marble Needle can be distinguished by the sheer and terrifying beauty of their precipitous flanks. Although they have received a number of brave ascents, several accomplished climbers have succumbed during these attempts.

CHAPTER TWENTY-THREE: SPINE OF THE NORTH CASCADES

To avoid a bivouac, hasten back in a northeastern direction, sticking as closely as you can to the western flanks of the ridge. To make it all the way back to your camp on the ridge at the col north of the Coccyx makes for a lengthy journey. Fortunately, campsites between the Backbone's various summits are feasible. It is unwise to attempt a complete descent until daylight, when you can visualize Stout Lake and the infamous brush you will need to descend in order to reach it. From the Lake, the remnants of the trail back to your vehicles at the Newhalem Road is a slog. The descent in itself requires strong knees and the strength to tackle brush as thick as in any National Park in the land. I recall a number of arm rappels off thick-enough trees to ease the pain. But rest assured you have experienced a trek worthy of any proud North Cascader.

There lie a series of sharp summits along the western crest of Backbone Ridge southwest of Stout Lake, including the **Newhalem Peaks (about 6,000'–6,475')**, the apex of a sub-range forming the boundary between Newhalem and Marble Creeks. I question the received opinion that all have been climbed. Although they have been approached, not all the points on this northern ridge have any records of ascent. However, they appear, especially on their western and southern slopes, to be accessible.

Attempts directly from Stout Lake have proven fruitless (at least for our parties) but a more direct and even pleasant approach can be enjoyed from the approach to Backbone Ridge itself, if time allows. At least 2 days are needed for the Newhalem Peaks; 4–5 days would be required to traverse all of Backbone Ridge and attempt the Newhalem Peaks as well. From above timberline, meadows sporting much lupine, paintbrush and purple alpine aster make for an agreeable amble through color to these summits from their eastern and northern aspects.

If contemplating such an adventure, it is best to first gain the Sternum, then traverse west from along a broad ridge to the first of these peaks, Point 6,210, then contour due west over a bump at 6,000' to reach the highest and western-most point along this ridge at 6,475'. Turn south from here to reach the ridge's last gasp, a sharp but easily gained point at about 5,800', one of the ridge's last prongs before tumbling south and losing any distinct definition. The third peak west along this ridge forms a curious circular summit between twin rock horns, perhaps borrowed from the Devil's traverse next door to the south. Stay south and west when this ridge narrows, thus conveniently avoiding occasional nasty steep northeastern cliffs. Few have ever contemplated, let alone achieved these inscrutable summits. Again, although this ridge can be climbed directly from Stout Lake, ferocious brush-beating is to be expected.

White Heather

Fortunately, not so for the aptly-named **Isolation Peak (7,102')**, on a spur extending southwest from Snowfield Peak. It appears it can be climbed without technical gear from the northern-most portions of Backbone Ridge but many up's and downs are to be expected. The approach we've taken involved following the east fork of Newhalem Creek, perpetually doing battle with the moderate west-side brush to reach red and white heather and open skies at around 6,000'. From that elevation you can wander south to the top without technical problems. There are unnamed peaks, somewhat ill-defined, just northeast of Stout Lake. From a saddle just east of the lake, one can forge through heavy brush to reach a ridge, where these points, all about 6,600', can be spied and ascended without calling upon technical skills or equipment.

Red Heather

The Haystack (7,102') far to the northeast of Stout Lake, can be climbed from the Newhalem Creek Road, though much brush is to be expected. Beckey may have described another nearby peak as he lists the elevation of Haystack at 7,139'. It is difficult to spot such a point along the ridge leading north from Dorado Needle or leading across the McAllistrer Valley. However, many of these peaks are best approached from the north in a 3–4-day outing from the Neve Glacier clothing Snowfield and Colonial Peaks. **Cat's Ear (7,560')** is the distinctive name of a craggy peak west of the Neve Glacier on Snowfield Peak and is best approached from that icy body. However, its sole climbing history involves battles on its east buttress, with facial rock, hand cracks and a traverse rated class 5.7. Our own sole attempt ended in rain-soaked misery.

It would appear from the topo's that an approach from the Ladder Creek drainage and then up the Neve Glacier would prove less technical but that route has not, to my knowledge, been explored. Other named points, include **The Needle (8,040')**, **The Horseman (7,760')**, **Styloid Peak (6,972')**, the descriptively named **Distal Phalanx (7,560')** and **Mantis Peak (7,614')**. These would best be approached from a traverse between Colonial and Snowfield Peaks on the broad Neve Glacier. Each has seen but a handful of successful ascents. It is wise, however, to realize that descriptions of ascents may well rely more on hazy, brush-addled memory than on solid reality.

While there are a bevy of peaks, needles, crowns, and summits along the saw-toothed ridges emanating from Eldorado in the south through Backbone Ridge all the way north to the snow-clad peaks which clothe Pyramid and Snowfield, there are too many to fully describe. All we can accomplish is to place a name to those without a clear climbing history, although Beckey's *Green Guide* provides helpful hints of their accessibility, or the lack thereof. I believe many await first ascents. Prepare for class-5 brush and remember that your cuts, scratches and scars bear witness to your well-worth-it struggles. Those who challenge and conquer these peaks can write their own epitaph: "I persevered in this desolate yet beautiful range, touching its tortuous spires and reaching its rarely-visited towers."

Regardless of the fact that these oft-neglected summits are enigmatic and rarely penetrated, should you relish incomparable viewpoints paired with an explorer's heart, I believe Backbone Ridge is the most practical and well-explored way to shepherd a 3- to 4-day weekend climbing party safely, if not always comfortably, through the amazing wealth of peaks in this, the western-most reaches of the National Park. The panoramas you will behold are both vast and incomparable. Dare great deeds and the rewards will exceed the efforts you endured and the accomplishments you most surely achieved.

CHAPTER TWENTY-FOUR

Guaranteed Sunshine East of the Crest

The McAlester Area Ridges:

Reynolds Peak
(8,512')

Rennie Peak
(7,742')

McAlester Mountain
(7,928')

and Mt. Gibbs
(8,142')

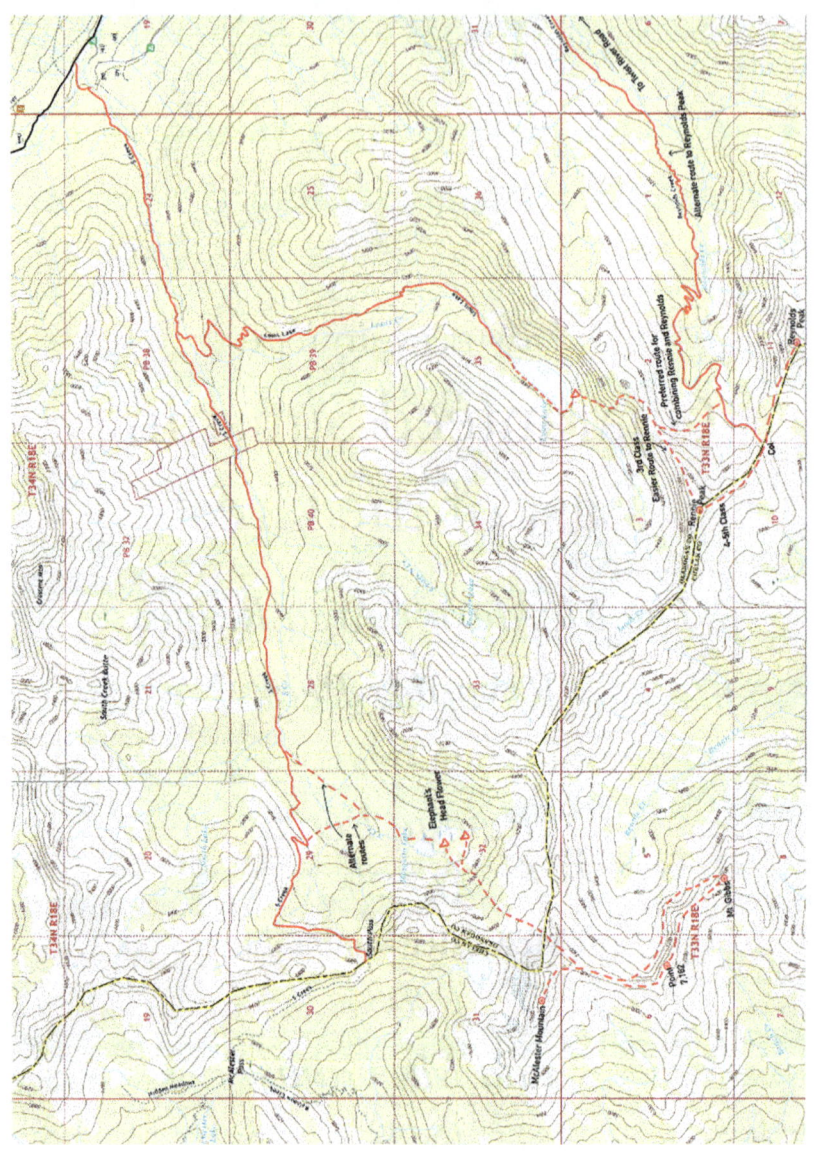

CHAPTER TWENTY-FOUR: GUARANTEED SUNSHINE EAST OF THE CREST

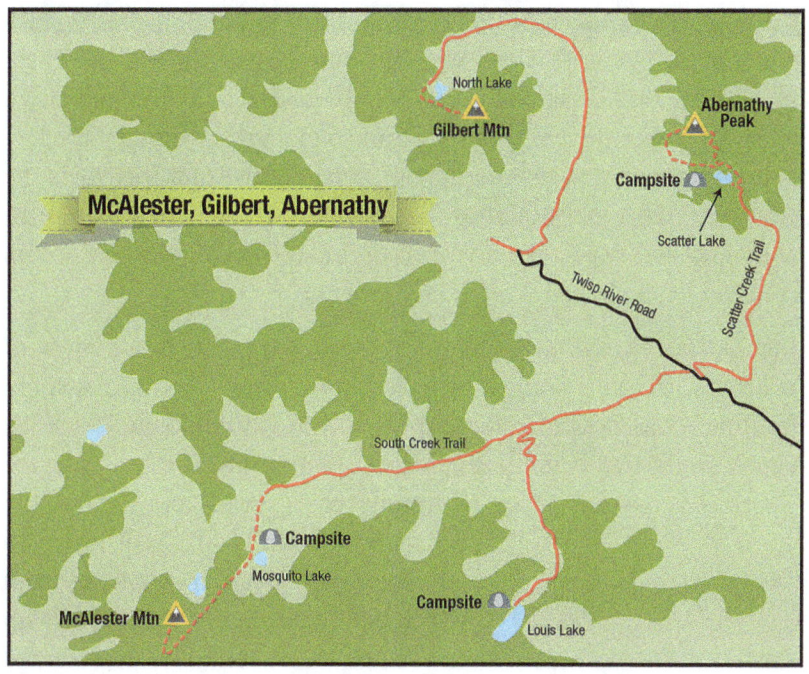

Craving east-side sunshine? Tired of west-side gloomy skies bleak as a blizzard? Then seek the sun east of the Pacific Crest by approaching these two peaks, rarely visited and often unknown even by experienced North Cascade veterans. Although Beckey urges approaches to the multiple peaks on McAlester Ridge via the Boulder Creek, then Rainbow Creek Trails, these would require an annoying and expensive boat trip up Lake Chelan, then a walk up the road leading northwest from Stehekin.

Instructions for climbing the McAlister area peaks in a variety of texts are about as simple as following a Venn diagram. A more feasible route to McAlester and Mt. Gibbs would be the Reynolds Creek Trail #402, beginning at Mystery Camp, about 18 miles up the Twisp River Road. If you're aiming for Reynolds and Rennie, the South Fork Trail, #401, will prove to be the best approach. It originates from the South Creek campsite, 22 miles up that same dusty but well-maintained road. Both trails advance gradually in forest, of interest as it differs slightly from the woodlands further west. Here, while second-growth Douglas Firs still abound, one can spot an occasional western larch and even some lodgepole pines, along with cut-leaf (or silver-crown) luina, with huge spiky leaves and dandelion-like yellow blossoms and white shooting-stars, all to let you know you really are east of the Crest.

Cut Leaf-Luina

If your goal is to conquer the mightiest summit in this range, **Reynolds Peak (8,512')**, lying to the northwest of Lake Chelan, by all means avoid Beckey's first choice, the War Creek Route, as it requires a longer approach hike via a well-used but horse-infested trail, then a descent (I try to avoid descending ground I have to re-climb later) followed by some bushwhacking, though more of an annoyance than a barricade. My preference would be to follow

CHAPTER TWENTY-FOUR: GUARANTEED SUNSHINE EAST OF THE CREST

the South Creek Trail for about 1½ miles, then turn left (south) on the Louis Creek Trail #428 for about 3 miles to camp at Louis Lake.

Try these in early summer or early fall seasons as, mid-summer, the bugs here are as numerous and occasionally as single-minded as the pundits on cable news TV shows. If your party is strong enough, you could haul your gear (no technical metal needed if your sole goal is Reynolds) up to the Reynolds-Rennie saddle to camp above the bugs, but the way is steep, lacks any semblance of a trail, and not a route I would recommend for the average party.

White Shooting-Stars

You could also take the Reynolds Creek Trail, embarking directly off the Twisp River Road. But beware: This route, while following a fairly well-maintained trail to this same saddle at first, quickly deteriorates, and by 3–4 miles, withers out in many spots as it is not well-maintained (as of 2024) and entails almost 3,000' of gain with full pack. This track makes sense to climb Reynolds if that is your major objective, and is quite feasible for strong parties. **Rennie Peak (7,742')**, just a mile to your northwest might also be feasible, but requires a traverse where rock protection is advisable.

If you allow sufficient time and plan your attack in early July, when the daylight allows you to tarry a bit to enjoy the views, hardy parties can gain both summits; however, the crest between them requires great caution. The Williams Creek Trail also provides access to Reynolds Peak, with a camp at (bug-infested) Williams Lake but would entail 5th-class climbing on the cliffs just west of the lake to gain Reynolds' south ridge. There is much dreaded up-and-down elevation change to eventually reach the southeastern slopes, where easy scrambling leads to the summit.

Following my suggestion, from a camp at Louis Lake, you can ascend Reynolds directly by aiming for the saddle between Rennie

Peak and Reynolds to its south. Then ascend meadows colored yellow by two species of daisy-like arnica's (the soft and meadow arnicas) to reach an initial saddle, sort of a pseudo-col before attaining a higher col between Rennie and Reynolds. Dance along Reynolds's northwest ridge, then head southeast along the steep but stable crest, avoiding its northern cliffs and a small glacier on its eastern fringe, to discover 3rd-to 4th-class rock on solid holds.

The summit affords rewarding views to the peaks outlining the west shore of Lake Chelan and the brooding hulk of Bonanza to the south in the distance. Further north, spy the Stiletto Range of peaks (see the next chapter), and beyond to the northwest, the titans of Mts. Logan and Goode, mocking many unsuccessful attempts. Silver Star, with its numerous saw-teeth pinnacles lies to the northeast, while the origins of the Cascade Pass Peaks can be glimpsed to the northwest and beyond, the massif of Dome.

Not a bad day's outing under hopefully lucid skies. These viewpoints are so atypical compared to those from the more popular summits further west that a comprehensive map, such as the National Geographic's North Cascades map or Pargeter's picture map and a handy pair of binoculars help in identifying the multitude of peaks lying before you, particularly those to your south along Lake Chelan's western shore.

Once back at the saddle, you can bag **Rennie Peak, (7,742')** by a direct route on the ridge leading northwest. This ridge may have been climbed, though records are sparse. It features aiguilles as sharp as a Nepalese pepper and exposure even an exhibitionist would envy. It also involves multiple protected pitches. Should you attempt to bypass this knife-like crest by traversing the headwalls of the pocket glaciers on its northern side, you must prepare for technical ice-work beyond the skills of the weekend scrambler. Nonetheless, if properly prepared, this traverse can be an exciting adventure.

However, for the average weekend alpine warrior, consider a second night at camp, then bagging Rennie the next day from base. This nontechnical ascent by the peak's north ridge, though steep at

CHAPTER TWENTY-FOUR: GUARANTEED SUNSHINE EAST OF THE CREST

times, is in the main, routine as it travels always upward through both white and red heather; purple asters; accompanied by two species of yellow daisy-like arnica's, the soft and meadow species, both solely alpine flowers; and the always-present partridge-foot, its name derived from the shape of its leaves. You will encounter steep drop-offs to the north, so stay on the ridge itself or, when technical difficulties demand, descend a bit on Rennie's southern flanks. Return to the saddle for the easiest passage back to base.

Although it appears on the map that **Mt. Gibbs (8,142')** and its connecting ridge to **McAllester's** multiple summits **(7,928'–8,142')** should be a short stroll from Rennie's Peak, a number of steep rock and ice pitches would need to be negotiated. A better course would be an approach from the South Creek Trail, then a climber's path to the woefully named Mosquito Lake. Unfortunately, to climb all the named summits on McAlester Ridge would prove a lengthy endeavor.

However, two additional peaks, forming a sub-range branching west from the Rennie-Reynolds divide, are not only worth the effort but offer slightly more abundant views, especially to the north. They form a separate drainage system, that of South Creek itself, above which these two summits, Gibbs and McAlester, arise. They must be approached from South Creek Campground, 22 miles in on the dusty Twisp River Road. Your goal is to reach Mosquito Lake (5,282'), ignoring its name. Follow the South Creek Trail #401 for about 5 miles before crossing its southern-most branch just before an abrupt right-hand turn northward; this should be at about 5,100'. Swing left and you will now be following the southern-most branch of South Creek; a climber's path and animal tracks can often ease the way, and fortunately, west-side brush is sparse here east of the crest. You can also leave the trail at 5,000' and track south-southwest to reach the same camping spot.

What tangled underbrush there is can largely be avoided by adhering to the creek's eastern side. You will reach open ground and lovely meadows just short of the lake. Note particularly, elephant head, a strange Snapdragon Family plant related to the louseworts and thriving in moist mountain meadows. Its flowers bear a remarkable resemblance to an elephant's head, ears and trunk included. Many alpine larches line the lake's banks. If it's off-season for the bugs, campsites are plentiful around the lake's northern and western shores. However, if the little flying critters are too bothersome, seek higher ground above the lake's southern shore.

Cliff Indian Paintbrush

The following day, to summit **McAlester (7,928')**, employ the main drainage gully southwest, over the ubiquitous meadows alive with subalpine cut-leaved daisies and alpine asters (the asters are taller but both are a purple-pink), then blocky talus that always seems to shift under my unsteady feet. This will deliver you to upper grassy meadows featuring even higher-altitude flora, such as the yellow senecios, brilliant crimson cliff paintbrush and light pink tufted daisies. From this point, at about 6,600', you will reach the saddle between McAlester and Gibbs.

To attain the rock-bound summit of McAlester, proceed up its southern ridge on mostly gentle slopes with no technical difficulties. Avoid the perpetual snow and ice below the summit. The climb is mostly gradual but you will have gained nearly 3,000' of elevation. Nonetheless, the views are worth the toil: south to Bonanza and southwest to the Dome complex, especially its eastern aspects, including Dark Peak and the aptly-named Sinister, then sharply-angled Agnes and Needle Peaks. To the west lie McGregor Mountain and the Seven Sisters (though I can only count six), and some of the Ptarmigan Traverse Peaks, such as Sentinel and Old Guard. To your northeast rise Goode and Logan over the blades of Memaloose Ridge. These sport glaciers on *both* their north and south flanks. Buckner hides shyly behind, but its twin tops can be spied and recognized with binoculars. Just north, glimpse Frisco

CHAPTER TWENTY-FOUR: GUARANTEED SUNSHINE EAST OF THE CREST

Mountain and, behind it, Cutthroat Peak. To the east, Rennie and Reynolds can be spotted but to the northwest, Baker and Shuksan are concealed by the Cascade Pass Peaks.

Beckey's *Green Guide* suggests a climb of McAlester's southern neighbor, **Mt. Gibbs (8,142')**, directly from the South Fork Trail. You must continue south ¼ mile to attain the higher summit of Gibbs. However, once you've succeeded on McAlester, the most direct pathway is simply to follow the ridge south from its summit. It should be noted that the Green Trails and the 1969 7½" topo series place Gibbs at an elevation of 7,782'. Our GPS and altimeters beg to differ; Beckey is probably correct.

Here, you will be dancing across nontechnical meadows with no need for fancy choreography. When steepness intervenes, rock and ice experts might want to try their skill on the eastern edge of the ridge but the western side offers easier and more rapid travel. With only occasional bouldering, you reach a point named by Beckey as Mt. Gibbs after an early explorer of these realms. It remains a conundrum that the highest point on this crest bears no official name, especially since it stands 300' taller than McAlester itself.

The ridge affords up-and-down travel but rest stops for views are in order, particularly since the views to the south come into sharper focus the further you progress toward Gibbs. This northwest route surmounts several bumps before arriving at the summit. A register was in place several years back, but, as you may know, the Mountaineers have attempted to remove these antique artifacts. This can be equated with the removal of bolts on climbing routes that have been "freed", but some registers are often secreted under summit blocks and do provide a purpose in recording ascents, along with the occasional sardonic, pithy, or sometimes bizarre comments of prior parties.

The views from the top-most point are similar to those from McAlester but Bonanza and its northern counterparts, including Dark Peak and Mt. Lyall, can be seen more easily. Over Lake Chelan's northern tip, try to identify Black Tower and, further south,

Dumbell [sic – more accurately spelled with two"b's" in some texts and on certain maps], Chiwawa, and Fortress Mountains. The relatively untraveled peaks lining Lake Chelan's western shore, including Castle Rock and Tupshin Peak, can also be spotted by the advanced North Cascader, or more likely by someone with a comprehensive map.

Try not to rush back to camp after the gradual descent from the saddle between McAlester and Gibbs as most "climbing" accidents actually occur on the long drive back home. Relax one more evening under skies not cloaked by urban light and track the many meteorites as they flash across the night sky. Try to comprehend the Milky Way, an arm of our galaxy and a source of wonder that it represents but a single (and minor) spiral nexus of the Milky Way Galaxy. In fact, many, if not most of what we can see from earth through amateur telescopes or even strong binoculars are not stars at all, but far-away galaxies in our incomprehensibly vast universe. The cosmos may be stranger than we now understand; indeed; it may be stranger than we *can* understand. Our brains evolved to help us survive on earth, and to propagate our species, not to necessarily totally comprehend the universe. These notions embellish the trip out to the South Fork the following day, and render the drive back on the Freeway insignificant compared with that of these nighttime wonders. But if you have accomplished these climbs on McAlester Ridge and its offshoots, you can at least take pride in reaching one small space on this earth, glorious in itself and one that few others have ever enjoyed. The pleasures of these out-of-the-way peaks, ridges and meadows will always refresh the climber after she or he reaches the more familiar asphalt, steel and silicon of the modern world.

CHAPTER TWENTY-FIVE

The Razor Blade Traverse

Scalpel Ridge

(7,065'–7,805')

HIDDEN GEMS OF THE WASHINGTON CASCADES

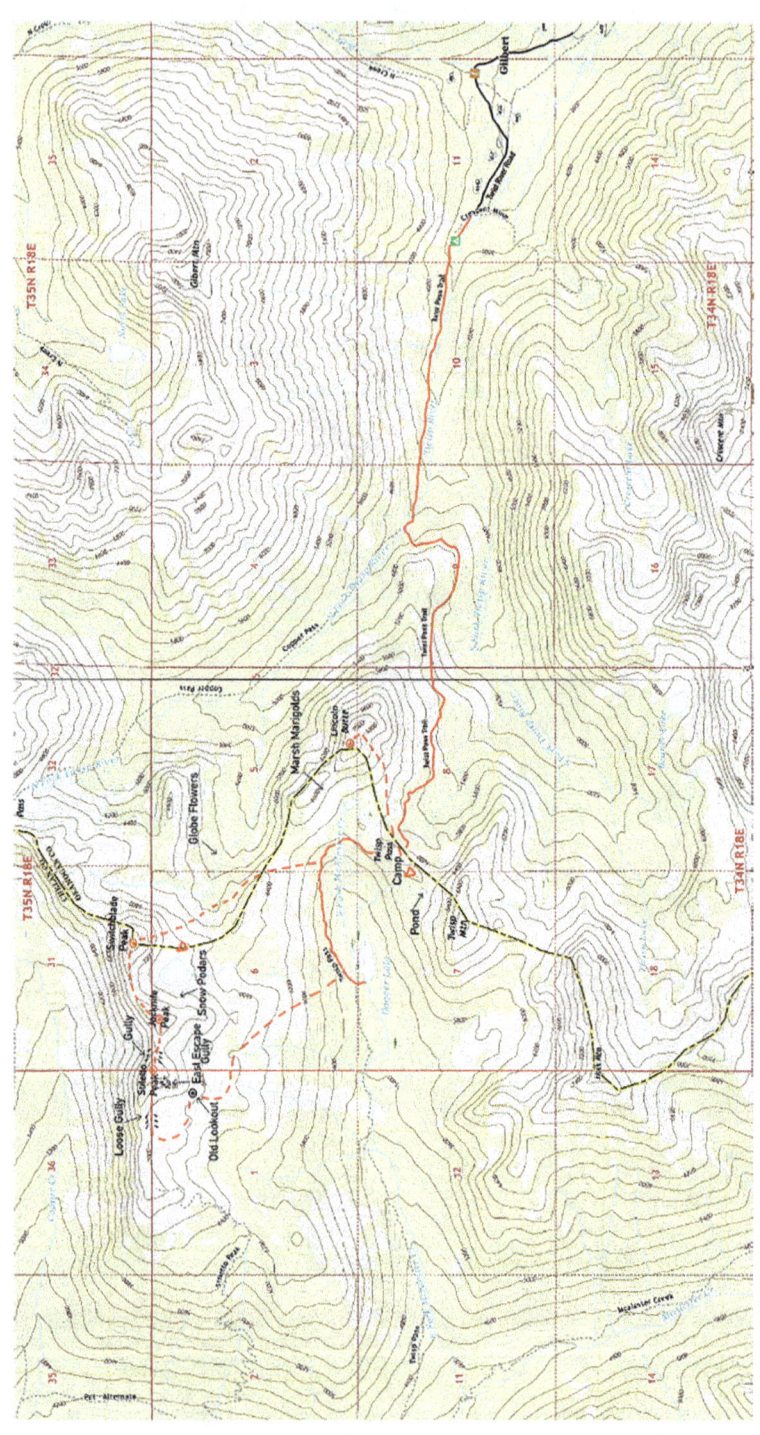

CHAPTER TWENTY-FIVE: THE RAZOR BLADE TRAVERSE

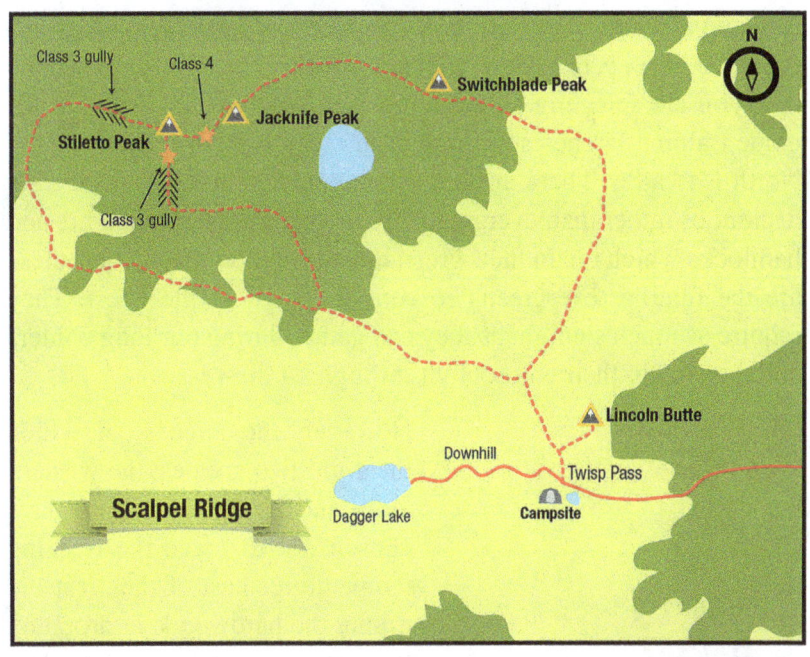

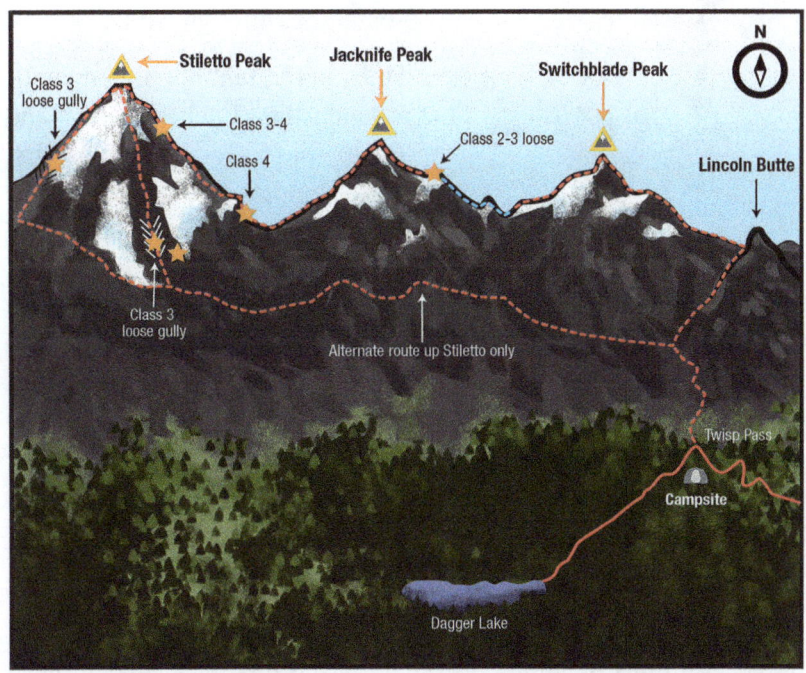

Remaining east of the crest is common for two major reasons: one, of course, is if weather dictates your choice, while the second is if you are selecting an autumn trip in order to luxuriate in the golden alpine larches so common in these eastern reaches of the North Cascades. There are but a few "needle" trees that are truly deciduous rather than evergreen. We are accustomed to the firs and hemlocks which retain their green hue throughout the winter; these are the familiar evergreens so common west of the Crest. They require as much sunlight as they can gather during our long winters and thus retain their chlorophyll throughout the year.

Alpine Larch

However, the larches, of which there are two species, the western larch and its alpine cousin, have chosen not to brave the freezing temperatures east of the crest but mimic the hardwoods in dropping their needles, now gilt, from late September through April.

Thus, in the fall, the high uplands around the Enchantments and Twisp Pass, for example, first turn a golden color, then forsake their branches and gild the ground with their orange-yellow needles.

It is a common error to use the phrase "turn" as in these needle-like larches and leafy hardwoods such as maples and alders, their leaves do not truly *turn* from green to yellow. They simply lose their green color and what lies beneath comes to the fore, usually the brown, orange and yellow that we so much associate with, and admire, every autumn.

Whatever the weather and season, a trip up to Twisp Pass, on the border of the Okanogan National Forest and the North Cascades National Park, will not disappoint any hiker, backpacker or climber. First, you must negotiate 25 miles on the dirt track of the Twisp River Road. Usually, however, this dusty thoroughfare is fairly easy

CHAPTER TWENTY-FIVE: THE RAZOR BLADE TRAVERSE

to navigate all the way to its end without having to use any high-clearance vehicles. Most cars can manage the ride without fear of bottoming out, as long as their speed is reasonable. You will reach, at road's end, an enormous parking lot filled with SUV's, Subaru's, and the occasional Prius and Volvo at 3,650'. Begin this journey from the parking lot on the well-marked Twisp River Trail, #432 and, at 2 miles, stay left at the junction with the steep Trail #426 to Copper Pass, a viewless saddle you should by all means avoid.

Continue on the relatively gentle Twisp River Trail, noting the abundance of the 3'-tall cut-leaved luina to your right, with huge palmately cleft leaves and topped with yellow dandelion-like heads. These, in the Aster Family, lack ray petals but sport numerous individual disk flowers. The Aster Family is the world's second largest in terms of number of species. Its success lies most certainly in its habit of floral charade: What appears to be a single blossom is actually many.

Cut Leaf-Luina

In most species within this family, such as the asters and daisies, each ray petal is actually a complete flower and each disk is also composed of a multitude of individual disk flowers, thus deceiving the many insect pollinators anxious to sip its nectar and unwittingly fertilize the next flower it visits by ferrying pollen from blossom to blossom. Although certain Aster Family species are wind pollinated (think of the dandelion), most are pollinated by flying insects. What's the world's largest family, in number of species? The Orchid Family takes that honor, with over 24,000 species and a seemingly infinite number of hybrids. The Aster Family comes second and counts approximately 23,000 species in all.

The trail begins in a benign manner but becomes a bit more adventurous ("steep") at around 3½ miles, then ascends to Twisp

Pass. Along the way, especially at 4,000' and above, glance to your left to appreciate the northern flanks of Hock Mountain, which appear too precipitous to attempt but, in reality, this foreshortened view belies a Class 3 ascent on its northwest ridge. At about 4,100', look to your right (north) to see the first of the climbable peaks surrounding the pass, sharply angled Lincoln Butte. Once you reach the pass at 6,084', gaze down at Dagger Lake but please do not, as the books recommend, make the 500' descent to its shores. Should you do so, you will only have to ascend that elevation again the next day, and you will be hounded by flying insects in such varied swarms that some species may have not yet been identified by entomologists.

Instead, stay on the eastern fringes of the lightly wooded ridge to your south; a mere 5-minutes' walk will bring you to a small pond (usually full throughout the entire climbing season), and with an outlet stream and flat ground on which to establish a base camp on the eastern fringe of the ridge and not in the National Park. You thereby avoid the requirement to obtain a camping permit at the Twisp Ranger Station. From this vantage point, you can see all the named and unnamed peaks on Scalpel Ridge (my appellations) to explore: one, **Lincoln Butte (7,065')**, can be easily climbed after you've established camp.

To do so, meander up grassy meadows festooned with spurred lupines; small-flowered paintbrush, the most common alpine paintbrush in the North Cascades, some of which are a dusky white, others a dull maroon; 1'-tall spikes of partridgefoot, its leaves an almost exact rendition of this bird's lower extremity; pink subalpine daisies; taller purple alpine asters; and exquisite white blooms of globeflower, whose 2' tall orbs emanate from muddy patches: a beauty arising from humble origins.

Globeflower

CHAPTER TWENTY-FIVE: THE RAZOR BLADE TRAVERSE

Climb through color, needing only hiking poles, to reach Lincoln's summit. The view to the west is partly blocked by the ridge of Stiletto Peak itself, but still encompasses the tops of Mts. Logan and Goode. To the north lie the remarkable rocky towers of the Early Winter Spires and Liberty Bell while to the northeast, Silver Star shows off the snowy mantle of its eastern and southern faces; not a bad 45-minute evening stroll up the Butte to work up an appetite.

The next day, the true fun begins. Most parties simply climb class-3 **Stiletto (7,660')** but for you, the brave buccaneer, the true test is to run the knife-like ridge in its entirety, thereby summiting all three of the named peaks and varied points in between. Although there will be precious little difficulty in either route finding (you will be above timberline the entire way) or the need for technical equipment, you will encounter some class-4 pitches with moderate exposure. Therefore, it is wise to consider your party's abilities when deciding upon what equipment to bring along.

From the pass, a trail begins that eventually leads to the ancient Stiletto Lookout (7,223'), now a heap of ruins. However, it offers a viewpoint far surpassing any from the pass, a worthwhile objective for hiking alone. The trail gives out in patches of alpine larches but can easily be followed simply by heading northwest to the knobby lookout. Along the way, note a relatively large lake, often lying at the foot of a permanent snowfield at the base of Stiletto's eastern aspect. The lake is a pretty sight and a reasonable destination but a bit out of the way inasmuch as it lies to the north, that is if your sole intent is to reach the lookout. However, for those who wish to climb Stiletto alone, then have to pack up and head home, it makes a suitable starting point. There is an obvious gully on the peak's southern aspect with solid holds for a class 3 scramble to Stiletto's top. An interesting descent is down a loose class-3 gully on the peak's west face.

Any of these routes will cross streams emanating from the lake just mentioned above and from snowfields on Stiletto's southern flanks. Watch for two buttercup family wildflowers along their courses: subalpine buttercup with shiny yellow petals and the

Ballhead Waterleaf

white globeflower, sprouting up seemingly from the midst of streams and marshes along the way. In the drier portions of your trek, note the comical ball-head waterleaf, a foot-tall plant with mottled leaves and flowers held below its leaves in a globe-shaped cluster, appearing as a lavender furry orb. Count yourself fortunate if it's autumn as the alpine larches turn a golden hue and drop their needles on freshly fallen snow. This wilderness is truly a photographer's paradise.

However, I recommend trying the full Stiletto Ridge; it's straightforward to ease off the ridge onto 3rd-class descent routes if the going proves too tricky. Otherwise, begin by tackling the full "Scalpel Ridge" (my moniker) by heading north from Twisp Pass. You can follow a stream-course, then bypass a lake (6,795') on its eastern shore. From this spot, you can spy the highest peak on this ridge, which bears an unjust indignity, remaining officially unnamed. Beckey, in his thorough manner however, and in keeping with the knife-like names on the ridge, applies the name **"Switchblade Peak"**, at **7,805'**. By aiming north-north-east, you can scramble class-3 rock with intermittent grass and heather, to reach its summit, the highest of this compact range.

Views abound in all directions: To the south, spy McAlester Ridge, with Rennie and Reynolds peaks in outstanding relief, their sharpest sides on their east and west ridges delineated most clearly. The peaks queuing the east and west shores of Lake Chelan arise in similar relief while the hulk of Bonanza broods in the far distance. Even Mt. Stuart can be spied to the southeast. To your east, a multitude of lakelets can be seen while to the west, the giants of Logan, Goode and Buckner are visible. It is to the north and northwest, however, that the views present aspects seldom gained from any other perspective.

CHAPTER TWENTY-FIVE: THE RAZOR BLADE TRAVERSE

Over Gilbert Mountain, take in the vast bulk of Silver Star, with its multitude of steeples and towers bearing the intoxicating names of wine varieties, such as Chablis and Burgundy Spires. To the south of Silver Star, discover Kangaroo Ridge, a saw-toothed line of jagged pinnacles which still to this day bear routes attempted unsuccessfully. Look north to those icons of North Cascades postcards, Early Winter Spires and Liberty Bell, with Cutthroat Peak just beyond. Breathe in these views as they will be the most extensive from this ridge.

There are too many summits to identify from this summit and, if your goal is to run the ridge, it's best not to tarry too long. To your west, note the sometimes-improbably jagged crest you must now assault. But the going is much easier than it looks. (Where have I heard that before?) Stick largely to the crest. Strange as it seems, the northern side is at times a bit easier when it looks too technical to stay on the ridge proper. Your goal is **Peak 7,700'**, baptized **"Jackknife Peak"** by Beckey.

This ridge, at times as thin as my wallet, trends southwest, then bumps along over several smaller mounds to reach Jackknife's summit. The scrambling between Switchblade and Jackknife is all on rock about as stable as a paranoid schizophrenic off his meds, but it does not require roped climbing; it's in the main class 2–3. From this mountaintop, all the same views can be had as from Switchblade, with the addition of Frisco, a sharply delineated summit forming the culmination of Fisher Creek Valley. Surely, a short rest and a snack are in order for it's the next brief section that will require nerves of Teflon, if not of steel.

To reach your ultimate peak on Scalpel Ridge, Stiletto, the distance may be small but the route requires a tolerance for moderate exposure and the patience to test hand-and foot-holds. Descend toward the saddle between Jackknife and Stiletto, facing in at one point to check out hand-holds. Next, dance across an exposed but steady class-4 section 200' above this saddle, bypassing a block on its south side. This choreography requires the accuracy of a delicate surgeon's blade rather than a chainsaw, but eventually gains you a broader ridge to tip-toe to the summit of Stiletto itself. Be certain in this ballet, however, that the tune does not become off-key. Steep drop-offs to the north could cause this foxtrot to topple.

However, the final class-3 scramble to the summit should provide no difficulties. It remains a mystery why cartographers chose to reward Stiletto a name while ignoring its higher brethren to the east. But since it has a lookout, which you can spot to your south on a rocky knob, perhaps early explorers felt the need to christen it with its knife-like moniker. Views abound, much the same as from Switchblade Peak, but a bit closer to the towers of Early Winter Spires and Liberty Bell, while the daggers of Kangaroo Ridge are thrown into sharper relief.

The descent can be negotiated by several class-3 gullies on the east side of Stiletto to the lake at its eastern base or down a tricky gully with loose chock-stones toward the west. The latter bears the advantage of a slightly lengthier but more scenic route back to base. You might pack out after all this razorblade ridge-running, but should you stay, you will be more rested for the drive home. All-in-all, gamboling across these knife-like ridges requires care but if you proceed with surgical precision, you and others who might dread any route above moderate 4th-class climbing can enjoy extensive and unusual perspectives of most of the significant summits in the northeastern sections of the North Cascades, both within and just outside the boundaries of the National Park.

CHAPTER TWENTY-SIX

It's Worth the Brush

Mt. Blum
(7,680')

HIDDEN GEMS OF THE WASHINGTON CASCADES

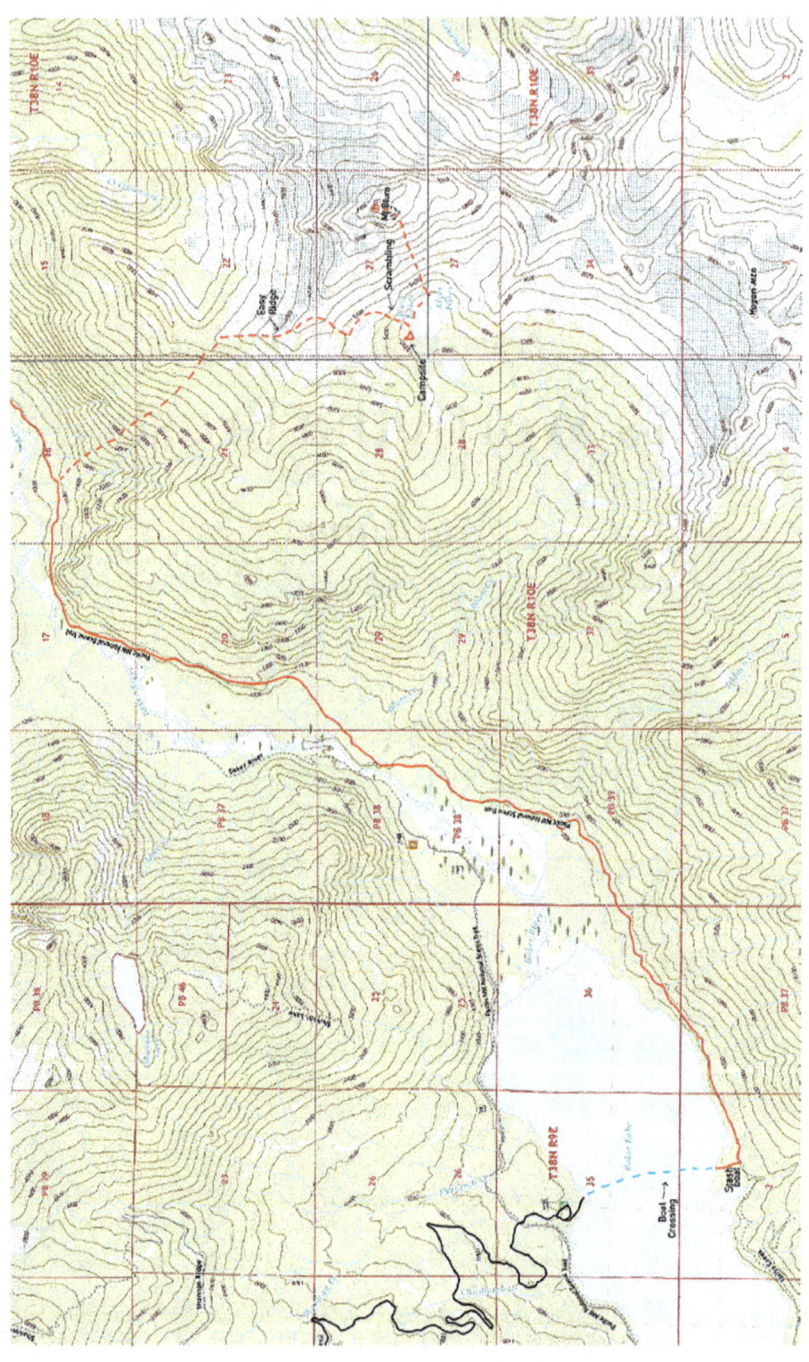

CHAPTER TWENTY-SIX: IT'S WORTH THE BRUSH

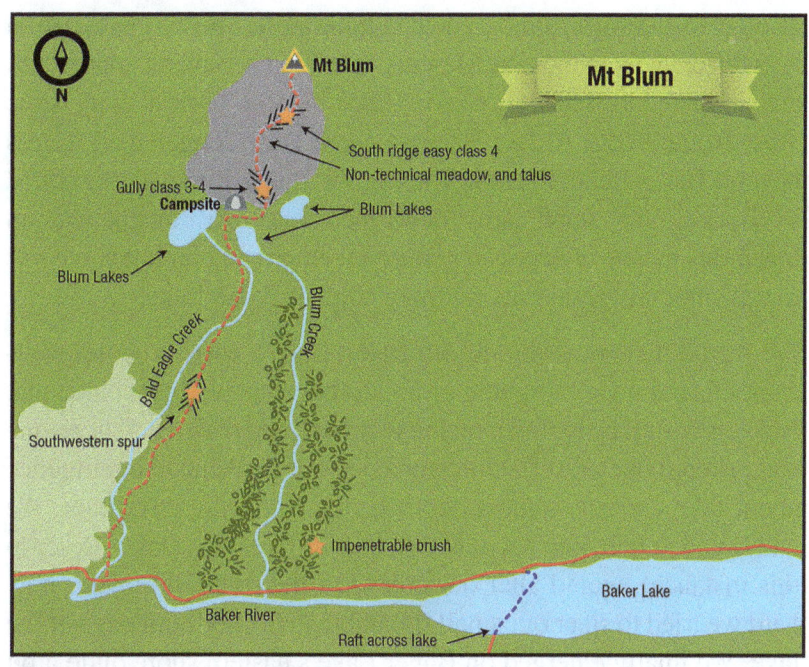

Though located at an almost equal latitude as the Stiletto Peaks, Blum is as different from those as Mercury is to Jupiter. Several approaches are suggested in Beckey's *Green Guide* but the "easiest" way is the West Route-South Ridge. Because there is no longer road access beyond Baker Lake, to avoid fording the Baker River, as suggested by Beckey, our small party developed what we thought was an ingenious means of accessing Blum by employing an inflatable raft to sail smoothly across the northern edge of Baker Lake.

We would then stow the raft on Baker Lake's eastern shore, well-camouflaged under a mound of brush (but so poorly concealed that we were fortunate to find it on the way back and discover that no one had pilfered our vessel). Unfortunately, our inadequate intelligence about lake currents almost doomed our sea-faring adventure. We had failed to take into account that a swift river (the Baker River in this instance), would alter our course to the south, no matter how hard we tried to steer our small inflatable to the northern edge of the lake. We finally emerged on Baker Lake's eastern shore quite a bit further south and much later than anticipated.

We then followed a fairly obvious tread toward our first objective, Blum Creek. This particular late July, the temperature at the town of Concrete was 107 degrees (a record), so we anticipated a difficult crossing of the creek. Therefore, to save weight, we had brought just one pair of flip-flops. Our bright idea was that the first person would use this footwear while crossing the turgid torrent, carrying socks and boots, then toss the flip-flops back across the raging creek to the next climber to use.

This splendid plan came to a pitiful end when the first climber tried to bridge the swollen creek, now more like an angry river, and promptly tossed the footwear back across it so high that it landed in a Douglas fir branch 40 feet above the furious stream. Putting boots and socks on our backs, the rest of us crossed barefoot. I believe my feet are still cold from that crossing. I know we could have crossed in boots sans socks but we wanted to keep everything as dry as possible.

CHAPTER TWENTY-SIX: IT'S WORTH THE BRUSH

Ignoring Beckey's instructions, we next ploughed through some of the most miserable brush imaginable trying to stay just northwest of Blum Creek. After all, shouldn't a stream named "Blum" lead naturally and most easily to Blum Lakes? We cursed the brush in red ruin, brawling with the spiny salmonberries; thorn-bulging Devil's clubs (no club I would wish to join); second-growth Douglas firs; stunted subalpine firs which incarcerated us in their knarled branches; fool's huckleberry (an appropriate name); salal; black hawthorn; trailing blackberry; and spiny gooseberry; all retarding the slovenly progress of our expedition. What could we make of such a country, tearing us asunder? We ploughed ahead in this steamy green hell, hotter it seemed than the surface of Venus, but never found Beckey's "informal trail" nor the "spur ridge east of Blum Creek". Studying the topo's and using GPS, we had placed cramming ahead of creativity: Our hopes often trumped reason and reality.

Salmonberry

Devil's Club

The tangled greenery we encountered formed a living rebuke, retarding our progress. We seemed caught up in a quantum world with a multiplicity of possibilities – all entangled. After fighting this brush of epic proportions for about 4,000' (we had begun at the lake's low elevation), it seemed we had reached a cul-de-sac of eternal brushy misery, with no present nor future - the sole certainty was that the past would keep repeating itself hour after hour. At one point, I whimpered about the heat but our leader, altering an old cliché', replied "It's not the heat, it's your stupidity". I was reminded of Schrodinger's cat: unseen, did the lakes really exist if, as it seemed likely, we would never actually catch a glimpse of them?

As we saw no immediate prospect of gaining open meadow or the Blum Lakes, and out of water in the overpowering heat, we had the wisdom to retreat; no need to turn attempt into tragedy. Our leader was a man of steel but even a star can run out of time. It was only later that we realized we were actually close to the lakes: scant solace in recalling being entombed in that prison of brush, and not realizing we were still in the wilderness and, in a sense, perhaps as free as we ever would be.

Once back at Baker Lake and after a prolonged search, now in the dark, we located our craft, paddled furiously back across the lake, always fighting the tide from the river pushing us southward. We aimed at lights from the Shannon Creek Campground and hit (literally) the west shore. Tripping over tents and awakening couples sleeping (or doing other things you can imagine), we disembarked but forgot the leader's boots. The last view, and the unforgettable image I have of our misguided adventure, is of his boots floating gently but quite out of reach, south-bound down Baker Lake. I can still see the scars of our battle with the brush and recall the stings of the salmonberry and Devil's club but in all honesty, I take perverse pleasure in these memories – at least we survived and on looking back, we were truly in the persistent pulse of nature.

There are more technically difficult routes to Blum including the north ridge (Grade III, class 5.9) and the south route (nontechnical but with a much longer approach). Blum's northeast spur has been climbed but it involves a brushy approach, then rock as loose as my ex-wife's use of credit cards. Our small group opted, for our second attempt, the western approach to the south ridge suggested in Beckey's *Green Guide, Mt. Blum Route*. This time, we were united in cheerful, yet defiant solidarity. And yes, we were in denial that we had completely ignored such a clearly labeled route the first time around. This proved that Beckey is more often correct than our

CHAPTER TWENTY-SIX: IT'S WORTH THE BRUSH

own mistaken instincts. Mistakes are forgivable; not learning from them is not.

We questioned the old saw that it was better to be wrong than vague. We dutifully followed Beckey's description on our second attempt, following Bald Eagle Creek, close to our first expedition but aiming for the southwestern spur. I cannot agree with Beckey's description of "an easy subalpine ridge" but the brush was not as miserable as on our first attempt. This route, while longer on the well-defined Baker River Trail, followed close to Bald Eagle Creek. We eventually crossed that river mid-way up, then headed first east, then south toward the spur, fortunately lightly forested. We traversed directly over Point 5,163 and reached pleasant strolling on the ridge heading south toward the lakes.

This spur is not the first one encountered, as steep cliffs block that passage. However, the second ridge leading due south will eventually deposit you at the lakes. We did encounter much brush but were able to gain the ridge Beckey describes, staying mostly on top of it to avoid as much brush as possible until we reached the lovely series of Blum Lakes. The largest of these was the third one south and this was also conveniently best positioned for our attempt on Blum the next day. We gazed ruefully down the steep slope and heavy brush in the valley of Blum Creek and were reproachful witnesses to the ravages we had endured on our initial attempt. We found the lakes to be surrounded by granite-like rock and snow, yet they afforded us multiple campsites and an evening stroll to explore the amazing scenery from this lofty perch, at around 6,307'.

And what a perch it was! World-class views south to Hagen and Bacon Peaks were up close and the jagged ridges separating them looked as evil as sharpened knives. That evening, as we peeked around a corner of the south ridge, a series of pointed towers and imposing minarets was spied, ending in Mts. Triumph and Despair. Their full silhouettes were not yet wholly visible, partially blocked by the cliffs off the crest, but nonetheless, their majesty, even in partial prospect, could be glimpsed. But it was the climb the next day that finally revealed the full bounty for which we had suffered this arduous approach.

On climb day, we think we found the gully Beckey mentioned above the lakes, but were never quite sure. Nor could we locate the "snow-cirque lake" he mentions but the latter may have been due to that lake being cloaked with snow (mid-July). Nonetheless, the route to the summit seemed straightforward as we boulder-hopped aiming for what we took to be the top-most point. Soon however, we were confronted by cliffs the size of skyscrapers, and realized we were hopelessly off-course.

Undaunted (well, partly daunted), we traversed south over easy 3rd-class rock to a higher 4th-class gully which allowed us to attain the south ridge, from which we ambled over easy rock to what we thought would be the apex of our climb. As so often happens in the mountains, what we had attained was a false summit (I hate that), merely a stony pyramid impersonating the top. However, a relatively easy traverse of the south ridge brought us to the true summit.

Adjectives cannot adequately convey the majesty of our view. The series of minarets and towers between Blum and its southern neighbors, Hagen and Bacon Peaks, seemed to have been arranged by a madman intent on thwarting any climbers' ambitions. Hagen has multiple heaps of angular spires as possible summits. We quickly realized that our plans of also summiting Hagen from Blum were a bit grandiose, although Beckey advises that it could be accomplished. Not by us, however.

Anyway, we were so enthralled by the panoramas unfolding before us that we were in no mood for what could have been a technical traverse. To our southwest, the needles of Teebone Ridge stood out in stupendous relief, while beyond, Eldorado's northwestern snow-laden slopes were surmounted by its northern ridges, culminating in the vertical pillars of Dorado Needle and the Austera Towers. Just beyond Bacon Peak, we could study the astounding step-like southern buttress of Mt. Triumph and to its north, the well-named and rarely attempted Mt. Despair.

CHAPTER TWENTY-SIX: IT'S WORTH THE BRUSH

To the northwest, the yin and yang concave cirques of both the south and north Pickets were resplendent in the sunshine. We argued about which was which but the unmistakable peaks of Crooked Thumb, Fury and Challenger cresting the northern range were agreed upon, although Luna was hidden by its taller neighbors. To the south, above the remarkable Crescent Creek Spires stood the McMillan Spires, Inspiration Peak, the frightening Mt. Terror and the distinctive Chopping Block. Further southwest, the Cascade Pass Peaks were mostly concealed by intervening ridges, although the top of Forbidden Peak was identified, but some among us doubted the attribution. Views north and northwest encompassed the two snow-blanketed giants: Baker, directly above Baker Lake, and to its east, Shuksan, everybody's favorite mountain (at least mine). Yet these views from the south offered us a unique glimpse of their southeastern slopes, no less intimidating than the more famous views from the ski area on Baker's eastern side.

The jagged ridge trending east from Shuksan, with its almost unclimbable Nooksack Tower, was clearly in view. To our northeast, Bear and Redoubt could be seen, the latter with its enormous southern-trending flying buttress, surpassing those of any man-made cathedral. However, the incisor-like Slesse was concealed by intervening ridges and peaks. We sat dumbstruck at the majesty before us. We were fortunate in having the luxury of a second night at camp, the sun playing with randomly scattered shadows, first highlighting one area, then the next.

Our dreams that night were punctured by needles, minarets and spires as dramatic as the views we had been privileged to witness that day. Our descent back to civilization in the form of beating back the brush, then bypassing the numerous campsites along Baker Lake, was unmemorable. But we will never forget our priceless experience, although back in town it also seemed everything had a price. This time we relished our success not chiefly in summiting Blum, but because we had seen firsthand much of the iconic nirvana that is the North Cascades.

CHAPTER TWENTY-SEVEN

Better Views of the Giants than Climbing Them

Fisher Peak

(8,040')

HIDDEN GEMS OF THE WASHINGTON CASCADES

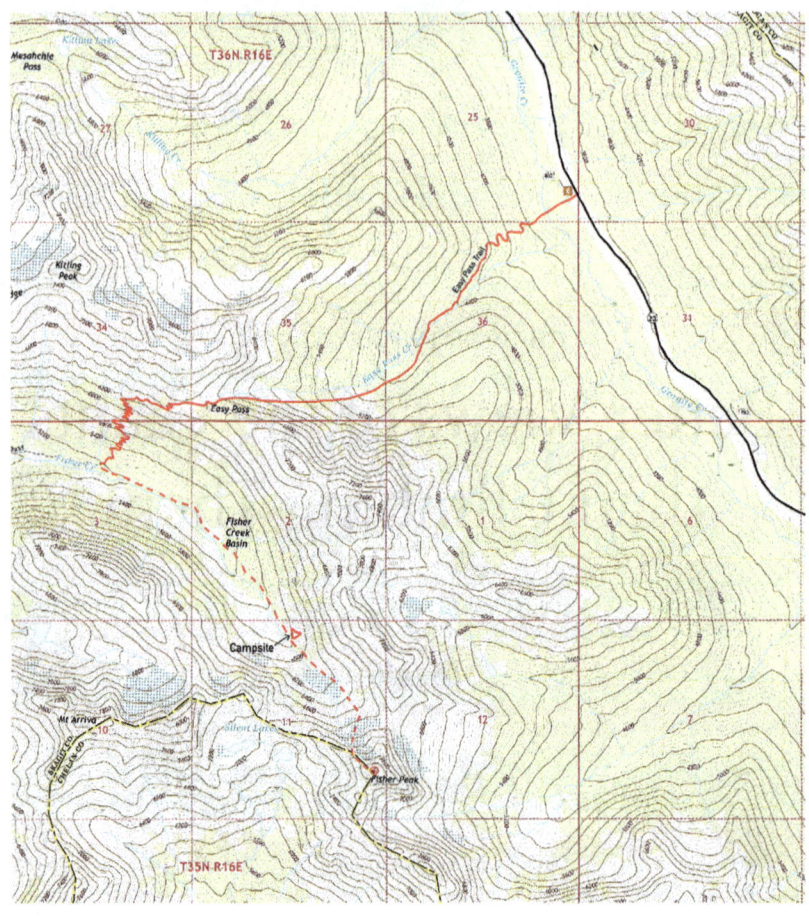

CHAPTER TWENTY-SEVEN: BETTER VIEWS OF THE GIANTS

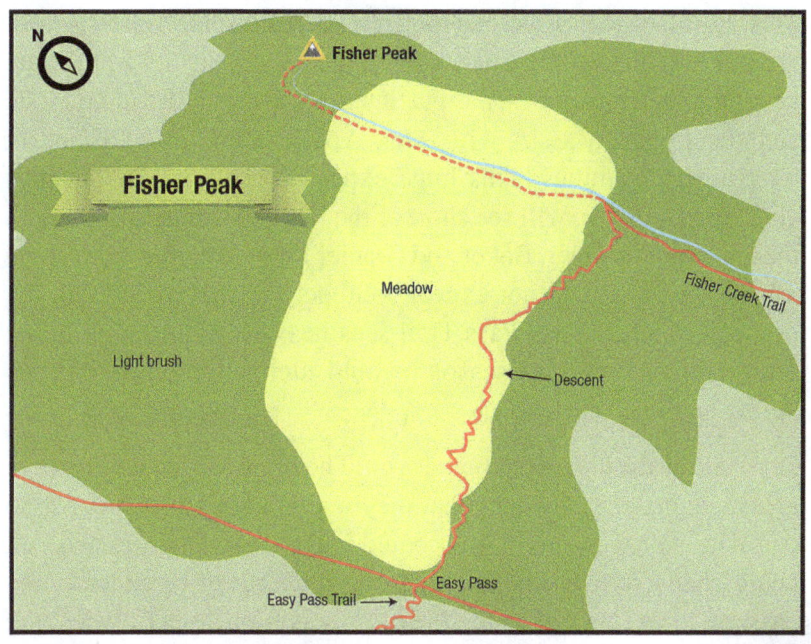

This thimble-like peak can be considered as the eastern-most capstone of the valleys beneath Ragged Ridge to its immediate west and the expanse of the glaciated north faces of Mts. Goode and the Logan Massif, with Mts. Arriva, Corteo and Black at its southern terminus. This huge expanse encompasses the most glaciated faces you will see short of the Range's volcanoes, such as those on Mts. Rainier, Baker and Glacier Peak. You may come here for the views but do not expect solitude. From Highway 20, the ironically named Easy Pass Trail sees heavy use during climbing season (at least the only season I would attempt these peaks), even during summer weekdays.

Don't allow the crowds to bother you. The more folks who use these areas, the better the chance that they will remain preserved, for no one with any measure of soul could leave these environs without being changed; even the most hardened abuser of these trails and passes will be touched by the fire of preservation, hopefully leaving only with a sunburn and the pack they carried in.

Scarlet Columbine

Despite its name, there really is no easy way to approach Easy Pass, then descend into the headwaters of Fisher Creek and climb Fisher without exerting stamina and perseverance. Also, beware if clouds become excited – this is a trip to be undertaken solely under sparkling skies. The Easy Pass Trail climbs steadily after crossing the bridge over Granite Creek (you used to have to ford it in earlier times). Note the many multi-hued columbines on your right as the forest gives way to open spaces. These, the scarlet columbines, bear a closer look: Turn the flower gently to marvel at its symmetrical yellow petals and crimson sepals retroflexed in support of the main flower. Its Latin species name (*formosa*) appropriately means "beautiful".

CHAPTER TWENTY-SEVEN: BETTER VIEWS OF THE GIANTS

After a crossing of Easy Pass Creek on stone and logs about mid-way up, you arrive in the open meadows of this splendid cirque, where no trees can withstand the annual avalanches rumbling down from the pass. Crimson paintbrush, blue lupines, yellow fan-leaf cinquefoils and subalpine buttercups, (especially near the all-season stream), along with the tiny purple Cusick's speedwell (a small eye will appreciate its delicate architecture), all vie for attention in liquid whorls of pigment, while the views north to Mts. Ballard and Azurite, as well as to the sharpened turrets of Cutthroat and Whistler Peaks, sear your soul.

Fan-Leaf Cinquefoil

I attempted to both admire the flora and scenery while trying, with full pack, to keep up with the leaders, who had evidently trained with Usain Bolt. But I finally attained the Pass, where vistas to the south and west will leave you agape. The heavily-crevassed glaciers of Mts. Goode, Storm King and Logan blanket their northern slopes while their serrated ridges and summits are laid bare before you, stunning in their breathtaking glory. Fronting these monsters are the sharp arêtes of Arriva, Corteo and Black Peaks (see the ABC Chapter later in the text). Look to the west to comprehend the saw-toothed Ragged Ridge, beginning at the pass and continuing westward to Red Mountain in a jagged line of peaks over 10 miles in length. Only the famed Pickets can compete with such a rugged horizon.

Lines of alpine larch hedge the pass itself, where the delicacy of the flora and fauna (watch for the fat marmots) demand no camping, nor, if your goal is to climb Fisher, would you want to. However, if you plan one other day to challenge the Ragged Ridge Peaks, a world-class camp can be attained by climbing the grassy slope to your right (south) 500' to a huge sandy flat, where at least four tents may be pitched on level soil. Snowmelt off its northern slope provides a year-round water source.

No matter where else you might wander in this mountain-filled universe, you will not discover grander views from any campsite. Here, you and your seven closest friends could take many days to discover Ragged Ridge's scores of wonders, including its tallest and most challenging peak, Mesachie. If peaks on Ragged Ridge are your focus, see a later chapter to avoid the criminal error, perpetuated by Beckey's *Green Guide*, in directing you to descend into the Fisher Creek Valley, a painful loss of 1,300' which you must regain the next day. These peaks can all be climbed from this spectacular vantage point noted above without injury to your knees.

You could also try to make a sort-of level camp above the pass to your east amongst the larches where some flat spots remain, but even that may well be teasing the Park Service Rangers into issuing you a ticket. To climb Fisher itself, however you have just one choice: that descent of 1,300' into the bosom of the Fisher Creek Valley. Fortunately, the views remain as you descend the well-maintained switchbacked trail which, at the bottom, meets the Fisher Creek Trail.

Fireweed

Most parties here will turn right (west) onto that broad Trail, which holds dozens of approved campsites along its considerable length until it reaches the Thunder Creek Trail miles away. This is not the way for the true mountaineer. Turn instead left (east) on a timeworn climber's path to head up-valley, where you will see, at its head, your goal: Fisher Peak standing proud above the many fireweed plants, not weeds at all, but beautiful dusky red in July and, by late August, shedding their flowers and turning into wooly strands that resemble clouds of cotton.

CHAPTER TWENTY-SEVEN: BETTER VIEWS OF THE GIANTS

Camp at the head of the valley, on gravel and sand at about 6,200–6,400' elevation; a number of bare patches exist. The bugs are not terrible at this altitude, especially early in July or late in August. Beware of a herd of voracious deer however, who fear no human. They were after my salty sweaty socks drying in the radiant sunshine late one afternoon, and, unfazed by my shouts nor by chasing them with an ice ax, they made off with several pair. From this campsite, several snow gullies lead south in about 1,000' to the twin Silent Lakes, a worthwhile and necessary endeavor for climbing Mt. Arriva, best left for a second day.

If your goal is to summit Fisher, camp as close to the steepening valley head as possible while still within reach of Fisher Creek or its many tributaries crisscrossing the valley floor. On climb day, aim southeast to gain Fisher's northwestern ridge. Snow will usually linger throughout the summer months to the north of this crest. At first, the ridge appears to offer an easy gradient. However, after about 500', it becomes steeper, and requires a traverse to its southern side, where in about 400', the ridge merges with the west face of Fisher, at about 7,500'. While the climbing on this face offers several enjoyable mantles and crack climbing, the majority consists of rock as loose as overhanging beach sand. Beckey rates it between class 3 and 4, but certain parties may wish a belay on anything solid you can find. Others forego the rope, believing it will only loosen rocky blocks falling at terminal velocity towards their helmets.

Persist, however, even though there are a few class-4 moves. If stumped, always look to your left as somewhat easier class-3 climbing can usually be found on the northwestern flank. Note that there exist permanent ice/snow basins on Fisher's northern inclines. From about 7,800', the moves to gain the summit consist of satisfying boulder hopping on sturdier stone. Should anyone in your party be nervous about 4th-class moves without a cord, bring a rope, harnesses, slings, carabineers and hard hats. Unless you plan a "shoulder season" ascent in late fall or early spring, no ice gear is required.

The views from that campsite I mentioned above Easy Pass are remarkable enough but in no way diminish what you can absorb from the summit of Fisher. Close in, Arriva, Corteo and Black dominate the southeastern aspect, while to the northeast, the five or so sharp-toothed peaks of Ragged Ridge bear close scrutiny. To the south, Heather Pass and even Lake Ann can be spotted.

But it is to the south and southwest that the stone-cold north faces of almost-unclimbable Goode, the rarely attempted Storm King, and, best of all, the Douglas and Banded Glaciers of Logan's north face, all stand out in resplendent frigid beauty. Mt. Buckner can be glimpsed beyond. Further afield, the views to the south encompass Glacier Peak, the Dome Range, and bulky Bonanza. Beyond Ragged Ridge, Ballard and Azurite stand tall, while further west, Crater Mountain, in sharp profile, fronts its more famous northern neighbor, Jack Mountain.

Just above Ragged Ridge, the top-most peaks of the Pickets can be seen, while to the extreme northwest, the iconic shape of Redoubt, with its famed southern flying buttress, is in view. To the far west, spy the top of Eldorado just above Mt. Logan, with its knife-edged northern ridge well-defined. Cutthroat lies due east, with Liberty Bell and the Early Winter Spires thrusting up in grand and precipitous splendor. This scene, once experienced, is hard not to crave, sort of like your favorite chocolate chip cookie, though requiring quite a bit more effort.

Try not to take the seemingly mandatory group photo of every member of your party attempting to smile while standing stiff as frozen flags un-buffeted by the wind. Yes, I hate those feigned smiling summit photos, which reveal nothing while trying to catalogue everything. The glory of these views cannot be captured on a smart-phone, no matter its number of pixels nor even by an SLR. Anyway, you know you have photo-obsessed friends in high places. Let them take the requisite photographs. I realize there is an elemental need to share these adventures; however, they cannot be captured by a camera but only by actually experiencing, enduring and sensing them.

CHAPTER TWENTY-SEVEN: BETTER VIEWS OF THE GIANTS

Hopefully, you will have the luxury of absorbing all these views in no haste as you have planned wisely not to attempt to descend the loose rock of this west face and ridge, pack up, re-climb the 1,300' back to Easy Pass, then take the trail out. Remember that it's not all downhill from camp. Do not allow haste to turn into tragedy by driving home after such a pack-out. Doing so may turn the statistical into the personal. Anyway, the experience of camping another night in the magnificence at the headwaters of Fisher Creek is an integral part of this mountain experience. After all, you cannot move this mountain, but surely, this mountain will move you.

CHAPTER TWENTY-EIGHT

The ABC's of the North Cascades

Arriva

(8,215')

Black

(8,970')

and Corteo Mountains

(8,080')

HIDDEN GEMS OF THE WASHINGTON CASCADES

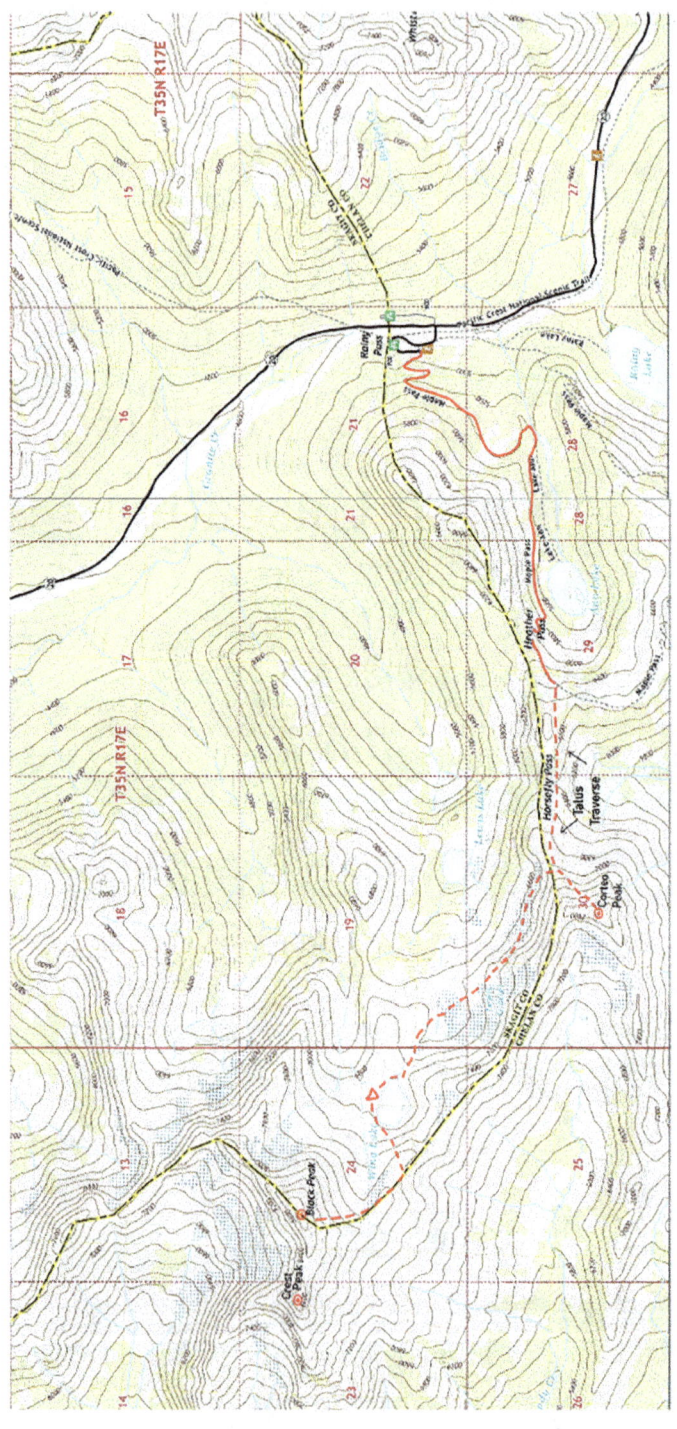

CHAPTER TWENTY-EIGHT: THE ABC'S OF THE NORTH CASCADES

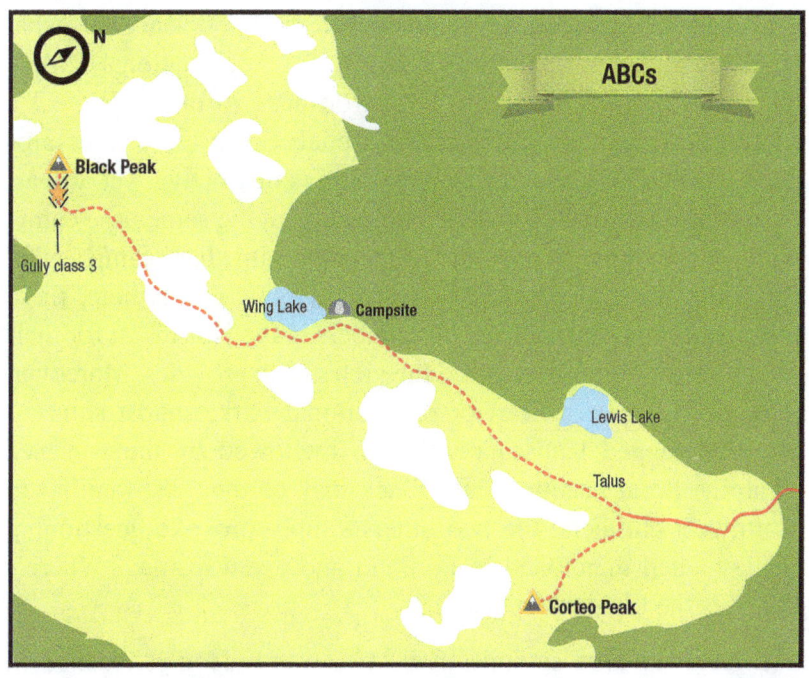

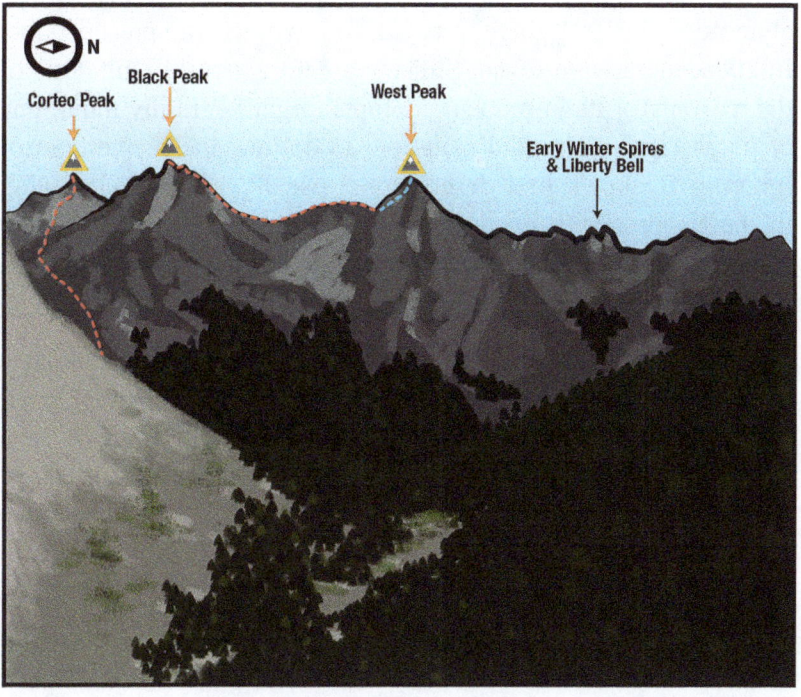

This trio of challenging summits offers the essence of what climbing and scrambling in the North Cascades National Park is all about. Initially speaking, I was fortunate in that each peak's first three letters are those of the alphabet, but these three alps share more than just orthography. Each is distinctive, yet at least two, Black and Corteo, can be climbed from the same base camp, while Arriva must be approached from the same base camp as that for Fisher Peak (Chapter 27). Rugged, rocky and remote, these three deserve attention from all climbers in the Northwest for their relatively moderate routes and the views each provides. Moreover, they sit at the very heart of the National Park, amidst some of its most rugged landscapes, though mellowed by the presence of alpine floral beauty. While Black may be the most familiar to Northwest climbers, the two others simply provoke questioning replies when mentioned in Portland and even Seattle: "Where's that?" is the typical response.

Mt. Arriva's true summit, at **8,215'**, was only first reached in 1966. When I arrived on Arriva (I have no idea of the name's etymology) in 1991, there were just four parties who preceded me. In 2006, there were seven. Still the ascent is not difficult. One of the reasons for its infrequent attempts might be, in my mind, one of its assets: its splendid isolation. I continue the theme here of ignoring Beckey's first descriptions, usually correctly implying the best approach. It may always be wise, especially on the easier peaks, to read his *Green Guide* in its entirety as alternative routes may prove more feasible.

For the approaches to Arriva, Beckey first mentions the east ridge or the eastern approach; this involves miles of tedious path-treading and much bushwhacking. Instead of the 15-mile trek he first recommends, the identical approach to Fisher Peak over Easy Pass, then a descent into the Fisher Creek Valley described in the preceding chapter, will prove to contain the least amount of toil. Simply ascend the sarcastically named Easy Pass Trail to the Pass, about 2,800' gain in 3½ miles, then descend the track to the Fisher Creek Trail, a drop of about 1,300'. Of course, on the trip out, you will have to regain this elevation, though with a lighter pack and hopefully after a second night at base camp to rest up for the trip out and the drive home.

Note the flora in the broad avalanche swath as you climb the Easy Pass Trail. Here, trees barely have the capacity to grow tall, as winter and early spring avalanches overwhelm tiny seedlings trying to survive in the harsh environment of this north-facing cirque. As you ascend the tedious switchbacks, you will be hiking through color, as the blue lupines, scarlet paintbrushes, spikes of white partridgefoot and yellow fan-leaf cinquefoils cheer you on. The tread is easy to follow but, near the Pass's crest, you will be walking on gravel rather than dirt. Not to worry; the views which open up at the Pass (6,500') are more than spectacular. The north faces of Goode, Storm King and Logan, with their glaciers heavily crevassed, are in close enough proximity that you may well hear them unload their burdens of icy seracs even though they are, in reality, miles distant.

Fan-Leaf Cinquefoil

If your goal is simply to backpack, you would be well-advised to climb the grassy hillock to your northwest (right, facing south) for, after a grueling ascent of 500' over tall grasslands, you will be well rewarded with a world-class campsite on bare sandy ground. It is sufficiently ample for 3–4 tents, so you can bring along a group of 7–12 of your closest hiking friends to share a view not soon forgotten. You will also be at the eastern terminus of Ragged Ridge and many of its peaks. Kitling Peak (8,003'), Peak 7690, New Morning Peak (7,230'), and

Patridgefoot

Cub Peak (7,985') are all within a day's journey without the need for any rock protection.

All offer even more miraculous views than from the pass, although that seems like a miracle itself. Unfortunately, the crowning overseer of Ragged Ridge, Mesachie Peak (8,795'), while attainable from this blessed camp in a single day, may require protection for many parties; however, it has been climbed solo (even by me...so, well you know....). Use your judgment about the skills of your party before attempting Mesachie and see the following chapter for an account of traversing the entirety of the full Ridge.

Should your goal be Arrriva, it may be regrettable, but necessary, to descend the 1,300' to the floor of the Fisher Creek Valley, though your way is cheered by purple subalpine daisies and alpine asters, growing tall on this well-watered southern slope. Moreover, you can also be cheered by the constant presence of the views south, which now include your objective – Arriva. It appears directly in front of you in the form of a blackened series of saw-like teeth, its twin summits at the western end of this rugged sub-range. Soon you are at the very bottom of the maintained trail, where most parties turn right (west) to multiple well-used but bug-infested campsites along the Fisher Creek Trail.

American Bistort

But not for you, the more adventurous climber/scrambler. Head left (east) on a climbers' track through delightful flower-filled meadows ablaze with pink Cascade and leafy asters, ubiquitous white spires of partridgefoot, and yellow arrow-leaf groundsel. Note the towering fireweeds all about. They can reach 7' tall and at their tops, pink blossoms appear by July, followed by cottony wisps as seeds later in August. You are free of the dreaded west-of-crest brush, so you can luxuriate in these flowered meadows and soon, you will reach level

CHAPTER TWENTY-EIGHT: THE ABC'S OF THE NORTH CASCADES

campsites amidst lupines, paintbrushes, bistort and valerian. Pitch your tent up-valley off the flora at around 6,200' to 6,400'. Stands of Lyall's (alpine) larch and subalpine firs offer scant cover.

Camp here for the night as the following day you must trek up the valley of Fisher Creek to a hidden snow-filled couloir and ascend this icy streak at a 35–40-degree angle, using crampons and ice ax during the summer months. After a climb of roughly 600–700' you finally arrive at the spectacular basin to the south of the col holding the twin Silent Lakes, at 6,960'. Note with care that this couloir is hidden from view at Easy Pass, and even from your camp.

Therefore, as you ascend the gentle valley heading due east, do not attempt the first couloir. It is the second snow and ice gully you must attack. Struggling up the other couloirs will only lead to misery unless you are anxious to tackle high 5th-class loose rubble and vertical headwalls. Once at the saddle cresting the couloir you can enjoy the quietest bodies of water you are ever likely to witness: the twin Silent Lakes. Listen hard as I could, I never heard more than the muted breeze rustling across the waters. In many summers, these lakes, ponds really but large for the North Cascades, are completely iced over, with a mantle of snow on top.

Serrated peaks abound from this col in all directions. Particularly ominous is the yellow and dark grey mass of Mesachie to the northwest; beautiful in its own wicked way, it is the apex of saw-toothed Ragged Ridge. The entire crest of Ragged Ridge can now be appreciated as well. (See the following chapter.) The brooding hulk of Black Peak lies to your southeast. The pinnacle directly to the east is Fisher Peak (in the previous chapter), a 4th-class climb rarely attempted, while to the north, sharp-angled Greybeard matches its color with its name.

Split the lakes and head south between them a few hundred yards to avoid an east-facing cliff, then begin a somewhat loose traverse west on Arriva's south side, at about the 7,200–7,400' levels. Here, you must negotiate several gullies of loose rock, the down-then-up climbing more tedious than difficult. This traverse eventually brings you to a passage through a vault of rock just before encountering the southwest ridge at around 7,750'. From here, a 4th-class jaunt brings you to the true summit. The eastern peak is 55' lower and a traverse would seem to require rock gear for protection. You have arrived at Arriva!

Views even surpass those from Easy Pass or the campsite above it. Besides the complete and jagged outline of Ragged Ridge to your north and northwest, Black stands proud to the southeast. The glaciers cloaking the north faces of Goode, Storm King and Logan are directly in front of you now, the closest you can come to this astonishingly frozen view. The thumb of Thunder Peak, a precipitous eastern outpost along the ridge between Logan and Storm King, is of particular prominence, while Eldorado can be spied in the western distance. The sole difficulty ahead may lie in the descent of the couloir from Silent Lakes back to camp. If snow-filled or icy, careful cramponing or facing inward may prove necessary to avoid a slip on the 40-degree slope, at least by August.

Our "B" peak, **Black (8,970')**, is a more popular climb, given its relatively trail-filled approach and its dominance over the surrounding ranges. Its reputation is well-deserved. Stark, even grim in its appearance, well-named Black boasts a relatively handy approach via the Maple Pass Trail (a highway) with the bonus of a view down to Lake Ann, with its iconic island, a single hemlock punctuating its serenity. Maple Pass is gained in 1,800'; the Pass itself lies at 6,600'. From here, a climber's path, really now more of a major throughway, heads west through Heather Pass (few additional views except to Corteo and Black itself), then meadows to the ill-named Horsefly Pass. Begin a short trek first on path, then talus, then meadows again, just before reaching Wing Lake at about 6,905', and about 1½ miles from Maple Pass.

Note that there are unnamed, but shriveling glaciers on Black's north and eastern aspects. The lovely, yet unassuming Wing Lake is most often a populated base camp, especially on many summer weekends. Go mid-week if you can. Expect curious mountain goats; they are not particularly interested in you, but in your pee; they

CHAPTER TWENTY-EIGHT: THE ABC'S OF THE NORTH CASCADES

relish the salt in urine and lap it up constantly, never thinking twice about how disgusting a habit it would be to its human progenitors.

The goal the following morning is to scramble up sand or snow to a saddle on Black's southern slope at 7,900', then contour around to reach a south-facing half-gully filled with loose SUV-sized boulders. (Hard hats please, and mind the parties above and below you.) Pleasant 3rd-class scrambling above concludes an enjoyable ascent on reasonable rock to the summit. And the views! These are even more expansive than those from neighboring summits as you are above most of them. The identity of many peaks from this vantage point is usually straightforward: Of course, Arriva and Corteo are the closest but Fisher Peak and Mt. Frisco stand out in the east, while to the southwest, the entire Buckner-Logan-Stormking-Goode Range displays its snowy white expanse of heavily glaciated ice fields, so close they are seemingly within your grasp. Ragged Ridge profiles the northwestern perspective, with a particular appreciation awarded to its master, Mesachie, the tallest on this saw-toothed crest.

From this vantage point, Crater and Jack Mountains are quite prominent to the north while even Baker and Shuksan can be spied over the Pickets in the northwest. It might be easier to name the mountains you *can't* see from Black, so wide-ranging are its views. Glacier Peak and the Dome massif are to your southwest. Then try to gain a perspective on peaks tentatively named by Beckey but not yet on the most recent topo's: Repulse Peak to the east (I can only imagine the derivation of its name); Indecision and Meulfire Peaks to Black's immediate south (this last named after an early explorer of this marvelous mess of mountains); then Fisher and Graybeard Peaks to the northeast. Try to identify Cutthroat Peak, with no easy route possible; then the nearly vertical walls of Early Winter Spires and Liberty Bell, all to the northeast.

You may not want to attempt **Black's West Peak**, at **8,820'**. Indeed, that sub-peak could deserve a day all to itself. While Beckey describes protracted approaches, we were able to traverse the western ridge of Black to reach this lesser summit. The ridge-walk is tedious because of loose rock at first and 4th-to-low 5th-class careful scrambling. It is wise, if attempting this route, to place protection carefully due to the loose nature of the rock, sort of similar to beach sand, although some quartz-diorite near the summit eases the nerves. The views mirror those of its taller sibling to the east, so little beyond peak-bagging can be gained.

The descent to Wing Lake includes a carefree glissade down the final snow slopes above. It's always best to camp again at the Lake but many parties hastily retreat back to civilization as the returning trek can be accomplished by headlamp. However, should you stay an extra night, besides enjoying the nightly movie of meteorites and satellites gracefully arching across the inky sky, no streaming necessary, you can climb **Corteo (8,080')** the next day. It is conveniently located within an hour's worth of time off the route and includes just one pitch of 4th-class rock on the South Face route described in Beckey. Drop your packs at Horsefly Pass (conceal them well) but take helmets and rock gear if anyone in your party is uncomfortable with 4th-class climbing. Aim for the southeast ridge over heather, then talus to attain the foot of this crest.

It is easy 3rd-class climbing at first up a ridge, which unfortunately gives way to the southeast face a bit too soon. Aim for whitish rock as you locate fissures and touchy holds – test them first. Despite reasonable rock (for our Range anyway) I managed a short fall when a hand-hold came loose (and yes, I didn't test it well enough). This resulted in a 20' fall, held on top rope and fortunately my worst injury in many decades in the mountains – a broken fourth finger. I attribute my good fortune in avoiding accidents to two key practices: avoid anything over 5.9 and never being the leader. Nonetheless, I've fallen enough to become an expert in falling; I've submitted an application to the Mazamas to teach falling in their Basic School but have not heard back for quite some time.

Several 4th-class moves over unstable rock on this southeast face bring you to a ledge, from which a 100' descent and climb westward reaches the southwest ridge, exposed but largely a pleasant hike to the boulder-strewn summit. You have now reached the third arrow

CHAPTER TWENTY-EIGHT: THE ABC'S OF THE NORTH CASCADES

in the quiver nominated as the center of the National Park. Several rappels bring you back to your well-hidden packs and a path down to the parking lot.

Even though this last of our ABC's is the lowest of the peaks, it still holds enchanting views of North Cascades' valleys, waterfalls, glaciers, snowfields, peaks and forest. Often, the best views are not from an airplane but from the lowlands, appreciating the scene of ever higher mountains in the vertical distance. Rappelling off Corteo, we had the experience of many climbers in looking back and thinking (rarely saying it outright) "I climbed that?"

Yes, it's a long drive home, and yes you really should take at least one day off and give these summits three days at least, unless you are attempting some sort of Tommy Caldwell speed record. But their sheer cliffs, gushing waterfalls, gleaming glaciers, turquoise lakes, mighty forests, and flowered meadows are worth the time. Here, a lifetime's exploration awaits the adventurous mountaineer.

CHAPTER TWENTY-NINE
Running Ragged Ridge:
Centerpiece of
the National Park
(7,310'–8,795')

HIDDEN GEMS OF THE WASHINGTON CASCADES

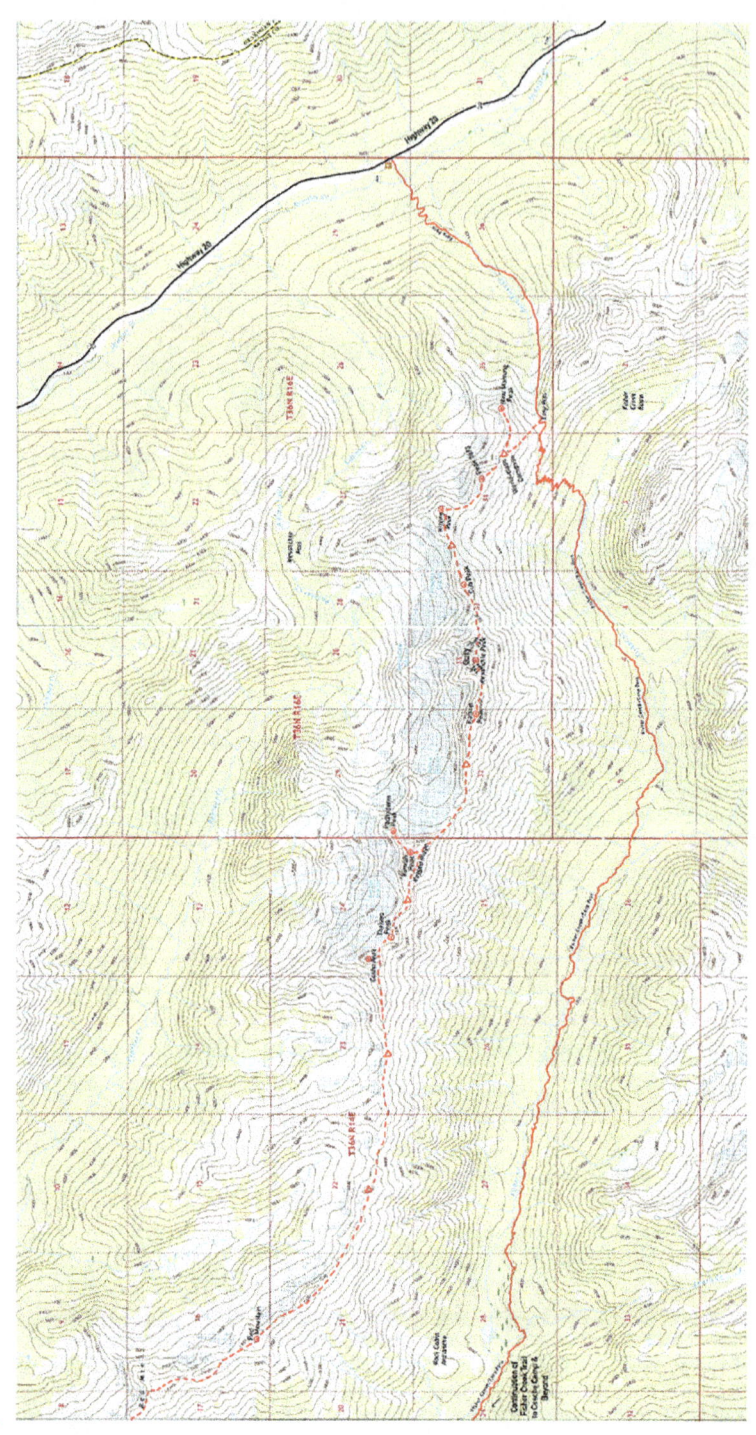

CHAPTER TWENTY-NINE: RUNNING RAGGED RIDGE

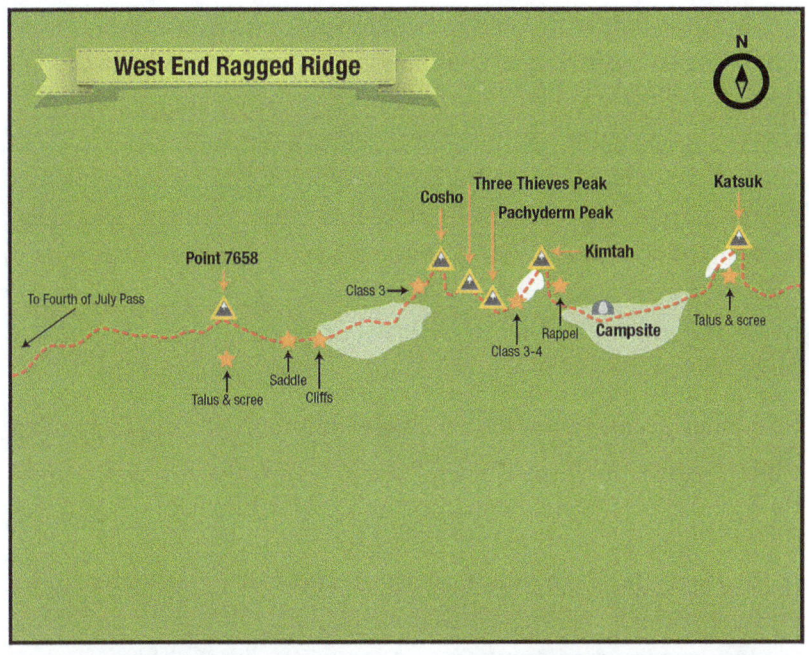

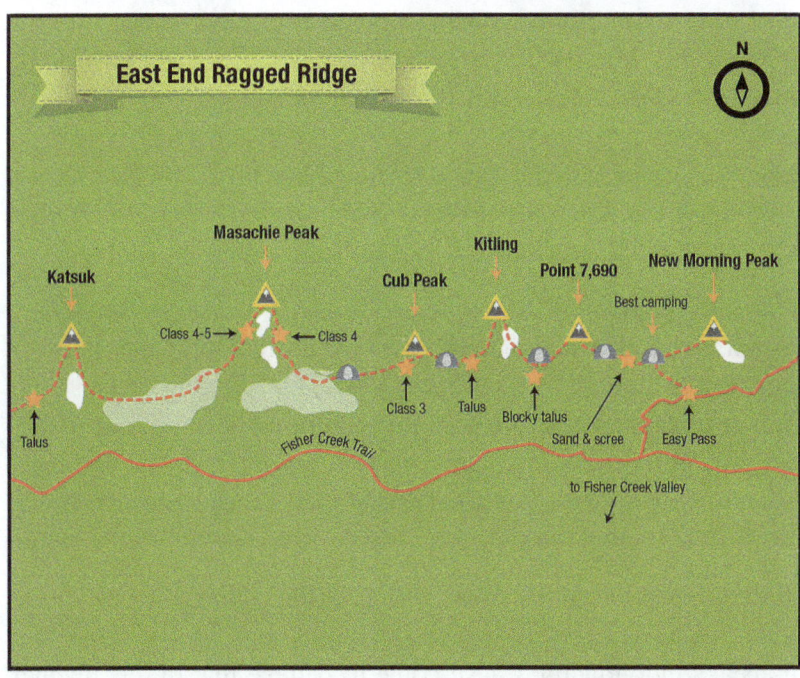

Aside from the more celebrated, and more well-travelled, Picket Range, there exists no finer continuous crest amongst these mountains than Ragged Ridge. This spine, though broken, is not random; its northwest-to-southeast orientation reflects the forces of similarly aligned tectonic plates off the Pacific shore. Compulsive types may not appreciate this inconvenient complexity, as many Cascades' sub-ranges do not conform to any consistent orientation because the tectonic forces underneath are not as unvarying as they are in other major ranges, such as the Himalayas or Andes, where up-thrust is more uniformly east-to-west or north-to-south, respectively.

Fortunately, you can climb its single summits or traverse wonder-filled Ragged Ridge completely, hitting all of its varied peaks in 3–4 days, without bashing through much brush, or you can obtain the same outstanding vistas by completing one or two of these view-filled summits without the need for any technical kit whatsoever. For the highest peak, Mesachie, some rock protection for less experienced climbers may be wise, although the toughest pitches even on this top-most peak entail 4th-class moves on solid granidiorite. The rewards are endless views of the National Park; indeed, Ragged Ridge itself not only rests entirely within the Park but near its very center. You will rejoice at the far-flung views from any of its summits and sub-summits. This 10-mile-long traverse requires elemental route-finding skills (on clear days), accurate GPS readings if cloud-bound, and skilled scrambling abilities.

Our earliest attempts to complete the entire traverse from southeast to northwest proved fruitless. We had no lack of plans, just the inability to implement them at the time. But adhering to the saying that you never have a future until you get over the past, our second try proved more satisfyingly complete. I will thus describe these ascents from northwest to southeast as this is the most feasible way to gain the high ground, then remain above it for 90% of the way.

Beckey's *Green Guide* takes the opposite approach, but having traversed this ridge on several occasions, and ascended each of its peaks individually, I have come to believe that in this manner, you will obtain a greater appreciation, not only of the character of

CHAPTER TWENTY-NINE: RUNNING RAGGED RIDGE

the Ridge, but also of the unique attributes each summit provides. Anyway, I will describe, for each major summit, the Ridge route approach I believe is best, but I will also explain how to climb each peak individually if that is your choice. Remember, however, that the approaches to each single summit may require some bushwhacking, but then again, what worthwhile ascent in the North Cascades doesn't?

For the easiest (read least brushy) climb of your first peak, begin with **Red Mountain (7,658')**, actually a series of bumps almost 4 miles in length, with numerous ups and downs but just entailing minor altitude changes. Begin your journey

White Heather

from the Colonial Creek Campground on the Thunder Creek Trail up the Thunder Arm of Diablo Lake. In just 1.3 miles, you will encounter Thunder Camp and a trail junction. Take the left path, which ascends, sometimes steeply, to Fourth of July Pass. (You can light a sparkler here but with due care.) Since this part of the trip is entirely on trail, you should arrive early enough for an ascent of Red Mountain the same day. Leave the trail at the pass's high point in a southeasterly direction, just before it reaches the "Panther Potholes", actually usually mud-saturated excuses for ponds, and ascend moderately steep but only lightly forested brush, aiming to remain on a broad ridge which tends southeast.

You should attain open ground, delightfully graced with both red and white heathers, as well as numerous pink subalpine daisies and yellow cinquefoils. You will now see the bumps and humps of the 4-mile

Red Heather

Ridge called "Red Mountain". The actual high point is the most southeast of these but any of these nano-summits are adequate to say that you've succeeded on Red. You have begun your traverse if that is your goal, but even if Red is the sole aim of your expedition, this is its most facile passage, rather than the Thunder Creek-Fisher Creek approach championed by Beckey. Stick to the south crest if technical difficulties arise, though these will be few and no higher than class 4. Most parties (and there will be few), by now losing their clout, camp at the saddle between Red and the next named peak to your southeast, **Cosho Peak (8,332')**. There are flat spots at this saddle, which is situated at approximately 7,100'. Water can always be found on the north side of the Ridge all along the traverse on permanent snowfields, glaciers or streams emanating from them.

You can recognize this saddle because it is unusually flat and straight ahead of you will be the angular profile of Cosho Peak; to your right is a minor unnamed knob at 7,533'. Even more startling is a lake, often frozen into August, just over the ridge to your north and also directly north of Point 7,533. You will inhabit fewer more awe-filled wonders at this beloved spot. Contrary to local topography, on Ragged Ridge the north-facing slopes can often be less steep than their southern counterparts. The views to your south include the northern aspects of Boston Basin, holding the huge and heavily crevassed Boston Glacier. This ice sheet is crowned by the jagged incisors and canines of Ripsaw Ridge, stretching from Boston Peak to Mt. Buckner. This wondrous display of tottering steeples and towers is tilted at impossible angles, all seemingly the design of a giant madman suffering a chaotic temper tantrum and determined to repel the advances of any would-be climbers.

One could also ascend Red, then Cosho, by continuing on the Thunder Creek Trail to its junction with the Fisher Creek Trail, then head up steepening and worsening brush for 2,500' before attaining any openings or views. This would place you, if you head due northwest, at the southeastern point of Red but would entail more brush, more elevation gain, and the missed opportunity to say you

CHAPTER TWENTY-NINE: RUNNING RAGGED RIDGE

began the traverse (if that is your goal – and a worthy one at that) at its northern-most origins.

From your camp at the Red–Cosho col the next morning, you must begin the climb up Cosho Peak (also called "The Ragged End"). Do not be afraid of Cosho's pyramidal profile, quite intimidating from this foreshortened aspect, as it has a class-3 route. To unlock its mysteries, counter-intuitively, keep to the *north* of the connecting ridge, thus avoiding severe cliffs on its southern aspect until just beneath its towering summit block. Here, a ledge on your right leads across Cosho's southern face (some exposure) to its eastern slope, where easier travelling over heather and boulders shepherds you to its summit. Beckey's alternative is to again attack the brush of Fisher Creek to gain the upper open ground. If Cosho is your sole objective, it is far easier to climb Red, then ascend Cosho from Red's multiple summits.

Moss Campion

The views from here are even more overwhelming than from Red, if that's at all possible. The north faces of Goode, Logan and Buckner can be identified, along with Ripsaw Ridge peeking through these towering giants. The vast expanse of the Boston Glacier is particularly striking; it is one of the largest ice sheets in the lower 48 states. Peeking modestly among the summit blocks are the flowers of Spiky Phacelia, adorned with purple and yellow bristles; the small white flowers with four cross-like petals are likely one of the recondite species of mountain draba's in the Mustard Family; purple alpine willowherb also can be found, also with four petals, along with white partridgefoot (named for its leaves); cutleaf daisies; deep crimson moss campion clinging to its rocky substrates, with leaves so tightly packed that the flowers appear to spring directly from compacted moss; cuteas-a-button Sitka Mistmaidens, hiding in crevices within the rock walls wherever any seepage of water nourishes these lonely but lovely floral denizens of the alpine world.

Descend the way you approached, reaching an abrupt saddle at about 7,800'. As opposed to the route to Cosho, now you must stay to the south of the ridge. However, a camp can be made on the southern aspect of this col. Try to spy what Beckey unofficially calls **"Thieves' Peak" (?7,800')**, a protrusion east of Cosho, and **"Pachyderm Peak" (7,310')**, another bump on the Ridge just to the northeast of Kimtah Peak, this last your goal for the following day. Peer over to the north side of the ridge to spy the impressive Kimtah Glacier, usually heavily broken up during climbing season.

The next day, aim for **Kimtah Peak (8,600+)**. Here, you will be just 4 miles from the striking north face of Mt. Logan, looming just to the south. However, to gain this prize may take a bit of intricate maneuvering as the southern and southeastern slopes between Cosho and Kimtah hold a series of spires and cliffs which Beckey says have been labeled "The Grotesque Gendarmes". It is unclear whether any of these have been attempted or successfully summited; however, it would appear that an ascent of any such steeples and pinnacles, indeed not unlike soldiers standing at attention, each just below the next, would require a ton of hardware and several more tons of steely nerves. To add to your problems, near-vertical cliffs drop precipitously off the southeast part of the Ridge.

Beckey's approach from the Fisher Valley is feasible if you don't mind 2,500' of rugged and steep brush. But you're already on the Ridge, my preferred route, so make the best of your elevation by tip-toeing the crest just above the Kimtah Glacier, skirting cliffs just beneath Kimtah's western ridge. Angle south, and even consider descending (I hate that) 300' into forest (easy travel), then, once you've reached open ground (meadows and boulders) head directly over 3rd-to-4th-class stable rock due north above the heather to reach the summit. This route maintains most of your altitude and connects with the Southwest Route in Beckey's *Green Guide* at about the 7,600' level.

CHAPTER TWENTY-NINE: RUNNING RAGGED RIDGE

If you're interested, Kimtah's northeast ridge has been successfully ascended partly utilizing the Katsuck Glacier, but again, the route begins deep in the Fisher Creek Valley, then crosses the Katsuk-Kimtah col to gain the abrupt ridge, a very long day indeed, requiring class 5.5 rock-work. The east face was climbed by the Skoog brothers but the ratings are unknown (nor would I wish to follow in their highly skilled footsteps).

One could argue that the views from Kimtah are even more majestic than from any other vista on Ragged Ridge. To me, that's similar to arguing about whether Mozart was better than Beethoven. Across the Fisher Creek Valley, glaciers of giants spew forth crevasses, seracs and avalanche tracks in close proximity. Logan's pinnacled rocky summit appears almost as a nunataq above the snows, with the Douglas (east) and Banded (west) Glaciers decorating these icy realms. Waterfalls can be traced from these bodies of ice, especially the one draining the Douglas Glacier to the north, which forms the headwaters of Logan Creek. The summits of Storm King and Goode rise to the south.

The Boston Glacier stands to the southwest, with Mts. Buckner and Boston serving as the eastern and western anchors for the jagged pinnacles of Ripsaw Ridge. Further southwest, Eldorado, the Tepeh Towers, Klawatti and Austera Peaks come into impressive view, soaring above the aptly-named Thunder Basin. Across Ross Lake to your north, Jack Mountain dominates the view but to your northwest, the spiny Pickets pierce the Cascades sky with their terrible beauty poised amidst their angular regularity. Descend east to a camp, which can be made in the saddle between Kimtah and Katsuk just above the steep headwall of the Katsuk Glacier.

The next named peak on this Ridge is **Katsuk Peak, (8,680'** – the US topo pegs it as **8,426'**). It can be most easily gained by ascending west over meadow and 3rd-class rock to its summit. I will not repeat the specifics of this view as it matches or even exceeds that of its close neighbor to the west, except to note that these outlooks are even more widespread from this vantage point. It's as if the views metastasize over unnamed ridges and summits in the farthest of distances. Of particular note are the summits due east to Whistler and Cutthroat Peaks and, beyond Easy Pass, to the Fisher Creek Valley's terminus in Fisher Peak. Arriva, Black and Corteo Peaks can also be identified.

You are smack dab in the midst of the National Park as far as viewpoints go, so please take the time to identity the hallmarks of this glorious landscape: the deep forests, the waterfalls issuing from the snowfields and glaciers all around, and the too-numerous-to identify saw-toothed ridges and jagged pyramids before you. Smart-phone photos, or better, SLR's are obligatory, and even the dreaded summit group photo, but no photograph will ever match this panorama. It will lie not only in your memory banks but in the effort it took to reach this glorious spot.

Katsuk is tall enough that Mts. Baker and Shuksan can be spotted to your northwest. Beyond Jack, the twin horns of Hozomeen are in sight at the northern head of Ross Lake, while to the northeast, past Ballard and Azurite, peaks in the Pasayten Wilderness can be seen, though their identification is a mystery to most North Cascaders. The most prominent of these is Robinson Mountain. Beyond Goode and to its north, the peaks off the Twisp River Road, including Gilbert and the Stiletto Range are in view. But the closest, and perhaps most fearsome outlook, is directly to your east, where the sharply angled profile of **Mesachie (8,795')**, your next destination, lies: enough vast beauty for one tough day. Descend either by rappelling directly to the col between Katsuk and Mesachie or down-climb Katsuk's east ridge to relatively flat ground at the saddle, where camp can be made.

"Mesachie" derives from the Chinook language meaning "wicked", a telling adjective for this, the tallest of the Ragged Ridge Peaks. To be honest, I first climbed Mesachie via the most facile of approaches: from the world-class campsite above Easy Pass. If Mesachie is your only goal, an approach from this 360-degree viewpoint is the most efficient. You must endure a "footsore" traverse over steep meadow to reach a snow-filled gully. Ascend this to a broad flat area where a pond can sometimes form. From this spot, find a gully trending northwest to reach easy scrambling to the top.

CHAPTER TWENTY-NINE: RUNNING RAGGED RIDGE

On the other hand, if you have been stout enough to have reached this col on a traverse, you have already accomplished an elevation of 8,250' and the somber vision of Mesachie's west ridge, although appalling from this viewpoint, beckons, or at least affords a feasible pathway to the summit. From the saddle, find a ledge which contours around the north edge of the ridge (mostly nontechnical) to enter a somewhat loose gully. Ascend this, a class-4 to mid-5th-class climb, which actually consists of a series of two couloirs. I clumsily followed our leader's guidance but slipped twice on belay, the result of both haste and ineptitude. Indeed, the gullies, composed of fairly stable granidiorite, reach easier ground for a class-3 scramble to Mesachie's apex. A summit register is usually present, filled with praise, poetry, pap and philosophical rambles of those who have attained this, one of the ultimate spectacles within the National Park.

Sometimes it seems that this world is too beautiful to justify humanity's presence, but without it (in the form of roads and trails, plus information from the earliest of explorers), you would not have reached this sublime place at all. We often pine for a pre-human quasi-mythical wilderness but, in fact, Native Americans had already altered these landscapes many centuries earlier. Much of what you can see among these forests are second growth planted Douglas firs. All animals alter the wilds as well, but we humans do not need to add to the damage. So yes, you can leave your mark in the register, if it still exists, and spend protracted time at the summit.

However, you have additional peaks to scale if you wish to complete the full traverse of Ragged Ridge. Descend down a gully to your southeast, following Beckey's directions in reverse, until you reach the 7,600' level. This entails mostly class-3 down-climbing. You will next traverse rocky ribs and gullies at this same level, until you can see a well-defined summit directly to your north. This is **Cub Peak (7,985')**. To be honest in your claims to have traversed the entirety of Ragged Ridge, climb the talus north to reach this small lump of a summit.

From the top of Cub, you may be wondering about camp, as it's been a long day, so most parties choose to rest before attempting to complete the entire traverse. Campsites can be eked out at the col between Cub and **Kitling Peak (8,003')**, though they may be a bit uncomfortable unless you enjoy stone as your mattress. Kitling's summit is easily visible from Cub Peak. To continue, whether this day or the following morning, climb blocky talus to reach the south slope of Kitling, where easy side-hilling and boulder-hopping brings you to the southeast across talus, scree and steep meadow. Ascend sand and talus about 100'. This will eventually deliver you to the south ridge. Stay to the south of the ridge to climb and again traverse meadow and talus, then easy boulders to Kitling's summit. The only other route described is a nontechnical traverse from Easy Pass. This will be your highest of the remaining summit-like peaks on this ridge.

From here, you can recognize your final destination, at least as far as Ragged Ridge is concerned, the campsite at 7,000', below and to your southeast. Also from this point, the Ridge takes a southwest bend. Yet there are other summits to attain in order to complete your traverse. The eponymous **Peak 7,690** is but a stone's throw from Kitling and does hold, just below its summit, not only broad views, but some flat ground for tents. Snow is always reliable just to the north of the Ridge. But you are close to those promised campsites above Easy Pass, wide and flat as a huge pancake, perhaps just 1–1½ hours away.

Try, then, to complete the entire ridge by ascending the terminal and ultimate summit to your east, anointed as **"New Morning Peak" (7,230')**, perhaps by a super speedy climber having breakfasted at the flat campsite above Easy Pass. The summit lies almost due north of the Pass. One could complain, rightly so in my mind, that this peak, due north of Ragged Ridge, is not duly qualified as a point on the Ridge itself, as it lies on a northerly spur. I believe you can ethically claim a traverse without climbing this peak, but it is a fairly easy-to-reach bump and provides a marvelous viewpoint from which you can spy the best (read easiest) route down to your final camping spot 500' above Easy Pass.

CHAPTER TWENTY-NINE: RUNNING RAGGED RIDGE

A traverse across meadow, talus, then steep sand, brings you to this incredibly flat and wide campsite just to the northwest of Easy Pass. Pray it is not tent city, or better than prayer, that it's mid-week. Even if you've got time to spare, I'd advise lazing the day away, resting up for the steep descent to Easy Pass and the trail back to the trailhead. After all, you've accomplished an amazing traverse and deserve to revel in the views and, hopefully, the sunshine before undertaking the descent, even at a glacial pace.

But this raises the dilemma all traversers face: You certainly don't want (or perhaps are incapable of) retracing your steps back to Colonial Creek, where you left your vehicles, even if you simply stayed on the Ridge and avoided its summits – a grim prospect at best. But you have been wise enough to have split your vehicles so that one or more are waiting patiently below at the Easy Pass Trailhead.

This traverse requires vim and strength, along with the days off work or school to enjoy this ultimate crossing. There is no need to rush; take your time to drink in the splendor of these ranges, occupying 4–5 days. But why subject yourselves to such rigors? The answers may be like leaves floating in the singing waters of Fisher Creek. The why's are hard to explain to your non-climbing friends.

Certainly, a sense of accomplishment urges us to undertake these adventures. But what a wonder-filled journey you have endured, even if you didn't reach all of Ragged Ridge's summits. There might be an elemental urge to share these experiences, though no one with whom I'm familiar has ever tempted fate to repeat a full traverse. You've chosen this quest to climb many unjustly ignored peaks in the center of the National Park.

This is the stuff of exalted mountaineering genius emerging from the day-to-day chaos of modern existence. This experience is now baked into the rigors of your daily lives. But of even greater importance, you've had an adventure permanently etched into your character, one it will be impossible to match and one which you will always remember and never fail to regret.

CHAPTER THIRTY

Heeding the Climber's Creed

Mt. Logan's North Face
(9,087')

HIDDEN GEMS OF THE WASHINGTON CASCADES

CHAPTER THIRTY: HEEDING THE CLIMBER'S CREED

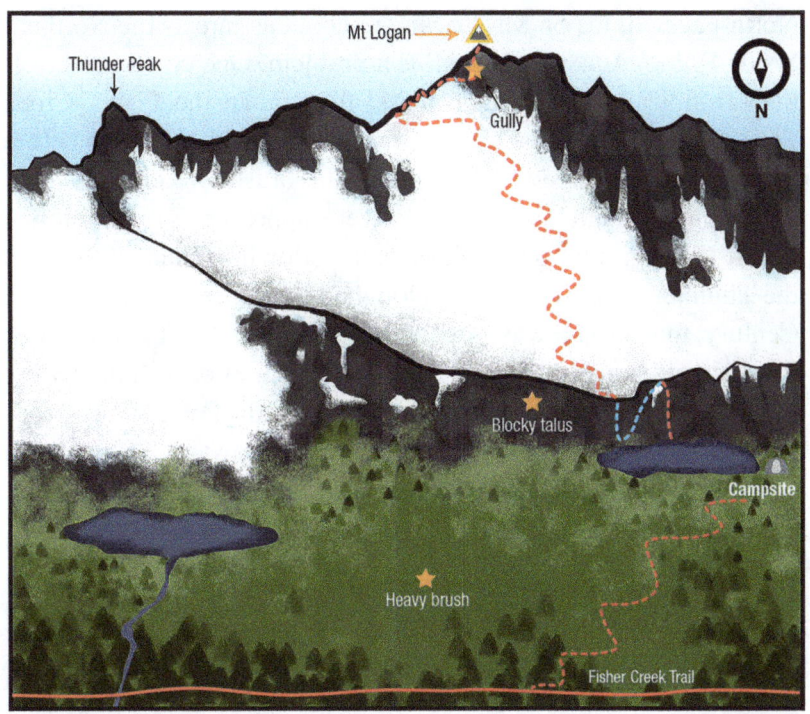

North Face climbs on Mt. Logan are about as rare as the Northern White Rhino. Access, as usual, is a problem. One could head over the sardonically-named Easy Pass, then down the Fisher Creek Trail about 5 miles, past Logan Creek about another 2 miles before attacking the north side of Logan up the brush. We chose a more tracktable, though somewhat longer, approach from Colonial Creek Campground off Highway 20, following Thunder Arm on the Thunder Creek Trail. First ploughed by miners in the late 19th Century, this throughway threads a route all the way to Park Creek Pass, should you choose to endure 19-plus miles of walking within the shroud of mostly second-growth forest. To be fair, the way opens up around 4,000', though grand views must await Skagit Queen Camp. Beyond, old-growth can be found, mantled by magnificent western hemlock, red cedars and silver firs.

However, to climb the north face of Logan, really the Banded Glacier Route briefly described in Beckey's *Green Guide*, you must branch off the Thunder Creek Trail at Junction Camp, a blister-generating 9.6 miles from Colonial Creek. Along the way, pass more named camps than biting black flies in July, such as Neve Camp (5.6 miles in), Middle Horse Camp (6.1 miles – you figure out the derivation of that name), McAlester Camp (7.1 miles), Tricouni Camp (8.6 miles), and finally Junction Camp (9.0 miles) and a thank-God meeting with the Fisher Creek Trail. (Note: the distances given in Beckey's green-covered *Approaches Section* appear to be over-estimates, according to the National Park and 7.5 series maps, as well as the carefully-measured *100 Hikes Guide to the North Cascades Region* by Spring and Manning.)

Yet your burden of hiking through forest will not cease here if your goal is to attain a position this day from which you can attack the Banded Glacier the next. Wiser parties rest here at Junction Camp, accumulating sinew and stamina for the trials ahead but we plodded on, weary but anxious to gain an enchanted yet unnamed lake that lies at the foot of the Glacier, mentioned in Beckey and visible on the 7½" topo.

The Banded became an object of curiosity after our leader, Eddie,

CHAPTER THIRTY: HEEDING THE CLIMBER'S CREED

had tried once and did not succeed. Failure had only prompted Eddie to greater heights of hubris, while his tales of steep yet accessible ice seemed riveting, motivating, but a tad intimidating as well. To us, it appeared that his reassurances were about as realistic as if the Pope admitted that perhaps Martin Luther might have been right.

Thus Eddie tried to convince us that, if successful, we would achieve a first direct ascent of the Banded, but even a cursory look would have shown that our climb, in the early 80's, would come more than a decade after a well-known, and probably much more proficient party had ascended the Banded. Gary Mellom, John Roper, and Reed Tindall climbed Thunder Peak in 1972 via this very glacier. Their description, however, failed to mention whether they had also summitted Logan itself as it appears that their main objective was Thunder. Regardless, they had the wisdom to make their original ascent in early July, when the Banded was not as broken as a worn-down barn. Our attempt was unfortunately in mid-August. We were gullible until we studied Beckey more carefully. We are still uncertain, however, if our ascent was the first true climb of the North Face but we'd like to think so. Personally, I doubt it.

Up the Fisher Creek trail, the grade gradually steepens a bit but views reward through first, silver firs, then more stunted mountain hemlocks and subalpine firs. We seemed to travel lightly on this part of the trek. Look left to the southern slopes of Ragged Ridge and right to the northern origins of Logan itself. Despite our heavy loads, we ascended the mostly gentle trail as rapidly as singletons at a speed-dating event. But where to leave the trail and plow up through the inevitable brush? From the topo, it appeared that about a mile after passing the remains of Rock Cabin and its avalanche path, and a few hundred yards after crossing Logan Creek (the largest thus far on the Fisher Creek Trail), the going appeared reasonable, at least in a North Cascades kind of way.

The mountain lords must have been with us as, after about 3 miles from Junction Camp and at about 4,200', we ventured forth (south), plunging into the brush to do battle with a lethal ferocity of predatory thickets packed with Devil's club, salmonberry,

White Rhododendron

white rhododendron and what-all as we dodged cliffs and labored with packs heavy with rock and ice gear. Our party of four shared methods and mindsets, though I, being merely mediocre, lacked their technical mastery. Happily, we finally broke free and slogged up to a parkland of meadow, grass, and wildflowers spotted here and there with subalpine firs. A lake lay magically where we had hoped, something which rarely happens to me in my solo wanderings.

Our leader, Eddie, usually an anchor of stability, emitted wry comments about my slow pace. Nonetheless, he seemed to have chosen just the right path (had he scoped out this route before?). It was twilight by the time we could lay our weary bodies to rest, with barely the vigor to down the cardboard of a freeze-dried dinner. They say that merely showing up is half the battle but in climbing, that's hardly true, as our real adventure lay beyond base the next day.

Leather-leaf Saxifrage

Our campsite was fringed by cheerful brooks and the largest gathering of leather-leaf saxifrage (then in seed) I've ever encountered. Unhappily, the flora did little to revive us. However, we were acutely aware that an early start would be necessary to avoid a bivy. We had barely scrambled over the fence of a dreamless sleep before alarms rang and a hurried breakfast of a roll with cheese saw us off at 4 AM. Fortunately, we had the wisdom to start early. Surprisingly, we first had to climb, then descend, a sandy ridge a few

CHAPTER THIRTY: HEEDING THE CLIMBER'S CREED

hundred feet to gain the base of the well-named Banded Glacier. We took this to be the remnants of an ancient terminal moraine. Streaks and slashes on the Banded signified the origins of its name.

However, wisdom had little to do with our choice of season to tackle this ice; it was the middle of August and, though the atmospheric pressure was high, our spirits couldn't match it as we threaded our precarious way through and around crevasses, tenuous snow bridges and teetering seracs. We believed we had averted a crisis by awaiting ideal weather, but in fact, we had merely postponed one. The creaking and cracking Glacier gave us pause but we continued upward following a less-then eloquent zig-zaggy line, trying to avoid the worst of the fragile snow bridges and deep crevasses, many of which seemed bottomless. During our wanderings in this frigid terrain, we often were caught in what appeared to be an island of ice with no way out (how did we get in?) as we danced across spans of snow that looked like they couldn't hold a stiff breeze let alone a heavily-burdened climber. The professors of ice could have used the Banded as a textbook.

The angle stiffened to an unnerving 45–55 degrees and double-ax technique was required. We swerved to and fro, creating a serac-lined passageway as devious as a politically-drawn gerrymandered district, caught in a turbulent icy ocean with swells of frozen H_2O. The pitiless truth of physics probed my balance; while never super, it was sorely tested as we continued our dalliance with danger, entranced by the charm, yet at times terrified at the peril, of our frozen journey. Route descriptions would be pointless here as the snow dictates your way. Unfortunately for me, hard as I tried, I could not escape myself and thus have no shame in admitting to a few slips, fortunately held by ice screws; the glacier was too far into summer to accept pickets.

We generally headed in a southwesterly direction, angling beneath Logan's Middle Peak (8,960') and the giant molar of Thunder Peak (8,800'), looming as a steep thumb anchoring the eastern edge of the ridge. The searing sun turned this approach at times into a rolling rock and ice minefield. Our goal was to reach the saddle between

Middle Peak and Logan's summit but the glacier dictated that we trend further west than Beckey's diagram, arriving on the rocky, but surprisingly stable, east ridge at about the 8,750' level. A 3rd- to easy 4th-class scramble un-roped up a gully on Logan's north face led to our prize.

Views were of the 360-degree sort, a veritable supernova of sights, tempering much of the misery in gaining such a lofty, yet central, spot in the National Park. Ragged Ridge fanned out before us to the south, crowned by the majestic Mesachie Peak, jewel of that vaunted crest. The rarely-climbed Greybeard Peak shot up its angled dark slopes to our southeast. Glorious as that perspective was, we could not ignore next-door Goode to our east, upon which no easy route lies. Arriva, Black and Corteo danced on the southwestern horizon while to the west, the outlines of Buckner, Boston, and the sawtoothed fangs of Ripsaw Ridge punctured the blue-bird sky.

Yet, on the summit I felt more trepidation than triumph. Not to tarry; it was painful but necessary to recognize that shadows were lengthening and a descent of the highly creased Banded would prove a test we might likely fail. It took almost as long to get down that Glacier as it did to ascend it. We were caught in terror between the tragedy of thin ice and the brutal tyranny of time. Nightfall loomed closer as we tried to avoid the multiple crevasses seemingly stretching across this band of ice. Off the Glacier, we finally reached the top of a moss-covered buttress we did not recognize, not a promising sign as we stared down the vertical slope with bridled emotions. Rappelling in the dark proved terrifyingly mysterious but the lake shimmering below gave us hope.

We reached our base at midnight and thoughts of food faded as quickly as the light as we simply bedded down, exhausted but prematurely happy – we still had the tortuous brush-filled descent, then the endless walk out on the trails.

At the end of that final day's trek out, one of our party's members undid her boots to reveal a red, blood-stained pair of socks. Cheerfully unaware until she saw her reddened feet, I thought at

CHAPTER THIRTY: HEEDING THE CLIMBER'S CREED

this juncture that ignorance wasn't just bliss but blisters as well. I should have felt pity, or happiness at my lack of such sores, but honestly, I was beyond numb, and could only look forward to return to our blaring world, and burgers, fries and a milkshake (I know – I'm not the beer guy) at The Buffalo Run back in Marblemount. For me, the Banded was a dream realized, but hardly a statement. Any middling weekend climber can master its ice, steep but not waterfall vertical.

However, I cannot in all honesty recommend the Banded unless your plan is to suffer, but what an adventure! And what memories, especially as the pain recedes with the years. You cannot airbrush this experience away. If the climber's creed is to endure pain, suffering and malaise, then have at it. The Banded will upgrade your mountain experience as well as your climbing résumé, and it contains the essence of North Cascades ascents: a long trail approach, a merciless brushy toil up to a parkland sited in a postcard fantasy, an icy climb climaxed by an easy scramble to a summit packed with ridiculously far-flung views only a few will get to witness in their lifetimes. What better way to spend a long weekend in this kingdom of a wilderness?

CHAPTER THIRTY-ONE

No Easy Way Up

Jack Mountain
(9,066')

HIDDEN GEMS OF THE WASHINGTON CASCADES

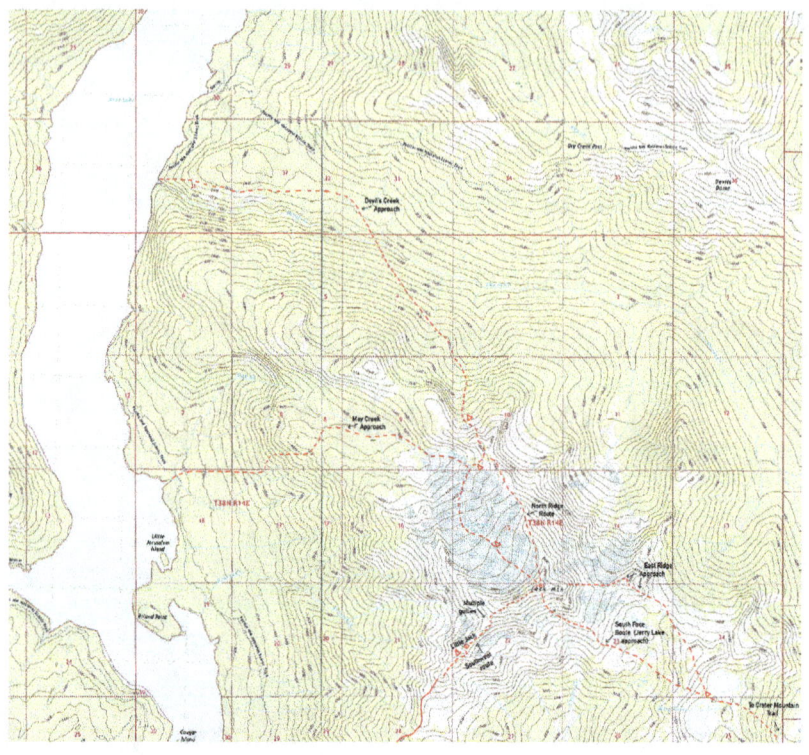

CHAPTER THIRTY-ONE: NO EASY WAY UP

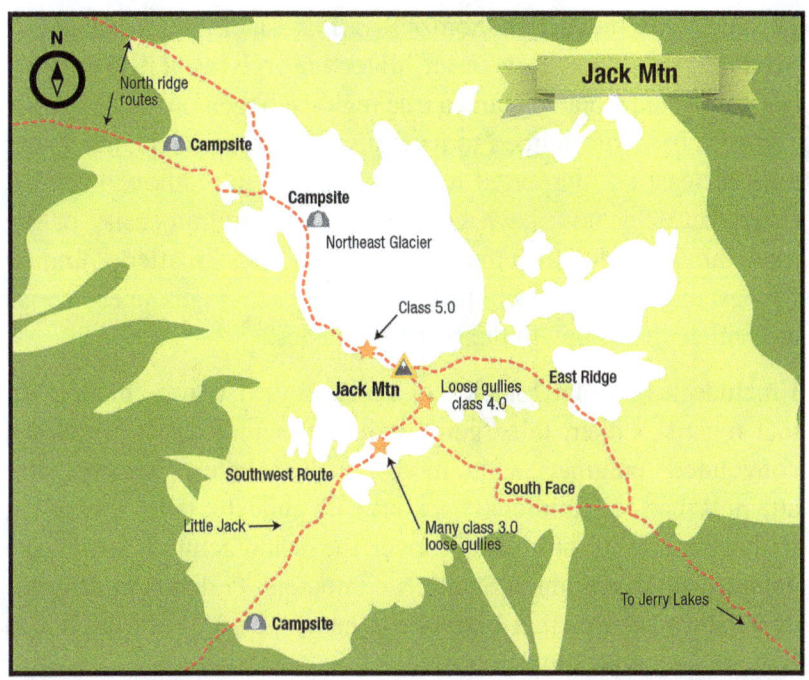

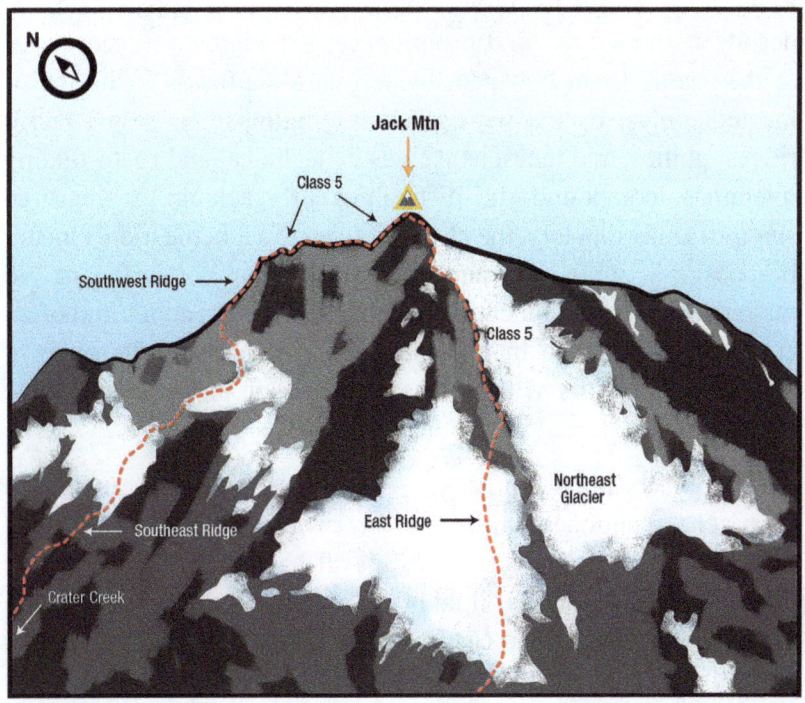

Lording it over the eastern shore of Ross Lake, Jack is like a teenager's first love: passionate at its onset, all too unforgiving at its demise. It is a raging and isolated giant, a true regional hegemon and not a few climbers have succumbed to its many glaciers and furrows. There exist at least six purported routes by last count, although several others must by now have been explored. The immensity of the mountain is not so much the problem as the tricky matter of finding the best angle of approach. Its complexity encourages an enterprise as challenging as any in the North Cascades.

I include it here not for lack of popularity; it is not "hidden" in that regard. Rather, this "gem" requires mention as it remains a convoluted enigma, with more proportionately unsuccessful attempts than Mt. Rainier. It beckons with guile due to its reputation, its height and its prominence over the manufactured Ross Lake dammed up to enlighten Seattle's computers. Perhaps it's because of my own failures that I include it here, though I've tried not to write merely a personal narrative.

Regardless, Jack's mention herein is more than appropriate, as, despite its popularity and prominence, it remains a monster, due to the seams sown between mystery and confusion in its multi-faceted routes. Bulky, with glaciers clinging to its sides, Jack's ridges, gullies, and faces, as well as its technical and route-finding dilemmas, compound the difficulties in reaching its treasured summit. Unfortunately, the closer you get to Jack, the more sinister it appears. Scoping out routes is necessary, but not sufficient. No matter which route you choose, it will provide strenuous and often complex approaches. In that manner, it often shares its prize of well-guarded crests with so many others of its brethren in the North Cascades.

Most climbers approach Jack via the South Face or Jerry Lakes approaches mentioned (in an altogether cavalier manner), in Beckey's *Red Guide*. Do not be deceived by his off-hand fashion of providing descriptive terms such as "light brush" or "broad alpine ridges" with "easy hiking". Jack is no easy climb, regardless of ability or route. Even the most stout and skilled parties have been repelled by its

CHAPTER THIRTY-ONE: NO EASY WAY UP

devious loose pitches and deceptive gullies, each requiring time-wasting descents and re-ascents along many of its routes.

There may be an easy way up Jack but in five attempts, I've yet to discover it. That may speak more to my own fallibilities and the collision with the reality of advancing senility. Nonetheless, I will describe the routes we've attempted and the reasons (? excuses) for our multiple failures. I do so with the realization that many climbers have succeeded on Jack and that I may well be too dramatic in describing its dilemmas. Unfortunately, our own interests in Jack were probably more intoxicated than insightful. They say that true knowledge is to know what you don't know; if so, I know a lot about Jack.

The Southwest Route:

All the hyperbole about Jack focused our attention on attaining its summit so we attempted a number of approaches. Ultimately, we experienced the same sequence of hubris, hope, then hurt which has haunted other parties. Our first attempt appeared to us to be the simplest and most direct: the southwest approach. You can hike the 3 miles on the East Bank of the Ross Lake Trail or charter a boat from the folks at the Ross Lake Resort thereby saving 1-2 hours on the flat Lake Trail, but costing you some cash. Either way will bring you to a small docking just southeast of the Ruby Pasture Horse Camp. If the latter, just be certain the boat company writes down when to pick you up; they have left us stranded more than once, thus forcing a 5-hour midnight march back to our vehicles on Highway 20.

The Jack Mountain Trail is not a high priority on the National Park's maintenance list. It begins just uphill from the landing, past several usually empty campsites, and is well-marked at its origins. Unfortunately, the path soon deteriorates so expect log hopping and a bit of brush, although the path is easy enough to follow, though often steep. It offers few views until you break out into heaven: heathery meadows seemingly planned by a benevolent and talented landscape artist; billows of lupine bend in the breeze, while scarlet

Sitka Valerian

paintbrushes are too numerous to count. Yellow meadow arnicas and smaller fan-leaf cinquefoils flourish here accompanied by white Sitka valerian and American bistort, the latter capped with a cylindrical bottle-brush of hundreds of dull white flowers in its conical head. The trail is supposed to lead to "Little Jack Mountain" but it appears to end abruptly just when you emerge from the forest, so placing a piece of surveyor's tape at the last mountain hemlock wouldn't be a bad idea as this opening is crisscrossed with goat and human trails.

It's difficult, wandering these high-sky pastures, not to stop and comprehend the views, first down to, and across Ross Lake (actually the dammed-up Skagit River); then west to the saw-like teeth of the Pickets. Ambling up and down this bumpy wonderland one truly feels that you really are traversing between earth and heaven, the burden now lifted of having ascended from the lake at around 1,600' to this alpine Eden, at 6,000' and above. Although the trail and maps designate a "Little Jack Mountain", any of these small hillocks, which seem to be of equal height, could be called thus.

Meadow Arnica

You'll have time to pitch camp, preferably as close to the monster of the real Jack staring at you (mocking you?) to the north, so linger here, have a snack and eat up this view; you may never return to this idyll. The goal is to place camp on duff, not flora, and a number of campsites

CHAPTER THIRTY-ONE: NO EASY WAY UP

have been utilized. Water is almost always available from the many streams flowing off snow-banks on the east side of these wonder-filled openings.

Subalpine Fir

The optimum campsites are at a saddle just before a stony gully, yet still on meadow and sand. It is from here that your travels and travails will begin the next day. An early start is advised because the route to the top of this brute masquerading as a mountain is not direct by any means. In front of you lie numerous stony and loose gullies separated by wicked stands of stunted subalpine firs in which you may well feel imprisoned.

The ups and downs on this largely east face traverse are more tedious than technical. We counted four such gullies, each requiring descents and re-ascents of 300–500', all around the 7,000–7,500' level, but with each, elevation must be regained. Cliffs to the left of you, rubble to the right - it seemed we were caught in a cruel rendition of a Jimmy Buffet song. We were in constant view of the summit and the south ridge, which looked so inviting. Once beneath the summit, at about 8,300', there isn't just a single gully to ascend, but several. Conflicts arose about the correct route. This led to a conversation best described as animated moderation. Compromise (no one achieving entire satisfaction) led to consensus (everyone unsure of the proper course).

We therefore must have missed the memo: Not knowing which to test, we explored each, eating into our turn-around time, but we thought we were so close. Yet each gully ended unceremoniously in a cliff requiring hardware and the skills we lacked. It appeared in retrospect, and after consulting wiser parties, that had we chosen the third gully more carefully, success could have been ours. It was as if there was an elevator available but we were taking the stairs. Too late to make it all the way back to camp, we endured a bivouac colder than a night on Mars.

Were it earlier in the season, some of these gullies might have been snow-filled; hence Beckey's advice for an ax, though by late July, we found no snow. Having been rejected by each gully, we were forced to bivouac half-way back to camp. We did not wish to repeat our attempt the next day and hastened down the trail in ignominious defeat. I'm certain, had we just tried the next gully over...but you've all heard that one before. I took some small measure of solace as we trod the descent of a frustrated party; I truly believe there is a class 3–4-gully leading to Jack's west ridge and a scramble to the top but it was not for us that day. It was then that I realized that the leading cause of failure in these mountains isn't the lack of technical skills nor fatigue, but rather the simple want of time.

The North Ridge:

Familiarity breeds intent. Our remit on Jack might have been redundant but it was unrelenting; unfortunately, our enthusiasm was blunted by our lack of foresight. So we thought perhaps an easier (read less tiring) route lay from Ross Lake's eastern shore further north. As is our usual practice, we ignored the warnings from other climbers, which proved prescient, and chose what appeared to be a line from the shores of Ross Lake; at least it appeared feasible on the topo. However, having been appropriately chastised by our earlier failure, we approached this undertaking with some foreboding. On this, our second attempt, we chartered a boat to drop us off at Devil's Creek Landing, then began a brushy, steep but achievable route up Jack's western slope, unlocking as best we could the brushy dungeons, and passing a small pond (not on the 7½" quadrangle).

We camped after a long day at about the 6,400' level in fairly open meadow. The next day, we descended a few hundred feet to the Nohokomeen Glacier and made camp on the glacier itself, with a broad view of the north ridge and what deceivingly appeared as a scramble to the summit. This rest day allowed us to scout a

CHAPTER THIRTY-ONE: NO EASY WAY UP

seemingly feasible passage. Gaining the north ridge the next day, we discovered the true nature of that mischievous boy named Jack.

The ridge consisted in the main of 3rd- to 4th-class fairly solid rock but we were forced to rappel down several 5th-class gullies to save time (and our bodily health), though with the realization we would have to climb them on the return. At the 8,900' level at 3:30 PM, we knew we would have to endure an uncomfortable bivouac on the way back, as agitated skies threatened. The route ahead was chock full of what appeared to be tricky low 5th-class maneuvers. Our pace matched that of our surroundings: glacial. We chose to again turn our backs on Jack and accept disgrace rather than risk injury. The hike down the brush the next day had us convinced of two things: We were probably off course and the brush had grown thicker over the past two nights.

When failure closed one door, we could not help but look for another that might stay open. Thus our next maneuver, which of course we thought was ingenious, was to try again from Devil's Creek, again from Ross Lake, but stay more to the south, closer to May Creek and not descend to the glacier. For me, this seemed like a wooly compromise or a choice between arsenic and cyanide. Nonetheless, we commissioned a boat for the May Creek Landing, realizing a tough (and hot – 103 degrees at Stehekin!) bushwhack lay ahead. Word had it that the slope was less angular and the brush more diluted. Word was wrong.

Our leader, usually spot-on, displayed a previously unrevealed distain for accuracy. We camped again on the glacier and the following day, trekked up it to merge with our previous route, arriving on the north ridge with what we imagined would take us to the top. Since this coincided with our previous attempt, in hindsight we should have guessed, rightly, that we would encounter the same problems on the ridge as we did the year before, except that we were a year older and not smarter but only slower.

As the day wore on, we again gained the north ridge too late to achieve the summit, although at 8,400', we did gain the base of the summit tower and could see the exposed snow traverse Beckey mentions. We could have blamed this failure on an approaching yet unforecast storm but in reality, had we been more adroit or willing to brave yet another bivouac, we could have persevered. But it was far too late in the day to attempt it and thus turn this farce into a tragedy. Anyway, a folly repeated is still a mistake. Nonetheless, I'm certain that more robust and skillful parties could easily reach the top via this route.

The South Face:

After three unsuccessful attempts, we were crushed but not yet defeated. The final result of our eternal struggles with Jack, we believed, should surely not be a loss of hope. Thus, could the south face represent the triumph of aspiration over experience? Isn't the southern route usually the easiest in the North Cascades? That's Mountaineering 101. The South Face might well be a solution to the Goldilocks dilemma – just the right measure of difficulty. We ascended the Crater Lake Trail in an inappropriately carefree manner, then worked around the Lake on a climber's path, and hit snow on the southeastern slopes. We crossed the divide into the Crater Creek headwaters, then descended and camped on snow (mid-July) at Jerry Lakes. Finally, we had it nailed. The following day, we followed a ramp (class 3) that leads above the Jerry Glacier to Jack's south ridge.

On easy snowy ramps, then steeper crystals of bright ice, we gained the frost-crusted ledge west of the summit. We were able to avoid cliff bands on this broad ridge, which, unluckily for us, seemed to narrow with each step. We were finally able to gain the southwest ridge, a bumpy affair requiring too much time to set up decent protection. We powered up the crest but were forced to turn our back on Jack yet again as we could not beat the clock, our attempts both reckless and feckless and, in the event, we melted back to camp.

We attacked Jack with brio, but we returned broken. It would have been wiser to have listened to our parents, Mother Earth and Father Time. Some of us were determined never to return, while others

CHAPTER THIRTY-ONE: NO EASY WAY UP

among us, the hardy-minded majority, vowed with equal resolve to continue attempts on this wicked and hideous gargoyle. I was not among them, refuting the aphorism that you either win or you learn. I failed on both options.

The East Ridge:

From our various readings along with collective amnesia, we studied this cruel peak through binoculars. It appeared to us that the east ridge offered the quickest, if not the easiest, route to Jack's topmost point. Indeed, several of my colleagues have now reported success on this route. They approached by the Crater Lake route, then gained the ridge at about the 7,300' level. They then ascended 4th-to-easy 5th-class moves on solid holds to gain the summit. Of interest is that they chose to descend via the Jerry Lakes approach, then down via the Crater Lake route. I (with some gall) congratulated their effort, although with a tinge of regret and chagrin as it was my sluggish pace that may have hampered our earlier attempts. My own attempt later that year with another party was again foiled by a retarded pace and an annoyingly advancing storm. I felt like I had been fishing for rainbow trout in the middle of the ocean.

If you are foolishly lured by Jack's rock and ice sirens, try the east ridge first; I truly believe that it offers the least bushwhacking and the most solid rock on the darn thing. With a sniper-like focus on gaining the ridge early, or even by headlamp in the middle of the night, this route may offer the best chance to summit. Unfortunately, like unruly children and soccer goalies, you're only noticed when you fail. We had our hopes crushed like a steamroller and learned that in these mountains, a 99% success rate is a 100% failure.

Other routes have seen success on Jack, including the southeast ridge, rated at Grade II, class 5.6; the northeast glacier, probably 5.4 but with heavily crevassed ice and a long brushy approach; and the southeast ridge (Grade III, Class 5.6). Age has convinced me not to try again. Too many attempts extinguished the fuel of adventure here. But whether from the summit or even as low as the Little Jack campsites, the views are stupendous. Not just due west to the sequence of crenulated teeth we call the Pickets but beyond to Colonial and Snowfield. Baker and Shuksan cannot hide their snowy beauty as Jack is sufficiently high that a 360-degree view is guaranteed. To the south, Glacier Peak and the Dome massif shine like brilliant jewels, while to the north stand the implausibly Patagonian sheer faces of Hozomeen, almost straddling the Canadian border.

These peaks excite the wonder of how slow but irrepressible geologic forces have created such angular forms. Northeast, the sharp angles of the Mox Peaks stand in stark relief against the south buttress of Redoubt, with Spikard just to its northeast. Ross Lake seems like a dream, so far below that it is difficult to imagine you began this marvelous journey from its shores. To the east, beyond Crater Mountain lie the rarely attempted Ballard and Azurite, while the Ragged Ridge peaks are outstanding to the southeast. But beware of Jack in inclement weather. Its height above Ross Lake means it will attract the fiercest of Pacific blasts; it is not a sensible place to withstand Cascade storms. Tempests can hide behind western ridges and advance, unseen, like a guard dog growling at an approaching stranger, heralding oncoming fury.

As I age, slowness has become one of my pathologies. Thus I continue, at a more leisurely pace these days, and, as I gaze ruefully up at Jack from lesser vantage points, I cannot help but feel a twinge of regret. My zeal for Jack has been successfully amputated and I have lost any appetite for a diet of revenge. Fate, combined with my clumsiness and overall sclerosis, have sealed the death warrant for any further attempts of my own. No Hollywood endings or redemptions for me as I collide with the realization that whatever climbing skills I had have atrophied over these years, along with my sense of balance.

There is no end of excuses. Yet climbers, in failure, are rarely sorry for trying. Beneath the bandage of time, our wounds heal, though slowly. Jack at the very least serves as a reminder to me that the mission of a climb may not always be to attain a summit; an equally vital goal lies in the effort itself. To quote a famous Polish poet,

CHAPTER THIRTY-ONE: NO EASY WAY UP

"The past is never dead. It's not even past." For now, for me, this behemoth of a mountain will remain a dream deceased, with no requiem. These days, in the morning from some obscure North Cascades ridge or campsite, Jack's shadow still haunts me.

CHAPTER THIRTY-TWO
At Last - An Easy One!
Crater Mountain
(8,218')

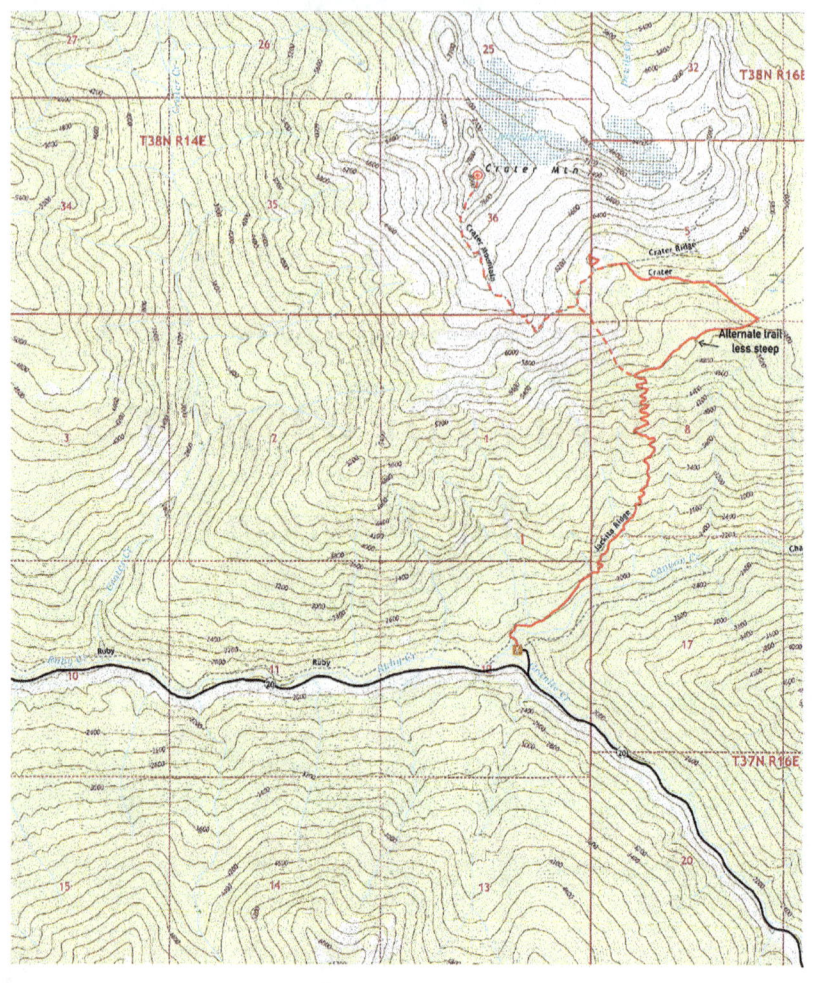

CHAPTER THIRTY-TWO: AT LAST - AN EASY ONE

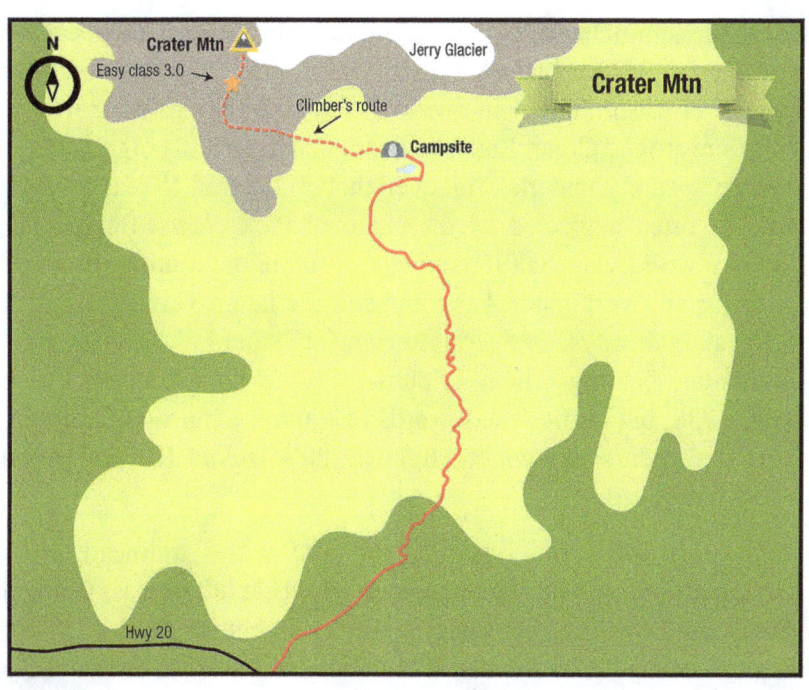

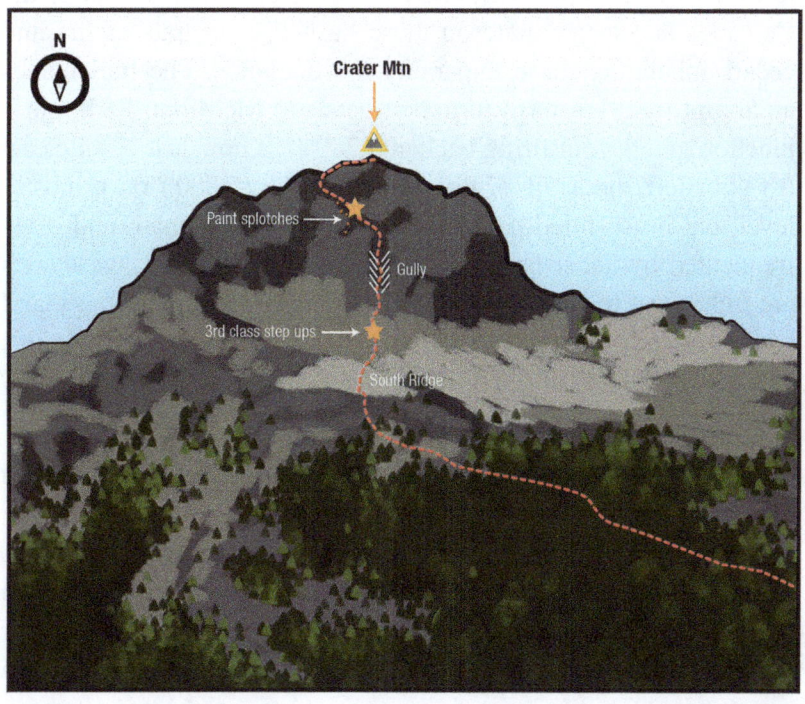

Ideal for scramblers, and with big-mountain views, Crater can be considered the runt of Jack's litter but I prefer to christen it a peak worthy of ascent, either in one long day of 6,000' gain, or from a campsite around Crater Lake. It cannot match Jack in height but it is a more leisurely undertaking, even though the trail to reach Crater Lake is often neglected by the National Park crews. Begin your journey with a daypack if you wish a single-day outing, or a full pack for an overnighter. I recommend the latter: Having climbed the peak both ways, an overnight camp at Crater Lake, 5,850', may necessitate bearing a heavier burden up the steep Canyon Creek Trail #738, but carries the rewards of a more unhurried climb the next day, then a descent to Highway 20's Jackita Ridge-Canyon Creek Trailhead.

Whichever you choose, begin your hike at this trailhead, cross Granite Creek on a substantial bridge, then bear left to cross Canyon Creek on a log bridge to begin a steep ascent on Trail #738 for approximately 3,100', rendered a bit more tractable via switchbacks toward its last 1,000'. Time here to savor the giant forests of the Cascades and to meditate on these hushed cathedrals of firs and cedars inhabiting these unparalleled woodlands. The trail makes an abrupt right (eastern) turn as it heads to McMillan Park, but a junction greets your tiring back at 5,280'. It's now just ¾ mile east (to your left) on Trail #746 to Crater Lake (5,800') on a mostly level, but brush-filled path. Although the lake is small, and often frequented by fisher-people camping on the lakeshore, these sites are unhealthy to the surrounding vegetation and both buggy and usually already occupied. Ascend 75' to the ridge toward the Lake's east for level sites off the flora.

A climber's path extends from this perch heading northwest. It traverses meadows alive with purple small-flowered penstemon and subalpine daisies; pinkish-to purple alpine asters (taller than the daisies); yellow mountain goldenrod and soft arnica; dull-white wooly pussytoes, looking for all the world like a feline's upturned paw; bird's-beak lousewort ("wort" is the old English name for plant), unfortunately named and not really a bane to lice, but a

CHAPTER THIRTY-TWO: AT LAST - AN EASY ONE

dull burgundy flower masquerading as a bird's snout; alpine paintbrushes, here more white than red; mats of moss campion, with startling pink flowers set against its carpet of mossy leaves; white low-growing heathers; fields of Lyall's (or dwarf) lupine, also known as Lobb's lupine), our most diminutive of the lupines but the prettiest, with silky palmate leaves topped by 1–2 inches of purple and white Pea Family flowers; partridgefoot, in clusters 4–6 inches tall, with frilly leaves bearing an accurate shape of this bird's lower extremities and with a stalk of white flowers; and our old friend, fan-leaf cinquefoil, the brightest yellow the sun allows.

But you've come here to scale a mountain, not for a botany lesson. The climbers' path tracks north-to-northwest from Crater Lake to a rocky ridge dividing Crater's south face. You do not have to return south to regain Trail #746, although many parties choose to do so as the way is frequently travelled and well-tread, not only to climb Crater but also as an approach to the Jerry Lakes and a base camp for Jack Mountain.

Bird's-Beak Lousewort

To gain the broad ridge, you must make an awkward 3rd-class move on stable rock for about 40'. From there, you will discover a unique series of man-made orange-yellow marks about every 50–100' on easy 3rd-class rock. These serve to guide you up the south ridge to about 7,850', where the ridge turns into a sand dune and a path leads you gently to the view-filled summit. Beckey mentions a "northwest flank" of the summit crag, but, honestly, the pathway follows the broad,

Lyall's Lupine

327

sandy southern route all the way to the top without any technical difficulties after that first awkward step at around 7,500' elevation.

Many would be indignant that these splotches of manufactured marks should point the way, while others take a more laid-back view that they may have guided early pioneers building a now-demolished lookout tower on Crater's wind-whipped summit. Finally realizing that the top of the peak, buffeted by western winds born in the Pacific and often obscured by clouds, was unsuitable for such a lookout, Rangers built a second fire lookout on Crater's east summit at 7,054'; ill-advised as well, that structure proved no more sturdy than the first and now stands in complete disarray.

Hopefully, you have reached Crater's broad summit on a bright sunny day. Bring a large map such as Pargeter's picture map of the North Cascades or the National Geographic's North Cascades map to identify the multitude of peaks visible in three directions from Crater's top. Unfortunately, Jack blocks the northward view to Hozomeen but Ross Lake sparkles directly below your boots.

Across the Lake, the Pickets thrust up their uniformly abrupt spires seemingly defying the laws of physics. To your immediate north, you can comprehend the conundrum of Jack Mountain, with its many ridges, gullies and the glistening snows of the several unnamed glaciers pocketing its northeastern slopes. The Jerry Glacier hugs the northwestern slopes of Crater. At its northern terminus lie the Jerry Lakes, often frozen throughout the early climbing season but picturesque when melted out. A few hardy subalpine firs mark the beginnings of the Jerry Lakes approach to climbing Jack. Be thankful your goal is not that objective this day (see the preceding chapter).

Views from the top to the southwest include the Colonial/Snowfield complex, while unobstructed vistas to the south reveal the Ragged Ridge peaks and beyond, Glacier Peak, fronted by the Dome massif. Baker stands snowy white in the northwestern view, though Shuksan remains shyly hidden by the Pickets, a fair trade-off in my opinion. Logan and Goode are blocked by Ragged Ridge but

CHAPTER THIRTY-TWO: AT LAST - AN EASY ONE

the Cascade Pass Peaks can be glimpsed, especially Bruckner, Boston and Forbidden Peaks, all bridged by the fangs of Ripsaw Ridge above the massive Boston Glacier. Eldorado and its northern associated needles are in the distant southwestern view while to the east, Cutthroat and the sheer domes of Liberty Bell and the Early Winter Spires are present and accounted for.

If you're intent on the full descent to the parking lot, it's best not to linger too long, as a 6,000' drop awaits. It's far better, if time allows, to spend another night at Crater Lake and perhaps snag a trout for dinner if you're lucky. Regardless, Crater offers the best of two worlds: a fairly easy scramble combined with far-flung panoramas of the finest the North Cascades have to offer.

Crater has been climbed (with skis) in winter after the highway closed. The ascent taken is more direct, ascending the broad southern ridge east of Crater Creek over snow-covered brush. A direct ski or snowboard descent was then manufactured toward Crater Lake and down the *voie normale*. But for me, it's more pleasant to avoid the frigid weather and bruised skies this fourth season brings. Such a journey must await more fit parties willing to suffer the consequences of an arctic environment. I am content to await spring through fall; under winter's snows, these trails will rest.

CHAPTER THIRTY-THREE

Jewels of the East

Gilbert Mountain
(8,023')

and Abernathy Peak
(8,321')

HIDDEN GEMS OF THE WASHINGTON CASCADES

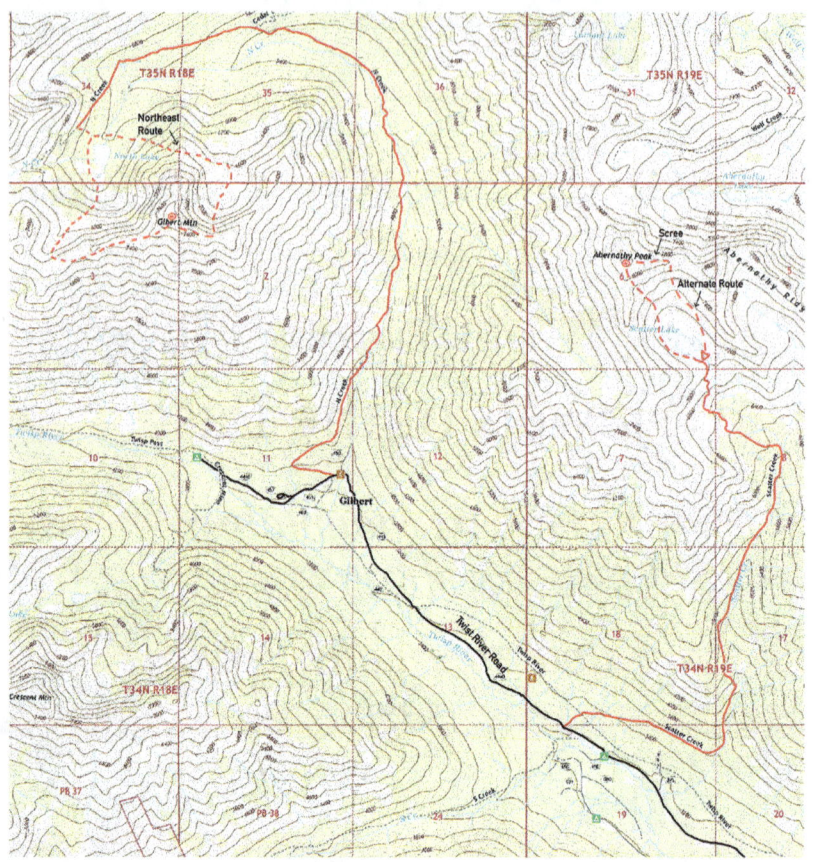

CHAPTER THIRTY-THREE: JEWELS OF THE EAST

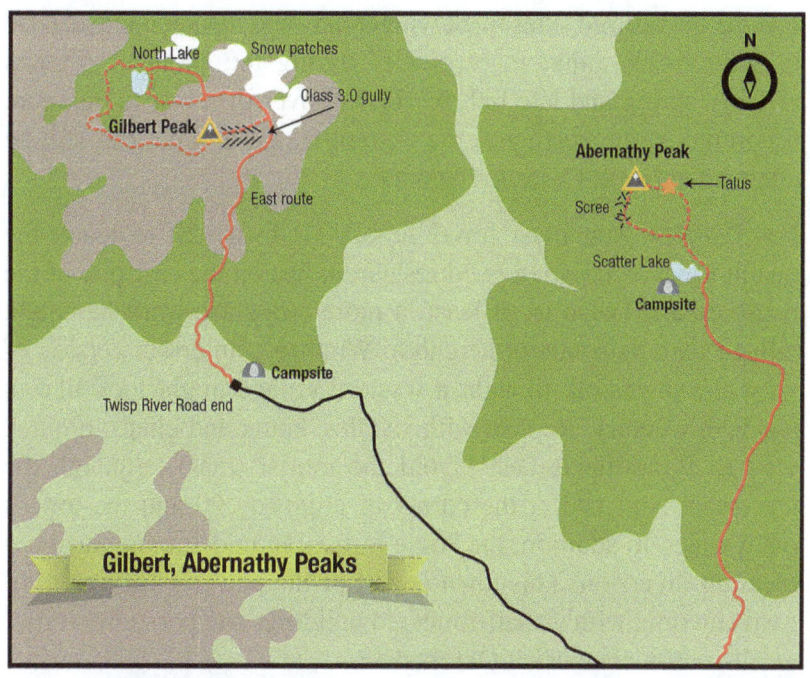

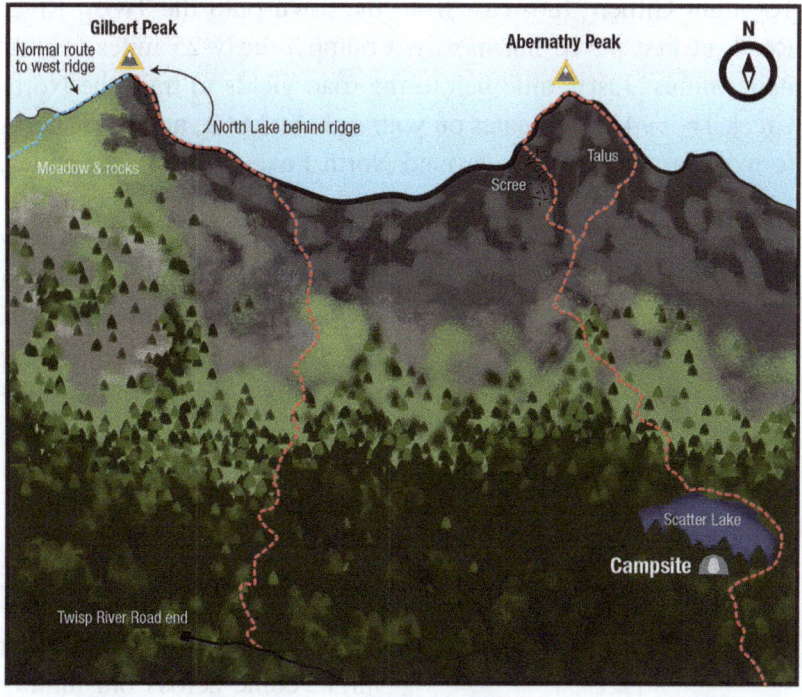

Escape the bruised skies thick with clouds and the unending drizzle of western Washington, especially during the shoulder seasons of early spring and late fall, by driving over the crest to the more accommodating weather at the eastern fringe of what can still be considered North Cascades country.

For **Gilbert**, you must travel across Highway 20 to reach the quaint town of Twisp (a good restaurant lies on the east side of the main street). Twisp is, at least, a more straightforward mountain village than its southern neighbor, Winthrop, an ersatz version of what the townsfolk thought a western village might look like in the 19th Century. Replete with saddles, spurs and chaps, a quick visit to Winthrop is best (avoid the tourist traps), although the ice cream isn't bad at the corner of Highway 20 and the town's main street. In addition, the fiddle festival in mid-summer is also a pleasant diversion. This town is sort of the cowboy equivalent of Leavenworth, with its half-timbered buildings and permanent air of an all-season counterfeit Oktoberfest.

To attain Gilbert, turn east from the town onto the Twisp River Road, at first paved but mostly a bumpy, dusty 25 miles to near its terminus. Just a mile before the road yields to trail, the North Creek Trail #413 originates on your right at 3,662', and heads north to make a northern loop around North Lake (5,760'), in 5 miles.

Puccoon

Although you could camp at the Lake, the sites are dusty and occasionally taken by horse people pretending this really is the old West. In addition, Gilbert is probably a climb to consume just a day's worth of adventure rather than a backpack.

Loop around the north side of North Lake, then follow the ancient mining trail south until it gives out. You'd think you might come across old mining

CHAPTER THIRTY-THREE: JEWELS OF THE EAST

equipment but we found none in several trips. The easiest passage is to gain the western ridge south of the Lake through a slight gully, nontechnical though steep, between 6,400' and 6,800'. Once on the broad ridge, light forest gives way to bouldery ground where a mix of western and eastern flora thrives. At this longitude, certain flowers not present further west appear, including the cut-leaf luina at the beginning of the trail described in the Scalpel Ridge Chapter; a white shooting star; pale yellow puccoon; and large-flowered collomia, with pale orange funnels as flowers.

Large-Flowered Collomia

Follow the broad crest, between 6,800' and 7,000' eastward, aiming directly for the easily visible summit. A few 3rd-class moves up the topmost boulders brings you to the south summit, the tallest; a ridge traverse of 3rd-classs scrambling could also land you on the north summit, 8,023', if you desire. One could also reach the top from the North Lake Trail by ascending the east ridge in light brush and subalpine larch (colored golden in autumn), staying north of Point 7,524 to avoid cliff bands due east of the summit.

This last route has been recommended in spring as it eliminates any brush, which is usually snow-covered until early July. It also avoids the mini-glacier, a permanent ice field cradling the north slope. The west slope has been ascended to attain the west ridge route without too much brush or technical difficulties. The entire north ridge has been climbed, first approached from the west and rated as class 5.0 at most, though route-finding from the base of Kangaroo Ridge might pose a muddle. In addition, there is quite a steep and loose section between 6,400' and 6,600' that would make for some unpleasant travel.

A more feasible route, and one our party once tackled, is to approach the north ridge by trending east from just north of the Lake up moderately brushy terrain to attain the ridge above its major cliffy portions. Our plan seemed reasonable, but what appears to be a practical decision may not always be prudent, as we were about to discover. We hoped to climb southeastward on class 3-to-4 crumbly rock and meadow, steering well clear of what appeared to be class-5 cliffs just southwest and southeast of the summit, then attain the north ridge at the 7,000'-to-7,400' level. A seemingly straightforward dash for the top morphed from light brush and sand into tangled underbrush amidst unstable boulders.

Unfortunately, our leader, ever the opportunist, chose to tackle the cliffs directly, despite our lack of adequate protection and my poverty of requisite skill. I struggled up the cliffs, making God-help-me moves across unseen stretches of unstable stone; it's funny how you gain religion at such precarious moments. Above these sheer walls, we finally gained the north ridge via one-step-up-two-steps-down scree at a notch between **Point 6,615** and the summit. From there, pleasant strolling across meadow and stone brought us to the top.

Unusual views this far east were our rewards: Crescent Mountain and the Reynolds-Rennie Ridge and McAllister Ridge summits stood out to our south; to our southeast, the Stiletto/Scalpel Ridge peaks were prominent; most outstanding were the panoramas northeast, where an unobstructed view of the spikes, turrets, and pinnacles of Kangaroo Ridge speared a tortured sky, angry with cumulus and stratus streaks and billows.

In fact, this view of the Kangaroos is the most complete I've enjoyed of these marsupials, as Silver Star and the Liberty Bell complex often obscure these leaps of the Kangaroo. In addition, from this perch Liberty Bell and the Early Winter Spires are visible through the clouds to the northwest, though Goode hid Buckner. However, the Dome Massif poked its steeples and glaciers above the South Cascade Glacier summits. To our immediate east, Abernathy stood proud in isolated splendor, while to the northeast, the sprawl of

CHAPTER THIRTY-THREE: JEWELS OF THE EAST

North and South Gardner predominated. Moreover, due north, Silver Star and its many wine spires were visible in their jagged entirety. North Lake shimmered beneath our feet.

Weather really bad? Need to head further east? You can (almost) always count on Scatter Lake and **Abernathy Peak** to be either clear or at least in the twilight under gun-metal streaks of overcast skies, visible if not sun-lit. The Scatter Creek Trail #427, leaves the Twisp River Road at about the 22-mile marker and in gently rising fashion, then a steeper series of switchbacks, reaches Scatter Lake in about 4 miles and about 7,000'. Dusty campsites are usually available but horse camps are not separated from people camps so your next-door neighbor might well be a filly or stallion.

Many climbers would be pleased to make Abernathy a one-day affair, but a more unhurried pace is nice if the cavalry isn't present. Although Beckey first mentions options to summit Abernathy from the North Creek Trail, and all of these are quite feasible, a more direct scramble can be had directly from the Lake. If you don't mind sliding scree too much, simply head north-north-west directly up the brushless slope forming the southern aspect of the peak to the top. If loose rubble the consistency of beach sand is unwelcome, trend northeast to a saddle between Point 7,910 and the main summit, then boulder-hop to the top, due west.

Views are similar as those from Gilbert although you can better see the sere corrugated hills and straw-colored grasslands of eastern Washington, similar to parts of eastern Oregon, where a painting of these landscapes could be turned upside down without much of a difference. Do not disparage these dry hills, where our apples and increasingly, our Pinot Noirs and Cabernets originate. To the north, peaks in the Pasayten Wilderness are visible, if not as familiar as those to the west. Tiny Scatter Lake reflects whatever sun can be glimpsed, but to be honest, if it's a typical mid-summer shining day, both Gilbert and Abernathy will leave you thirsty as a parched prospector. At least the outflows from both North and Scatter Lakes can be relied upon, though with heavy-duty filtering.

Anyway, screeing down these southern exposures is fun, even if a rock or two squirrels into your boots on the way down. While the hardened climber might consider Abernathy prosaic, it's a nice way to spend one or two days on this most eastern crest of the Range if the weather further west turns churlish.

Beckey mentions a peak enticing merely for its name: **Belly Roll Peak (7,002')**. He never allows a hillock, bump or hump to go unnamed. Belly Roll may be a pointed peak just northwest of Abernathy Lake (not Scatter Lake). The route lands a stout climbing party on Abernathy Ridge, near the saddle of the same name. It is best approached by a lengthy jaunt south from Highway 20 on the Cedar Creek Trail, then a brush-filled battle to a north-facing wall near the terminus of the south fork of Cedar Creek and to the west of Abernathy Lake. Dihedrals, crack-climbing, friction moves up to class 5.9 with some aid, all combine to render this the stuff best left to the experienced rock climber.

We lesser scrambler/low 5th-class climbers can be content in reading about such endeavors and wishing we could change our fantasies into realities. Nonetheless, climbing either (or both) Gilbert and Abernathy offers great exercise (remember those scree slopes) and unique views. We could all use the drizzle westward as an excuse to be lazy sloths or instead drive the extra miles to enjoy what the east-of-the-crest has to offer, thus turning a nickel of a day into a dime. But visit nearby Winthrop with caution. Its bogus wild-west shops overflowing with cowboy artifacts are off-putting to most climbers. Nonetheless, although tourist-stuffed and over-priced, the ice cream in town may still be worth it.

CHAPTER THIRTY-FOUR

Icon of the North Cascades

The Picket Range
(6,819'–8,207')

HIDDEN GEMS OF THE WASHINGTON CASCADES

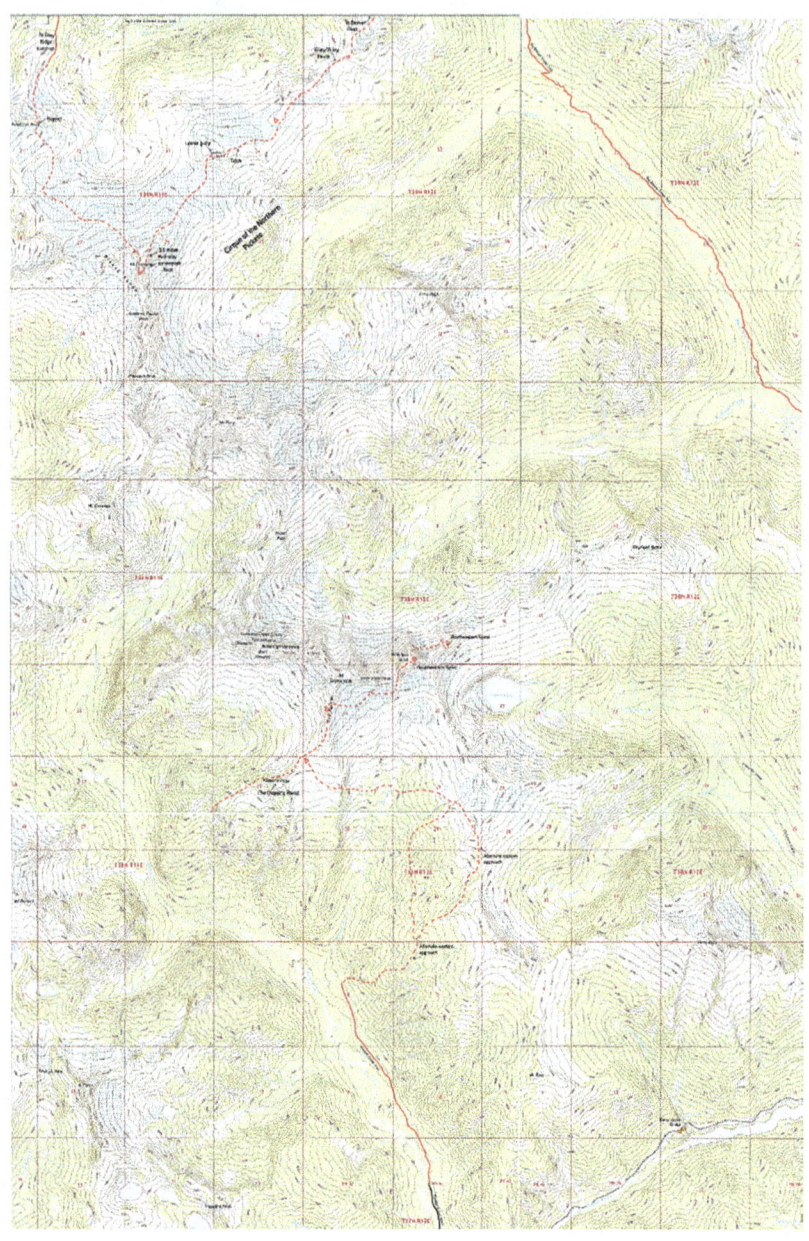

CHAPTER THIRTY-FOUR: ICON OF THE NORTH CASCADES

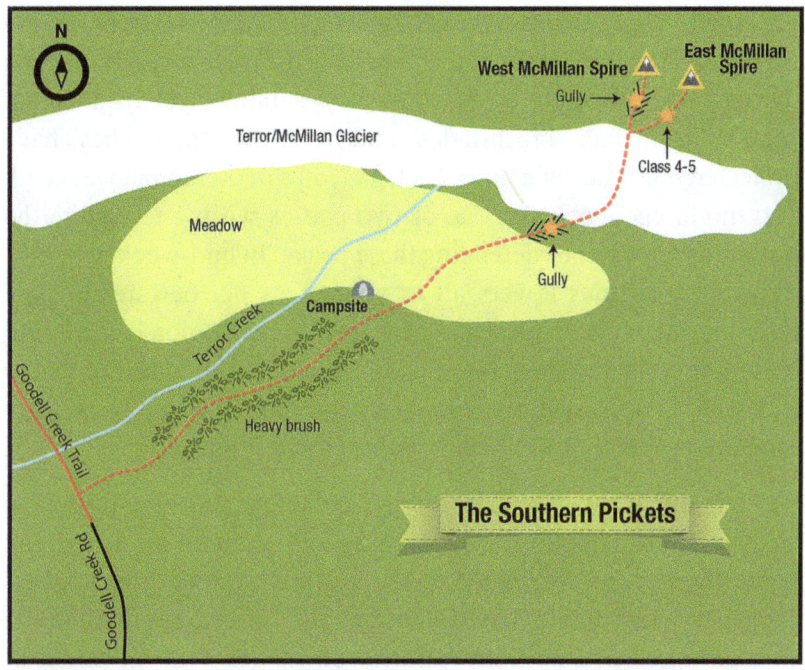

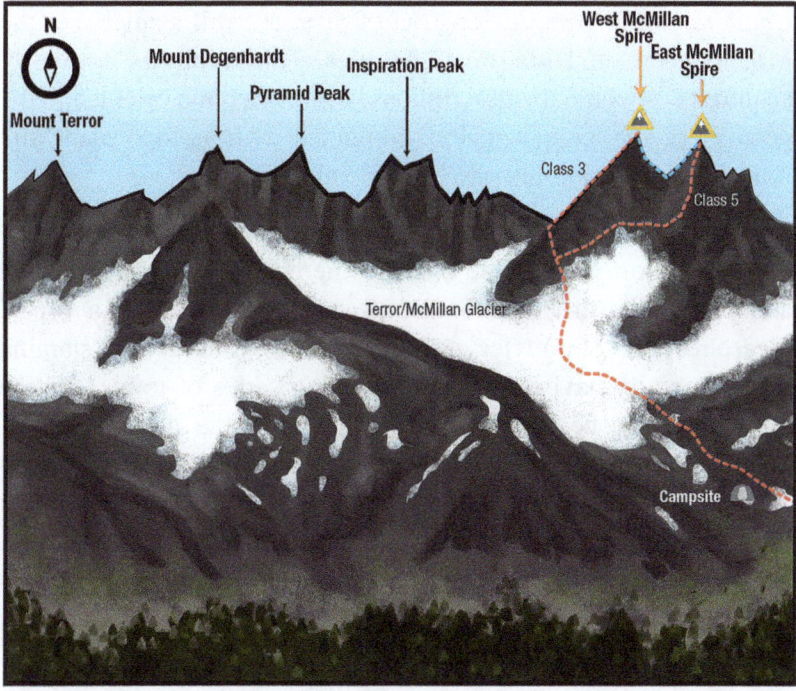

One could argue that the famed Pickets, crème de la crème of the National Park, are not "hidden gems". Superlatives have been exhausted in attempts to describe their sublime, yet frightening, beauty. But their brush-laden and tortuous approaches have protected this fence of a range such that, on a mid-summer weekend, you might encounter but one or two parties willing to endure the notorious approaches defending these peaks. In mid-week, you may have these famous towers all to yourselves but beware: Beckey describes it as "the wildest and most unexplored region in the North Cascades" (and probably in the continental U.S.). It is as impossible to not be in awe of this range than it is to be unborn. Their mere mention is synonymous with both heroics and suffering.

Indeed, authoring an exhaustive and complete narrative on access to these peaks is equivalent to writing a law school thesis arguing about the Second Amendment. The earliest explorers, geologists-turned mountaineers, R.W. Tabor and D.F Crowder, provided the first glimpses of this sharply furrowed range. If at all possible, try to acquire their 1968 classic, *Routes and Rocks in the Mt. Challenger Quadrangle*, long out of print but still available in the Mountaineers' and Mazamas' libraries. This trophy is not easily acquired elsewhere. Its descriptions, while brief and oriented to the geology of this unique region, combined with its topo maps and routes punctuated in red, are beyond value at any price.

Best also to heed their advice that "all [these] off-trail routes are in the vast majority...suitable only for the hiker who is experienced and physically fit...with boots, ice ax, crampons and a rope." Please respect their advice, as sagacity is just as critical as stamina in successfully navigating this staggering series of towers. These passages must be well-planned and within the abilities of all members of your group. Whichever pathway you choose, you may encounter brush of Biblical proportions, especially the approaches from the eastern and western low valleys draining these slopes. While you don't have to be a geologist to grasp all the complexities of tectonic subsidence, some understanding of the forces that govern the creation of such majestic ranges only enhances their allure.

CHAPTER THIRTY-FOUR: ICON OF THE NORTH CASCADES

It is difficult to write about the Pickets without resorting to overused adjectives. Of course they are spectacular, not so much in height as in verticality; spines, towers, horns, pyramids, glaciers, waterfalls, flowered meadows – they are all here. The names of the individual peaks bear witness to the struggles and fears climbers have endured in attempting to scale them: Mt. Terror, The Chopping Block, Twin Needles, The Rake, Ottohorn, Cooked Thumb, the Crescent Creek Spires, Mt. Fury, Phantom Peak, and, to top it all off, Mt. Challenger, the northern-most anchor of this remarkable Range. Seemingly frozen in snow, rock and ice, the Pickets appear as a riveting fantasy that turns into a reality as you approach closer and closer. Though these curving ranges have been divided into southern and northern groups, they really combine a southeast-to-northwest chain whose regularity in height of each peak, combined with their mostly even spacing, leads to the resemblance of a white picket barricade.

Yet this is no benign guardian of house or garden. All should be mindful of the dangers involved. Nor should casual scramblers attempt these peaks without adequate guides and the skills and equipment required to ascend technical rock and ice. Seeing the power of these peaks should give shape to your fears. Their terrifying symmetry was not created by chance, but by design: the slow grinding of tectonic forces and the equally ponderous power of erosion. Nonetheless, you will not infrequently hear parties begin their adventure with a collective eclipse of reason, planning to "knock off" Terror, the Twin Needles and Frenzel Spitz or to conquer a complete traverse of the southern or northern sub-ranges. Unfortunately, these dangerously elastic plans are often like streaming a Netflix movie: with high expectations but weak plots, inadequate acting, and predictable endings. You underestimate this Range's treacheries at your peril and you must recognize your own borders of the possible.

Thus, many parties return days later, summit-less, exhausted and defeated by the thick brush and technical rock and ice encountered. Plans in the Pickets may prove more provocative than definitive.

Speed and power are necessary in the Pickets but these qualities are not merely sufficient. Careful research combined with clarity of mind and an unbending will to achieve, are all additional ingredients for success. Ramparts of brush, rock and ice guard the peaks above well, effectively stanching the flow of would-be ascensionists thwarted by apocalyptic barriers both cruel and unmerciful.

Yet for those sufficiently brave and resourceful, the alchemy of tin can approaches can turn suddenly into the gold of meadows and memorable views no other heights in the continental U.S. can match. Each summit encompasses its own stellar world. To conquer such forbidding peaks requires a dire commitment from those climbing for their lives, or for whom climbing *is* their life. Neglect these risks at your peril.

The summits of the main groups are rather uniform, not only in their rugged character and height but in their synchronized spacing. These razor-sharp summits and their satellites show a harmony of structure unmatched in our Range. It is as if some Giant gardener planted the seeds of these spires all in a curvilinear row; this ground, then, must be abundantly fertile as up sprouted an array of evenly spaced, equally tall, icy towers, icons of the North Cascades. Two grand cirques, amphitheaters both broad and steep-walled, lie at the feet of both the southern and northern sub-ranges. Each is concave to the east and each is brush-choked, with major streams emanating from both, including McMillan Creek from their southern reaches and Access and Luna Creeks from the northern glaciers.

All flow into Big Beaver Creek, actually more of a river, which eventually makes its way to Ross Lake. Flows from the western peaks, including Goodell and Crescent Creeks, drain directly into the Skagit

Red Cedar

CHAPTER THIRTY-FOUR: ICON OF THE NORTH CASCADES

River. These valley basins bear the weight of the continuous avalanches of rock and ice from the hanging glaciers above. Both eastern and western approaches must therefore do battle with almost impenetrable brush, thick as the trunks of the magnificent cedars lining Big Beaver Creek at the 3,000–4,000' levels. Thickets of slide alder, arctic willow and vine maple impede progress in the many watery gullies, while white rhododendron, black currant, Labrador tea, and Devil's club thwart access on both eastern and western slopes.

Labrador Tea

Nonetheless, this serrated and staggered Range has now seen all its main summits achieved; indeed, an entire traverse of both the southern and northern sub-ranges has been accomplished, and some movie-hero madmen, part lunatics, part supreme athletes, have completed a traverse of the entire crest, first in 1963 in a 10-day miracle of miserable stamina. It then seemed impossible: "lies" said their competitors; "an underestimation", said their friends.

A full span has rarely been attempted since but such a traverse has occasionally been repeated, often by mountain champions, those rootless vagabonds who devote their lives to seemingly impossible adventures. This passage requires careful navigation and an early season approach because the glaciers slathering the Picket slopes have become increasingly crevassed. Many ventures have been turned back; crack climbers are resilient, but not immortal. This traverse has indeed become a warehouse of failed attempts. To my thinking and experience (admittedly limited), this traverse represents almost the outer limits of climbing achievement. And yes, I've completed a traverse of the southern Sierra, alone and without the need for any pro. Rock, sweat, and dust were my only companions.

The approaches to any Pickets' peak all begin from low altitudes, and all are heavily guarded by brush-choked ravines, steep valleys and stony buttresses. All require protection, whether on glaciers or class-4–5 rock. Both the southern and northern groups are arranged in broad U-shaped basins. The rock is mostly gneiss and often surprisingly solid. Several blocks of granite on Mts. Fury and Challenger are a welcome change from the loose basalt and granidiorite so commonly found elsewhere in these parts. The Picket glaciers are heavily crevassed and can be said to be "hanging" in that they tumble over tortured near-vertical rock walls, in the main on eastern and northern faces. The largest of these, the Challenger Glacier, however, is rather gentle in angle, at least from its foot, though by late summer above 7,000', it too can become quite steep and broken.

Because of the rugged nature of this Range and the infamous difficulty of its access, it is surprising that it is so compact, just about 6 miles in length. Yet there are so many turrets, spires and mountain massifs to tackle it seems less compressed than one might think after a glance at the map. This aspect may hold, for the climber, a beguiling allure, similar to a flesh-eating Venus fly-trap, first welcoming insects, then trapping them inside and consuming them before spitting out their remains. The analogy may seem melodramatic, but if you think so, you haven't yet met the Pickets; this Range embodies to the extreme what the North Cascades are all about.

Climbs of Luna Peak's southwest ridge are gaining in popularity, as are those of the west ridge of Mt. Terror. I've shied away from those here and, with over 20 summits to attack, I will concentrate on the two I know best: one from the southern group: the McMillan Spires; and one from the north: Challenger itself.

The McMillan Spires (both ~7,990'-8,000'): Even today, with many parties having accomplished the western ridge of the West Spire, among the easiest route in all these 20-odd summits, the approach to these spires is complex and laden with brush and much off-trail scrambling up thickets rife with slide alder and vine maple. It is a western passage exposed to the fury of the Pacific winds and all the soaking, dripping, drenching, and waterlogged

CHAPTER THIRTY-FOUR: ICON OF THE NORTH CASCADES

vegetation that signifies. Do not be lulled into what appears at first a well-trodden track up Goodell Creek, which can accommodate high-clearance vehicles for about one mile from the highway at Newhalem; from wherever you park, the overgrown logging road can be easily followed on foot for another 3 miles, watching carefully for surveyor's tape just after crossing a small stream. If you arrive at a raging rock-hopping torrent, you've gone too far as that is probably Terror Creek, an ascent up which any sane individual would want to avoid.

Vine Maple

The "trail", really un-maintained and easy to lose, wastes no time in ascending opaque brush-filled slopes; continue to watch for surveyor's tape. You may encounter a labyrinth of paths but even should you try to follow one, you, in all probability, will still become "lost" at some point as these trails begin to blend with the brush seamlessly. The brush is not new; what is are the clumped-down vegetation patches marking the "trail". You may encounter the orange-red streamers of climbers marking the way. But beware – these may also be the detritus of parties off the actual route. Your goal is to aim left (north-northeast), staying well clear of the Terror Creek drainage. As an elderly climber at that point, I continually realized that, with age, one does not become stronger, just better able to tolerate pain. Perseverance amid suffering, with a dash of resilience, can propel you forward, even in your "classic" years.

An alternate approach, landing you at the same camping site, begins from the same point off the Goodell Creek Trail but branches from this sometimes-trail at about 4,200' and aims for, then stays largely on, a minor ridge, thus avoiding some (but never all) of the brush of the route described above. An animal/climbers' trail occasionally makes the going a bit easier on this ridge. This, however, is its sole advantage, as it involves more ups and downs. It heads due north once relatively open ground is reached at 5,800' and intersects the more western approach at about 6,300'. One advantage of this approach might be its distance from the formidable cliffs of the Barrier but the western approach is more direct. Both approaches stay east of the Terror Creek drainage after crossing the two southern branches of that raging stream, and not the main creek itself.

Yes there will be blood; more likely surface scratches. But if you remain on the broad forested crest east of Terror Creek until it branches, at about 5,600', you will eventually reach open ground, actually meadow, though still steep. At this elevation, traverse north, crossing streambeds, including the upper reaches of Terror Creek, and gullies, but always ascending to about the 6,300' level, where several bumps come into view to your right.

You are now in the cradle of Crescent Creek, but fortunately, you will be above timberline all the way and will not have the pleasurable agony of trying to cross "The Barrier" if McMillan Spires are your goal. Crossing this rocky cliff with full pack is equal to class 5 climbing; do not be so gullible as to believe climbers' stories of finding a "magic" class-4 breach in this barricade, which must be surmounted if Mt. Terror is your goal. In these ranges, there are many mysteries, but precious few miracles.

Climb northeast on meadow with occasional clutches of mountain hemlock, first over several bumps on the ridge to flatter ground beneath **The Chopping Block**, also labeled **Pinnacle Peak (6,819')**. This table-topped squared-off summit is unmistakable from the view up Goodell Creek from Newhalem. Cliffs below (part of the Barrier) may intimidate you but at this level, you are above the technical lower reaches of the Barrier. Here, heather benches are quite passable at the 6,300–6,400' levels. Scramble to a crest at 6,450' to view both Azure Lake 4,000' below and then out across the McMillan Glacier to both McMillan Spires, followed sharply to the north by **Inspiration Peak at 7,780'** (you will need all the inspiration you can get after this approach) and **Mt. Degenhardt (~8,000')** with associated spires and towers in between. Descend southwest from this minor ridge about 100' to sort-of-level campsites at about 6,350' and pleasant streams in meadows festooned with subalpine buttercups, fan-leaf cinquefoil, American bistort, Sitka valerian, and Gray's lovage.

You have gained about 6,100' with full pack to reach this paradise, but with views unequalled in our Range except from outposts of the northern Pickets. To the northwest identify Mt. Terror and the Crescent Creek Spires, best left for those with a rage to climb and the ability to match. Betting on me making those summits is like shorting a stock...you never know. To the south, Eldorado and its associated towers, along with Colonial and Snowfield Peaks poke their jagged heads above Mt. Terror. Equally severe is the northern branch of the Pickets, with Mts. Fury and Challenger reigning supreme above hideously uneven crevasses on their eastern slopes.

Gray's Lovage

Rest well, for the next day, though with a lighter burden and shorter distance to cover, you will nonetheless encounter no easy mission. **McMillan Spire's Southwestern Summit** is easiest and should be your first objective. Climb back up to the saddle, then drop 200' to the Terror/McMillan Glacier and make an ascending traverse toward the fully visible West Spire. Aim for the col between McMillan and Inspiration Peak; the snowy ascent is not steep but crampons are advised throughout the summer. If snowmelt has occurred, the saddle can be reached by a gully and scree. Once at this saddle, proceed northeast up what is described as relatively easy 3rd-to-4th-class moves on solid rock. I detected what I thought were some easy 5th-class moves but my sniveling was rendered pointless by its futility as I struggled to finally gain (in an ungainly manner) the summit.

Views abound, although vistas of the Pickets follow the rule that the taller or closer you are to other crests, the views are not as spectacular. Nonetheless, Inspiration Peak and **Mt. Terror (8,151')** are either frightening or motivating, depending on your state of mind as well as your level of prowess. **The Crescent Creek Spires (~7,000–7,880')**, sharp as the heels of a diva's shoes, can be seen along with Challenger peeking out beyond **Mt. Fury (8,280')** to the north.

Beyond lie Bear and Redoubt, their forms bespeaking their difficulties of access and ascent. To the west, Shuksan and Mt. Baker are well-defined, while to your south Triumph and Despair melt in the distance. Colonial and Snowfield show their handsome faces again to your south, while to the east, Jack Mountain predominates. Gaze down to appreciate the well-named Azure Lake, and out to the southwest for views of the rarely challenged Blum-Bacon-Hagen complex. While the south face, north face, and southeast face of this Spire have all been climbed, those 5th-class routes are usually on slabby rock, where it has proven difficult to place adequate protection.

Not to dawdle should the **Eastern** (really the **Northeastern**) **Spire** be your ambitious objective this day. Lower by about 10' from its western sibling, you do not have to approach it from the east, as Beckey suggests, because a route exists from the McMillan/Inspiration col mentioned above. To turn a common cliché topsy-turvy, we hoped that a pound of success was worth an ounce of risk. Thus we dropped down to the Terror/McMillan Glacier we had ascended for the West Peak, then scrambled, gradually at first, then more steeply (of course – it's the Pickets) to a point just beneath the south face of the East Spire, where a 4th-class gully (loose) allowed access to its south face.

Aim for a notch on the east ridge, then track left on sloping class-5 ledges. The aim is to return to the south face via a small rock rib (solid 5.6). Here, the climb became an argument with the rock; the holds for me were as slippery as a wet bar of soap. This task would require delicacy but all I could muster was brute strength when precision and control were required. Unfortunately, footholds for me have often proven positively puzzling. I gazed in awe as the

CHAPTER THIRTY-FOUR: ICON OF THE NORTH CASCADES

more skilled among us pranced up these pitches at what appeared to be a shuffle while to me, they presented more of a stretch and a leap. I could have retreated, demonstrating apathy and fear, then regret, or expose myself to the terror facing me.

Happily, our leader recognized a passageway, a veritable hole through the rock and motioned us onward. I wondered, amidst the darkness between the rocks, whether the light at the end of this tunnel was more like that of an oncoming train. However, an ascent through this stony hole led to the reasonably solid east ridge, less broad than on the Southwest Spire but only involving class 3 to low 5th-class moves with some exposure, especially to the north, to gain the Northeast Spire's top. For me, the summit was an achievement but one dispatched more by luck than skill. I rarely celebrate at the top; after all, one wouldn't declare victory at halftime. We chose the more direct east face as a rappel route; fortunately, even the Bible has a Book of Exodus.

Views are similar to those mentioned above, but now encompass more of the southern sub-range, including the Crescent Creek Spires and Mts. Fury, best left to those with a rage to climb those towers and pinnacles. Mts. Terror and Challenger rise above the northern crest-line. It is now time to return to base camp, but think more than twice about packing out. You've enjoyed the luxury of scaling two of the illustrious peaks in the Pickets; try not to rush out, down 5,000', perhaps in twilight or gloomy darkness with barely a trail to follow, and in an area that was never meant for a headlamp.

The north face, north buttress and south face of the McMillan Spires have all been climbed; each requires steep ice up the east-facing McMillan/Terror glaciers and rock (difficult to protect at times) between classes 5.6 to 5.9. Longer, tougher challenges remain in this vicinity, including a tricky traverse to Inspiration Peak and Mt. Degenhardt. We eyed these towers but, from these angles, they appeared better left for more tireless climbers.

We had briefly pondered an attempt at these objectives but realized that there are marvels here but no mysteries; it was clear that natural talent combined with a super-athlete's training and prowess would be needed for those summits. At first, we actually gave Degenhardt a faltering try but we retreated, feeling like a cake had been delivered but we would have to wait for the frosting a week later. Anyway, rock stars (not the kind who sing) considering these peaks may be made of the ice and stone they ascend; I will, in all likelihood, not be among them.

Mt. Challenger (8,207'): While not having the honor of being the tallest peak in the Pickets (Luna Peak is higher by about 100'), Challenger anchors the north sub-range of the Pickets and also enfolds its largest glacier. For those of average ability in the mountains, Challenger is a worthwhile and achievable objective, but one not lacking protective barriers. There are two main approaches to this northern sub-range. You can choose a long and tedious approach by trail over Hannegan Pass, a ford of Little Beaver Creek, then a climber's path through meadowed heaven on Easy Ridge. Once above the tree-line, campsites on Easy Ridge offer not only gorgeous views, but level ground and fresh water. This northern route is variously informed yet, in the main, accessible with strength and a bit of luck.

The next day, on this approach, you can follow the ridge east but then you must descend east toward Perfect Pass, 600' below. This trip alone will consume much of your energy as it involves a variety of frustrations, some trivial, others tragic. Unfortunately, many (read most) parties can spend a day trying to locate the most feasible route past the steep slopes, really cliffs, on the southwestern face of Whatcom Peak. There have been not a few who have turned back in frustration here, after a two-day approach.

Alpine Aster

The ones who made it have told of a multitude of attempts to find

CHAPTER THIRTY-FOUR: ICON OF THE NORTH CASCADES

a gully which doesn't require upper 5th-class moves with equipment-heavy kit. Here, you must temper enthusiasm with patience and reality. Yes, there does exist a feasible gully, one of the last you will see, that leads you up loose class-4 rock to what will likely be your second campsite (world-class) at Perfect Pass (6,240'). This, the saddle between Whatcom Peak to your north and Challenger itself to the south offers far-ranging views of both the northern and southern sub-ranges of the Pickets, and a masterful overlook of the Challenger Glacier below to the east. Alpine floral jewels carpet the meadows surrounding the Pass, featuring alpine asters and subalpine daisies.

Subalpine Daisy

From the pass, usually on the third day of your outing, descend steep ice onto the middle of the Challenger Glacier, where the angle of the snow and ice eases. You must re-ascend some ground but this traverse, roped and cramponned, is feasible for average climbers Aim southeastward on your ascent to the saddle between Crooked Thumb and Challenger, occasionally encountering steep ice at 40–45 degrees. You should strive to traverse this glacier at the 6,800–7,200' level before climbing more steeply to the saddle. It is from here that you can gain the summit pinnacle, a near-vertical spire best attacked on its southern aspect and rated at 5.6. Fixed protection mid-way up and near the top is reassuring, as is a bolt on the summit for a rappel.

Views are as striking as you would expect. The entire cirque of the northern sub-range stands proud before you to the south, featuring Crooked Thumb, Phantom Peak and Mt. Fury, this last with no easy route to its fearsome summit. The names of these peaks are surely apt as they score a jagged line towards the southern cirque of the Pickets, with **Mt. Terror (8,151')** and **Luna Peak (8,311')** outstanding. Beyond this sub-range lie Triumph and Despair, along with the hazy outlines of Colonial and Snowfield; to the east, over Ross Lake, Jack dominates, but the rugged peaks of Ragged Ridge can be glimpsed as well to the southeast; northward lie Spikard, rarely attempted; then to its west, Bear and Redoubt, the latter with its famous southern ridge a "flying buttress" which would dwarf that of any medieval cathedral.

From this vantage point the westward view is now unobstructed, affording the awesome sight of photogenic Mt. Shuksan, with its eastern ridge punctuated by the digit of Nooksack Tower, said to be the most difficult pinnacle to climb in the entire North Cascades. In high relief, the white hulk of Mt. Baker secures the western front of the North Cascades.

Many North Cascade climbers might disagree but I believe there is an "easier" route up Challenger, from the east. Crowder and Taylor name it the "Wiley Lake High Route" though it is also called the "Eiley-Wiley High Route" as well. It entails an arranged (and not inexpensive) boat ride up Ross Lake, then a 13-mile trek to Beaver Pass, all on a gentle creek-side trail but burdensome with heavy pack nonetheless. I packed the lightest gear I could muster, for once outpacing my more heavily-laden companions. Nonetheless, they soon discovered my deceit; I was made to carry the ropes the rest of the long way.

While I much prefer to be above the trees in heavenly meadows ripe with flowers and views, this long but gentle trail is anything but monotonous. Boredom is not the same as irrelevance. On this long but delightful trek aside Big Beaver Creek, you will pass magnificent cedars and then the sardonically-named Access Creek: an approach to the northern sub-range, but brush-choked, its climbers' path obscured amidst thick shrubbery and ill-placed boulders. Its name is as impressive and overstated as its route is both inefficient and often forbidding.

Along the main trail, glimpses up the valleys from the west make spirits fly, with jagged pinnacles and snow-bound glaciers

CHAPTER THIRTY-FOUR: ICON OF THE NORTH CASCADES

aplenty. Giant firs and cedars create an awning through which sunlight diffuses the colors of the forest as if through a cathedral's stained-glass windows. Continue on the path until you eventually reach Beaver Pass in 13 mostly well-graded miles; here a first camp should be made.

The second day is really the most taxing of this three-to-four-day outing. From 100' shy (south) of the pass, begin what can only be described as the pain of the brush: a tortuous 4,000' bushwhack (rated 5.15 for brush) as you fend off the familiar villains of the North Cascades, including Devil's club, salmonberry, white rhododendron, multiple types of blueberries, slide alder and vine maple, while carrying both rock and ice gear. You are entering a Troll forest, replete with rank ferns and the gloom of an ever-present canopy which thwarts the light from above, root-ridden, steep (up to 60 degrees), squat and dank, with creepers and clingers, all picturesque in a strange way. Almost impassable but not impossible, this brush chains you like an iron fence. Unfortunately, the ratchet of North Cascades shrubbery turns in only one direction: against wherever you need to go.

Red Cedar

We began this bushwhack with high hopes that quickly turned to low spirits, and rests at 100' intervals. Resolute in the face of adversity, our pace turned from rabbit-like speed to that of a tortoise extending its head from its shell while making slow cautious progress. We were breathing air but it seemed suffused with the vapors of strife. Chained by the brush, at times we were coerced into throwing our bulky packs over varied obstacles, such as a log or up a cliff (3rd-class); at other times, we became anesthetized to the shrubbery and to our brush-choked approach. Since I always wear shorts on summer climbs, I suffered the stabs and arrows of barbed-wire brush piercing my skin and blood pooling on my socks like coagulated grief.

Due to our differing paces and odd obstacles, we separately encountered this green centrifuge which, at times, flung us further and further apart, like blood cells separating from serum. We were proving Heisenberg's Uncertainty Principal in reverse, unsure where we were due to the slow pace. Our leader, Eddie, thick-necked and slippery as a used car dealer, enjoyed a fetish for brush; although he did better than the rest of us, even he seemed to invent new curse words as we all struggled with a tsunami of greenery that seemed to reach to infinity. His eyes remained placid but his face twisted into a maddening grimace that signaled just two words: "Damned brush!"

The way on the map appeared straightforward but the brush was toxic. We were like a spider caught in its own web. I tried to lighten our mood, if not our packs, by commenting that we were in understory purgatory. No one laughed. In fact, nobody smiled for the entire 4,000' of brutal brush-whacking. Boasting about surviving this verdant hell is like bragging about having a clean face in a pizza-eating contest.

Moss Campion

As we slowly progressed through this agony, we had to remind ourselves that our goal was no less targeted, but also no less brutal. However, after 10 hours handcuffed to the vegetation, we had the clout to reach eternal bliss: a heavenly kingdom of heathered meadows festooned with lupine, paintbrush, subalpine buttercups, yellow cinquefoils, American bistort, Gray's lovage, Sitka valerian, cut-leaf and subalpine daisies, and alpine asters. Tiny purple Cusick's speedwell and bright pink-purple mats of moss campion eased the pain of the bushwhack as we treaded slowly up these parklands in

CHAPTER THIRTY-FOUR: ICON OF THE NORTH CASCADES

the sky. We were exactly where we were supposed to be; Eddie had chosen a decisive and well-aimed route. In that one moment of breakout above the cruel thorny brush, it seemed as if our blood and tears, through some miracle of alchemy, had turned into the finest of wines, so sublime were the views; we drank in the spirit of the mountains themselves.

The unparalleled scenery along this upper way offered salve for our brush-beaten wounds. Quite suddenly, before us lay a circumplex of dark, improbable spires and glaring white snow and ice which even squinting could not diminish. Now our idea of reaching heaven turned into the ideal into reality. Our aspirations, once atrophied, were now inspired by an airy traverse over heather and talus. We passed Eiley Lake on bench and flowery pasture, then established a base camp at about 6,500' on the broad ridge between Eiley Lake and, to its southwest, Wiley Lake.

For all the campsites I have ever visited, on all the continents in which I have climbed, this ranks in my memory as the most spectacular which I've been fortunate to occupy. (I apologize for the cliché's; our adjectives remain exhausted, a testament to the poverty of words as opposed to these views). It is only rivaled by campsites above Egg Lake called Silesia Creek camps; book those early – both sites are in the National Park and are usually sold out by late winter of the previous year.

Gazing in silent awe, we were stunned at the panorama, like a herd of deer suddenly realizing a group of hikers were approaching as they grazed. We were accompanied on one trip by a well-known Himalayan climber; she agreed. Spread out in front of our tent doors was a wet dream for the true North Cascader: the full backdrop of the northern sub-range with its glorious cirque holding the majestic Challenger Glacier, topped by Mt. Fury as a southern outpost, then Phantom and Crooked Thumb Peaks and capped by Challenger itself, separated from us by the immensity of its gleaming Glacier.

Yet to our happy surprise, the southern sub-range was also in view, with its prominent peaks of Mts. Terror and Degenhardt,

Inspiration Peak, and even the topmost rocks of McMillan Spires. Towers, steeples, spires, incisors, arêtes, crowns and pinnacles too numerous to count inhabited our entire view to the west, while the shimmering waters of Wiley Lake glistened below. The photos in Beckey's *Red Guide* do this landscape some justice, but if you can find a copy of Crowder and Taylor, the view on the cover and the first photo before the Foreword provide an even more striking idea of this tortured yet beautiful terrain. Words have not yet been invented to adequately describe these scenes.

American Bistort

The next day, we traversed southwest over meadow and talus, featuring American bistort and Grey's lovage, then descended a loose gully 100' to reach the eastern fringe of the Challenger Glacier. Here, the angle was not severe, though above 7,000', the slope increased. However, the Glacier on our late July trip was not heavily crevassed. We were able to use French technique, ankle-sore but feasible, and occasional front-pointing, to gain the Crooked Thumb-Challenger col, from where the 5th-class summit pinnacle was successfully attained with a few well-protected and reassuring iron bolts. Views abounded in all directions but they are the same as those described above. Nonetheless, they repeated our oft-considered understanding that the mighty forces uplifting this range were like a hurricane in slow motion and reminded us of how puny are the efforts of mankind in the face of Nature's unhurried fury.

We were young then and ambitious, so, after summiting Challenger, we climbed its mostly snow-bound northwestern summit, which Beckey calls **"Middle Peak"** (**~8,000'**). It is just northwest of the summit and usually cloaked in snow up to about 100' of its top-most point. Though the ramp of snow leading to the rocky top was steep

CHAPTER THIRTY-FOUR: ICON OF THE NORTH CASCADES

in places, it was relatively easy to gain the base of its pinnacle. Class-3 scrambling led to its pointy zenith and far-flung views comparable to those from Challenger itself. We spent a third night back in camp admiring the stupendous view, visible in marvelous outline even past midnight. The stars never shined more brightly for us than on that moon-less eventide, memories forgotten of the harrowing descent to be undertaken the next day.

The following morning, we dreaded the descent, believing it to be more complicated than a Mars landing. However, we needed to face our inhibitions and get on with it. Employing the judicious use of tree-assisted arm rappels and ferocious thrashings, we arrived back at Beaver Pass, then endured the long tedious slog down the Big Beaver Trail with some haste in order to meet our boat 13 miles away at Ross Lake. Hobbling along the trail, we barely made it, fortunate because missing it would have entailed a further 9-mile walk on the West Bank Trail to Upper Baker Dam. Come to think of it, we never did see a large dam-building mammal like the big beaver on this, my second attempt on this route, but what we did see is seared into our memories as spectacles we will never forget; incredible settings no human could ever have imagined nor created. I still cherish my scars.

At the end of such an encounter, the battle of the climb, with all returned safe and sound, is beautifully resolved. While most climbers prefer a beer after such a climb as a reward, for me, a burger, fries and a chocolate shake brings nirvana; so much so I sometimes fear these delicacies may be listed as Category One drugs by the FDA.

Other routes to Challenger's apex exist, including the east face and the south ridge, all involving the usual brush and poor rock, and all necessitating mid-class-5 climbing on rubble. I believe I'm being a pragmatist, even a masochist, but had I the youth and strength of years past, I would still choose the Eiley-Wiley Route, with all its thickets, thorns, scrub and undergrowth, as the "easiest" means to summit Challenger. Through the marvelous misery we endured came the most sublime moments I have ever achieved in these mountains. Indeed, to my eyes, the Pickets remain the benchmark against which all other ranges on the continent should be judged. A tour of any part of the Pickets is like eating your favorite foods again and again without ever feeling full or gaining weight. All who can should try; ample rewards will surpass your struggles.

CHAPTER THIRTY-FIVE

Massive but Unjustly Ignored

Mt. Spikard
(8,979')

HIDDEN GEMS OF THE WASHINGTON CASCADES

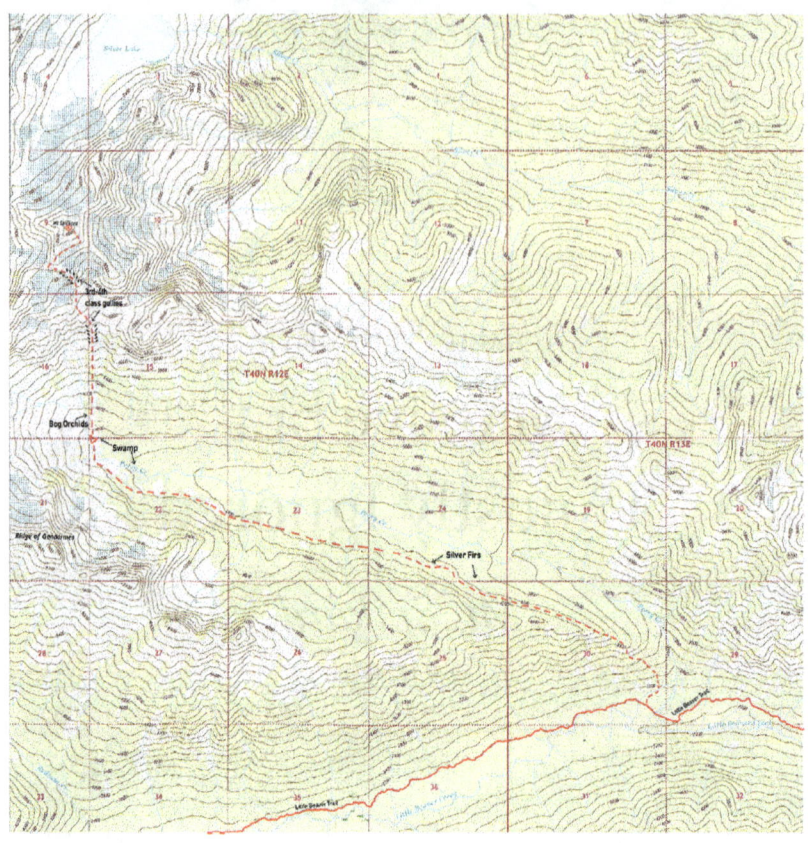

CHAPTER THIRTY-FIVE: MASSIVE BUT UNJUSTLY IGNORED

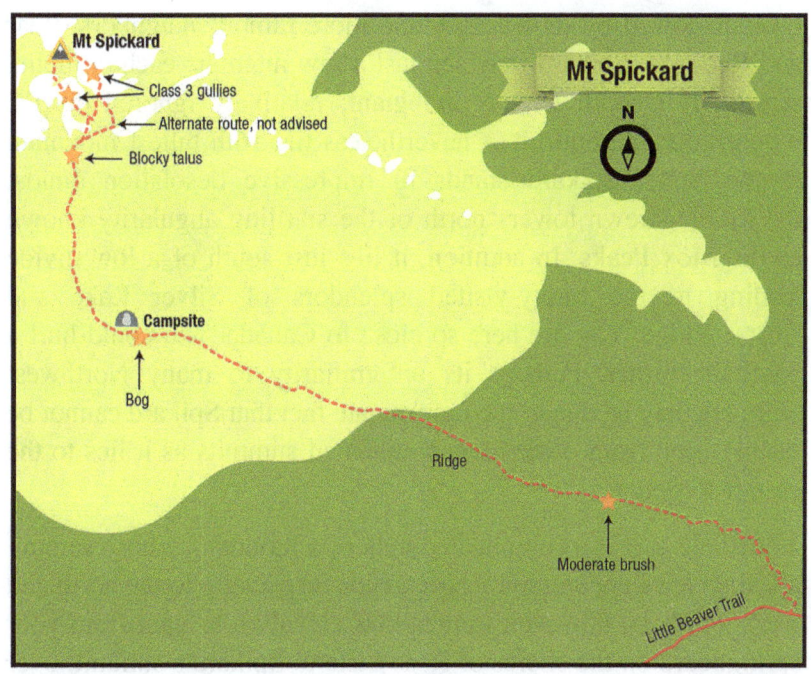

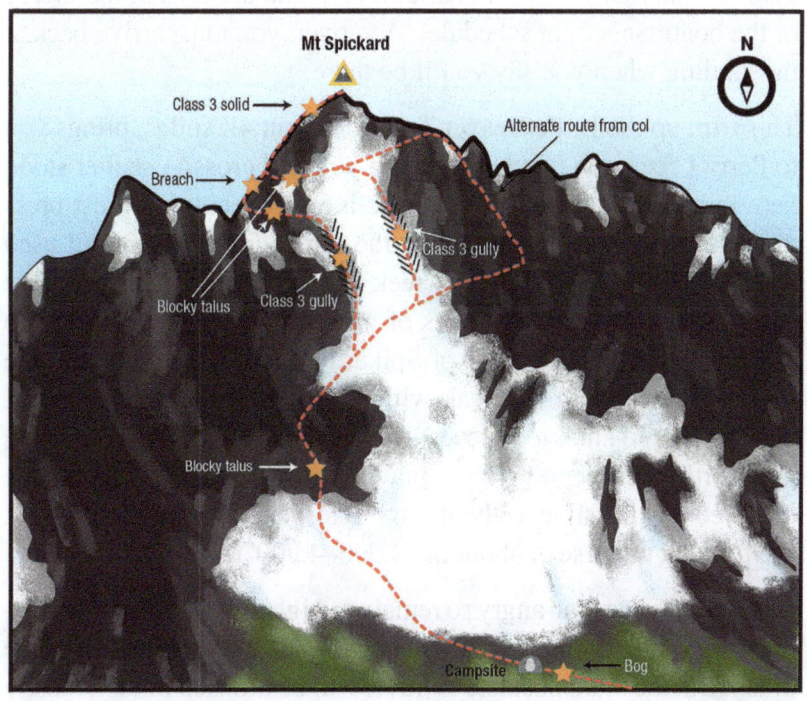

Overshadowed by its westerly and more famous neighbors, Bear and Redoubt, Spikard may see just a few attempts each climbing season. It is both gnome and giant; relatively ignored despite its considerable bulk, it is nevertheless the 16th tallest mountain in the State. Spikard stands in impressive desolation amidst the rubble-strewn towers north of the startling angularity known as the Mox Peaks. In addition, it lies just south of a low divide leading to the rarely-visited splendors of Silver Lake and Custer Ridge. You are here so close to Canada, you could hurl a baseball further. Perhaps its unfamiliarity to many Northwest climbers may be due to the unfortunate fact that Spikard cannot be readily seen from other more frequented summits as it lies to the east of Redoubt.

Nonetheless, it is a complicated hulk of a mountain whose summit affords views uncommonly spectacular, especially to the north and west. There is, however, tremendous elevation to gain from your springboard on the shores of Ross Lake to Spikard's summit: over 7,000'. And yes, you must charter a boat and are thus at the mercy of the boatman's tight schedule. Moreover, you must arrive back at the landing when you say you'll be there.

This trip, up the Little Beaver Trail for about 4½ miles, brings you to Perry Creek, the first large stream you will cross. A shelter stood here in ancient days and a campsite is visible, but you must press on if your target is Spikard. Now the fun begins: An old trail used to exist partway up the Perry Creek drainage but if it did, we were hard-pressed to find any traces of a passage-way. Your goal is to attain a campsite at the base of Spikard's south face route, the sole means of ascending the peak without a highly technical track. It seemed best to stick to the west side of the gushing creek, heading first north, then bending west, staying as high on the ridge above the Creek as possible without having to gain, then lose elevation. We found a traverse at about the 4,000–4,300' level best.

Better to be wise than angry so remain as high as you can on the west-trending ridge. Even so, you will occasionally be hobbled by some brush. But the main obstacle to travel will be downed timber, mostly

CHAPTER THIRTY-FIVE: MASSIVE BUT UNJUSTLY IGNORED

silver firs, but also western hemlocks, Douglas firs, and alpine larches further up the valley as well. Birds twittered above; how I envied their gift of flight! At times you may be obliged to temporarily abandon your pack in order to crawl under or leap over the deadfall before reaching back to retrieve it. Snow load, fires and avalanches have lightened the understory, but have also created ingenious barricades that only Mother Nature can devise. Sometimes, in this forest what you do to correct a problem ends up aggravating it.

Silver Fir

It is about 5 miles of this bushwhacking torture; we wanted to howl against the tyranny of the brush, almost pushing us backwards, but we eventually reached the headwaters of Perry Creek, at the forefront of this hanging valley. Unfortunately, campsites are few. Numerous feeder streams from the Ridge of Gendarmes and the Mox Peaks have created a swamp at the base of Spikard, yet this is where you want to be. As is so typical of North Cascades summits, it's the approach, filled with its anguished irregularities, rather than the climb itself that presents the most difficulty. Seek the few spots elevated above the quagmire of surrounding bogs and muck but do

not expect a perfectly dry campsite. Alpine marsh marigold thrives in these besotted bogs, with (usually) two pristine white many-petalled flowers above pear-shaped leaves clustered about its base.

No matter: You are ensconced in one of the least frequented yet awe-inspiring deep "holes" of all the North Cascades, festooned with enough marsh-marigolds (Buttercup

Alpine Marsh Marigold

365

Family) that you cannot help but trample at least a few. To your left (south) sits the Ridge of Gendarmes, with its multiple spires threatening to repel any climber daring to reach their summits. Beckey has applied temporary and unofficial names to a few of these towering steeples, including Consolation and Tranquility Gendarmes but several of the lesser minarets are not only nameless but may never have witnessed a successful ascent. The history of this breathtaking area has not been fully written; authors are needed. This serrated ridge ends in the Mox Peaks (also called Twin Spires) jutting at acute angles and rarely attempted, for obvious reasons. Indeed, the east face of the northern peak has only recently seen a triumphant ascent, rated at 5.12, and serious enough to warrant publication in a national climbing magazine.

But it is to the north that you must gaze, for your route lies here the following day. Spikard was named for an early climber who perished on the descent of the northern face of one of the Mox Peaks. Not an auspicious appellation but, despite very steep faces and ridges on western, northern and eastern aspects, Spikard's southern slope offers the scrambler/climber a reasonable chance to summit. Begin by ascending talus and heather benches at increasingly acute angles, until a series of gullies, loose but just class 3, present themselves. Either of the two eastern-most gullies will do.

Angle eastward to reach a small saddle, a breach in the southwest ridge. Here snow or ice (really a nano-sized glacier sans crevasses) leads upward to the east, where the summit blocks can be gained. Once you've gained the ridge, turn eastward to scramble the class-3 blocks to Spikard's apex. This is the only level of difficulty you're likely to encounter, though if you are facing class-5 gullies or ridges, you are off-route.

Views from the top are as inspiring as they are singular. To the immediate south, one can appreciate the many routes on the Mox Peaks and the Ridge of Gendarmes, so sharply do they pierce the sky. Luna stands tall in the Pickets, and both their northern and southern sub-ranges can be seen. Westward, the immense hulk of Redoubt can be appreciated in its entirety; especially impressive is its southern "flying buttress", steeply angled at its origins, then topped by a roof as level as your dinner table. Bear, with its prodigious north face, lies just to Redoubt's south. It has provided technical champions many opportunities for first ascents, both on its blackened ridges and icy north faces, plastered with chilly frost and hidden from the sun for much of the summer; these all require front-pointing mastery.

Madeagle and Nodoubt are the sharp spires to the north of Redoubt. Well to the west, Shuksan and Baker shine, snow-clad but clearly identifiable. To the northeast, the Silver Lake peaks sharpen the sky above its shimmering waters. As difficult to identify as they are soul-stirring, these clusters include Mts. Custer and Rahm, Thompson, Finlavson and Whitworth Peaks. Silvertip and Rideout lie just across the border and, further north, the Cheam Range impresses. Thompson, Leewood and Kleslika Peaks lie to your northwest and, on clear days, even Garibaldi can be gleaned to the far northwest. The east, unfortunately, offers no illustrious ranges, though Jack can be identified to your southeast. The serene hillocks and meadows of the Pasayten Wilderness provide a restful aspect due eastward, though across the northern tip of Ross Lake, the startling sight of the twin Hozomeen Peaks shatters the tranquility.

Time to descend. Down-climb the identical route you climbed; there is no need for rappels but you might have thought ahead and marked the correct gullies with cairns or tape just to be certain. Contemplate a second night at camp, for you will, in all probability, not be so fortunate as to appreciate this view again. Anyway, the trek out is just as tedious as the march in. Try to begin above the melancholy swamp bottoms of Perry Creek's headwaters. One climber I know (alright – it was me) stepped completely out of his boot, mired in the muck trying to traverse the mud just 50' from camp. Also remember the time you told the boatman to meet you at the Little Beaver landing. Being stranded this far up Ross Lake after your climb and descent will entail no amiable stroll back to civilization on the West Bank Trail.

Should you be more adventurous and able to handle low-to-middle 5th-class rock, there exist several other routes to consider. The northwest ridge and north face must be gained from Silver Lake, as arduous and terrifying an approach as can be imagined. Both entail mid-5th-class rock work plus steep north-facing ice. The southwest couloir is rumored to be straightforward, but requires a long traverse from Depot Creek, beginning in Canada, then demanding adroit route-finding and an extended glacier traverse.

Spikard, because of its remote location, combined with its onerous approach and the fact that it can rarely be identified as it lies in the shadow of Redoubt and Bear, meets the criteria set out in the Introduction to this book. Should you crave lack of crowds combined with unbeatable and distinctive views, give Spikard a try. Your rewards will outpace your efforts in this seldom-visited northeastern reach of the North Cascades. Plus, you will have glorious tales to tell. Just make sure you lace your boots tightly, don't step completely out of them in the muck at the head of Perry Creek, and be certain you've allowed sufficient time to meet your boat ride back to civilization at Ross Lake.

CHAPTER THIRTY-SIX

A Northern Outpost of Mt. Baker

Hadley Peak
(7,515')

HIDDEN GEMS OF THE WASHINGTON CASCADES

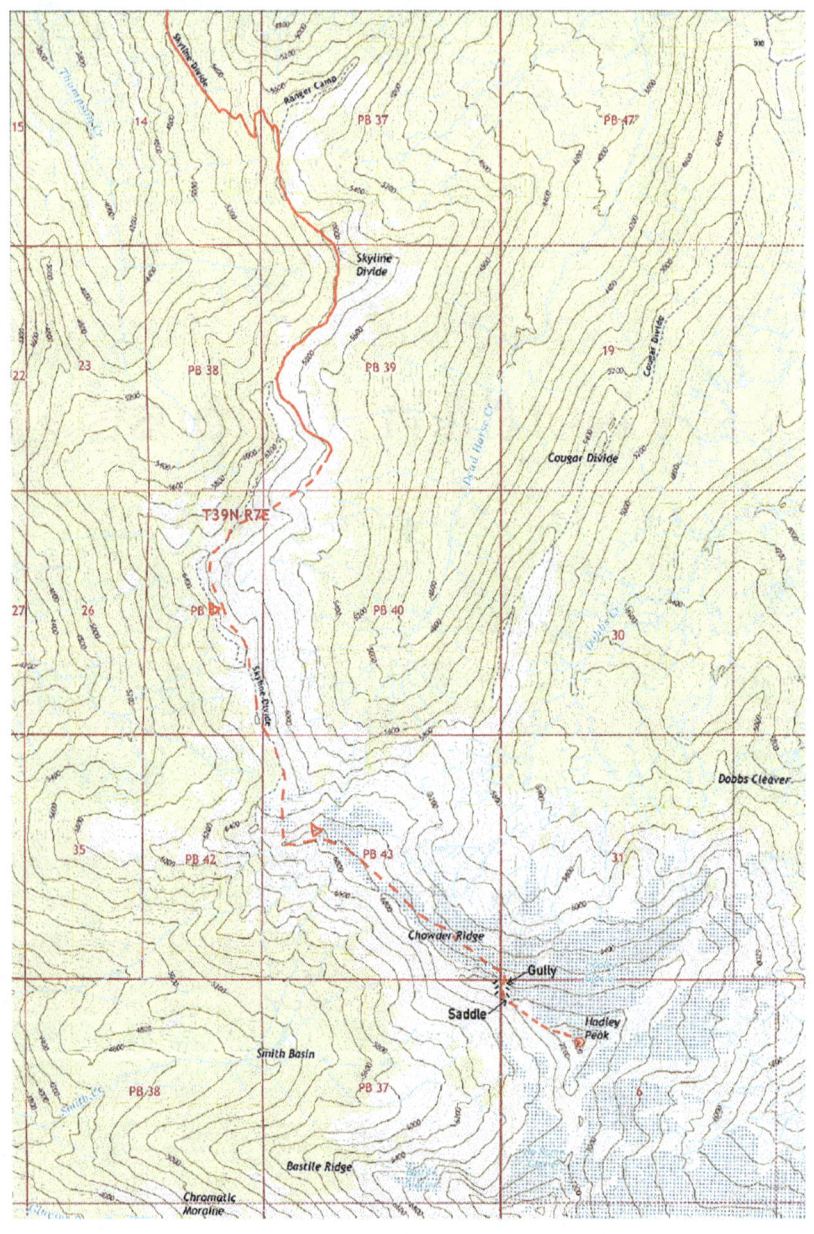

CHAPTER THIRTY-SIX: A NORTHERN OUTPOST OF MT. BAKER

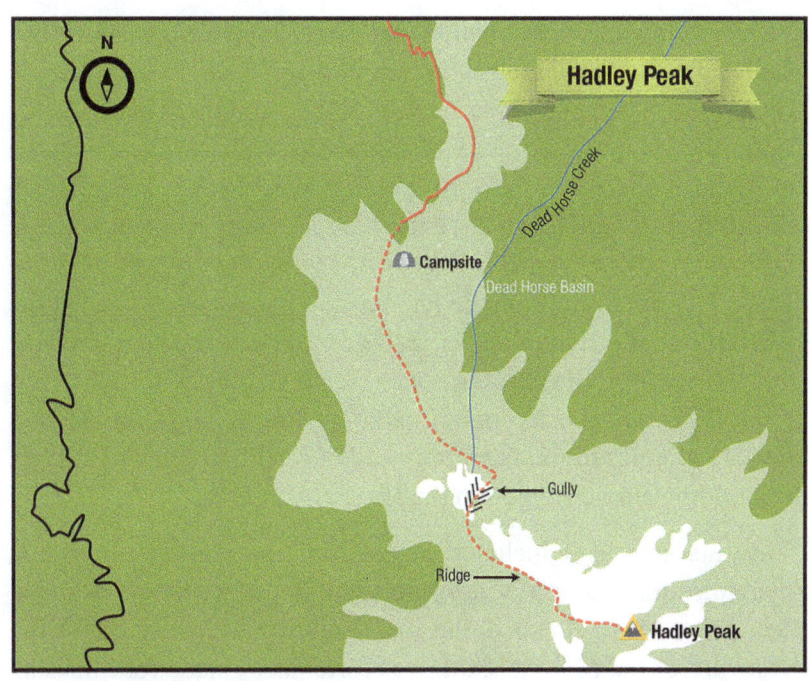

Despite being a northern outlier, even just a satellite of Mt. Baker, Hadley Peak is becoming more popular since the Skyline Divide Trail offers the best up-close views of Baker's northern face. Hadley forms the southern terminus of three converging ridges: Skyline and Cougar Divides to the north, and Chowder Ridge entering from the northwest. Still, few will venture to its summit, content with the glorious meadows and icy vistas of Skyline Divide, yet unaware that world-class campsites lie just beyond the eastward bend at the official trail's terminus. The road and trailhead are accessed just past the town of Glacier; turn onto Glacier Creek Road #39, then just 100 yards later, a left onto Deadhorse Road #37. It's another 13 dust-laden miles to the large trailhead at 4,300'. Thank the loggers for building a road so high in the sky.

Why this area isn't included in the National Park is a mystery, though a small portion of it to the south is designated a "National Recreation Area". A map of the area demonstrates that an extension westward of the National Park was fortunately made for Shuksan. I'm hopeful this area's inclusion in the Mt. Baker National Wilderness will provide adequate protection.

While it is possible to climb Hadley in one day, that would require a party both equipped with only day packs and a powerful one at that. Better to tread the path up Skyline Divide, past or over several knolls, then, following a pronounced eastward bend, find several campsites on duff. Neither the 7½" topo or the Green Trails maps depict the Skyline Trail continuing up Chowder Ridge, but the path up Skyline Divide and Chowder Ridge is now a highway, even a two-track one at that. The effort up this trail, emerging from the forest at about 5,900', will be but a distant memory because, even though you know it's going

Meadow Arnica

to be there, the awesome view of the snow-bedecked north face of Baker, lording it over these flowery meadows, is one of the obligatory spectacles in all the North Cascades.

Skyline Divide leads to one of the premier amphitheaters of Mt. Baker. As you progress up or around three "bumps", really small hillocks, you will trek across a calico of meadows endowed with white and scarlet paintbrushes; yellow fan-leaf cinquefoil; tiny white spikes of partridgefoot; blue lupine; yellow meadow and broadleaf arnicas; white American bistort; Gray's lovage; and Sitka valerian. It is raining color, all while the white gleaming behemoth of Baker is right in front of you. There is no finer view of Baker's north face than from this perch. One could also approach this point by taking an old trial up Cougar Divide, but recent attempts have noted the absence of a clear path, with much brush and more altitude to gain.

Broad-Leaf Arnica

As Skyline Divide and Chowder Ridge meet, a left turn eastward soon brings you to the ideal campsites, mentioned above, at about 6,400'. These sites must be rated world-class, encompassing views not only of the north face of Baker but the thorned aspects to the north and east of the Border Peaks – American and Canadian, as well as the Patagonian fang of Slesse. Snow for water is usually present but if not, you must descend about 300' to the headwaters of Deadhorse Creek. Despite its cadaverous name, we have drunk from these streams without subsequent illness. However, you will probably prefer to filter. Should you descend into the basin below, be sure to note the relatively rare broad-leaf willow-herb, also known as alpine fireweed or, more appropriately, as river beauty. It grows on the gravel slopes descending into Deadhorse basin

Broad-Leaf Willow-Herb

and resembles fireweed but with a much shorter habit (1–2') yet even larger flowers of a pinkish-purple hue.

These ornaments glorify the otherwise barren slopes and signify that water has either been there earlier in the season or moisture lies beneath. In the basin by the creek, look closely to find elephant's head, a perfect miniature rendition of the beast for which it is named. As nighttime falls, you can still see the white outline of Baker well after dark. The next day, continue east through scree, talus and gravel as you follow a climber's path. It soon gives way to trackless meadow as you descend slightly into the headwaters of Deadhorse Creek; despite its name, a heavenly basin holding many species of mountain flowers congregate in these damper realms. These include the shiny yellow petals of subalpine buttercup and dusky-red birds-beak lousewort, along with the aforementioned alpine fireweed.

Elephant's Head

Look to your north to find a sketchy, rude, but clear-cut upward path and shallow gully to your south which at times requires handholds but, in a short ¼ mile, lands you onto the crest of Chowder Ridge. Mark with tape or a cairn the exact spot the trail meets the ridge, as there are several gullies trending north following this junction which could lead you down onto the Cougar Divide, Dodd's Cleaver or even the brush of Dodd's Creek (remove tape when you descend). On one trip, as we reached the ridgetop on a return from the summit, the largest herd of mountain goats I've ever encountered could be seen to the west but still on the ridge; we stopped counting at 55.

CHAPTER THIRTY-SIX: A NORTHERN OUTPOST OF MT. BAKER

Now hop boulders and scree, but stay firmly planted on the top of Chowder Ridge, aiming southeast toward its highest point, Hadley Peak. This traverse of about ½ mile could also lead you to a saddle between two summits if you've steered too much to the north. Both appear to be about the same height. The correct one is to your left (west). Beckey mentions an "easy connecting ridge" to **Peak 7,842**, taller than Hadley but probably not much different in terms of views. He believes the route would take you due south over the Bastile Glacier but actually it would require a trek across the most easterly branch of the Mazama Glacier. Late in July through September, both these ice sheets would require crampons, ice axe and rope; thus I cannot recommend it. In fact, there is, or used to be, permanent ice to the north of Hadley Peak, called by some the "Hadley Glacier". Warming has reduced it to a mere blot of frigid crystalline snow.

Anyway, the views from Hadley are reward enough. Of course, your eyes would first strain against the brilliant crystals of Baker's north face (bring sunglasses). From this vantage point, you can identify the huge expanse of the Roosevelt Glacier. To its west, the Black Buttes color their spires in darkest ebony; Colfax, Lincoln and Seward Peaks can also be identified. The Roman Wall, actually the headwall of the Coleman Glacier, a tough technical ice route, rears due south, followed by Sherman Peak, then the apex, Grant Peak, topping them all. The Boulder Glacier can be seen to your southeast, the most difficult ascent I've enjoyed on this not-so-extinct volcano. If of a certain age, you will recall the closure of Baker to all climbers in the 70's due to menacing rumblings from its crater. Fortunately, it's now open for business but you can never be certain.

Yes, the views are spectacular southward but don't fail to look west and north as well. From Hadley's perch, Shuksan can be seen in its famous western-face profile, its northern glacier-clad slopes menacing ice climbers of suitable ability. Mt. Sefrit anchors its western ridge, riddled with towers, some of which remain unexplored. To the north, the striking fang of Slesse (I apologize but we really can't use any more appropriate noun) straddles the Canadian border, while American Border, Canadian Border, Goat, Tomyhoi, and Larabee Peaks, plus the Pleiades, all tattoo the northern skyline with their fantastic angularities. To the west, the Twin Sisters raise their reddish iron-rich peridotite rock, which contrasts nicely with the grays, whites, greens, and blacks all round.

The trip back requires some care in locating the correct gully/path, but it's not much of a problem if you have to search, as the area is small. We angered a ptarmigan protecting her chicks on one trip. An ice ax was required to dissuade her from a vicious attack. Views of mountain goats are also often seen hereabouts. Fortunately, no extra fees are required for the wildlife. Once at camp, there's ample time to pack up and out. This comprises a glorious excursion with minimal effort and views far exceeding the work you put in. Yes, there will be crowds on the Skyline Divide Trail, and the standard slow vehicles in front of you as you swallow the dust of 13 miles in your car or SUV, but there's really no rush. You've spent a blissful several days in the elegance of this Eden, and odds are, you'll come back, dust and all. There is no patent on these views.

CHAPTER THIRTY-SEVEN

Even Better Views than from Ruth

Icy Peak
(7,073')

HIDDEN GEMS OF THE WASHINGTON CASCADES

CHAPTER THIRTY-SEVEN: EVEN BETTER VIEWS THAN FROM RUTH

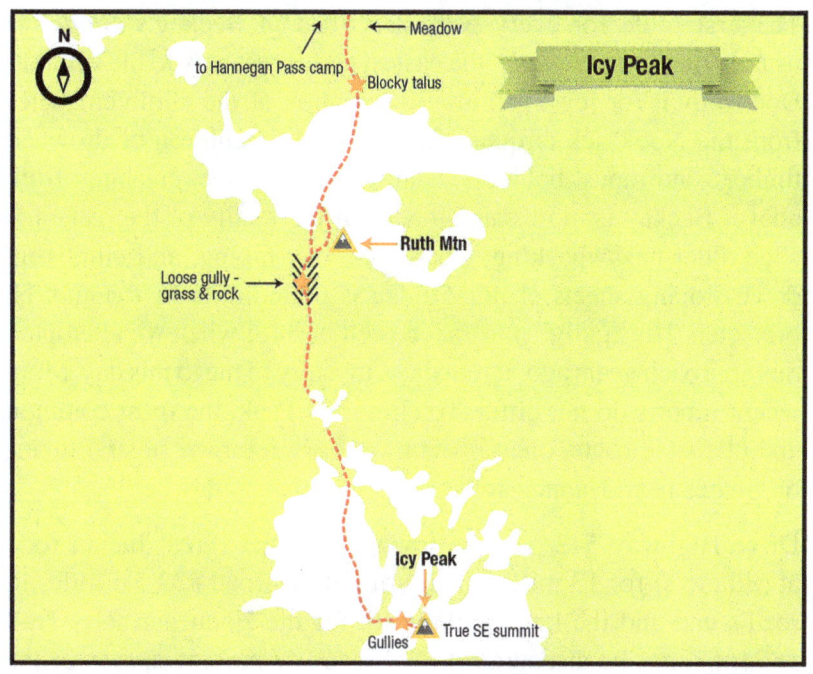

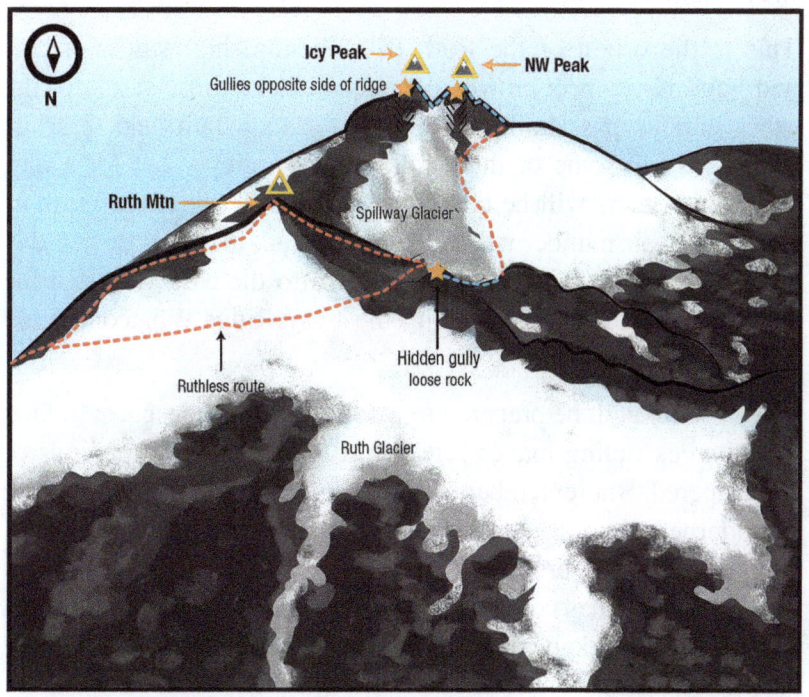

The first route for every peak described in Beckey's *Guides* is usually the *route normale*, the easiest and surest way to the summit. Don't buy it for Icy. His initial description of the climb emanates from the Nooksack cirque, a giant witches' cauldron of drowned timber, enormous boulders, and islands of ice crashing from above. Beckey is more sanguine about the reality of the fearsome slide alder-bushwhacking, wet-socks river-hiking, and climbs up down-sloping sheets of 4th–5th-Class granidiorite that cannot be protected. His "gully" must have been bashful when we attempted this approach years ago; it remains a mystery to me to this day. More recent reports do not differ. To climb Icy Peak, the most common and plausible route, one to which we have returned several times, originates from Hannegan Pass, congested as it may be.

Drive Highway 542 past the town of Glacier (great Italian food at Milano's) for 13 miles, then turn left on Road #32 5½ miles to road's end and the large parking lot for the Hannegan Pass Trail #674. Do not be discouraged at the lack of parking spaces or the many vehicles forced to park ½ mile before the trailhead.

This is the origin of the Ruth River-bottom highway of a trail and you must expect crowds the equivalent of those at any of the other famous pass trailheads, such as Snoqualmie and Cascade Passes. While some of these folks will be simply out for a day, and many others will be climbing Hannegan Peak to the north of the pass, a fair number will be climbing Ruth in a one- or two-day excursion. A few will be heading down to the east to hazard the long approach to the Pickets up the Easy Ridge/Whatcom Peak/Perfect Pass approach.

If it's a weekend, be prepared to jostle for a parking space; in fact, a mid-week outing makes sense if crowds make you nervous or ill-tempered. But remember too that all these folks are appreciating a wilderness, just inside the western border of the National Park, that must remain protected; once they experience this beautiful approach, each may come that much closer to voicing their concerns should this remarkable landscape ever become threatened.

CHAPTER THIRTY-SEVEN: EVEN BETTER VIEWS THAN FROM RUTH

The Hannegan Pass Trail is distinctive in that it is largely in the open all the way to the pass. Although the trail is a through-way, by no means is it without its charms. Splendid views to the south encompass Mt. Sefrit to Shuksan's west while Jagged Ridge and the pillar of Nooksack Tower extends to its east; this last appears almost unclimbable.

Leafy Aster

Behind you, Goat, Tomyhoi, and Mt. Larrabee loom.

Straight ahead, Ruth, with its anomalous expanse of snow-white glacier gleaming in the sun is stunning; Ruth's relatively low elevation (7,115') belies such a large body of ice, even given its northern exposure. Soon, switchbacks signal that the pass is near. Yellow mountain arnicas, pink leafy and Cascade asters, American bistort ("bottlebrush"), Gray's lovage and Sitka valerian accompany you as you ascend. Unfortunately, the pass is a bit of an anticlimax. Western hemlocks and Douglas firs block most of the views, although Bear and Redoubt are visible in the distant east.

Not to worry, for dazzling panoramas are now easily within your grasp. If you have the time, take the well-defined trail (unsigned) to your left (north) to **Hannegan Peak (6,187')**, an hour's worth of sometimes-steep trail work, but rewarded with heathers, both white and red, and views north and west over Mamie Pass to twin-summited Goat

Cascade Aster

Mountain and beyond to Larrabee and The Pleiades. Ruth and Jagged Ridge, along with its founding father, Shuksan, shine as brightly as the sun will allow, all capped by the snows of Mt. Baker in the western distance.

Back at the pass, where to camp? The Mt. Baker Wilderness officials disallow any camping in such a fragile and well-frequented site. You could have taken advantage of the few campsites aside the trail below the pass, but these are usually full, and beset with bugs so numerous that I'm convinced there are species, and even genera there, yet to be identified. Moreover, the only views you'll have are the ones you've already encountered on the trek in. You really should begin at the pass, then take the boot-worn almost vertical path to the south, and proceed up the hill to discover a small lake on your left, often dry by late summer, where legal sites on duff offer pleasant camping, though preciously few views – those darn trees again!

Or, even better if your party is sufficiently robust, continue past the small basin holding the lakelet and climb the quite precipitous double-tracked path leading due southeast. It's a haul, but what a vista awaits: Bypass Point 5,963 on its eastern side, where the path levels to a meander through these parklands and, with luck, chance upon 3–4 campsites underneath subalpine firs, between about ¾ and 1½ miles from the Pass. These are balanced just north of the National Park; therefore, no permit is required. Best to hope and pray these are mostly empty, thus the suggestion to go mid-week or in shoulder seasons.

There remains a possibility, however, that even on a summer weekend most parties will not have endured the hardship to reach these glorious sites. Their loss – your gain. Brown bears frequent these areas so watch your sweets. Water may be difficult; most parties drop west into a basin holding the headwaters of Ruth Creek to obtain it. In early summer, snow may linger on the eastern slopes.

But it's all worth it. The views, to be explained later, are nothing short of stupendous. You are on a broad flowery ridge open both to northern, southern, and western views. Although some other

CHAPTER THIRTY-SEVEN: EVEN BETTER VIEWS THAN FROM RUTH

North Cascade campsites are as overwhelming, a precious few in the Northwest surpass these blissful spots above the Pass but beneath the gleaming snow and ice of Mt. Ruth. Look deep into the awesome maw of the Nooksack Cirque, with ice cascading down into the valley bottom with disarming frequency. The floor of this wicked basin is littered with house-sized boulders and chunks of ice. Jagged Ridge is now in starkest relief while the north face of mighty Shuksan, clothed in the ice of the Price and Nooksack Glaciers, dominates this scenic overlook.

Stay up as late as you can to savor the nighttime movie: stars you never knew existed, lazy satellites looping across the sky, brisk meteors, the Milky Way and the silence of air falling on trees; they all compete for attention in this isolated locale, far enough from urban light pollution to fully appreciate these Atacama Desert-like conditions. The astronomers in your group may try to identify the many points of light but most will simply lie back and view what the true night sky must have appeared to Native Americans.

Trying to comprehend the vast oceans of space and the paradox of the quantum world, which apparently rules not only the small, but our everyday existence as well, makes one appreciate that our brains evolved to help us survive on earth, not to grasp the complexity of the cosmos. Indeed, our universe may be not only stranger than we imagine; it may be stranger than we *can* imagine.

But you must also rest as the next day's ascent of Icy awaits, and it involves both a loss, then again, a gain of altitude. Begin by heading southwest, just to the right (west) of **Ruth's summit (7,115')** and either climb its final blocky summit rocks, a 15-minute diversion to your east, or bypass it, thereby becoming Ruthless. Just over Ruth's western arm, head east to the Ruth-Icy saddle, then descend an obvious though loose, heather, rock, and grass-filled gully (class 3) to gain, in 200', the Icy Glacier. From here the three rock peaks of Icy stand out almost as nunataks, blanketed by the glacier's expanse.

Climb step-by-step up the glacier's northwest slope. Opinions about equipment and safety here diverge, as they do on the route up the Ruth Glacier. It's always wise to rope up, even on Ruth, with nary a crevasse in sight. Recently, however, warming has broken these once-smooth expanses of snow such that crevasses are not uncommon, even on Ruth's seemingly gentle ice.

I would recommend rope, ax, and crampons, even if you see other parties casually ascend without any technical equipment. It's your call - the safer option is often the best. Now your aim, in full view, is to ascend the rising but fairly gentle Icy Glacier toward the rocky outposts at its head. Stay on the western side of the rocky peaks until you can traverse at about the 6,600' level in order to eventually gain the southern aspect of Icy's three upright spikes.

Most parties at this point ascend a gully, one of three consisting of loose 4th-class sand, talus and scant vegetation to reach **Icy's Northwest Peak (7,062')**. The proper gully has been a matter of debate on CascadeClimber.com but the easiest one is the furthest right (east) as you stand due south of all three pinnacles. The true top-most apex of **Icy**, however, is the **Southeast Peak (7,073')**. The purist would therefore aim for the true summit, about 10' taller than the Northwest summit. To do so, take the far east (right-ward) gully noted above, reach the ridge, and ramble over 4th-class boulders and sharp spines heading east to attain the true summit.

Regardless of which crag you choose, you will be well-rewarded for this prize. There are no adjectives to adequately describe the views south to the Blum-Hagen-Bacon Group; to the southeast spy Triumph and Despair; east to an easily-attained close-up of the sun spotlighting both the northern and southern slivers of the Pickets; Bear and Redoubt to the northeast; westward, and some would argue the premier vista, to Jagged Ridge, seemingly within touching distance, and headed by the singular totem of all the Cascades, Mt. Shuksan, with its intimidating northern glaciers spilling repeated avalanches of rock and ice onto the floors of the Nooksack Cirque. This is surely the most terrifyingly glorious basin in all our mountain ranges. Almost as imposing, or more so, are the views to the north, past Ruth to, in west-to-east-fashion, Canadian and American Border Peaks, Larrabee, the Pleiades, and

CHAPTER THIRTY-SEVEN: EVEN BETTER VIEWS THAN FROM RUTH

the unequalled shaft of Slesse, whose vertical walls both tease and tempt the Class-5 athletes among us who would challenge such a precipitous monster. Here, one is awed by the overpowering beauty of the North Cascades.

If you plan on a 2–3-day outing and must descend to the parking lot, it's best not to linger, though it's difficult to forfeit such a viewpoint. You will, in all likelihood, never behold this remarkable tableau again unless you return, despite that 200' gully you must climb just west of Ruth's summit to get back to camp. And who could blame you if you did return? (Perhaps only those who still insist that Ruth has the best views.) At the trailhead, remember where you parked and beware of oncoming vehicles on the drive back to civilization. Do yourself a well-earned favor and don't miss a meal at Milano's – you've more than earned it!

CHAPTER THIRTY-EIGHT

Tip-toe Across the Ridges North of the Western Giants

The High Divide/Keep Kool Lakes Traverse

(4,350'–6,415')

HIDDEN GEMS OF THE WASHINGTON CASCADES

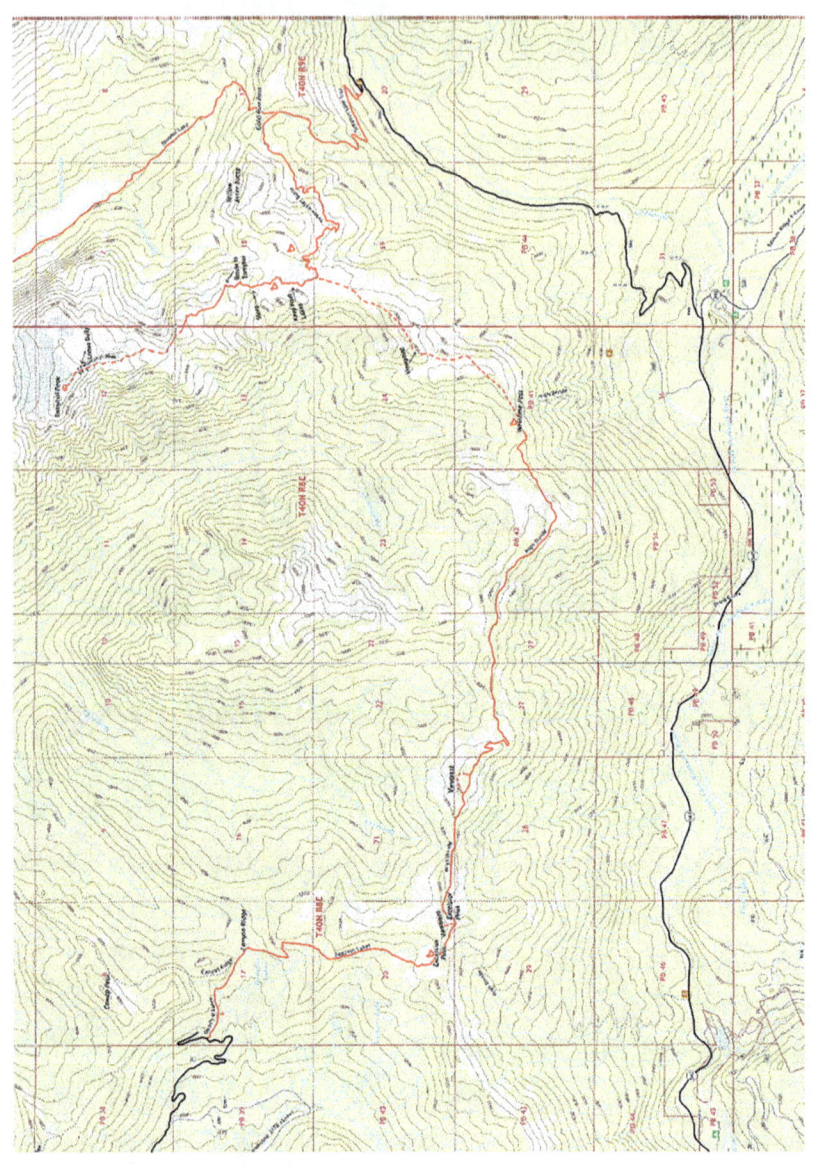

CHAPTER THIRTY-EIGHT: RIDGES NORTH OF THE WESTERN GIANTS

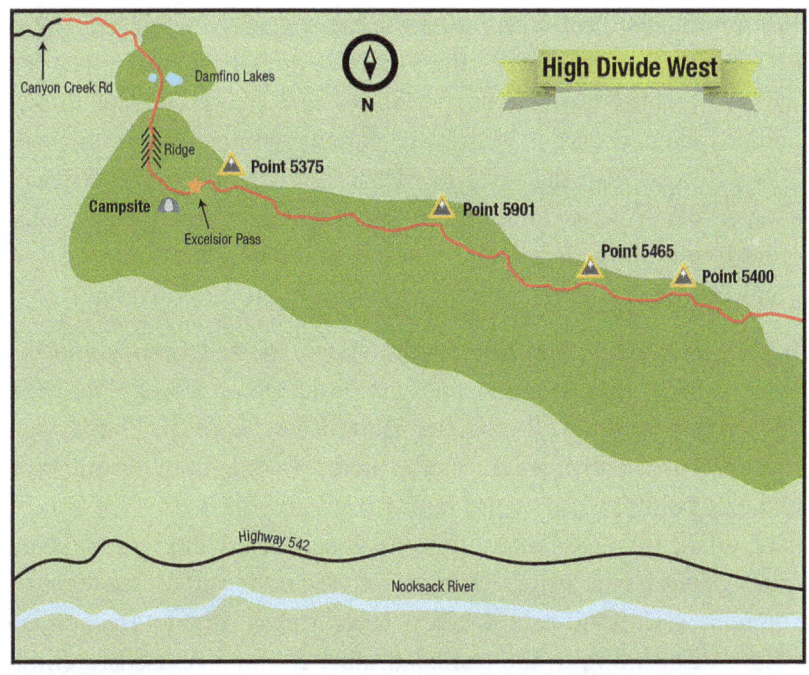

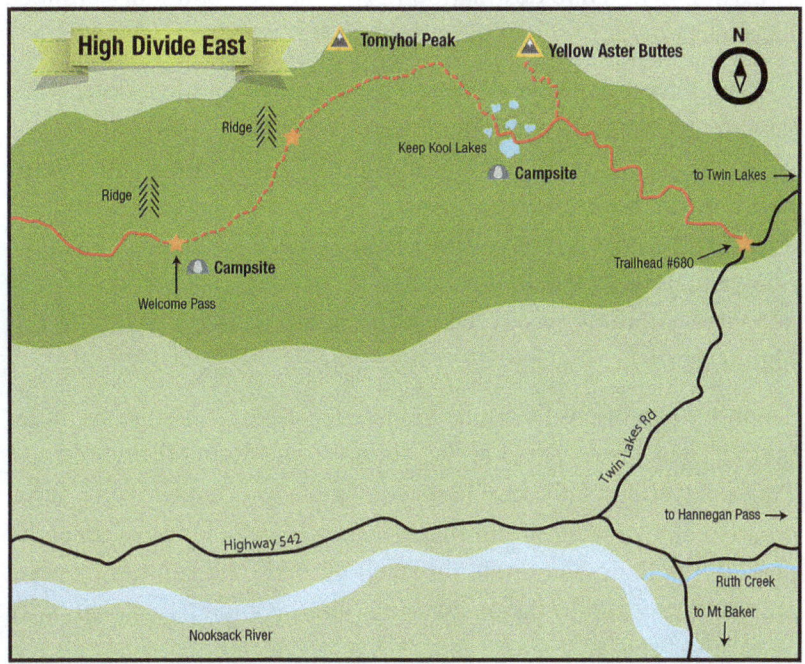

While you may not climb many notable peaks on this, the most scenic of traverses north of the Pickets, you will be well-rewarded with on-and off-trail travel over miles in a playground of flower gardens planted by our greatest of parents, Mother Nature herself. You will also reap the rewards of a 3–5-day journey you will not soon forget. Yes, you may think this traverse, which never comes close to climbing an actual mountain, is really a fool's errand, but you would be mistaken only if peak-bagging is all you covet.

For the rest of us, the flowers, the views, the blueberries and the lakes suffice. Beginning at the Damfino/Canyon Creek Trailhead and ending at the Yellow Aster Butte/Keep Kool Trailhead, you must prepare in advance to have vehicles ready at both the entrance and exit points, but they are both within an hour's drive or two of each other; plan well and enjoy the unparalleled and unobstructed miles of views in all directions on this traverse. If in the heat of summer, also anticipate a Keep Kool Lakes' dip to freshen up before descending to the trailhead most commonly used to climb Tomyhoi, a valuable destination itself, but too commonly climbed these days to merit much discussion in this text.

Although there is some elevation to be gained and lost during this passage, you can skip all but an ice ax to burden your pack, as you begin the trek at an elevation of almost 4,400', thus guaranteeing you'll soon be above the forests blocking your views. Indeed, 85% of this trip is above timberline, where unblocked vistas to Shuksan, Baker, the Pickets and the border peaks soon almost become so common as to render you numb with the beauty of this high traverse.

Begin by leaving at least one vehicle for a party of four 4½ miles up the Twin Lakes Road at the Yellow Aster Butte/Tomyhoi Lake Trailhead #686. This is where you hope to complete this aerial traverse. On a sunny summer weekend, vehicles are generally parked a mile up and down this well-graded road (up to this point anyway), with the major parking area completely filled with Subaru's, Prius's, Volvos, and SUV's of all the major brands. So it's best to time your beginning early in the week and thus your

CHAPTER THIRTY-EIGHT: RIDGES NORTH OF THE WESTERN GIANTS

hoped-for arrival here on a Thursday or Friday. Take your time on this traverse; haste will only dampen your delight. Expect solitude; it is unlikely you will meet too many other explorers on this backcountry crossing.

Travel back in your approach vehicle (with all participants within) west on the Mt. Baker Highway, #542, to the Canyon Creek Road #31, about 2 miles east of the Glacier Ranger Station and turn north. While Road #31 tricks you at first into believing any low-clearance vehicle, such as your recently-purchased Maserati or Aston, can easily handle this dirt boulevard, do not be deceived. Based upon the generosity, or lack thereof, of funding for road maintenance, after about 3–5 miles the track becomes bumpy, to put it mildly, with wash-boarding, stemming from the regular up's and downs of the many trucks and campers also hoping to make it to the road's end.

After 14 miles of hitting your head on the vehicle's roof, avoid Road #3170, and stay left on Road 31 to just before a severe left switchback at 15½ miles, where there should be a trail sign and a small parking area for Trail #625, labeled "Damfino Lakes, Boundary Trail, Canyon Rim". The road may have shattered your nerves, let alone your forehead, but it has perched you at about 4,350' of elevation, not a bad start for the incredible journey which awaits.

It shouldn't take long (½ hour) on this trail to reach Damfino Lakes, actually more like tarns, where you turn due south on Trail #625 for 1½ mostly agreeable miles, some in the open, to meet Trail #630 at Excelsior Pass, and campsites if you're tired or just awed by this aerial transit. If not (it's only been about 4 miles in thus far), turn abruptly south on Trail #797, heading to Welcome Pass, 3 miles distant and about at 5,000'. But what a 3 miles they are! Most of this walk has been pure alpine meandering, floating in the sky with what seems like air beneath your boots.

Try to hang a left (north) at about 1½ miles from the last junction to a clearly visible hillock just 200' high for a snack and the requisite photos south to Baker and Shuksan. The latter displays its fearsome north face, with the Price Glacier appearing almost vertical and

American Bistort

heavily crevassed; Price Lake nestles at its base. At about 1½ miles further on this blessed traverse look again north for another hillock, at about 5,930'; it barely seems possible but this viewpoint encompasses more spectacular views. But more about these later.

Thus far, the traverse has been mostly on trail in meadows graced by a complete flora of the North Cascades: Platoons of tall purple asters contrast nicely with the beds of white, red, and yellow (sticky) heathers. Here and there white and red paintbrushes dot the landscape, always accompanied by their friends, broad-leaf lupines (some taxonomists would insist these are "arctic lupines" but they look the same to me – and other botanists would agree); while mats of multi-colored phlox decorate the rock gardens so plentiful in early summer. American bistort is the white foot-tall "bottlebrush" plant more densely populated here than anywhere else in the range.

Orange Agoseris

Along the streams rushing down from the ridge-top snow-banks, startling rose-colored Lewis's Monkey Flowers and huge yellow Tiling's Monkey Flowers mark the watercourses. Also find delicate partridgefoot, named for its multi-cleft leaflets sporting 6"-high white flower clusters; and moss campion, with shockingly pink tiny blossoms emerging from velvet mats of moss - actually tiny bunched-up leaves plastered against the granidiorite whitish rock-fields. An occasional orange agoseris pokes up, displaying

CHAPTER THIRTY-EIGHT: RIDGES NORTH OF THE WESTERN GIANTS

a color not often seen at this elevation; it actually resembles an orange dandelion.

Camping at Welcome Pass, at 5,160', offers an ideal site to take photos of sunsets and sunrises. There are sites off the greenery and snowmelt persists until late summer. There's time to scale a hill ½ mile northwest and 200' above the Pass for even better views. These encompass the overpowering views of the north faces of Shuksan and Baker, this last with the Roosevelt and Mazama Glaciers in full view. The Roman Wall rears up at the head of the Coleman Glacier as well. Shuksan's fierce north face tosses a challenge to ice climbers of all calibers, with the Price Glacier in full glory. Jagged Ridge, extending east of Shuksan's summit, features dynamic views of its high points: Nooksack Tower, whose flanks appear designed to tease, then dash the hopes of scaling it successfully; Cirque Tower; and secured at its eastern end by Seahpo Peak.

As magnificent as these southern lookouts are, to my eyes, the views north are even more striking, although less icy. From your left (west), Canadian and American Border Peaks (to be described as climbs in the next chapter) showcase prominent vertical reliefs partly hidden on their northern flanks; but even their eastern and southern aspects have given fright to the average scrambler. However, truth be told, they are not technically as challenging as they appear. Larrabee comes next, a pyramid of reddish rock with whitish gullies streaming down its southern slopes. Next door, the multi-summited Pleiades, sharp as dog's-teeth, create ripples against the North American sky, all ending in the exclamation point of Slesse, a shriek frozen in stone. It lies just north of the border, a fang as sharp as a shark's tooth, and as deadly; no easy route yields to any summit-bound party.

Church and Bearpaw Mountains anchor the western skyline, along with The Sisters, while to the east, Goat Mountain offers twin summits featuring vistas as glorious as from Welcome Pass. Famous Redoubt, beyond to the east poses no problem in identification, what with its abrupt southern buttress seeming to fasten its walls and support its sheer summit. Look beyond snowbound Ruth Peak to your southeast to view the Pickets, a platoon of neatly serrated pinnacles receding in the distance. The highway can be spotted 4,600' below. It's sort of fun at night to see the ski run lights blink on at sunset around the Mt. Baker Ski Area.

The next day begins a trek into true wilderness, as, after ½ mile on the High Divide Trail, you must exit the familiar manufactured tread by turning north, leaving the trail as it starts to drop south at around 5,000', then follow the broad ridge north, gaining 400' of elevation as you run the ridge to several of its high points, at around 5,500'. Some game trails (marmots?) and possibly ridge-running humans have marked the way but these trails always run out.

Tiling's monkey-flower

At this point, I must write about an anecdote, though I detest these in most route descriptions. This day on our traverse, the temperature was 105 degrees in Concrete. The snow was gone as it was late August and we had foolishly slurped all our water well before noon, believing there had to be a stream somewhere. It was at that point that my meager botanical knowledge became a practical, rather than academic, asset. "There's a stream over there", I cried out, pointing to a yellow streak coursing down a hillside 500 yards away. How did I know? Because of the Tiling's monkey flowers that always accompany a running stream. We marched over and slaked our thirst, filled our bottles and proceeded, ignoring my boorish preening about how basic scientific knowledge is often of practical benefit.

Regardless, from this point, your goal is easy to spot: it's the Yellow Aster Buttes just northwest of Goat. Here and there are sprinkled groves of alpine hemlock and subalpine fir, but most of the track you'll encounter is above timberline, affording you an uninterrupted motion picture of unrivalled beauty. Some up's and

CHAPTER THIRTY-EIGHT: RIDGES NORTH OF THE WESTERN GIANTS

downs are gentle enough to pose no problem. Keep a bearing north-northeast and you will soon begin to view tiny to moderately large lakelets below, the Keep Kool Lakes, and, if you are wise, these will be your final camping destination.

It's true that here you will have company at the Lakes, even in mid-week. However, these are mountain folk, adventurers such as yourself (there are no fish in these lakes as they dry up by September). You can always share your adventures and theirs. While the campsites are plentiful, they are also partly hidden in tiny alcoves and trees such that you don't get that crowded-in feeling. You may hike up either or both of the Yellow Aster Buttes for spectacular views but in truth there are no yellow asters; budding botanists may have confused them with the Tiling's monkey flowers shouldering many steams in this paradise. The rough trail up from the lakes, through an avalanche of corn lilies, is the same one you must haul full pack up the next day so you can also simply relax and gaze at the splendid scenery, or, if it's hot, take a dip in the largest of the lakes. An all-season stream gushes forth at the northern end of the meadows.

Subalpine Huckleberry

By mid-August, you may also wish to partake in the swarms of Cascade (AKA subalpine) huckleberries (*Vaccinium delicosum* – really!) thriving in these wondrous meadows. The best are hiding amongst the rocks, perhaps fearful of being plucked but more likely because the stones retain daytime heat better than the surrounding meadows. Groves of this low-lying fruit have delayed many summit attempts at Tomyhoi – the base-camp for its ascent amongst these Lakes. Although in any direction you look, there is no bad view, try to catch the alpenglow on the west sides of Yellow Aster Buttes. There is no more intense green that the sun can create than in these magnificently verdant meadows; who knew that the blue of the skies and the meadowed green could merge so beautifully?

By this, the third or fourth day, you may be ready for a pack-out, a vehicle, and a shower, not to mention burgers, fries and a beer. Climb the arduous trail up to a saddle just south of the **"Southern"** (actually the **Western**) **Yellow Aster Butte, (6,134')**, drop packs and scramble to both of their summits for even more far-flung scenery, but only if you can tolerate even better dioramas; at this point, you may well be sated enough with the views you may just wish to descend. Should you scramble up the **Northern** (actually the **Eastern**) **Yellow Aster Butte (6,241')**, see if it's still a marmot toilet. The few times I've been there, marmots (not mountain goats) have defecated profusely at the tippy top of the North Butte: In anger? Out of pure spite? As a decoy? Who knows? Just don't sit in it, and lunch elsewhere.

Corn Lily

Take the well-graded Trail #685.1 down to its junction with the Tomyhoi Lake Trail; track right through the last of the glorious meadows, filled with corn lily, valerian, and purple asters, then descend the forest to where you left your vehicle at the Keep Kool/Yellow Aster Butte Trailhead, hopefully still there. I hid cans of real, not diet, coke in the stream across the road and this time, they were still there, unmolested by humans or bears. I drank 2 full cans in 2 minutes: soda never tasted so sweet.

To seasoned North Cascade travelers, this high traverse combines ease of access, no technical difficulty even if you combine it with a climb of Tomyhoi (though some might prefer a rope down the last ascent gully, a class-3-4 furrow), and a trip in which you could burn a candle at both ends – its brightest is in the middle. I took no photos on two such traverses, muttering about the

CHAPTER THIRTY-EIGHT: RIDGES NORTH OF THE WESTERN GIANTS

time wasted in pictures which can never match the real experience. Nonetheless, these vistas provide an antidote to the gentrification of the soul. These scenes remain forever etched into my brain, and will last until the day I die.

CHAPTER THIRTY-NINE

Few Goats, but Spectacular Gardens and Views

Goat Mountain
(6,840')

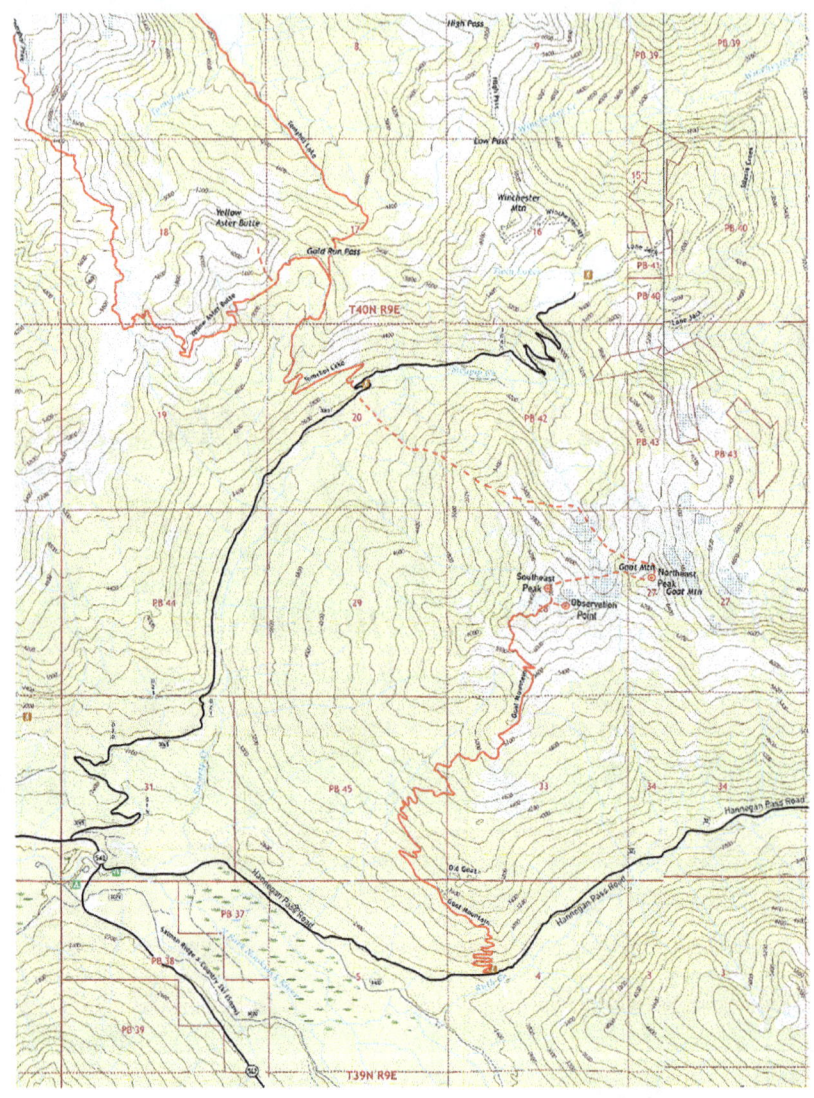

CHAPTER THIRTY-NINE: FEW GOATS BUT SPECTACULAR GARDENS AND VIEWS

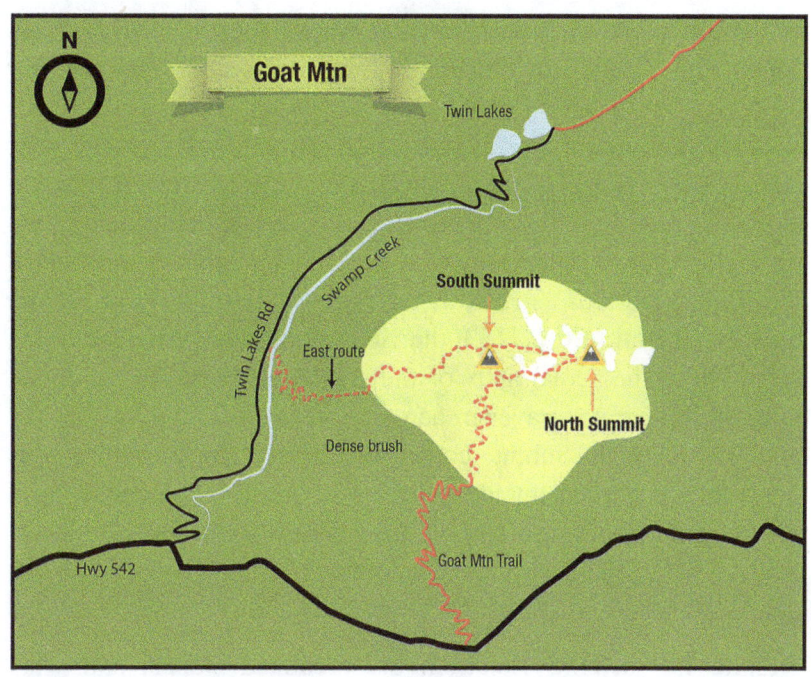

Is there a range in North America which doesn't have a "Goat Mountain"? There are four in the North Cascades. One lies far to the east, at the head of the Methow Valley and has a trail; it's a handy lookout on an otherwise rain-splattered day on the west side of the crest. The two others are actually encompassed in a single description in Beckey, but could be considered two distinct peaks because almost every hiker/scrambler stops at a viewpoint, glorious as it is, at the foot of the true top of **Goat's Southwest Summit (6,725')**; the views don't really improve if you scramble to the actual apex of the southwest peak, but to do so, you will have to traverse across some dicey ice, so an ax and/or crampons might come in handy. Once across this north-facing permanent ice patch of about 100', scramble up a messy gully facing southwest to gain the bonafide Southwest Peak. Either choice offers panoramas far and wide, to be described below.

Despite its seeming isolation, brush-choked slopes, and what appears to be first-growth forest, much of Goat had already been explored by frustrated miners, and its timber cut by greedy loggers in the early years of the 20th Century. The would-be miners were searching for gold beneath their feet, oblivious to the true treasures which lay above: priceless vistas free for all. There is also no need for such arduous labor these days. Begin on the Goat Mountain Trail, which begins just 13 miles east on Highway 542 from the town of Glacier and another 2½ miles on the well-maintained Hannegan Pass Road #32.

Small parking spots on your left, and a bigger one to the right, lie just beyond the trail, but these have failed to account for the burgeoning popularity of this area, so vehicles are usually strung out along the road east and west. You begin at an elevation of 2,550', so plan on a steep ascent, but one well worth the labor involved. Spring and Manning's *100 Hikes* book mentions a turn-off on this trail at an anonymous junction at about 3,700', which, if found and followed (an adventure in itself), reaches a crag where a lookout tower once perched. I've missed this junction on three attempts;

anyway, the views, as usual, are finer higher up - better a pragmatist with a small measure of cynicism.

You reach open slopes at around 5,600' but corn lily, Cascade asters, and the occasional orange agoseris, in association with unnamed tall grasses, block not only the views outward but conceal the trail's path. Step carefully; there are a few built-in steps constructed eons ago, but from here, the trail is hot, scrubby and inconsiderate. After about ½ mile of this overgrown torture, however, unadulterated joy is yours. The path leads up to Goat's western ridge and

Cascade Aster

a brief aerial trundle to the lower view point where the majority of hikers will gladly settle. If you'd rather enjoy a bit of solitude, cross the ice to your left and scramble the 75' gully to truly say you climbed Goat, or at least its Southwest Summit. View the brilliant textured meadows below; they seem almost a mirage, as green and radiant as the brightest emerald, in contrast to the snowy faces of peaks all about.

A better adventure awaits, however, if you're up to it: the **Northeast Peak (6,840'**, but which the Green Trail map puts at 7,060'). Purists would argue that this represents the valid summit. It looks fairly far away because it is, though most able scramblers can cover the ¾ mile in about an hour or less. Though there are no technical difficulties, the trek eastward across these meadows, flecked with a complete menagerie of alpine blossoms, involves a short descent of about 250', then an amble in the sky heading straight for the obvious true-blue top-most pinnacle of Goat – its Northeast Peak.

I've exhausted all the adjectives in my limited vocabulary so all I can say is that you will not soon forget the inexpressible beauty of a straight-on view south to Shuksan's mighty north face, so readily adorning calendars and postcards. The Price Glacier tumbles down in what appears (and in late summer is) an un-climbable snarl of ruined seracs, ice blocks and boulders bigger than temples; Price Lake lies at its foot, collecting icebergs as if they were marshmallows. Slivers of the Crystal and Nooksack Glaciers vie for attention, all heavily crevassed. Jagged Ridge propels itself east from Shuksan's summit, punctuated by Nooksack Tower and terminating in the exclamation point of Seapho Peak - its eastern conclusion. All this above a sweeping expanse of wildflowers in endless profusion, a salve for the soul far from the troubles of urban toil.

Rejoice here in whatever religion or belief you hold dear (or not) for this is the best view of Shuksan, that icon of a mountain, you can gain, aside from the tourist/calendar photo from the lake near Artist's Point. Baker puts on its snowy show to your southwest, proving that it is indeed, the most heavily glaciated peak per unit of volume in the lower 48. Its Park and Boulder Glaciers (both climbable by weekend scramblers like me) are clearly visible, along with Coleman Pinnacle; then Sherman Peak to the left of the true summit; next the Cockscomb, peeking sheepishly above the ridge, leading to Grant Peak, the actual top-most point at 10,281'.

To the southeast lie the staggering array of the Pickets while due east, Bear and Redoubt rear up swiftly from low west-facing flanks. It is from here that the Easy Ridge/Whatcom Peak approach to the northern Pickets can best be appreciated. But the view north cannot be ignored without committing a grave error. Not only can the spikes of the Border Peaks, Canadian and American, be spied; but Larrabee; the spires of The Pleiades; and the tusk of Slesse, which intrudes as a sheer-walled tower as impossible to miss as it is unlikely to be climbed. To my eyes, it has always personified mountain mayhem. Certainly, many parties succeed on this Patagonian spire, with fixed protection and low-mid-5th-class routes, but one glance often sends shivers down the spines of even the most accomplished of climbing combatants.

Other routes up Goat have been accomplished, though not without brushy difficulty. On a subsequent outing, our party, unified in

CHAPTER THIRTY-NINE: FEW GOATS BUT SPECTACULAR GARDENS AND VIEWS

deference to Beckey's authority yet motivated as much by curiosity as conviction, descended from the Twin Lakes Road about 1/4 mile before the Yellow Aster Butte Trailhead, plunging across the well-named Swamp Creek. In retrospect, we had an attitude instead of a strategy for what turned out to be an exquisite torture of a climb. Cautious, but trying to be collaborative, we fought the jungle, twisted and coated in this ghastly beauty, to reach the snow-slopes just north of the Southwest Peak.

To describe the shrubbery as dense would be assigning to it a dignity this west-side thicket hardly merits – an understatement of the highest order. This day, the brush was in its angriest mood, thick as a body-builder's biceps and heavy as a Soviet tank. Man plans but Nature laughs. This shrubbery presented a green Rorschach test we could only rarely discern. Once for me on this alternative was sufficient – a baleful toil through fraying brush leaving scars still visible 20 years on. It appeared that, in these shrub-filled gullies and slopes, the future seemed to predict the past, but on this route, we escaped some of the brush by angling east up a steep snow finger, aiming directly for, then finally attaining the **Northeast Peak's summit**. The views are about the same as from the more accessible Southwest Peak without the same level of mutilation. I still believe that much of my skin is hanging over brush where I never really belonged. Nonetheless, as in both climbing and love, the heart is often master of the mind.

Folks who are not familiar with the North Cascades should really take this hike/climb up the Southwest Peak if they have but a single day to spare. Yes, others will argue for Cascade Pass or Mt. Ruth but, to these aged eyes, you cannot go wrong in pleading the case for preservation and admiration of this, America's most neglected National Park, than to showcase the climb/hike/scramble up Goat. This adventure represents a study in alpine splendor and grace, where, in no other place does the blue of the sky blend so seamlessly with the greenest of meadows you will ever encounter. A single visit turned friends of mine, Rocky Mountain parishioners, into true believers in the vaulted cathedrals of the North Cascades.

CHAPTER FORTY

Close Encounters of the Fourth Kind

Bear Mountain
(7,942')

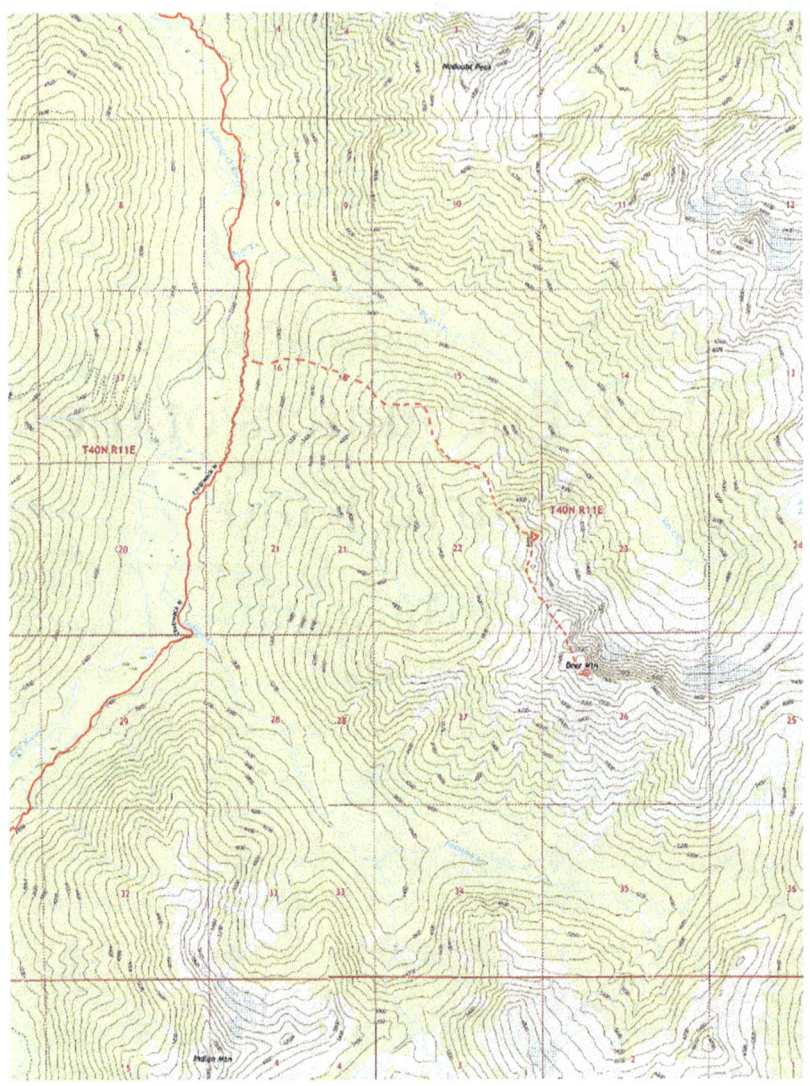

CHAPTER FORTY: CLOSE ENCOUNTERS OF THE FOURTH KIND

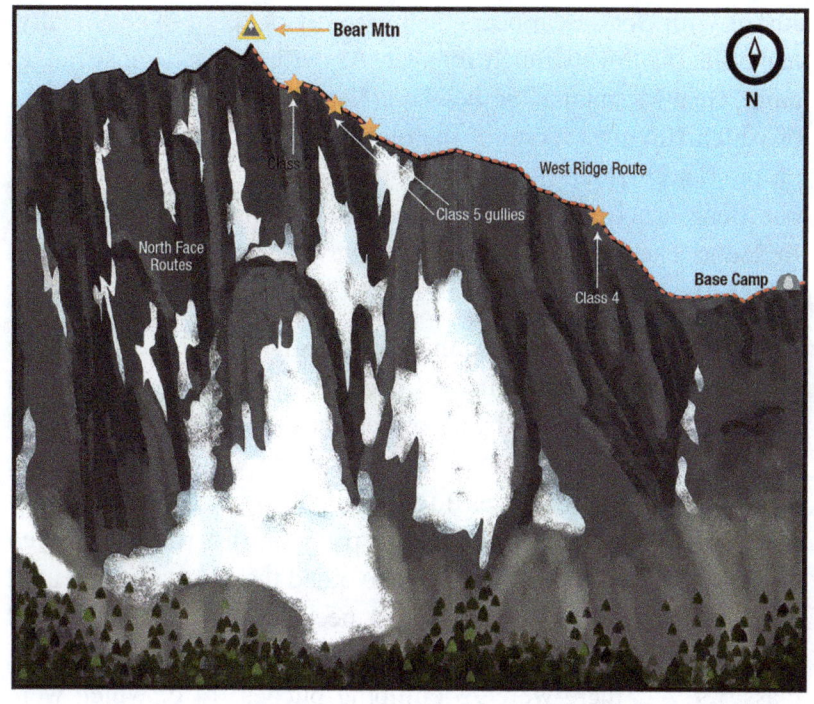

Just as with Goat, Bear bears the ignominy of being so generically-named as to thwart much interest. As with "Goat", most ranges have "Bear Mountains" somewhere; the North Cascades have three of which I'm aware; one of the others may be an unofficial name on the bump which rises northeast of Hannegan Peak. Moreover, our Bear has been overshadowed by its taller northern cousin, Redoubt. There can be no doubt, however, that this ursine hulk is more Grizzly than Brown or Black.

As rugged as it is remote, in recent years Bear has gained the attention of serious ice climbers because its northern face poses a complex of thin and sketchy ice routes, the scene of many a mangled drama. Depending upon conditions, these can vary from Grade III, class 5.8 (Northeast Buttress) to Grade IV, class 5.8, A2, or 5.10a (North Face Buttress). The original party on that route employed 44 pitons but more modern parties avoided the fixed gear and used a "variety of chocks and cams, but needed a pendulum to avoid placing fixed gear". The North Buttress Direct was rated Grade V, class 5.9, A2; there were 23 climbing pitches, 14 of which were above 5.0. The well-named Diamond Route, completed in 1988, required 18 days of climbing and re-climbing, after which this first ascent party rated the climb Grade VI, class 5.10, A3. There is no Grade VII in the North Cascades.

These artists of rock and ice speak the language of ambition, as foreign to me as Urdu or Swahili. My companion, a paragon of first ascents, suggested just such a north face line but as I contemplated his desires, I could only deem such an enterprise as either laughable or, more likely, tragic. It would have been akin to my trying backflips on the edge of a cliff. Fortunately, he agreed. I recalled that my sole attempt on Bear's north wall, years earlier, brought to mind both a vivid disaster and the memory of my first patient in Anatomy Class: a cadaver. To me, a repeat of that fiasco would be as impossible as trying to visualize a new color. It was scant solace that not to try was the biggest failure of all.

Other routes abound. The cutely-named Ursa Minor, on a route just to the east of the Diamond, involved more rock than ice as it clung to

CHAPTER FORTY: CLOSE ENCOUNTERS OF THE FOURTH KIND

the buttress separating the two main ice sheets on the north face. The initial party encountered loose rock (surprised?) and rated the climb Grade III, class 5.8. Our party attempted a repeat, ending inevitably in an ignominious rout after just a single day's push convinced us that this route lay beyond our meagre resources and abilities. The Ursa Major Route ascended the eastern-most buttress. This party remained mostly off the ice, and rated it Grade IV, class 5.9.

The East Ridge has been climbed at least once that I know of; it presents problems with an extensive brushy approach, but low 5th-class rock was reported as reasonably solid. The percentage who actually attempt such routes amounts to a rounding error among us climbers. My leader's suggested approaches to the north face evoked both alarm and apathy: alarm on my part that we would attempt anything with sustained rock exceeding 5.7; apathy on his part that we would have to accept the more benign West Ridge Route in our planned attempt.

Other, supposedly less severe routes have been described. Unfortunately for weekend punters and scramblers, the southern route, typically the easiest artery to a summit, requires an approach of about 15 miles from Hannegan Pass on the Chilliwack River Trail in order to reach the Indian Creek crossing, then unimaginable bushwhacking through at least six stream ravines, each mandating steep forested gully ascents of 2 miles and 2,500' or more before encountering low 5th-class rock as unstable as a bipolar patient off his meds. We found that the fourth gully east provided the easiest track. Careful route-finding is required here with the goal of aiming for a notch between a sharp-pointed crag and the true summit. Unfortunately, the top cannot be seen from this point and, in my limited experience (two attempts here, one successful), mid-5th-class work must be accomplished from the 7,500' level to reach a ridge via a strenuous crack system (stemming helpful here), and ultimately, the easier summit blocks.

To be honest, should the summit be your sole goal, the more convoluted courses outlined by Beckey above may represent a triumph of style over substance. The "easiest" route to Bear's top, the West Ridge, lies in the Bear Creek drainage. My fourth attempt on Bear, and second success at gaining its blocky summit, succeeded on this track. However, do not believe Beckey's description of "a less brushy route" here, a distinction without a difference. You must first cross the border and drive down to the southern end of Chilliwack Lake, where campsites are abundant. Rest well as the next day will require much class-5 brush, almost requiring aid, with a few cliffs thrown in for good measure. Begin by following the Chilliwack River Trail south across the International Boundary (marked by a post), thereby becoming an illegal immigrant in your own country.

The path is river-bottom, thus fairly easy to navigate quickly, an excellent idea as once you reach Bear Camp, in about 4 miles, you will be on your own. While Beckey mentions an "old fire trail" for about 1,000', we could only make out its origins at the camp. Then it was back to bushwhacking non-compliant technical brush for about 2,500'. We were pitched headlong into a multi-hued tangle of jungle thicker than a sumo wrestler's belly. Red marked our wounds while shades of green encrusted everything else in this forest, completely surrounding us.

Time moved almost too slowly in the brush; being elastic, it seemed to rush on by on the easier travels above timberline. Of interest, evidence of the 1977 Bear Creek fire was dissolving but blackened silver and Douglas firs served as reminders of that rainless summer's conflagration. At any rate, our goal was to attain Bear's northwest ridge, ridiculously hoping a ridge would provide easier going. Instructions in Beckey were neither all that instructive or inspiring.

Once on this ridge, we probably mimicked a cardiogram of movement, with seizures and rhythm abnormalities severe enough to warrant resuscitation. But happily, we could occasionally spy Bear

Thimbleberry

CHAPTER FORTY: CLOSE ENCOUNTERS OF THE FOURTH KIND

and Redoubt to the northeast, while white rhododendron, thimbleberry (delicious), Devil's club, false azalea, serviceberry, Labrador tea, crowberry, and subalpine fir, all of which rudely interfered with our progress, or lack thereof. My leader scowled at my sclerotic pace but finally we passed tiny Ruta Lake at about 5,100' (its name an irony; "ruta" in Italian often means highway) but campsites were nonexistent, so we pushed on, finally camping once we stumbled upon a piece of level ground, at about 6,200' on the ridge. Forced to haul water from a nearby tributary of Bear Creek, we settled into slumber; my nightmares were of greenery alive, vicious, and climber-hungry.

Crowberry

Climb day was actually quite pleasant. The ridge eastward opened up considerably, with marvelous views across Bear Creek and Bear Lake to the mighty fortress of Redoubt. Full-on and close-up, its famed southern flying buttress seemed impossible, but a 1989 party scaled its walls, though not exactly in a direct line. They rated that climb at Grade IV, class 5.9. We approached Bear's Northwest Ridge easily at first, with surprisingly solid granidiorite offering us class-3–4-foot-and-hand-holds.

I knew this was too good to be true. In my case, these kinds of statistics are like a drunk under a lamppost – employed more for support than illumination. As I feared, a near vertical crack dictated medium cams but fortunately just at two spots. My stone-faced leader, dour and much more skilled in rock work than I, seemed to levitate up the tough parts with lithe and grace; he laughed when I reported these moves as "class 5.7". I didn't question him further but appreciated his cam placements, distant though I thought they were. My skill set required tactics rather than technology. I followed meekly. Climbing texts and schools emphasize balance, especially on your foot-holds; I must have missed that lesson as I have never transformed that theory into practice. Fortunately, easy class 3–4-moves thereafter up chunky blocks led us to a summit offering dizzying vistas in all directions.

I could look down and just imagine the icy artistry required to scale those famous north walls of snowy crystal and brittle stone. Redoubt stood as haughty and contemptuous as ever, only closer. Below, Bear Lake twinkled in the clear sunlight. Though Redoubt eclipsed views further north, the views west and south compensated: Goat and the Hannegan peaks towered over Copper Mountain's lookout tower while to the south; battalions of both the northern and southern crescents of the Pickes punctured the North Cascades' sky and were easily identified. Particularly prominent was the Challenger Glacier, pierced by the triple spires of Challenger itself, along with its middle and north peaks.

Subalpine Blueberry

Our eastern view encompassed the spiky, spectacular Ridge of Gendarmes, and beyond, Spickard, from this angle more impressive than from its south. The twin spires of the Mox Peaks seemed close enough to touch, but from this angle I was relieved their summits weren't on my climb list anytime soon. We rested and ate, then rappelled back to camp to eat some of the best blueberries in these mountains: the Cascade, blue-leaved or subalpine blueberry. (Many plants have multiple common names.) Despite this mountain's name, we saw no sign of any type of bear on any trip.

There is no way around it: To descend any route on Bear, you will have to fight the brush, sometimes as tough as ascending up

CHAPTER FORTY: CLOSE ENCOUNTERS OF THE FOURTH KIND

it. Full-pack rappels down a waterfall, combined with occasional arm rappels off stout firs (complete with my sardonic comments) brought us back to Bear Camp and out, crossing the 49th Parallel again, this time into Canada. The long drive home (to Portland) was by far the most dangerous part of our international journey. After 400 miles, I asked my friend, a well-accomplished rock hound, if he could take over the driving chores. Too bad I could never awaken him to see if he would agree.

You may have noticed that the elevation given in Beckey's Red Guide differs from that above. I believe the topo map's elevation is correct based on my altimeter and GPS combined with my friend's GPS. No matter. An excursion up Bear by any route is a passage into the relatively untrammeled wilderness of the National Park. I wouldn't advise shorts even on the hottest of days (my legs still hurt years later just thinking about it), and I would not go alone, as route-finding can be a chore, although a GPS or SPOT-like device can sometimes, but not always, substitute. Still, why deprive your climbing cronies of this so-typical North Cascade's outing? Trail, followed by brush, followed by more brush, capped off by rock, then followed by brush, then more brush, and finally brush, until you descend to the trail. And don't forget the extended drive home; I hope you have plenty of caffeine or a more alert companion than did I to share the driving chores.

CHAPTER FORTY-ONE

An International Feast for the Eyes and Soul

The Border Peaks: American
(7,994')

and Canadian Peaks
(7,516')

HIDDEN GEMS OF THE WASHINGTON CASCADES

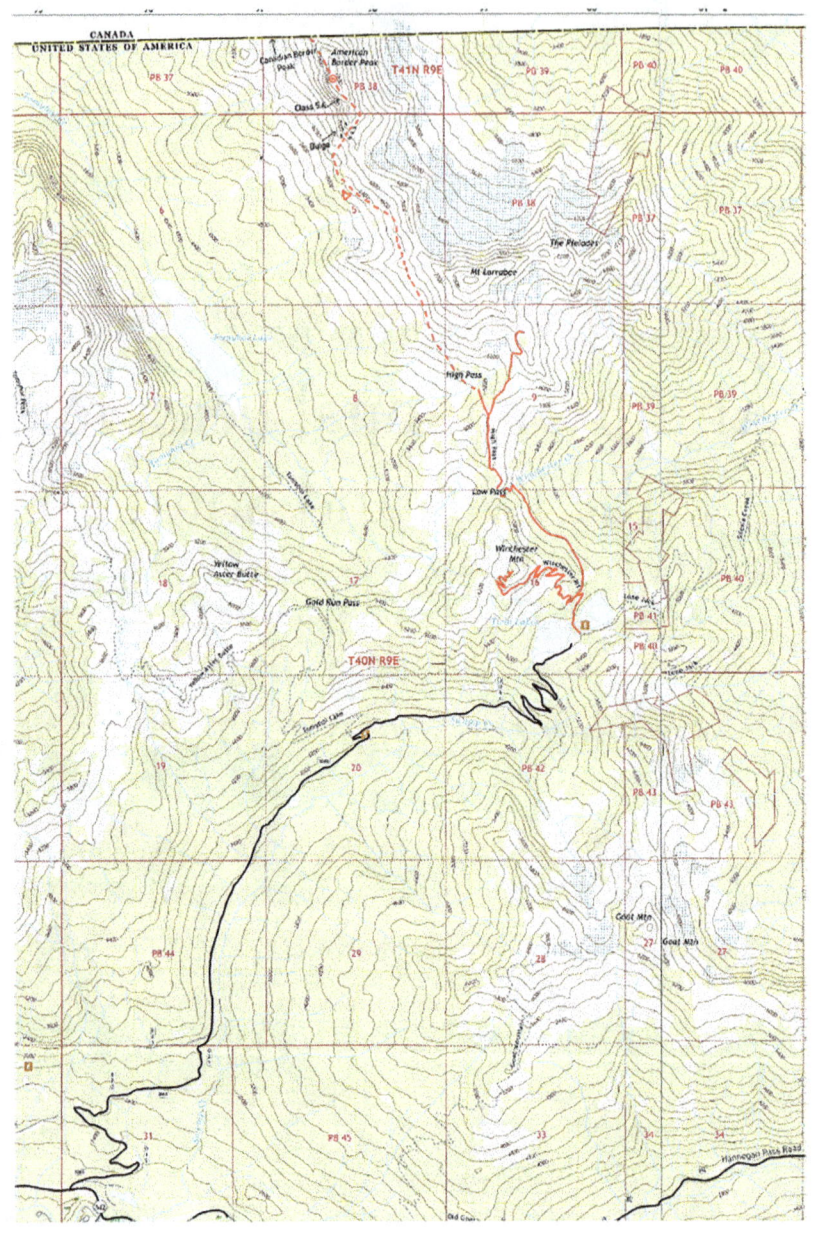

CHAPTER FORTY-ONE: AN INTERNATIONAL FEAST FOR THE EYES AND SOUL

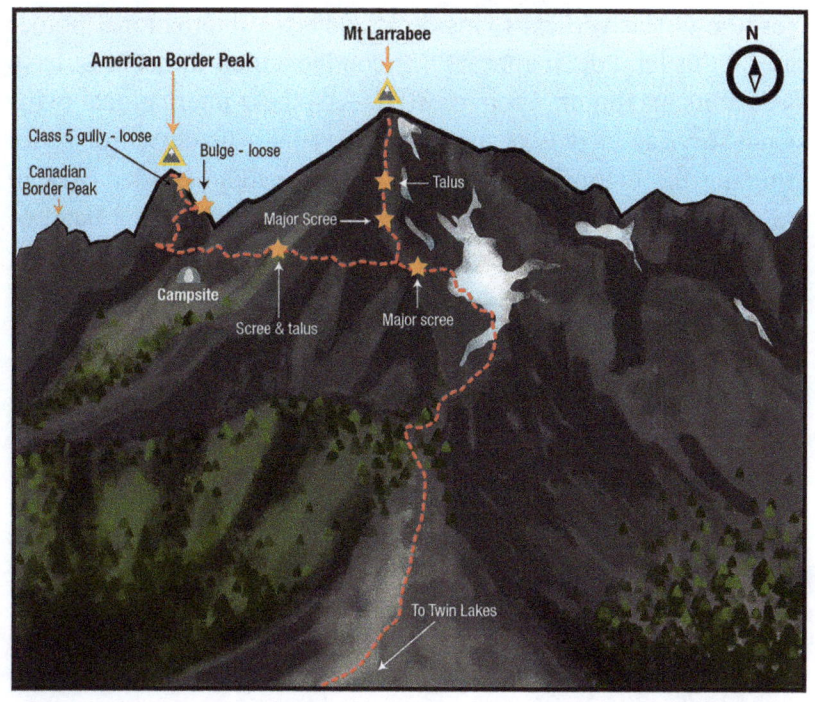

Yes, these near-vertical twins do straddle the international border and, at this latitude, it appears that continental up-thrust must have been at its maximum. From most aspects, these international twins could serve as models of mountain mayhem. The cluster of peaks rimming the international border, from Canadian Border Peak in the west to Slesse and Hozomeen in the east, present a band of vertical geographies of Patagonian proportions, stark, foreboding and as challenging as any in the North Cascades. The 49th parallel surely embraces the most angular and spectacular of all our peaks.

Not that the Border Peaks described here are that tough to climb, but, from many angles, they arise because of ferocious shifts in the continental plates girdling our restless planet. These up-thrusts resemble the roar of the lion, yet many of their actual ascents resemble more the meow of your common housecat, or at least the muffled hiss of a bobcat or lynx.

Nonetheless, access, that frequent bugbear, along with distance from major centers of population, render these two northern outposts infrequent, yet worthwhile, endeavors. Gazing at this maniacal panorama, these peaks appear to have been created to repel mountain masters, with deranged angles, sheer yet crumbling rock walls, yet less snow than equally tall summits 500 miles further south because of their vertical walls adorning most aspects. Yet they can be tamed by those who challenge their crazed slopes.

Our leader's suggestion of tackling these summits had been sparked by prior failures here; these only added fuel to his fire to return, sort of like gas poured on flickering kindling. An additional allure for all of us in the party was their beautiful isolation and the infrequency with which they've been attempted.

American Border Peak, the continental country's northern-most true mountain, can be accessed by bouncing and jouncing along the Twin Lakes Road (actually much improved in recent times), originating from Highway 542 about 13 miles east of the town of Glacier. By the way, this rough village represents a true mountain town and seems proud of it, with no ersatz cowboy or Swiss

CHAPTER FORTY-ONE: AN INTERNATIONAL FEAST FOR THE EYES AND SOUL

mimicry. Turn north off 542 onto the Twin Lakes Road, the same one you would access to reach the Tomyhoi Lake/Yellow Aster Butte parking area in about 4½ miles.

Up to that point, most any vehicle can navigate the wash-boarding and ruts common to all trail-access byways in the Northwest, unless your approach car is a Ferrari Panamera or a Lamboghini Aventador. The 2½ miles to Twin Lakes beyond, however, may send you bouncing and pouncing as it is a beast of a different hue, furrowed, wrinkled, and weather-beaten. Most vehicles can make it these days, but a high clearance SUV is recommended. In certain (forgettable) years, we've had to walk the road from the Tomyhoi Lake parking area to Twin Lakes but that's uncommon these days.

Twin Lakes (3,600') is almost always overpopulated, mostly by camper-vehicles replete with their own generators, assaulting the surrounding terrain, spectacular though it may be, with rap and heavy metal music, or the TV accounts of the Seahawks' latest attempts to trade, barter, and bully their way into a top draft pick. Parking is adequate. You will quickly wish to leave this camping city on the Winchester Mountain Trail, just to the west of this madness. In just 5 minutes, take the High Pass/Garget Mine Trail rightward, descending a bit, then climbing at a mature pace through thick stands of corn lilies, pearly everlastings and lupines furring these meadows.

Pearly Everlasting

The trail is in good shape and easily followed; best of all, it is always above timberline. Views only improve, as if that's possible. As you head north, leave the side-hilling and gain a wide ridge at "Low Pass", 5,600'. I must admit, I'm never quite certain where this pass is, as the trail simply plods along, aiming for "High Pass", 5,900'. However, should your goal be to climb American Border Peak, you

Smelly Socks

must leave this trail about ½ mile before High Pass, at about 5,800', and descend into a basin just beneath Mt. Larrabee, the pyramid in front of you with rock of reddish hue and a white gully up its southern aspect (see the following chapter).

Snow often lingers in this basin but be prepared for a foot-sore series of talus-hopping, screeing, and general unpleasantness as you begin a traverse across this stone-cold landscape. Climb up out of this basin, then descend again into a second, then a third bowl, where you must lose some elevation to avoid fearsome cliffs guarding American Border's southern face. You will occasionally encounter stands of mountain hemlock but in the main, you're in the clear, which is good in that you can see where you're heading but bad

Mountain Hemlock

if you (like me) hate the up's and downs of these wobbly rock crossings. That short dull white flower you're trying not to trample on is smelly socks (AKA known as dirty socks). Stoop and sniff to discover its etymology.

Luckily, it's this third valley that holds both some greenery and the stream which sustains it. This should be your base camp, well-deserved after such gravelly shenanigans. There do exist two level campsites within the trees on a ridge to the west. Unfortunately, it took us most of our first day to

CHAPTER FORTY-ONE: AN INTERNATIONAL FEAST FOR THE EYES AND SOUL

accomplish this approach but that was probably because of my sluggish pace mixed with my caustic comments and constant complaining. After a look at our surroundings, however, these cheered even me. Our objective, American Border Peak rose in a ferocious display of perpendicular cliff and slab, seemingly well beyond my rock-climbing skills, while Canadian Border Peak, next door to the northwest, appeared almost Slesse-like, a series of spires and angular precipices rearing up from low soundings. I hesitated at these sights, but reticence doesn't climb mountains.

Yet there is salvation here on American Border, as we learned on climb day. Follow the streambed, often the only sign of green on this southern aspect, up into the inevitable gully, aiming for the saddle between it and Larrabee. The climbing here is mostly class 3, loose as a bull released from its pen a bit too soon. However, we also encountered some solid class-5 moves; possibly (probably) we were off route. But success is about resolve as well as strength and, persisting, we reached Beckey's notch.

From this point, proceed northeast to reach a prominent bulge on the southeast face itself. Beyond, a second class-3 chute reaches the southeast ridge proper. A permanent snow couloir can be seen. It provides access to yet another gully, actually more of a snow ravine. Its top provides a view, dreadful as it appears, of what Beckey calls the "Great Chimney", actually an evil-looking but approachable objective, yet another pothole on our road to the top.

While you could elect to climb this chimney (class 5.4), fearful of falling and fatality, we elected to bypass this obstacle on its eastern side, finding our salvation in a broad class-4 channel leading to a notch atop the dreaded chimney, and a view of our main objective – American Border's summit. Yet another gully to our west led to the ultimate crest, first a 4th-class boulder problem, then an easy talus hop to the top.

Views were, to say the least, striking. To the south, just behind snow-clad Ruth and Icy, stand Baker and Shuksan, both displaying their fierce and icy north walls. Beyond, the fence-like Pickets rear their sky-piercing summits. While one would think there could be little to see to the west except a textured hilly landscape, the spectacle of Canadian Border Peak rears up in opposition, perhaps envious of American Border's superior elevation. Look to the far west beyond corridors of crumpled greenish corduroy: the Olympics can be seen along their main chain, with Constance standing as the tallest within view. Southeast lay Larrabee, more impressive from this perspective than from Twin Lakes, and to the immediate south, the rarely climbed or appreciated Bearpaw Mountain, with its steep north face lying just northeast of popular Church Mountain.

But the views east and north claim both surprise and delight in full measure. Tomyhoi glares in fearsome profile, both its south and north walls now exposed from this unique perspective. Past Larrabee lie The Pleiades; though partially blocked by Tomyhoi, one can gain an appreciation of their abrupt and rugged character. Just beyond, the canine of Slesse lords it over valleys so low they appear in perspective as if beneath sea level. Just to Slesse's east, one can make out Middle Peak, then Bear and Redoubt, though distant and partially obscured by the multitude of intervening ridges and peaks. To the north, try to identify summits within the Cheam Range in British Columbia, Welch and Foley Peaks being the most conspicuous. Far to the northwest, you may well spot the snows of Garibaldi.

Take your time from this singular perch, just 0.2 miles inside America, to identify peaks largely unknown, even to the seasoned North Cascades explorer. But descend you must, down-climbing or rappelling gully after gully to reach base. By that time, most climbers call it a glorious day and forego the up and down "pleasures" of beating it back to Twin Lakes. And why bother? Few campsites will be as private yet as eye-filling as this one. Besides, for us anyway, we had our fill of gullying and talus-vaulting on climb day. Rest under a night sky and leave the return tasks, though view-worthy, for another day. Intricate, often loose, and approached with difficulty, you must agree that American

CHAPTER FORTY-ONE: AN INTERNATIONAL FEAST FOR THE EYES AND SOUL

Border Peak remains a lofty goal as much for its far-ranging views as for its relative obscurity.

Alternate routes have been achieved on American Border: A Northeast Face party encountered a 45-degree ice gully and some mixed class-4 to easy class-5 climbing to reach the top; the East Buttress has been scaled from a Canadian approach (called the "Illegal Entry Buttress"), with much brush and steep ice on the northeast glacier. However, any route which attains American Border's summit will be rewarded not only with distinctive views but with a well-earned sense of accomplishment, plus the title of a gully-master to boot.

Canadian Border Peak, its shape weird but wonderful, lies just 0.4 miles north of the border. Its outline against the western sky is as mesmerizing as it is difficult to define, sort of like an Escher drawing with not-quite repeating blocky, then vertiginous competing angles. It forms a mix of most peculiar mountain topography, the opposite of the pyramidal shape a child might sketch when asked to draw a mountain. Indeed, from a southwestern perspective, its greenstone slate and phyllite slopes appear as a staircase with giant steps leading to the sky above. Depending on your frame of mind, its silhouette can be seen as playful yet malevolent. From most perspectives, it appears to consist of blocky wedges leaning to and fro but always up, and always sheer: a vertical meridian marked on a map but missing from most guidebooks (except the northernmost Beckey Guide).

Yet fierce appearances on the major routes up Canadian Border are more cosmetic than challenging, given that one follows the correct track. Loose slates and greenstone, not known for their reliability, predominate, so do not allow too much latitude in following the present recommendations. Trying to decipher Beckey's approach directions proved as dizzying as a carnival ride, though no fault of his. We might as well have been consulting a Ouija Board. This is one of the toughest approaches to master, a muddle of old logging roads (many gated), severe brush, recently logged tracts that could challenge an Olympic hurdler, and a confusing agglomeration of intersecting ridges and gullies, all seemingly placed strategically to frustrate would-be ascensionists. It took our meager party three attempts merely to set foot on the peak.

We finally drove the Chilliwack Road to Slesse Creek, then the road paralleling the Creek, as Beckey advises for the northwest ridge route, realizing he knew better than we about such approaches. These logging roads, some still open, took our SUV as high as this abused vehicle could bear - to about 3,600'. We soon realized that this approach would be as unusual as it was difficult.

Although we had hope, faith is not a strategy. We began a bushwhack south up a just-logged patch of downed timber. This involved hours of hauling packs over downed logs to reach forest, still choked with brush. Our efforts seemed strong, but often indirect as we swerved this way and that. However, we eventually reached a campsite at about 9 PM, at 5,750', just above timberline. If you agree that tackling Canadian Border can be better approached by any route other than its northwest ridge, please publish it.

From a sloping camp the next day, we gained the northwest shoulder, all above timberline, without breaking out any technical gear. Although Beckey then describes entering a cirque, then climbing a "snow-filled gully...adjacent to the northeast face", a simpler approach, though one filled with the need for rock protection, would be to aim directly toward the northwest ridge, avoiding the gully, which appeared frighteningly loose and bare of snow. I feigned courage but, in truth, I was naked to the reality of movement up these next sections. I needed protection but our leader simply emulated perfection.

Luckily, his solid placement of pro was like heaven from above as I clumsily managed a few mid-5th-class moves over loose stone. Finally, this brought us to the ridge proper. Climbing this proved at times a pleasant scramble, though steep; the route consisted mostly of Dr. Jeckel heather and grass, but at other points, it metamorphosed into a Mr. Hyde gully-ridden mess of loose flakes requiring rock protection and, *de rigueur*, hard hats.

CHAPTER FORTY-ONE: AN INTERNATIONAL FEAST FOR THE EYES AND SOUL

This crest soon devolves into a series of gullies; the easiest course is to bear west as the northeast face is alarmingly steep. Take 4th-class gullies to meet a pile of rubble at the base of what appears to be an insurmountable (at least to me) 90-degree wall 100' below the summit. Although Beckey promotes finding a narrow crack to the east of an inside corner, we found it easier to stay west, work around the wall on broken ledges (vast exposure at class 5.5 – rope up here), then surf on air and ultimately scramble the final blocks to Canadian's top. No summit register greeted us.

The views are mostly identical to those of American Border Peak so I will not bore you with repetition except to say that the views of American Border Peak itself, just to your southeast, make it appear almost sheer from all angles (take plenty of photos here). The enchanting Cheam Range beckons further north and Garibaldi shines in the distant northwest.

Other routes probably exist. The Northeast Rib has been ascended by the indefatigable Canadian strongman, Dick Culbert, who noted a "long class-4-5 climb". To me, this rib appeared startling in its abrupt angles and complex abutments of leaning towers. On our descent, we made attempts to down-climb and rappel what we assumed were our ascent gullies. This unfortunately revealed that we were completely out of our league; a chilly bivouac followed before locating the correct descent route the next day and a welcoming base camp.

It's odd and ungainly proportions combined with its bizarre box-like shape, when compared with our Ranges' handsome and photogenic masterpieces, such as Rainier and Shuksan, will in all likelihood, garner neither popularity nor affection However, following our climb, I can definitely say that this peak, despite its crazed geometries, deserves our respect.

Should you succeed on both peaks, you have conquered, in a fashion, two countries, or at least two adjoining rugged border peaks, though their names are, to say the least, uninspired. You will not be disappointed if you're up for the ardors of approach, the rigors of route-finding, a high tolerance for talus, respect for rocky inclines, and a gusto for gullies. You will be among the few who have explored and prevailed over the furthest reaches of our glorious mountains, a true evangelist for the North Cascades.

CHAPTER FORTY-TWO

Best Views for the Effort in the Entire Range

Mt. Larrabee
(7,861')

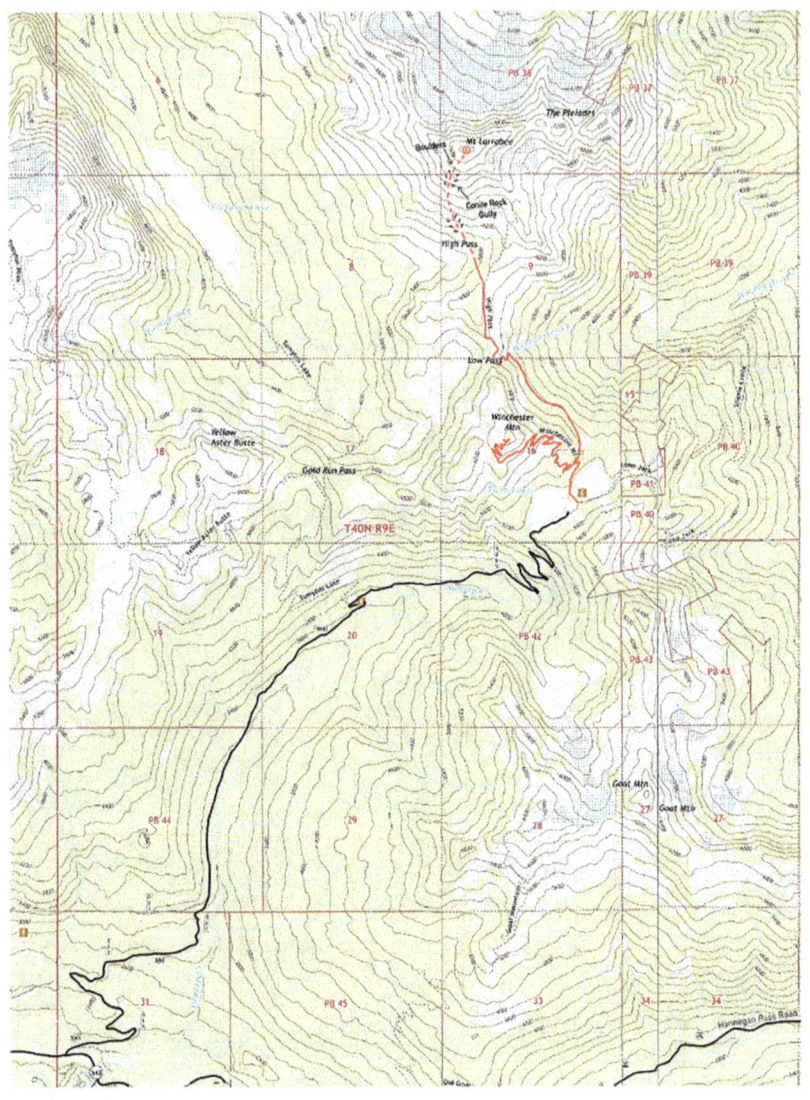

CHAPTER FORTY-TWO: BEST VIEWS FOR THE EFFORT IN THE ENTIRE RANGE

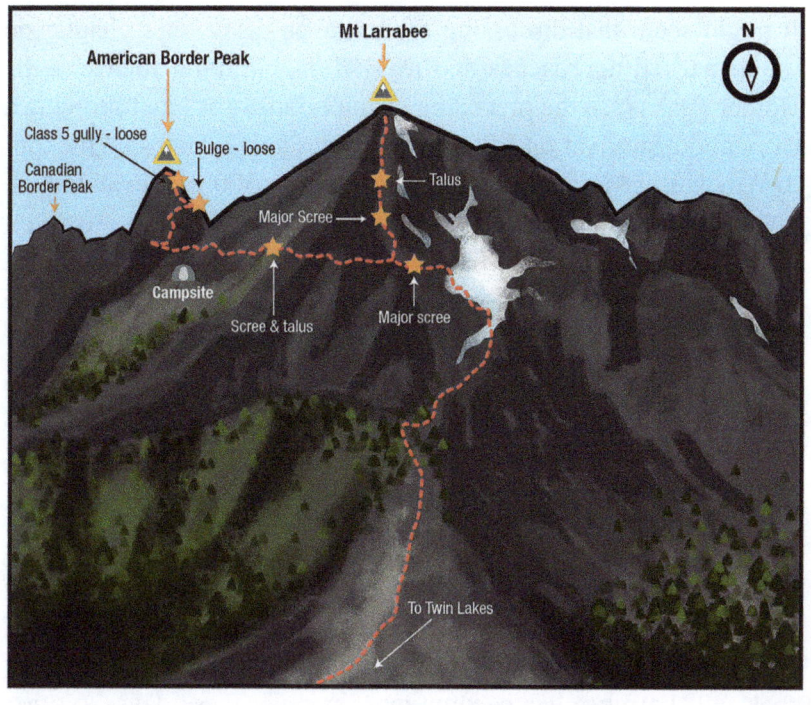

It might seem that discussing Mt Larrabee just after a chapter on the aggrieved approaches and mysterious climbing routes of the Border Peaks (see the preceding chapter) is sort of like following a story about survival on K2 with anecdotes about romps up the trail to Winchester Mountain (2 miles and about 1,300' of elevation gain on a highway of a trail). However, the reddish pyramid staring you in the face north of Twin Lakes asserts its own charms; nor can it be considered a trivial pursuit. The reason it resembles a volcano is due to the same laws that shape such mounts: gravity. While Larrabee will never erupt, nor does it hold hidden fiery fumaroles, its top-most rocks have tumbled to its bottom on all visible sides, much in the same manner that overweight climbers do as well.

Although an ascent of Larrabee is a one-day nontechnical affair, one piece of equipment should always be carried: a sturdy helmet. Its rocks are as loose as a convict's opened cell guarded by a sleeping officer. If climbers are above you, or if you are but one in a party, seamless cooperation will be necessary to avoid the hazards of rock-fall. Larrabee has become more popular these days, so other parties may be overhead, especially if you meander up the High Pass Trail in as leisurely a fashion as I do. Even if you are in the lead, or alone, most climbers have come to accept the uncomfortable fact that the value of a helmet is as much not bumping your head while looking up to see the route as it is from falling stone.

Cascade Penstemon

For the approach to Larrabee, drive the Mt Baker Highway #542 east about 13 miles from the town of Glacier, then suffer the jarring drive up the Twin Lakes Road about 7 miles to the abomination of a campground at the Lakes, whose only saving grace may be their open-air toilet. Campers, the kind you see being pulled behind SUV's,

CHAPTER FORTY-TWO: BEST VIEWS FOR THE EFFORT IN THE ENTIRE RANGE

have sprouted up as fast as the corn lilies, lupines and Cascade penstemons, which have been beaten down by thousands of little footfalls engaged in Frisbee contests while their chair-bound parents enjoy a few beers. Yes, this is elitist; at least these folk are, hopefully, appreciating the outdoors. Leave this tent city as quickly as possible by beginning on the Winchester Mountain Trail #685.1, then after about ¼ mile take a right branch heading to High Pass on Trail #676. (Note: The Spring and Manning *100 Hikes* book labels this trail as #626 in the text but #676 on its picture map.)

After several switchbacks through tall green corn lilies, purple asters and Cascade penstemons, accompanied by blue lupines and the occasional crimson paintbrush, you will gain a glorious crest, with unmatched views of your objective, Mt. Larrabee. It appears as an almost perfect pyramid, nestled next to American and Canadian Border Peaks to the west, their potential ascent routes a seeming enigma. Next door to the east lie the complexities of The Pleiades, with their jagged crests of serrated peaks seeming to almost pierce the sky. Travel the trail north until you spy a basin at about 5,900'. If you've reached High Pass and the old tailings of the Garget Mine, you've gone too far. There had been reports long ago of gold on Larrabee's eastern slope, yet subsequent mining activity revealed little of commercial value: an unfortunate finding for the miners but a happy defeat for those who would be apoplectic at the desecration of one of the North Cascades' superior views.

Drop into the basin at its farthest end, as descending too soon will enmesh you in more talus hopping and elevation loss than you need to suffer. If early enough in the season, around late June through mid-July, this basin may be snow-filled, enabling lucky you to glide over the tedious talus. At this bowl's lowest point, an all-season stream will be your last certain source of water. You now should aim for a southerly ridge, quite broad, directly to your west. Climb loose rocky blocks and steep grass to reach it. Then ascend the crest until you reach a series of loose gullies (are there any other kind?) which run in almost parallel fashion, trending northeast and pointing toward the top. I usually aim for a dike of firmer whitish rock, but gullies on either side should do; if you run into 5th-class rock, you've gone too far to the left (west).

Unfortunately, you will encounter falling rock even if no parties are above; perhaps an errant seagull has flown over too swiftly or one too many ladybugs have decamped from above. That's all it takes, it seems, to liberate falling flakes of phyllites and greenstone. Keep alert and, if like me, you would like to descend the same easy route you've just climbed, do not be ashamed to place some cairns with surveyor's tape to mark the proper descent route. (Remove it climbing down.) This is no idle recommendation: Alone with my fears, I have discovered that straying too far to the west or east leads to one of several gullies ending in a vertical abyss.

Once the gullies run out on the climb, simply scramble over talus, then scree (an actual climbers' path often can be spied) to reach the summit boulders. And what a summit it is. It seems almost manufactured for climbers to simply sit on the top's broad seat-like rocks and swivel around to enjoy one of the most spectacular and all-encompassing views to be had for the least technical difficulty in all the range – the visual equivalent of eating an ice cream sundae with hot fudge sauce, all for free.

All the major northern peaks of this most rugged landscape in our Range are haloed around Larrabee's modest summit. The word "panoramic" must have been invented here. North, the Cheam Range displays its many rocky summits above forests of Western Hemlocks and Douglas Firs still left in the chainsaw massacre known as southern B.C. Beyond, the glistening slopes of Garibaldi can be glimpsed. To the west, the Border Peaks stand tall; from this vantage point, the vertical complexities of both American and Canadian Border Peaks can be appreciated and begs the question of why they bear such mundane names. Further west, beyond the littoral gleanings of Puget Sound, the Olympics stand clear.

Swivel in your stony lounge chair to appreciate an unexhausted sky. Gaze east, where the Pleiades, a constellation of sharp spires belies the secret that a class-3 route from near High Pass exists. These

CHAPTER FORTY-TWO: BEST VIEWS FOR THE EFFORT IN THE ENTIRE RANGE

spires were named after seven stars whose ascent in the night-time sky was a signal to ancient Greek sailors that it was time to embark. Just beyond, the vertical walls of Slesse give pause to even the most accomplished of rock champions. Redoubt and its southern cousin, Bear, can be spied in the eastern distance.

Swivel again (I'm serious – you can sit on the top-most rocks and simply turn 360 degrees) to comprehend the enormity of the Cascades' northern outposts, now to your south. Savor the north flanks of both Baker and Shuksan. The latter, favored by ice connoisseurs, begins in an icefall infested basin, and, in my sole attempt, provided me the opportunity to carefully place my boot-steps in the leader's more capable hands (and feet) on a mid-June ascent of the Price Lake Route. For views equally impressive, spy the saw-toothed eastern extension of Shuksan, featuring the Nooksack Tower and Mt. Seahpo amidst innumerable jagged minarets. Of course, the Pickets, just behind Ruth and Icy, cannot be ignored.

Larrabee's north face sports an unnamed glacier and has been climbed but must be approached from Canada via the Chilliwack/Slesse logging road complex. Its eastern buttress has been described as a long alpine route with considerable exposure on class-5 moves. The southeast ridge/east face involves steep ice and a commitment to class-4 rock of questionable stability. I prefer the certainty of a 3rd-class scramble if, like me, your goal is to achieve a summit featuring rich views without undue drama.

I have spent hours on this summit, then regretted not marking my descent route as I delved into a labyrinth of sliding plates of rock before choosing the correct series of gullies. The trip out demands many backward views of Larrabee and its more jagged neighbors. Among the many peaks described herein, this one I believe, is best accomplished as a day trip.

Despite the view from its loo, I would strongly advise against camping at Twin Lakes; moreover, it's best to start early so that you needn't drive the rutted Twin Lakes Road back to the Highway in the dark. Reward yourself at Milano's in Glacier on the way back home (their fettuccini in walnut sauce is heaven), and dream all night about the vast mountain kingdom you've been privileged to penetrate. In these North Cascades, there is no shortage of majesty, and you can truly claim that you are the queen or king of this noble and lofty realm. There are few views this grand in all our ranges.

A List of Several World-class Campsites in Washington's Cascades

HIDDEN GEMS OF THE WASHINGTON CASCADES

1. On the Pacific Crest Trail above Waptus Lake

From the trailhead at Cooper Lake, ascend the gentle Pete Lake Trail #1323 for 4½ miles to gain the Lake. From here, turn right onto the Waptus Pass Trail #1329, steep but only in short sections, then leave this trail in about 2 miles on the Escondido Lake Trail #1320 and climb at a somewhat more acute angle, to the tiny eponymous Lake, often bug-infested in what appears to be a steeply-sided viewless hole. Do not abandon Hope (or any other of your companions). Turn to the northeast and ascend moderately steep, but light, brush and tall grasses to reach the Pacific Crest Trail in about 1½ miles. Turn left on the PCT and shortly find a wide gravelly opening, an official but lightly-used campsite with readily reachable streams.

This adventure eliminates a many-miles trek (which would probably take several days) on the too-populated PCT from Snoqualmie Pass and affords amazing views of all the major Snoqualmie peaks plus those not often viewed or visited. These include not only the well-known Mts. Thompson and the sharply pointed Huckleberry Mountain, but, even more spectacular, the vertical and enticing walls of this region's emperor, Chimney Rock, along with its five-fingered southern neighbor, Lemah, and, just as astonishing, close-up views of the underappreciated Summit Chief, Little Chief and Bear's Breast Mountains.

From this vantage point, these seldom-visited peaks are at their sharpest while views to the south, west, and north are unimpeded. In fact, a nontechnical route up the southeastern ridge of Summit Chief can easily be obtained, should you be so inclined. As Beckey advises in his *Cascade Alpine Guide, #1* (brown cover): "This is the shortest approach [to Summit Chief] from a road".

2. Upper Leroy Creek Basin

From the Chiwawa River Road, branch right onto the Phelps Creek Road and ride its choppy terminus. Take the Phelps Creek Trail #1511 for a little over 3 miles, then turn up the abrupt Leroy Creek Trail, which apparently ends in about 2 miles in the Lower Leroy Creek Basin, at 5,200', with its mighty waterfall to your northwest.

However, a climber's path leads right across the Creek (easy passage), then, in about 25 yards, watch for this path to turn abruptly uphill (left, to the north) and ascend through pleasantly placed subalpine firs and larches to attain the Upper Basin (~6,150'), where the light forest succumbs to a grassy, flower-bejeweled rolling meadow.

Ample sites abound amongst larch-crested hillocks but I prefer the more open sites on gravel close by the stream, the headwaters of Leroy Creek. You can trace the creek even from a distance by noting the brilliant spectacle of shining yellow Tiling's monkey flowers shouldering the stream. Views to the north and east are blocked by Maude and Seven-Fingered Jack (both of which can be ascended from here), but are well compensated by those to the west of the Buck Creek Pass area, such as Fortress, Chiwawa, and Dumbell [sic] Mountains, and to the southwest, of mighty Glacier Peak. From here a rare sighting can be enjoyed of its northeastern glaciers and its eastern icy extension to Tenpeak and Clark Mountains.

Tiling's monkey-flower

The ambience comprised of wilderness, lightly forested hillocks, rustling of the bright green needles of alpine larch, rushing streams, gorgeous wildflowers, the views noted above, the brooding presence of Maude's hulk just above combined with the sharp aretes of Seven-Fingered Jack to your Northwest, all combine to provide a peace as far removed from the bustling business of the city you've wisely left behind.

Alpine Larch

3. Camp at the base of Little Devil Peak

The Lookout Mountain/Monogram Lake Trail #743, heads north from the Cascade River Road after about 6½ miles from the Marblemount bridge. It's steep in places but, at 3 miles and 4,200', you will encounter a T-branch junction; turn right (left takes you to Lookout Mountain) as if you were progressing to the Lake. Do not descend all the way to Monogram Lake, however, as Beckey advises. Rather, after about 2/3rds of a mile, head northeast at about a 30-degree angle through mildly brushy meadow, aiming for a well-defined ridge at about 6,300'. Views are ample as this route is well above timberline. Keep to the ridge's south side but stay close as, after about one mile of traversing, you will reach a surprise: a broad and level gravel expanse seemingly manufactured (by Nature) for camping; at least six tents would fit easily.

It just so happens that you are now directly under Little Devil Peak, a painless 30-minute scramble from this site. Views to the north encompass the entire Teebone Ridge, with its sharply angular peaks jutting out from snow-bound footings, then beyond to the northeast, Snowfield, Colonial, Pyramid and Pinnacle Peaks (they must have been running out of nouns), and northeast to portions of the Cascade Pass area peaks. To the south, beyond the shimmering waters of Monogram Lake (4,800') 1,500' below, Snowking hides the Buckindy Range but a few of the Ptarmigan Traverse peaks can be spotted, or at least their very tippy-tops, including Spider, Formidable, and LeConte Mountains to your southeast.

But it is to the direct east that will attract your utmost awe. The entire western façade of Eldorado is splayed before you as if it were handed to you on an icy silver platter. Its snow gullies discharge countless turbulent waterfalls into Marble Creek while all the main spires stand in sharp relief against the Washington sky: Flower and Oliphant Towers just to the north of Eldorado's snow-crested northern ridge; then the Spires named Bandana and Dean's; followed by the sharpest aiguilles of Dorado and Marble Needles; then the climax of the Tepeh Towers pointing the way to

A LIST OF SEVERAL WORLD-CLASS CAMPSITES IN WASHINGTON'S CASCADES

the mysterious and rarely-attempted Klawatti, Austera, Primus and, just beyond, Tricouni Peaks.

You will not find a more astonishing, complete, yet disquieting display this close to a famous wall from any campsite in the North Cascades. Catch the alpenglow on this face as the sun sets in the west. As a bonus, check Chapter 22 in the text for a description of the climbs available on Teebone Ridge from this spot; that is if you can pull yourself away from this breathtaking look-see of mighty Eldorado – well-named as the source not so much of its rumored golden metal as for the magnificent diorama it provides from this miraculous perch in the sky.

4. Just 500' above Easy Pass

About 32 miles east of Newhalem, on the south side of Highway 20, find the large parking area for the ironically-named Easy Pass Trail. In a bit over 3½ miles of first, pleasant forest shade, then increasingly steep wild flowered-filled meadow, all culminating in a well-packed trail through scree, you will attain the Pass. On the way up, don't hesitate to glance back north to the sharply-angled faces of Cutthroat Peak across Highway 20, bordered by Whistler Peak and, further east, the well-named Needles; in the northern distance, rarely attempted hulks of Ballard Mountain and Azurite Peak can be spied.

But it is from the Pass (6,520') that a southern view astounds: Arriva stands directly across, with a dizzying number of apparently vertical dark walls topped by numerous turrets and spires; to its south lie Corteo and the brooding Black Peak; further south, the ice-bound northwestern aspects of three giants of the National Park's eastern fringe, Logan, Goode, and Buckner, dominate these overpowering vistas.

Enough for one day? Never. Head northwest up from the pass over a steep but negotiable grassy and trackless hillside to reach a broad sandy saddle, perched just below the eastern terminus of Ragged Ridge. Tent space is almost always available, so large is this spot, seemingly manufactured by nature (with a little help from previous backpackers). Water is always available throughout the summer from streams emanating from the site's northwestern snowfields but even if it weren't, the all-encompassing views, the proximity to Raggged Ridge's multiple crowns and the views south, west and east, already described above, are even more eye-filling than from the Pass, even though that seems impossible, a landscape defying imagination.

You can use this spot to climb several of the Ridge's summits, even its highest, Mesachie, or you can simply relax after pitching your tent and absorb what you are witnessing, blessing the Mountain Gods and Mother Nature for allowing us all the opportunity to fill our eyes, minds and souls with sights you may see in photographs but never fully appreciate until you have reached this true Heaven on our bare earth.

5. Above the Eiley/Wiley Lake Approach to Mt. Challenger, Northern Pickets

Views of the serrated regularity of tooth-like summits within both the southern and northern cirques of the Pickets are not easily attained (see Chapter Thirty-four in this text). It's as if, like in life, the best outcomes are the toughest to achieve. To savor the ultimate flavors of the North Cascades, you must sustain the agony of west-side brush at its most cruel. If you want the best, you must charter a boat up Lake Chelan, hike 13 miles up the Big Beaver Trail (the first day – that's enough!), then next day suffer the heartless ascent west from just below Beaver Pass, through 1,000' of seemingly impenetrable thorns and thickets to reach alpine nirvana, at about 6,500'.

Openings and views only become more incredible as you gently ascend over meadow and talus to just above tiny Eiley Lake, then southwest to larger Wiley Lake, where campsites on the ridge beyond and just to the west provide level (finally!) sites off greenery (at around 7,100'). Water is never a problem at these heights. The meadows hereabouts feature an abundance of the dull white bracts of small-flowered Indian paintbrush.

The sole conundrum is which way to gaze first. No matter – views in all directions encompass the best the North Cascades can offer: Directly across the cirque rise the fangs and spires of the well-named Mt. Fury. Beginning from low soundings as a wedge, it rises in howls of fractured ice and rumbling black rock walls apparently designed to repel any attempts to scale it from this east-facing prospect. In truth, none of its other aspects offer any easier route to its summit. To its southwest, Spectre Peak is largely ice-bound, with a near-vertical western wall.

Fine-tooth Penstemon

To the north rise a series of steeples, spires and turrets, variously named Swiss, Phantom, and Ghost Peaks, along with the wicked asymmetry of Crooked Thumb. The appropriate northern culmination of this cloud-piercing assemblage is Mt. Challenger itself, cloaked in the beautiful mantle of the Challenger Glacier, a sheet of largely unbroken lower slopes ascending to steeper ice, a severe (in most years) bergsgrund, and finally a series of three steeples of which the middle is the summit of this masterpiece of a mountain. You can climb Challenger from this spot in one long day (again, see Chapter Thirty-four), but that is almost a side excursion, perhaps the mountaineer's excuse to inhabit these lofty realms.

Views in other directions are no less spectacular, including the surprisingly flat-topped Luna Peak at the head of the cirque, then south past Mt. Terror and the jagged southern Pickets to the Cascade Pass peaks, Triumph and Despair, and even, in the often-hazy distance, the Dome Massif and Glacier Peak. Just to the northwest lie the iconic Mt. Shuksan and the snow-cloaked southern slopes of Mt. Baker.

All the adjectives one could pry from a thesaurus would only be repetitive cliché's unworthy of these views, indeed hardly adequate in our feeble attempts to describe what cannot be gleaned from words alone. Perhaps it was the trouble attaining these heights, perhaps it's the combined majesty of being able to view all the Pickets from this spot, but whatever the combination, you will never regret attaining these flowered highlands and these alarmingly magnificent visions. We were intoxicated and spoiled by these views. This spot on a map represents, to me, the definition of mountain glory.

6. Easy Ridge

For those of average ability in the mountains and sufficient stamina, campsites this close to the iconic Pickets and north to Bear and Redoubt, plus all the goodies in between, may offer one of the best opportunities to get close to the spectaculars of our Range amidst the finest scenery the North Cascades have to offer. While extended in mileage, Easy Ridge is a worthwhile and achievable objective, but not one without the recognition that long days and significant elevation with full pack will be required. Four days are obligatory; a week is even better. It is only when you reach the heavenly open-lands above the Chilliwack River and Brush Creek that you will be grateful, in full realization that your efforts have proven well worthwhile.

There are two main approaches to this northern sub-range. You can hike the 13 or so miles to Beaver Pass, then hike another 6 miles on the Little Beaver Trail (I've never seen either size of beavers hereabouts) pass Whatcom Pass, then about 5 more miles up the Brush Creek Trail, past the junction with the northerly trending Chilliwack Trail, then head 4 more miles south on the southern arm of the Chilliwack Trail to the junction with the Easy Ridge Trail. I count roughly 28 miles of forest-bottom trail to this point, which would take me about 3 days.

Your other option, and the one I recommend, is also a long and tedious approach by trail over Hannegan Pass, but involves only about 10 miles, first over Hannegan Pass (see Chapter 37 and Campsite #7, below) then a descent to the Chilliwack River Trail. The junction with the Copper Mountain Trail (Campsite #10, below) arrives at about 1½ miles down from Hannegan Pass and thus 5½ miles from the original trailhead. Continue on past Boundary Camp and turn right into the jungle of the Chilliwack River Valley at this junction. Best to carry on another 2 miles on trail to Copper Creek Camp and settle in for the night; enough accomplished for your first day.

You have now lost 2,300' of elevation and, yes, you will have to ascend that exact amount to return but do not despair – or despair only a little. I certainly did. Best to make camp here, despite being in a tree-bound valley and possibly being attacked by swarms of flying critters.

The following day, continue down the Chilliwack Trail 2½ miles; notice that a major creek, Easy Creek, swooshes down the slope to your right, the second major creek after Copper Creek Camp. Here find a climber's path on your right (south) that is easily seen through the tall grass and trees. Unfortunately, the path simply leads you to the Chilliwack River, which you must cross, a daunting feat in early season. Go later in August for an easier crossing and look upstream for a log jam that often eases the transit.

The trail picks up again on the south side of the River and is readily followed, though the Forest Service does not afford it high priority; prepare for some log hopping and overgrowth along the way. You next switchback 2½ miles, at times steeply, ascending a mostly dry forest of Douglas firs and western hemlocks, but the trees thin as you reach 4,800'. The first full views come at around 5,250', and, after gaining 2,600' from the Valley floor, they are most welcome.

Western Hemlock

You now can traverse through meadowy heaven on Easy Ridge. You reach a saddle at 5,200' but please consider continuing to an ancient lookout site on a 5,600' knoll. The trail largely gives out here, although a climbers' sometimes-path can be discerned here and there. Once above the tree-line and past the knoll, wander heaven on earth, seemingly between sky and air. Continue to ascend the gentle Ridge (finally "easy" has a meaning), and note a second hillock at 6,100'. At its base, a tiny tarn offers fresh water and sites off the shrubbery. The best campsites are here, at the base of this knoll on the Ridge or 100 yards along the Ridge, where a few subalpine firs give scant cover.

Fan-Leaf Cinquefoil

Not only do these sites offer gorgeous views, but level ground, alpine gardens, and fresh water. Yellow fan-leaf cinquefoils, white partridge-foot and pink and white heathers abound. Look for the rare small-flowered Indian paintbrush, often dull white with a tinge of red or yellow. It is endemic to the North Cascades. But the main prize, and the reason you've labored this hard, lies right in front of you: first-class seats to the glorious spectacle of the Picket Range, the special symbol of what every mountain-loving adventurer dreams about. This iconic serrated crest represents what any hiker/climber would picture as the essence, the ideal, of what a range should be. You have found here, to your immediate south, the closest you will come to mountain heaven.

Yes, Shuksan and Icy Peaks to the west, and Baker beyond, are thrilling sights. Bear and Redoubt stand proud to the north. But it is the Pickets, their icy secrets now laid bare before your eyes, so close you could dream of touching their slopes, that makes every tortuous step you took to attain these heights worth the effort. Of course,

Challenger is most prominent, with its icy glacier in the forefront, but Crooked Thumb, Phantom Peak, and Mt. Fury penetrate the heights of the northern sub-range. The southern sub-range is also easily identified beyond Picket Pass, with the Crescent Creek Spires pointing the way to well-named Mt. Terror, while the Spires of Degenhardt and McMillan are easily identified.

It is relatively painless, this day or the next, to scale Easy Peak's heathery slopes (6,613'), often snow-bound but gentle enough for the average scrambler. The view only improves with the additional height, as if that were possible. This is a trip, as Michelin would say, not only worth a detour or even a day's travel, but a journey in itself. It doesn't get more three-starred than this.

Patridgefoot

7. The North Arm of Mt. Ruth

Lugging your pack 2,000' up to Hannegan Pass, 5 miles and a bit over 5,000', is actually a grand tour, with largely open views along the way to the south over raging Ruth Creek. While the scenery up to the Pass is magnificent, with Mts Sefrit, then Shuksan and its eastern arm, Nooksack Ridge, providing icy entertainment along the way, the Pass itself is a bit of a let-down, an understatement compared with the views which accompanied you up to this spot. Douglas Firs and thick Mountain Hemlocks block views north and south, while just a glimpse east peeks through to Redoubt and Bear.

Not to worry; you have choices; climb steeply at times on a rough but easy-to-follow trail to your left (north) one mile to the top of Hannegan Peak (6,187') for grand vistas south of Ruth, the shoulders of Icy, and the unforgettable western and northern faces of Shuksan. Beyond, snow-clad Mt. Baker rears high, its snows befitting its reputation as the most heavily snow-laden peak in all the contiguous United Sates. Or gaze northwest to the striking towers of the border peaks, such as Tomyhoi, American and Canadian Border Peaks, and the unmistakable tusk of Slesse, described previously herein as a shriek made of stone. Back at the Pass, many folks are aiming to climb non-technical Mt. Ruth, either as a long day trip or a two-day affair. A few may be attempting Icy, usually requiring at least one night of camping.

Camps, however, are prohibited here so some parties opt for a bug-infested stay at multiple sites below the Pass at about 4,600', just as the trail begins to steepen. Not for you, however, should you be seeking either a climb of Ruth or Icy, or simply want to inhabit one of the North Cascades' most glorious campsites. Head south on a climber's path, broad at first, to a small lake about 300' above the pass. Yes, it's possible to put down your tent here (water is usually available at the outlet stream, though late in summer you may have to haul it from streams emanating 100–300' below on Ruth Arm's west slope).

Red Heather

However, should you wish to attain campsite bliss, continue on the steep double track continuing south, contouring east around a hillock, to reach Ruth's northern arm. Here, wander in the sky, past subalpine blueberries, wildflowers, and heathery slopes on a fairly level trek you will not soon forget. Tucked into diminutive clusters of subalpine firs are several gravelly campsites perfect for one or two small tents and with access, though hundreds of feet distant, to streams on the Arm's western fringe.

From these camps, you will have a premier look-see into the grandest of hollows in the North Cascades: the north-facing sweep of Shuksan's Nooksack Cirque, a beautiful but terrifying void with nothing but air separating you from the mighty northern extension of Shuksan's ridge, cradling the headwaters of the Nooksack River and the terrifying vertical walls of Nooksack Tower. Listen to the crashing of icy seracs, loosened by the afternoon sun and plunging from the Nooksack Glaciers into the bottom of this awesome hole, littered with remnants of ice the size of apartment buildings.

White Heather

To top it off, study the nighttime sky absent urban glare: The stars, satellites and meteorites never shined more brightly. The Big and Little Dippers, the North Star, Orion and the Milky Way – our arm of the Galaxy – brighten this jewel of a site even, and especially on, a moonless night. You will thank me, or more probably your lucky stars, for discovering these rarely-used, but astonishing campsites, unique, and as view-filled and enchanting as any in our mountains.

8. Skyline Divide - North of Mt. Baker

From the Mt. Baker Highway, #542, to just past the town of Glacier, begins a dusty 13-mile drive. It begins with a right turn first onto Forest Service Road #39, then after 100 yards, a left onto the ominously-named Deadhorse Road #37, and pray that a camper or logging truck isn't ahead of you. You will reach the trailhead for the Skyline Divide Trail #678 in about 45 minutes to an hour. It hosts a large parking area; no wonder as its popularity derives from the relatively short, though occasionally steep, 4-mile trail to alpine bliss: the meadows just north of Mt. Baker. The vast majority of folks hiking this trail will be day-trippers, perhaps unaware that a bit further along the Divide, where it meets Chowder Ridge, a bevy of campsites suitable for multiple tents awaits. The trail, once in the open at about 3½ miles, provides eye-popping and unobstructed views of the north face of Mt. Baker.

Even though you know it's going to be there, you cannot help but be staggered by the contrast between the greenest of green meadows topped by the immense glaring whiteness of Baker. The trail, which appears on the USGS topo to end around 6,400', actually continues in quite obvious fashion, either looping around minor hillocks and bumps or scrambles over them, a bit of a chore with overnight pack, but nothing severe.

Expect crowds here, even mid-week. Continue on the well-marked trail to the point where it turns from a southeasterly direction to an eastern one, at about 6,200', past one minor knoll (6,450') on its north side, then begin to search for the best sites you will find to camp on this ridge, actually at this point an extension of Chowder Ridge. You can put down about 200' from the knoll on gravelly flat ground or, if sites are taken, continue past the next promontory to a second site, as flat and rewarding as the first. (Also see Chapter 36 for this route as it is the approach to climbing Hadley Peak.)

What to see? Of course, your eyes would first strain against the brilliant crystals of Baker's north face (bring sunglasses). From this vantage point, you can identify the huge expanse of the Roosevelt Glacier. To its west, the Black Buttes color their spires in darkest ebony; Colfax, Lincoln and Seward Peaks can also be identified. The Roman Wall, actually the headwall of the Coleman Glacier, - a tough technical ice route - rears due south, followed by Sherman Peak, then the apex, Grant Peak, topping it all. The Boulder Glacier can be seen to your southeast, the most difficult ascent I've enjoyed on this not-so-extinct volcano. If of a certain age, you will recall the closure of Baker to all climbers in the 70s due to menacing rumblings from its crater.

Fortunately, it's now open for business but you can never be certain…

While the views are spectacular southward, don't fail to look west and north as well. From this perch, parts of Shuksan can be seen, particularly the northern portion of its famous western-face profile, and its northern glacier-clad slopes menacing ice climbers of suitable ability. To the northeast, the striking fang of Slesse straddles the Canadian border, while American Border, Canadian Border,

Goat, Tomyhoi, and Larabee Peaks, plus the Pleiades, all tattoo the northern skyline with their fantastic prongs and needles. To the west, the Twin Sisters raise their reddish iron-rich peridotite rock, which contrasts nicely with the grays, whites, greens, and blacks all round. Watch the sunset turn the west face of Baker an embarrassed but glorious salmon. Its profile can be glimpsed throughout even on a moonless night as its snows glisten despite the darkness.

The sole problem with ridge camping can be access to potable water. Occasionally, streams off the north-facing slope can be found but, by the prime summer months, even the northern basin holding Deadhorse Creek below may consist solely of dry scree. Bring a water bag and descend 300' to Deadhorse Creek, in the basin. While I have drank its headwaters without hesitation, others, perhaps due to its cadaverous name, prefer to filter. Those brightly colored red-to-pink flowers, almost the only ones gracing the sere hillside, are dwarf fireweeds, also known as broad-leaf willowherb or, more poetically, as river beauty; these are close cousins of the giant Fireweeds seen at lower elevations. They signify that snow must have been here earlier in the spring or that water, perhaps underground, still persists.

Broad-Leaf Willow-Herb

Should you descend into the basin, also note a cornucopia of alpine meadow flowers, including the shiny yellow petals of subalpine buttercup, the dull red flowers of bird's-beak lousewort, and the curious and comical elephant's head. Look with a small eye to appreciate that each small

Elephant's Head

blossom of this close relative of the louseworts features an almost perfect impersonation of a pachyderm's giant forefront. Speaking of mammals, it would be unusual not to spot congregations of Mazamas (not the climbing club, but the animal) gamboling across the distant meadows and on the ridge itself. I have counted over 50 in one such herd and bragged, as is my wont, about that number until a zoologist studying mountain goats counted a herd in this vicinity of over 70 such beasts!

This base camp, at the junction of the Skyline Divide and Chowder Ridge, combines a relatively facile approach, sans brush, with unforgettable views not easily attained elsewhere in our Range. No North Cascader should deny themselves a peek at these peaks, so grand and memorable, yet so accessible. You will dream of Baker for weeks to come.

9. Welcome Pass

Canyon Creek Road, #31, is not as well-traveled as many of the other approach roads north of Mt. Baler. It begins off the Mt. Baker Highway, #542, about 2 miles east of the Glacier Ranger Station. While the 15 miles of Road #31 tricks you at first into believing any low-clearance vehicle can accomplish the dust-laden journey with ease, after about 5 miles, ruts and bumps are as frequent as rainy days in December. Nonetheless, this approach to Welcome Pass, via the Damfino Lakes Trail beginning at 4,200', is a facile means of access to the highlands above. It is described more fully in Chapter 38, the High Divide/Keep Kool Traverse and thus will not be repeated in detail here. Briefly, you pass access to forest-bound and bug-infested Damfino Lakes in ½ mile, then climb gradually to tree-line at about 4,500' and reach Excelsior Pass (5,300') in another 2 miles.

A somewhat steeper, but more direct approach to Excelsior Pass (through which you must pass to reach Welcome Pass in the first of these three approaches) emanates from Highway 542 about 8 miles east of the town of Glacier. Here, a small parking lot marks the beginning of Trail #670. Starting at a deceivingly moderate grade at first, it steepens to reach Excelsior Pass in 4 miles. While more precipitous than the Damfino Lakes approach, it is shorter and also provides awe-inspiring views once above the forest, at about 4,300'.

Yet a third approach exists, also east of Glacier, this about 12½ miles east of town. A rugged logging road, #3060, leaves the Mt. Baker Highway and can be negotiated to around 2–3 miles, depending on your vehicle's clearance. It soon becomes a trail at one point, and a steep one at that. However, it is the most direct approach to Welcome Pass, attaining the Pass in 4 miles after 67 switchbacks! (Beckey may have counted them; I have given up after about 30 of these.) It avoids Excelsior Pass but at the risk of a backbreaking ascent with full backpacking gear.

Whichever way you reach Welcome Pass, prime yourself for nicely prepared flat campsites and awe-inspiring views. Camping at this Pass, at 5,160', offers an ideal site to take photos of sunsets and sunrises. There are sites off the greenery and snowmelt persists until late summer. There's time to scale a hill ½ mile northwest and 200' above the Pass for even better outlooks.

These encompass the overpowering views of the north faces of Shuksan and Baker, this last with the Roosevelt and Mazama Glaciers in full view. The Roman Wall rears up at the head of the Coleman Glacier as well. Shuksan's fierce north face tosses a challenge to ice climbers of all calibers, with the Price Glacier prominent and ending in an icy basin holding Price Lake. Jagged Ridge, extending east of Shuksan's summit, features dynamic views of its high points: Nooksack Tower, whose flanks appear designed to tease, then dash, the hopes of scaling it successfully; Cirque Tower; and the whole secured at its eastern end by Seahpo Peak.

As magnificent as these southern lookouts are, to my eyes, the views north are even more striking, though less icy. From your left (west), Canadian and American Border Peaks (described as climbs in Chapter 41) showcase prominent vertical reliefs partly hidden on their northern flanks; but even their eastern and southern aspects have given fright to the average scrambler. However, truth be told, they are not technically as challenging as they appear. Due north is Tomyhoi, a largely 3rd-class scramble growing in popularity. To its east lies Larrabee, a pyramid of reddish rock with whitish gullies streaming down its southern slopes. Next door, the multi-summited Pleiades, sharp as dog's-teeth, create ripples against the North American sky, all ending in the exclamation point of Slesse, a shriek frozen in stone. It lies just north of the border, a fang as sharp as a shark's tooth, and as deadly; no easy route yields to any summit-bound party. Church and Bearpaw Mountains anchor the western skyline, along with The Sisters, while to the east, Goat Mountain offers twin summits featuring vistas as glorious as from Welcome Pass itself. Famous Redoubt, beyond to the east poses no problem in identification, what with its abrupt southern flying buttress seeming to fasten its walls and support its sheer summit. Look beyond snowbound Ruth Peak to your southeast to view the Pickets, a platoon of neatly serrated pinnacles receding in the distance. The highway can be spotted 4,600' below. It's sort of fun at night to see the ski run lights blink on at sunset around the Mt. Baker Ski Area.

Whichever way you arrive at it, Welcome Pass exceeds in scenery and mountain meadow wildflowers whatever effort it took to reach it. You may choose to extend your journey for even more adventure, including an off-trail jaunt to Keep Kool Lakes (car shuttle required – see Chapter 38) or simply retrace your route. Other loops are possible as well if vehicles can be left at differing trailheads.

These vistas of our northern highlands don't come cheap – you have to climb with full pack to achieve them; but few campsites are so rewarding while avoiding the dreaded North Cascades brush. Evening time offers perhaps the best prize: the alpenglow off the western slopes of Baker, Shuksan and the Yellow Aster Buttes to the east. This is the stuff of a Galen Rowell photo anthology. You will thank me a thousand times…well, maybe not me, but surely Mother Nature herself, for recommending this heavenly spot, unsurpassed for ease of access and a viewpoint almost unmatched in Washington's northern reaches.

A LIST OF SEVERAL WORLD-CLASS CAMPSITES IN WASHINGTON'S CASCADES

10. Silesia Camp

While I can't honestly say I've saved the best for last since all of these campsites are spectacular in their own way, Silesia is definitely in the running for top honors. In the National Park, and thus requiring permits, the hassle will be well rewarded. Yes, it takes a while to reach this marvel, but every step is worth it, and, to boot (excuse the pun), it's on a trail the entire (long) way. See Chapter 37 for a more detailed description of the approach but it's the same as the one to Hannegan Pass (about 5,060', depending on where you're standing). While the Pass falls short of views we've come to expect at other famous passes, you could take a side trail left one mile to the top of Hannegan Peak, but I wouldn't advise this detour as there's still some ways to go.

You must descend about 600' (I know – it's a grunt on the return) towards the Chilliwack Valley, though not all the way to the River. At Boundary Camp, 4,400', take the Copper Mountain Trail to your left rather than the Chilliwack River Trail. You will be traversing high above the River on its precipitous northern slope but this trail is mostly an up-and-down affair without gaining or losing too much altitude. Sometimes switchbacking, it climbs over, then avoids, intervening hillocks, mostly in forests of mountain hemlocks and Sitka mountain ash, but openings become more apparent as you progress. You traverse a slash in the forest called "Hell's Gorge" at about 6 miles from the trailhead, though honestly there doesn't appear to be anything devilish about the crossing. Soon thereafter you enter open parkland, with glorious views back to Baker and Shuksan. Copper Mountain's lookout tower, still in use, can be spied straight ahead.

Sitka Mountain Ash

Red and white mountain heather, fan-leaf cinquefoil, Cascade asters and subalpine daisies brighten your way as you approach the 8-mile

Fan-Leaf Cinquefoil

mark and, shortly thereafter, the pygmy side-trail down 100' to viewless Egg Lake. If you have been fortunate enough to snag permits at the Marblemount or Glacier Ranger Stations for Silesia Camp (5,640'), thank your lucky stars. There's little point in camping at sites around the tiny Lake, viewless and inhabited by a multitude of flying insects whose species have yet to be identified. You really need to apply for those Silesia permits early, such as in early March for the following summer.

You'll be thankful if you can garner one of the two campsites at Silesia; they rest just to the east of Egg Lake and off the main trail, thus on the side of the ridge. These are flat, off greenery and with astonishing views south toward the Pickets, each tooth, precipice, tower and fang in the sharpest relief from this unique vantage point. Camping here, we honestly didn't know whether we were in Heaven or on Earth. Both the Northern and Southern sweeping arcs of the Pickets can be pinpointed, along with their fiercely broken glaciers and waterfalls tumbling into the jungles of their respective basins in thunderous fashion. To the southwest Shuksan, the Nooksack Ridge and Baker can be seen.

While the view north is blocked by the ridge guarding the northern flanks of the Chilliwack, due east is Copper Mountain, and beyond, to its north, sharply-etched Middle Peak and to the northeast, Nodoubt Peak, both of which are seldom-visited. They stand tall and seem to guard the approaches to the Depot Creek summits, still visible to the east: Bear and Redoubt, the latter with its famous southern flying buttress well displayed. Even the top of Spikard (Chapter 35) reaches above the intervening ridgelines. These views are even more pronounced as you are perched thousands of feet

A LIST OF SEVERAL WORLD-CLASS CAMPSITES IN WASHINGTON'S CASCADES

above the steeply walled northern flanks of the Chilliwack River, lending an air of vast distance and the fine-edged atmosphere of a tremendous void, minus any fear of actually crashing down into it.

Take the following day to climb the trail another mile to Copper Mountain's lookout (6,260'), where the views noted above are even more grand and encompass Canadian ranges all but unknown to climbers of both British Coulumbian and Cascadian adventurers. While the sharply-pointed Twin Spires, or Mox Peaks, are hidden behind intervening ridges, the Silver Lake Peaks north of Spikard, including Mt. Rahm, can be seen, or at least their top-most points. Behind the hazy distance to the east, both Jack Mountain and the twin towers of Hozomeen, both east shore residents off Ross Lake, are also included in this gift of Nature, all from a fairly easily-reached campsite and lookout.

Gaze northwest for far-off but impressive views of Goat's twin summits, followed by the Pleiades, Larrabee and American Border Peaks. Three days' stay should be the minimum for this trail-bound journey, absent the dreaded North Cascades brush and combining the best that Washington's Cascades have to offer: sharply-defined peaks, glacier-clad summits, glorious forests, thundering waterfalls, flower-filled meadows, and the knowledge that you've achieved a hallowed spot amongst the giants of our Range. Memories may fade a bit with time, but this odyssey, this journey, this adventure, will leave you changed forever.

Epilogue, with an Apology to Fred Beckey

In the hopes of widening the experience of North Cascades scramblers, explorers, and climbers, I have attempted in this text to feature peaks and routes which, while mostly acknowledged in other guides and online, have, in the main, been unjustly ignored. It's a wonder that, despite the increasing hordes of visitors to this unparalleled region of sharp peaks, flowery meadows, towering waterfalls, and gleaming glaciers, the North Cascades have not been overrun with adventurers. However, as increasing numbers of climbers visit this area, a certainty because of the rapidly rising population of the Portland/Seattle/Bellingham corridor and the blossoming of its tech industries, it becomes more and more urgent to raise awareness of the need for preservation of these wondrous lands. This marvelous Range serves as a tonic for the soul.

Yet, more people do not equal more destruction of wilderness; it is hopefully just the opposite. Who could not appreciate the enduring lure of these landscapes, with vistas only a visit, not a photograph, can achieve? Who could ignore the scientific certainty of global warming, so prominent among these glaciers? This wilderness and the National Park cannot be treasured from Washington, D.C., nor even from Olympia. It is only by the actions, voices and votes of concerned citizens who visit and appreciate these remarkable mountain domains that they can forever be preserved. The Cascades of Washington State comprises a society of climbers and mountains so tightly bound they cannot be prized apart.

Members of our species appear immobile, static, tethered to the land upon which we stand. In reality, to be human is to constantly move, explore and ascend, to surmount the barriers we all will surely face. What child can resist surmounting a pile of boulders or scamper over a fence or a hill, just to see what's on the other side?

Yet in the future, we all might be tempted to accomplish such climbs employing virtual reality; simply peering into specialized glasses could lead you up even the most difficult of routes without your having to exert even a single muscle fiber nor know the difference between a carabiner and a cordelette.

The hope of most climbers today is that the virtual is but a diversion and that the actual remains a priority. At the end of each wilderness day in the real world, you may scan the multicolored sunsets and find the serenity of mountain rhythms which bind you to the land. It is my belief that no photographs or electronic devices will ever compensate for the real experience. It is in the mountains that you will find majesties larger than yourself.

There are surely errors in this guide. An explorer cannot travel these ranges, then author a perfect narrative. It is rarely in the interest of those in the wrong to pretend that they hold flawless memory banks. I would be most appreciative for any feedback readers with even more experience or skill in this area than I, can offer. Conditions change rapidly in our increasingly warming planet and this, combined with mistakes caused by my confusion or faulty memory, could have magnified any inaccuracy or oversight in the present text. Corrections will be welcomed and can be emailed to me at wldflr@comcast.net or sent via the publisher, although the latter will only amplify my embarrassment. Your comments will be highly regarded and gratefully accepted.

Certainly, even what appears to be untouched wilderness has rarely remained free from the hand of man. Over millennia, Native Americans explored these regions, blazed trails, and even logged and burnt the land in order to survive. Over millions of years, churning continents have in the past, and will in the future, alter these domains. That should not deter our continuing efforts to shield what we possess now: a rugged complex of peaks and valleys; flowers and ice; streams, waterfalls and clear lakes unmatched in all the world.

The North Cascades National Park, in particular, is constrained

EPILOGUE, WITH AN APOLOGY TO FRED BECKEY

by unusual exclusions, including the Monte Cristo's, the South Cascade Glacier Peaks, much of the famous Ptarmigan Traverse, and a majority of the Dome massif. These omissions should be remedied. To preserve an unsullied future for these lands, we should look back at a relatively unspoiled past and become as active as possible in the political present. Those studying the fields of botany, microbiology and ecosystem evolution often are glued to their electron microscopes and mass spectrometers when some of the most significant contributions in these fields have been made by amateurs simply getting outdoors and observing the larger picture of our mountainous environments.

There are certainly other peaks which could have been included in this text. Forgotten Peak, not really ill-remembered, is a delightful scramble near the Monte Cristo's with superior views of that compact range. Whitechuck, with its stellar outlooks of Glacier Peak, could easily have been included. Snowking is another, although not really "hidden", as a number of parties ascend its super-steep approach trail, then climb its gentle northern snow-laden slopes from spring throughout early fall. Booker Peak, just southeast of Buckner receives short shrift in most guidebooks and promises superb views of all the major Cascade Pass peaks along with the Logan-Goode Complex; it is rarely mentioned and even less frequently attempted.

Further east, Frisco Peak, east of Easy Pass, may see a handful of attempts each summer, while the same could be said about Whistler Peak, across Highway 20 and just west of another challenging but often ignored group: The Needles. The well-known brush to gain the summits of Primus and Austera, north of Eldorado, have repulsed many climbers from even planning trips; it is still true to this day that these grand peaks may count but a handful of successful ascents. Imagining the views from these summits north of Eldorado and its many sharp aiguilles has left many North Cascade veterans drooling. However, this text can merely describe one of many tranches within the Washington Cascades, much of which hold equally neglected forays into our wilderness.

The peaks both west and east of Dome, such as Spire, the well-named Sinister and Gunsight entertain few adventurers hardy enough to endure long approaches and largely untrodden and ill-described routes. Bacon and Hagen Peaks, just south of Mt. Blum, are paid little heed, as problems of access repel most climbers. Thornton and Trappers Peaks are fairly populated, though worth a day trip even so, as their views of Mt. Triumph and the Pickets due east are unforgettable. Further northwest, Tomyhoi has achieved greater popularity, and rightfully so, given its gorgeous base camp at Keep Kool Lakes and its usually rope-less route to the top. To the northeast, Redoubt is hardly "hidden" but Red Face Mountain and Middle Peak provide Pickets' views of soul-stirring beauty, while Ballard and Azurite, to the west of Grasshopper Pass, are as commonly admired from the passes south of Highway 20 as they are neglected by climbers.

Mt. Robinson, lord of the Pasayten Wilderness, also deserves more attention for its views of the soothing calm of this road-less landscape, with green rolling meadows and gentler peaks, a respite from the ferocity to its west. The twin towers of Hozomeen beckon at the head of Ross Lake; despite their Patagonian appearance, class 4 routes have been described for each spire. Imagine the awe you will receive from your hiking, climbing, or city-bound friends and neighbors when you can point out these seemingly impossible skyscrapers and, in a nonchalant manner, say that you've truly stood on their rocky summits. Many would-be explorers do maintain a passionate ambivalence toward these peaks, sometimes known by name and proximity to more celebrated summits, but rarely attempted.

However, there are too many other peaks besides the standard bellwethers of the North Cascades to add to this already lengthy tome. It would prove tedious for the author or reader to mention them all. The fun is in exploring these relatively untrodden forests, meadows and rocky summits, not as popular as the hulking volcanoes or the peaks guarding the famous passes over which countless travelers have passed. Perhaps these "hidden gems" are a bit more distant from the increasingly accessible peaks closer to well-maintained trails and roads which crisscross these mountain chains. There is a reason, of course, why the volcanoes are often the first peaks the apprentice attempts, as they are close to access roads, have well-defined climbers' paths trodden in the snow, and are the most familiar and easily recognized of our mountains. Moreover, they are the tallest peaks in our Range.

There is also ample justification for why such celebrated summits as Whitehorse; Dome; Eldorado; Sahale; Forbidden; Logan; Goode; and even one of the Pickets, Luna Peak, are so in demand, and their routes well-described in the standard guidebooks. They deserve our attention because of the combination of relative ease of access (of importance to the Monday-to-Friday employee or student), lack of fearsome brush (at least in most cases), and spectacular views. For those newly encountering these ranges, these summits will be the first to attempt.

It is for those who know the North Cascades well and seek to explore the more remote and isolated outliers of these magnificent mountains that this book is intended. They may not be the Rembrandts or Vermeers of the North Cascades, but they surely qualify as the slightly lesser Braque's and Klee's, Stella's and Hockney's: newer variations on the more famed old masters of this Range.

A final, humbling note: I have perhaps too often besmirched the writings of Fred Beckey's Bibles: his brown, green, and burgundy *Cascade Alpine Guides*. In fact, I fervently believe that a door opened in Heaven and Fred free-rappelled down to found the North Cascades. His successes did not arise solely from his obsessive study of topo maps and archives, but from tough-edged experience. He has had the intelligence of a lexicographer, the heart and patience to share his wisdom, and the soul of a true mountaineer. Portrayed, falsely, I believe, as a predator of peaks, I believe he was more of a hunter setting traps, patiently waiting for which routes or summits might be caught waiting in his shrouded lair.

He was not only a genius in his first ascents but a wizard in his written words, especially in his opus on the geology, history and glaciology of our Northwestern Ranges, in which his ability for linguistic lubrication eased readers' ability to swallow technical concepts with some measure of ease. He was also brilliant in his ability to help us discover what he already knew; but, in the main, a magician in revealing this secret world, this magnificent mountain range. He and his companions were of an ancient race, laden with iron and steel bereft of out titanium lightweight gear of today, as natural in the mountains as a bird flitting through the air. For us climbers, he is neither brook, steam nor river, but an almighty ocean of wisdom. He not only climbed mountains, then described them, one felt he could also move mountains as well.

Meeting him, you are face-to-face with the history of North American mountaineering. His body, thin and angular, would not betray him as a super-athlete. Yet watching him flow up a wall with impossibly thin holds, you witness a movie of grace and fluidity few could ever equal. Without his impeccably researched volumes, the best mountain guide books ever published, few of us punters would have ever been able to appreciate the glories that Fred and his stalwart companions opened up for us.

For him, the foreign rules of *lese majesty*' still apply for immeasurable lengths of time; his passing leaves us sad, but his good works will never die. To quote Ben Johnson, "He was not of an age, but for all time". I will always cherish my memories of meeting this quixotic but quietly heroic technician of ice and rock while on some wild adventure. Though always resilient, he has often been accused of filching food (which we were loath to share) and begging for rides (which we were more than happy to provide). His main concern was an answer to the question mountaineers have been asking for centuries: "What's the weather report?" His blue eyes sparkled with wisdom barely known in times before him and with a deep understanding of a wilder world, fast vanishing. He is gone but his memory remains to guide us to adventures as yet unimagined. Go in peace, Fred – you have always led the way.

EPILOGUE, WITH AN APOLOGY TO FRED BECKEY

Note: As a scientist I have always abhorred anecdotes. They pepper pseudo-studies, the chatter of pundits on cable news and the speeches of politicians – usually about their families. Data and statistics are more applicable to the real world. But I must admit that anecdotes do lend a humanizing touch in getting a point across.

So allow me this last story: A well-known climber (no, not me...I know what you're thinking) suffered from acrophobia as a youth so he faced this fear by first scrambling around local boulders. He then progressed to increasingly tough hikes and hill walks. From there, he tackled climbs in the Olympics, then the North Cascades. Subsequently, he has made countless ascents on all of earth's continents, including many first and solo climbs. So face your fears. Embark upon your outdoor adventures rather than experiencing them vicariously as an electronic voyeur. Make no small plans. For most people, fear will come knocking on your door. Answer it and there will be no one there.

Most climbers labor to breathe during their ascents; it is ironic that once they reach the top, they are breathless because of the views.

BIBLIOGRAPHY

Beckey, F. (2000). *Cascade Alpine Guide - Climbing & High Routes 1: Columbia River to Stevens Pass* (Third Edition): Seattle, WA: The Mountaineers Books.

Beckey, F. (2003). *Cascade Alpine Guide – Climbing & High Routes 2: Stevens Pass to Rainy Pass* (Third Edition). Seattle WA: The Mountaineers Books.

Beckey, F. (1995). *Cascade Alpine Guide – Climbing and High Routes 3: Rainy Pass to Fraser River* (Second Edition). Seattle, WA: The Mountaineers Books.

Copeland, K. and Copeland, C. (1996). *Don't Waste Your Time in the North Cascades*. Berkeley, CA: Wilderness Press.

Goldman, P. (2001). *75 Scrambles in Washington: Classic Routes to the Summit*. Seattle, WA: The Mountaineers Books.

Goldman, P. (2004). *Washington's Highest Mountains: Basic Alpine and Glacier Routes*. Berkeley, CA: Wilderness Press.

Kearney, A. (2002). *Classic Climbs of the Northwest*. Mukilteo, WA: Alpen-Books Press, LLC.

Majors, H. M. and McCollum, R. C. (undated). *Monte Cristo Area: A Complete Outdoor Guide*. Seattle, WA: Northwest Press.

Nelson, J. and Potterfield, P. (1993). *Selected Climbs in the Cascades*. Seattle, WA: The Mountaineers.

Nelson, J. and Potterfield, P. (2000). *Selected Climbs in the Cascades, Volume II*. Seattle, WA: The Mountaineers.

Smoot, J. (2002). *Climbing Washington's Mountains*. Guilford, CT: The Globe Pequot Press.

Spring, I. and Manning, H. (1999). *100 Classic Hikes in Washington*. Seattle, WA: The Mountaineers.

Spring, I., Spring, V., and Manning, H. (2000). *100 Hikes in Washington's Alpine Lakes*. Third Edition. Seattle, WA: The Mountaineers.

Spring, I. and Manning, H. (2003). *100 Hikes in Washington's Glacier Peak Region*, Fourth Edition. Seattle, WA: The Mountaineers Books.

Spring, I. and Manning, H. (2000). *100 Hikes in Washington's North Cascades*, Third Edition. Seattle, WA: The Mountaineers.

Stephenson, S. and Bongiovanni, B. (2004). *Summit Routes: Washington's 100 Highest Peaks*. Mukilteo, WA: Alpen Books Press.

Tabor, R.W. and Crowder, D.F. (1968). *Routes and Rocks in the Mt. Challenger Quadrangle*. Seattle, WA: The Mountaineers.

Turner, M. and Gustafson, P. (2006). *Wildflowers of the Pacific Northwest*. Portland, OR: Timberline Press, Inc.

U.S. Department of the Interior. (1986). *North Cascades: A Guide to the North Cascades National Park Service Complex*. Washington, D.C.: Division of Publications, National Park Service, United States Department of the Interior.

www.ingramcontent.com/pod-product-compliance
Lightning Source LLC
Chambersburg PA
CBHW070605030426
42337CB00020B/3696